The Political Economy of Italy's Decline

Italy is a country of recent decline and long-standing idiosyncratic traits. A rich society served by an advanced manufacturing economy, where the rule of law is weak and political accountability low, it has long been in downward spiral alimented by corruption and clientelism. From this spiral has emerged an equilibrium as consistent as it is inefficient, that raises serious obstacles to economic and democratic development. *The Political Economy of Italy's Decline* explains the causes of Italy's downward trajectory, and explains how the country can shift to a fairer and more efficient system.

Andrea Lorenzo Capussela received a PhD in international law with a thesis concerning competition policy. After some years in the private sector, he served as the head of the economics unit of Kosovo's international supervisor, the International Civilian Office, in 2008–11, and then as the adviser to Moldova's minister of economy and deputy prime minister, on behalf of the EU. He is a visiting fellow at the Department of Government of the London School of Economics, and is the author of *State-Building in Kosovo: Democracy, Corruption, and the EU in the Balkans* (2015), and of *Declino. Una storia italiana* (2019).

The Political Economy of Italy's Decline

Andrea Lorenzo Capussela

OXFORD
UNIVERSITY PRESS

OXFORD
UNIVERSITY PRESS

Great Clarendon Street, Oxford, OX2 6DP,
United Kingdom

Oxford University Press is a department of the University of Oxford.
It furthers the University's objective of excellence in research, scholarship,
and education by publishing worldwide. Oxford is a registered trade mark of
Oxford University Press in the UK and in certain other countries

First published 2018
First published in paperback 2020

Published in the United States of America by Oxford University Press
198 Madison Avenue, New York, NY 10016, United States of America

British Library Cataloguing in Publication Data
Data available

Library of Congress Cataloging in Publication Data
Data available

ISBN 978–0–19–879699–2 (Hbk.)
ISBN 978–0–19–886662–6 (Pbk.)

To Corrado Stajano, first teacher, through the *Eroe borghese*, and then friend.

Contents

List of Figures

List of Tables

List of Boxes

List of Abbreviations

CGIL	Confederazione generale italiana del lavoro (Italian General Labour Confederation)
DC	Democrazia cristiana (Christian Democratic Party)
ECB	European Central Bank
EMS	European Monetary System
EMU	European Monetary Union
ENI	Ente Nazionale Idrocarburi (National Hydrocarbons Agency)
EU	European Union
GDP	gross domestic product
GRECO	Group of States against Corruption, Council of Europe
ICT	information and communication technologies
IMF	International Monetary Fund
IRI	Istituto per la ricostruzione industriale (Institute for Industrial Reconstruction)
ISTAT	Istituto nazionale di statistica (National Statistics Institute)
NATO	North Atlantic Treaty Organization
OECD	Organisation for Economic Co-operation and Development
PCI	Partito comunista italiano (Italian Communist Party)
PD	Partito democratico (Democratic Party)
PDA	Partito d'azione (Action Party)
PISA	Programme for International Student Assessment
PLI	Partito liberale italiano (Italian Liberal Party)
PRI	Partito repubblicano italiano (Italian Republican Party)
PSDI	Partito socialista democratico italiano (Italian Social-Democratic Party)
PSI	Partito socialista italiano (Italian Socialist Party)
R&D	research and development
TFP	total factor productivity
VAT	value added tax

Acknowledgements

This book seemed too ambitious an idea. I owe the decision to write it to my conversations with—in chronological order—Corrado Stajano, Gherardo Colombo, Branko Milanović (City University of New York), and Gianfranco Pasquino (Bologna, emeritus; Johns Hopkins), and to Adam Swallow's encouragement, who at Oxford University Press received the book proposal favourably and supported me throughout.

Tony Barber (*Financial Times*), Marco Doria (Genoa), Pietro Fioruzzi, Martin Heipertz (German Federal Ministry of Finance), Marco Magnani (Bank of Italy), Guglielmo Meardi (Warwick), Branko Milanović, Gianfranco Pasquino, Karl Gunnar Persson (Copenhagen), Dani Rodrik (Harvard), Francesco Silva (Milan Bicocca), Zoran Solomun, Adam Swallow, Guido Tabellini (Bocconi), and Renata Targetti Lenti (Pavia) read all or part of the manuscript and gave me comments both careful and insightful, which showed me links I had not seen and implications I had overlooked. Among them I am particularly grateful to my schoolfriend Guglielmo, whose closeness was also a source of confidence. I thank also Gilberto Seravalli (Parma), whose reservations on early drafts of Chapters 1–3 proved stimulating.

Besides many other ones, to Fabrizio Barca I owe a conversation on the strategic choices that underpinned the coalition which governed Italy in 1976–9. Valerio Onida (Milan, emeritus) shared with me his views on constitutional reforms. Tim Parks (IULM, Milan) translated the passages by Gadda and Calvino that are used as epigraphs, respectively, of the book and of a section of Chapter 7. Guido Rossi (Bocconi, emeritus) discussed with me the resistance he faced in persuading parliament to adopt a modern competition law. Paul Rössler (Regensburg) enlightened me on an aspect of Germany's linguistic history. Enrico Tosti (Bank of Italy) assisted my research on balance-of-payments data. Their help was more important than they probably imagine.

I was equally privileged to have the assistance of Daniele Guariso and Nicolò Tamberi, researchers at Sussex University, who prepared all the tables and figures, advised me on the selection of the data to be presented, and conducted the underlying research.

I am very grateful also to Adelphi, Editions Gallimard, and Flammarion, for their kind permission to reproduce the texts that appear in the Epigraph.

Acknowledgements

I have been greatly aided by two collections of essays, finally, both published by Oxford University Press. One is a history of the Italian economy since 1861, which sets out the results of a research project conducted under the aegis of the Bank of Italy (Toniolo 2013a). The other is a comprehensive analysis of Italian politics since World War II (Jones and Pasquino 2015). As they allowed me also to be parsimonious in quoting from the vast literature they rely upon, I thankfully commend them to the readers who wish to go beyond the often summary remarks that they shall find here.

Levanto, September 2017

Epigraph

De 1450 à 1650... l'Italie aux diverses couleurs, éclatantes toutes, a rayonné au-delà de ses limites propres, et sa lumière s'est répandue à travers le monde. Cette lumière... se présente comme la marque d'un destin exceptionnel.

[Between 1450 and 1650... this Italy of diverse colours, all gleaming, has radiated beyond its own confines, and its light has spread across the world. This light... stands as the mark of an exceptional destiny.]

(Fernand Braudel, 1989)

L'atto di coscienza con che nu' dobbiamo riscattarci prelude alla resurrezione, se una resurrezione è tentabile da così paventosa macerie... il transitus da follia a vita ragionevole non potrà farsi se non prendendo elencatoria notizia delle oscure libidini, che hanno scatenato gli oscuri impulsi.

[The act of conscience through which we must redeem ourselves is the necessary condition of our resurrection, if resurrection from such appalling ruins is feasible... the transition from madness to a life of reason is impossible if we do not first take careful stock of those dark lusts that have unleashed our darkest impulses.]

(Carlo Emilio Gadda, 1944–5)

Il y a longtemps qu'on sait que le rôle de la philosophie n'est pas découvrir ce qui est caché, mais rendre visible ce qui est précisément visible, c'est-a-dire de faire apparaître ce qui est si proche, ce qui est si immédiat... qu'à cause de cela nous ne le percevons pas.

[We have long known that the role of philosophy is not to discover what is hidden, but to render visible what precisely is visible, which is to say to make appear what is so close, so immediate... that, for that very reason, we do not perceive it.]

(Michel Foucault, 1978)

Carlo Emilio Gadda, *Eros e Priapo* © Adelphi; Michel Foucault, 'La philosophie analytique de la politique' © Editions Gallimard, Paris, 1994; Fernand Braudel, *Le modèle italien* © Flammarion.

Preface to the Paperback Edition

MARCELLINA: *Tutto ancor non ho perso: mi resta la speranza.*
[I haven't lost everything yet: hope still remains]
(Mozart-Da Ponte, *Le nozze di Figaro*, 1786)

The first edition of this book went to print one month before the election of 4 March 2018. The vote and the events that followed it were momentous. Seen through the lens under which we have coerced Italy's history, however, they seem less surprising. For if the prevalence of continuity after 1994 explains the country's subsequent malaise, continuity prevailed also after the rupture of 2011–13. What is striking, rather, is that continuity also characterized the choices of the coalition formed by the winners of that election, the 5SM and the League, which had campaigned on a radical critique of the mainstream parties. It was only partial continuity, veiled by their demagogic rhetoric and cruel immigration policies, but was remarkable nonetheless.

In a land prone to earthquakes, seismic metaphors abounded after the preceding election, in 2013, which delivered a parliament profoundly different from its predecessors. Parliamentary turnover approached, and electoral volatility exceeded the exceptional levels reached in 1994, as we saw, one quarter of the electorate abstained, one in four voters chose the 5SM. In 2018 turnout dropped further, falling below 73 per cent, and both electoral volatility and parliamentary turnover rose again, if below the levels of five years earlier. The parliament that these shifts have produced bears even less resemblance with those of the previous two decades. Compared to the 2008 election, in particular, the combined vote share of the two pillars of the post–1994 party system—the PD and Berlusconi's party—was halved, to just below 33 per cent: the same share as the 5SM's, which in 2008 did not yet exist.

So the metaphor reappeared, in the image of a seismic swarm (Bordignon et al. 2018): a succession of shocks, encompassing both polls, which transformed the party system (Valbruzzi and Vignati 2018; Bressanelli and Natali 2019). Few analyses welcome this transformation, many warn that further tremors are likely, most argue or imply that the 2018 election has most probably been a 'watershed' one (Pasquino 2018).

Another reason for this assessment lies in the geography of the vote, which revealed two clear fractures. Both have roots in Italy's history, although neither had hitherto taken such stark political colours, and both are likely to be more persistent than the swings we have just mentioned. One is the cleavage between the South, dominated by the 5SM, and the North, dominated by the right, and, within it, by the League (the only regions where elections were frequently competitive are the central ones, which for decades had been the stronghold of the left). The other fracture is that between the largest cities, where the mainstream parties—and especially the PD—have their highest support, and the less urbanized or more peripheral territories, including the outskirts of those same cities, where their challengers were strongest.

None of these phenomena has solely domestic causes, naturally. They depict a rebellion of 'forgotten places' and 'losers of globalization' similar to those that tilted the 2016 Brexit referendum, for example, or the US presidential election of the same year. There is debate on whether the causes of this tendency, common to many Western democracies, are chiefly economic or cultural. The most persuasive analyses invoke both, citing the consequences of globalization and technological change, the rise of economic inequality, the hollowing out of the middle classes, the Great Recession, and, in the EU, the sovereign-debt crisis, the surge in migration from the Mediterranean, and the tension between national liberation and European integration. In the most exposed territories and social groups many turned against the political elites that had presided over those dislocations, to support parties that promised them economic or cultural protection, and that frequently sought to turn their disquiet into acrimonious animosity against external targets, such as migrants or the Union. Particularly hit were the social-democrats, perceived as having neglected or even betrayed their traditional constituency.

Italy too endured those dislocations. There too the left was punished, falling to the lowest share of the vote since the Second World War. There too the 5SM and the League offered economic and cultural protection to vulnerable social groups. But while in France, Germany, Holland, Sweden, and elsewhere demagogic, nationalist, or radical-right parties have risen, rifting the hegemony of the mainstream ones, in Italy they took power.

This difference mirrors the divergence illustrated by Figures 1.1 and 1.2 in this book, and is mostly explained by it. Except Germany, no large European economy shone during the past quarter of a century: but none suffered as much as Italy did. The main reason for that difference therefore is the continuity of the politico-economic equilibrium described in the foregoing pages, comparatively inefficient and unfair, which depressed growth, exacerbated the effects of those dislocations, and progressively reduced also the quality of the country's elites. The criticism that the 5SM and the League hurled at them was often hypocritical or superficial, supported by no coherent analysis of the underlying social order: but in the winter of 2018 the mainstream parties were so vulnerable that those attacks overwhelmed them.

And yet in domestic policy the performance of the 'populist' coalition displayed remarkable continuities with the praxis of those elites. Having reviewed the main facts, we shall attempt an explanation.

The 5SM's manifesto offered citizens political and economic protection. The movement campaigned on a condemnation of representative democracy, accused of sustaining a party system deaf to society's demands, and placed greater emphasis on poverty reduction and employment protection than on its earlier criticism of the euro, its fiscal rules, and the Union itself: its main proposal was a comparatively generous transfer to the lower classes, named the 'citizenship income'. The League inversely pressed primarily on cultural, law-and-order, immigration-control, and sovereignty issues, adopting a virulent xenophobic rhetoric, and proposed two similarly expensive policies: a reduction of the retirement age, which had gradually raised since the 1990s, and the shift from progressivity in the taxation of personal income to a flat tax.

The 5SM won about 35 per cent of the seats in parliament, the League 20 per cent, the PD, Berlusconi's party, and its neo-fascist allies 18, 16, and 5 per cent, respectively.[1]

The 5SM-League cabinet took office on 1 June 2018. The process for its formation was one of the longest in post-war history, less because of the multiplicity of possible alliances than because the two parties were divided by their rhetoric, visions, aims, and constituencies.

In part, continuity was welcome. Despite this difficult context, the formation of the government unfolded according to the established rules and conventions: the 5SM bowed to them.[2] This suggests that Italy's basic political institutions remain 'solid and resilient', capable of 'accommodat[ing] new actors and [binding] them to play according to the rules of the game of a parliamentary democracy' (Pasquino 2018, 357; 2019).

But once in office the coalition embraced also some of the worst consolidated practices. Recourse to decree-laws remained lax, in particular, and the transgression of parliament's prerogatives persisted. It touched a new height when the Senate was given a handful of hours, in the night between 22 and 23 December, to read and vote upon the bulk of the 2019 budget, which had been

---

[1] Reference is made to the seats in the Chamber of Deputies, and no account is taken of subsequent moves of deputies from one parliamentary group to another (at the time of writing, three dozen such shifts had already been recorded: see the discussion of *trasformismo*, in Chapters 5 and 9).

[2] With the significant exception of the party's unwarranted and disorderly reaction to the veto posed by the head of state to the appointment of a minister, on 27 May.

extensively rewritten by the cabinet after protracted negotiations with the European Commission.

Fiscal policy is precisely the sector in which continuity was most pronounced. Like most previous ones, both the initial and the final version of the coalition's budget reflected no serious effort to either make public expenditure more universalistic, by reforming the system of selective inclusion that we have often discussed, or to improve its composition, by shifting resources towards items more apt to raise potential growth, such as education or public infrastructure. On the contrary, the reduction of the projected public deficit that was agreed with the Commission—equivalent to less than half a percentage point of GDP—was also achieved by drastically cutting the planned increase in public investment (IMF 2019, 1).

The ruling parties simply grafted onto an essentially unchanged budget the three policies on which they had campaigned, each heavily revised to accommodate them into the available fiscal space. The proposed flat tax became a tax cut for the self-employed and the smallest businesses, which reduced the equity of the system, without clear justification, created a fresh disincentive for firm growth, and 'add[ed] to a history of numerous marginal changes to the tax system, exacerbating uncertainty, eroding the neutrality of the tax system, and damaging the business environment' (IMF 2018, 17). The pension reform was an even more targeted benefit, offered to a specific and already comparatively privileged cohort of workers: a generous early retirement option, which is likely to lower both labour force participation and potential growth (IMF 2019, 2). Thus the coalition did not merely decline to reform the system of selective inclusion it inherited, but burdened it with more inefficient particularistic privileges.

The citizenship income is a universalistic measure instead. Reflecting a widespread opinion, in its yearly analysis of the Italian economy, completed while the budget was being written, the IMF (2018, 16) argued that the country 'needs a modern, guaranteed minimum income scheme targeted to the poor', similar to those adopted by most European states. This was the initial idea, apparently, but it was distorted by the coalition's contentious, uncoordinated approach to policy-making, itself a consequence of its heterogeneity: what parliament eventually approved is a measure that aims also at contrasting unemployment, which implied the setting of conditions that conflict with the purpose of reducing poverty, and distributes benefits unequally, again without plausible justification (Gorga 2019; IMF 2019, 2).[3]

[3] The transfers are comparatively high—equivalent to the relative-poverty threshold estimated for the Centre-North—at the top of the scale, targeted to single tenants without income, but decline fast as family size grows (Gorga 2019, figures 2 and 3).

Consistently with the practice of the previous half-century, finally, the coalition passed both an amnesty for tax evasion, wide and relatively generous (Gorga 2018), and an amnesty for illegal construction, applicable to the provinces hit by two recent earthquakes (Legambiente 2018; Italia nostra 2018). It also adopted a law potentially useful to contain corruption, but this alone, in the presence of such contrary signals, is unlikely to change citizens' expectations and strengthen the rule of law.

Two main reasons explain these continuities. The first is that this coalition was exposed, no less than the previous ones, to the incentives flowing from the spiral that we have described. And the history of the past seven decades suggests that those incentives will all the more easily override even genuine reform aspirations when they, as in this case, are supported neither by a plausible analysis of the equilibrium upon which Italy rests, by reasoned public debate about it, nor by intermediate organizations capable of coordinating citizens' political action. It is true that 5SM's foundational message was a (demagogic) call for cleaner politics and stronger political accountability: but that party too is vulnerable to those incentives, as we said, because it lacks a defined political culture, has weak internal democracy, and is relatively closed to grassroots participation.

The other reason, more visible, is that the League is cut from the same cloth as the elites it claims to oppose. It is Italy's oldest party, founded in 1991. It was in government for most of the past quarter century, with both the right (1994, 2001–6, 2008–11) and the left (1995–6). And with few exceptions all its strategic choices—from its opposition to the 1991 electoral referendum, to its firm support for the laws facilitating impunity for economic crimes adopted during the 2000s—attest that the party is fully aligned with the logic of the country's social order, in much the same way as Berlusconi's party ever was. Not even demagogy sets them apart, but merely its style. What hitherto distinguished the League, and created frictions with the nationalist inclination of Berlusconi's party and its neo-fascist allies, was its pledge to represent the interests of the North, which underpinned its federalist and fleetingly secessionist stance (Passarelli 2015). Its recent effort to shed its image as the Northern party of government to hold itself out as an anti-system nationalist one was successful (Passarelli and Tuorto 2018), and won it unprecedented support in the Centre-South, but brought little change in the interests and core constituency that it seeks to represent, as the tax cut and tax amnesty it obtained suggest. More credible is the increase in its xenophobia, which inspired numerous executive and legislative measures, and, ominously, was no obstacle to the progression of its remarkable surge (its support rose from 4 to 17 per cent between 2013 and 2018, to 34 per cent at the 2019 European election, to almost 40 per cent, according to the opinion polls of the summer of 2019). The League remains a demagogic status-quo party, whose priority is the preservation not of Italy's culture or traditions but of its politico-economic equilibrium, from which much of its core constituency—Northern self-employed workers, professionals, small entrepreneurs, and their employees—draws rents. Having absorbed much of its electorate, it now serves the same function as Berlusconi's party.

In early August 2019 the League abruptly withdrew from the coalition and invoked an early election. It presumably counted on winning enough votes to govern alone or with the neo-fascist party, growing and increasingly close to it. The 5SM and the PD avoided the dissolution of parliament by forming a government together. The League joined the rest of the right into opposition, taking its lead. Opinion polls suggest that support for the party fell closer to 30 than to 40 per cent.

When the PD first approached it, immediately after the 2013 election, the 5SM rejected any form of cooperation and for five years it intransigently opposed three PD-dominated cabinets. Talks between the two parties nevertheless also began after the 2018 polls, and proceeded a little further, but this time it was the PD that ruled out any alliance, equally adamantly. Policy compatibility is somewhat wider between them than it was between the 5SM and the League, especially in the fields of fiscal policy, social protection, and the rule of law: plainly, however, the main rationale of their coalition was that in August the far right did indeed seem likely to win an outright majority at the otherwise inevitable snap election.

The new cabinet took office on 5 September. Its draft 2020 budget was more prudent than its predecessor's but again reflected no serious effort to improve the composition of public expenditure. Policy-making remained fairly erratic. And the political alliance that supports it was confidently defeated—57 to 37 per cent—by the League-dominated right in a region, Umbria, that had been a stronghold of the left ever since the creation of this layer of government, in 1970.

The coalition between these two weak, defeated parties might nevertheless have opened a somewhat quieter phase, in which public discussion could shift from immigration and law-and-order onto Italy's real priorities. In office the League repeatedly used executive power to steer public debate on those issues, and raise its tension: in his capacity as interior minister, in particular, its leader frequently exacerbated or manufactured crises, primarily by closing Italy's ports to ships carrying migrants rescued at sea. The party is also an effective campaigner in opposition, but this tactic is no longer available to it. Without the aura of public office to support them, its attempts to change the connotation of words critical for public discourse might equally slacken: 'rescuing the shipwrecked' need not become semantically equivalent to 'helping human traffickers', just as insisting on taxes be paid has not been taken to mean 'harassing the country's producers', despite the persistent efforts of a wider front than the League.

The change in government may also have spared the nation a discussion over its unity. The electoral fracture we mentioned earlier, between North and South, has deepened precisely when three large regions of the Centre-North— Lombardy and Veneto, governed by the League, and Emilia-Romagna, led by the PD—demanded a very significant increase in their own powers and budgets. Although both the 5SM and the last PD-dominated cabinet bowed to these demands, sanctioned by regional referenda held in late 2017, they are now likely to be shelved or blunted. Its opponents argue that this form asymmetrical devolution would lower per-capita public spending in the South and could endanger the political unity of the peninsula. The latter concern might be overblown, even though the apparent polarization of the country along that axis (Vecchi 2017) lends it credibility, but there is no doubt that a political struggle between richer and poorer regions would distract a society that needs above all to reflect on its own organization.

The phase that has now begun might thus prove more hospitable to the debate envisaged in the Conclusions of this book. Should it breed fresh political alternatives, the volatility of their electoral preferences suggests that citizens will give them a hearing.

London, October 2019

Preface

Italy's decline and the risks it entails – 'Bits of paper', violence, and 'little oligarchies' – The stagnation of productivity – Political problems – Illegality – A sketch of our interpretation – Outline of the book – The reasons for this book – Invisible facts and petrifying ones

Italy's Decline and the Risks It Entails

Italy is declining. The observation scarcely needs illustration. Between the turn of the century and crisis that began in 2007 the performance of most rich countries was relatively disappointing. Italy's was distinctly the worst (IMF 2017, fig. 1). The vitality of its economy, as measured by the average per capita real growth rate, has never been lower since the country's industrialization began to gather pace, during the last years of the nineteenth century. The global financial crisis, the 'Great Recession' that followed it, and the European crisis of 2010–12 struck a society already enfeebled by an illness of its own.

Other countries suffered more, in 2008–9 and again in 2010–12. But during the past decade Italy nonetheless recorded 'the worst average [per capita] growth rate *in the world*' (Vecchi 2017, 289), its post-2010 recession was the longest in the Eurozone, and its recovery the weakest. In 2016 gross domestic product (GDP) was still well below the pre-crisis peak, which France and Germany surpassed already in 2010, and is not expected to regain that level before the mid-2020s, by when the rest of the Eurozone is projected to have grown cumulatively by 20 to 25 per cent relative to 2007 (IMF 2017, 4). The country seems set to lose two decades, and see a wide income gap open with its peers.[1]

---

[1] Depending on the context, 'peers' refers to either the world's, Europe's, or the Eurozone's other large advanced industrialized economies, or to the world's or Europe's other large established constitutional democracies. So in the context of Europe we shall normally compare Italy with Britain, France, and Germany, and with the latter two in the context of the Eurozone; even though its economy is smaller and its democracy and industrialization more recent, we shall include Spain too in our comparisons.

This book is an attempt to diagnose that illness. Its causes are deep, we shall argue. They lie in the manner in which Italian society is organized, in the logic that shapes the incentives of citizens, firms, public authorities, and political actors. It is an idiosyncratic malaise, at least among Italy's peers, but a similar logic might be retraced in countries that failed to change their social order as their economies transformed. For both reasons its roots have not yet been well identified.

Our interpretation is ambitious in scope but incomplete in demonstration. Should it be judged plausible it shall have to be formalized, along the lines set out in Chapter 4, and tested. Our aim is to suggest that it would be ignored at the analyst's, Italy's, and also Europe's peril.

For the country is a threat to the stability of the European Union (EU). Its public debt is the third largest in the world, in absolute terms, and is equivalent to more than 130 per cent of GDP. It was less its size, however, than its combination with economic stagnation and the unbalanced architecture of the European Monetary Union (EMU) that led the international financial markets to fear that Italy's debt could become unsustainable, in the second half of 2011. As bond spreads approached prohibitive levels the country swiftly replaced a discredited government with a technocratic one, which made a stiff structural adjustment to its budget. But it was the extraordinary policies later adopted by the European Central Bank (ECB) that resolutely quelled those fears and safeguarded the integrity of the Eurozone, and, indirectly, also of the EU.

Since then the Union has seen only partial reform, and Italy neither decisively lifted itself from stagnation nor began addressing its root causes, despite the reformist inclination of its governments. Both remain vulnerable, exposed not just to unpredictable shocks but also to entirely physiological, indeed desired developments. Sooner or later growth will accelerate in the Eurozone, in particular, and real interest rates could rise: should Italy lag behind, as on current form it seems likely to, its fiscal position could deteriorate and doubts might again arise about the sustainability of its sovereign debt. But if a fresh crisis erupts it cannot be assumed that hurried budget adjustments and extraordinary ECB measures will be as effective in restoring the markets' confidence as they were in 2011–12. Until the country has found a solution to its present predicament and begun acting credibly on it, its listless economic performance is likely to remain a latent threat to the stability of the EU.

The equilibrium on which Italian society rests might be approaching the limits of its sustainability, moreover, as the spread of discontent and populism suggests. 'Key social indicators are challenging', the IMF (2017, 7) writes in its latest assessment of the country's economy: '[a]t around 29 percent (in 2015, before social benefits), the share of the population at risk of poverty or social exclusion is well above the euro area average [and] poverty rates reac[h] 44 percent in the South.'

While this is a dangerous moment, therefore, it might nevertheless ease Italy's transition onto a more efficient and fairer equilibrium, five decades after the last serious attempt. For change seems urgent, and would happen, if it does, at a time when both the EU and Western capitalism face a similar alternative between reform and instability, regression, or even decay (see, e.g., Rodrik 2011, Brummermeier et al. 2016; Milanović 2016; de Grauwe 2017). Italy needs innovative ideas, we shall argue, and the battles of ideas that those debates will hopefully spark could give impetus to the discussion about the country's social order. If it will begin to change itself, mirror-like, the country is likely to be freer than many of its partners to spur reform in the EU. Whatever the intentions of its governments, conversely, in its present shape Italy is rather likely to be a hindrance to the Union's progress.

'Bits of Paper', Violence, and 'Little Oligarchies'

One character in Alessandro Manzoni's *The Betrothed* ([1840] 1972) is the elderly priest of a parish above Lake Como, who bows to the order of a lesser feudal lord not to join the two protagonists in marriage. The society in which that order was issued and obeyed—the Lombardy of the seventeenth century, then a dominion of the Spanish crown—is described thus (pp. 35–7):

> the forces of the law gave no protection to the tranquil, inoffensive type of man, who had no other means of inspiring fear in anyone else. We do not mean that there was any lack of laws ... There was a glut of such laws [but they only served] to provide a pompous demonstration of the impotence of their authors. If they had any immediate effect, it lay principally in the addition of many new harassments to those which the pacific and the weak already suffered from their tormentors, and an increase in the violence and cunning shown by the guilty; for their impunity was an organized institution, and had roots that the [laws] did not touch, or at least could not shift. [Such were] the privileges attached to certain social classes, which were sometimes recognized by the forces of the law, some-times tolerated in indignant silence ... Of the men who were deputed to see to the enforcement of the [laws], some belonged by birth to the privileged classes, and others were in a state of feudal subjection to them. Both groups had imbibed the principles of the privileged ... and would have thought many times before setting out to offend them for the sake of a bit of paper [i.e., a law] stuck up on a street corner. ... A man who wishes to hurt others, or who is constantly afraid of being hurt by them, naturally looks for allies and companions. That period accordingly saw a very marked development of the natural tendency for men wherever possi-ble to keep themselves grouped together into associations ... The clergy were alert to maintain and extend their immunities, and similarly the nobles with their privileges and the military with their exemptions. The merchants and artisans

were enrolled in guilds and fraternities; the lawyers and even the physicians had their own associations. Every one of these little oligarchies wielded its own special and particular powers [consisting of] the combined strength of many.

With Dante's and a few other works, this novel forms the core of the nation's literary canon. In schools every chapter is dissected and commented on. One question that students are often invited to discuss is whether the novelist was describing the Lombardy of the 1630s, when Italy's long decline began, or was speaking also of his own times, the early nineteenth century, when Habsburg rule had been restored over the region and his own city of Milan after a brief interlude of republican government, during the Napoleonic wars. This book argues that in several respects contemporary Italy is disturbingly similar to the society that Manzoni described, more so than is commonly accepted.

The uncertain supremacy of the law, privilege, patronage, particularism, and the power of private organized violence can all still be observed in the peninsula, if in different form and degree, and the logic that binds them together equally remains, in essence, that which generated that order. These features are well recognized, and few analyses view them as episodic pathologies. But their links with the country's decline remain largely unexplored.

The Stagnation of Productivity

This book moves from the observation that about two decades ago the productivity of the Italian economy—its capacity to produce every year more and better goods and services from a constant amount of effort and capital (see Box 1.1)—effectively ceased rising. The modest per capita growth recorded between the early 1990s and 2008, about half the Eurozone average, was due almost entirely to capital accumulation, to investment.

We shall return to it, naturally, but the point merits a few more words. For capital accumulation is neither a desirable nor a sustainable growth model for an advanced economy. The reasons are intuitive: how can capital be accumulated year after year, enough to sustain a respectable per capita growth rate, if productivity stagnates and additional investments consequently produce only more or less proportional increases in output? Conceivably, investable savings could be drawn by reducing the share of national income that is distributed to labour, as wages, but this strategy is likely to lower domestic consumption, and might be politically unsustainable in the long term. Investment can also come from abroad, but why would foreign capital increase its flows into a relatively unproductive economy?

In short, over the long run the rise of living standards depends on productivity growth, and the latter, especially in an advanced economy, depends on continuous innovation in both the organization of production and the technologies used. Hence the importance of the rules—the 'institutions', as we shall define them in Chapter 2—that organize the economy and shape the incentives to innovate.

The material basis for the 'lumière' that Braudel ([1989] 1994, 10) evokes in the epigraph, the 'agile et conquérant' early capitalism of Italy's cities, stood for perhaps three centuries on the world's productivity frontier because it was restlessly innovating. The peninsula approached this frontier again around the 1980s, after two or three centuries of decline or stagnation and a long, admirable process of convergence. Its high point was Italy's post-war 'economic miracle', during the first half of the 'Golden Age' of Western capitalism (1950–73), which in a dozen years transformed a still distinctly agrarian economy into an industrial one. The engine of this transformation was productivity growth, fuelled by the absorption of superior foreign technology and by a vast transfer of labour and capital from agriculture to manufacturing. Once this epochal process of 'structural change' neared completion it was physiological that the wheels of that engine would decelerate. But after the 1980s they slowed down to the point that they became almost motionless. So the peninsula again began insensibly falling away from the productivity frontier.

Until 2008 decline was rarely discussed in public debate, however, and has since been eclipsed by the Great Recession.[2] The paradox is that the downturn was particularly harsh and protracted precisely because productivity growth was already falling. And while some expansionary measures appear to have attenuated the recession, there is scarcely any sign that the policies of the past few years are close to restarting those wheels.

One reason may be epistemic, for the analysis of Italy's economic malaise often stops at its proximate causes, such as the small average size of firms (e.g., Calligaris et al. 2016, 7–10), or at slightly deeper ones, such as the inadequacy of the judicial system (e.g., Giacomelli and Menon 2013). But the links between such inefficiencies and the country's other illnesses have not yet been investigated systematically.

Political Problems

Political discontent is not merely the effect of stagnating real incomes and relatively high unemployment, and arose well before disenchantment for the

---

[2] Toniolo (2012, 1) remarks that for years Italy's economic decline was 'swept under the carpet', also because those who wrote about it in newspapers were often viewed as 'traitors'. This and all other quotations from non-English sources are given in our translation (except as otherwise indicated in the Acknowledgements section).

contemporary forms of democracy diffused across the Western world (e.g., Rosanvallon 2006). A grand reform of the political system was at the centre of public debate already in the second half of the 1980s, during happier times than these, and important reforms were enacted. The authority of the executive and the prime minister was strengthened, in particular, and in 1993 the purely proportional electoral system that Italy used since 1946 was replaced by a predominantly majoritarian one. One decade later the balance between the powers of the central authorities and those of regional governments was also altered, in a federalist direction.

The watershed, again, was the early 1990s. One by one the five political parties that had ruled the country since 1948 dissolved, under a wave of popular anger at the pervasive corruption unveiled by the so-called *Mani Pulite* ('Clean Hands') investigations. In September 1992, a few months after the flood of prominent arrests began, a dramatic currency and financial crisis demonstrated also the vulnerability of the country's macroeconomic equilibrium, and, together with the Maastricht Treaty, profoundly changed the framework for economic policy. Struck by an unprecedented number of high-level convictions, finally, in 1992–3 the Sicilian mafia responded with a strategy of previously unseen ferocity, which employed explosives to kill its adversaries and terrorize the country. When calm was restored, after the March 1994 election, this politico-economic rupture was christened as the birth of a 'Second Republic'.

The high expectations it aroused were soon disappointed, however. Trust in the political authorities again began to fall, following a trajectory that roughly tracked that of productivity growth, and now stands near the lowest levels recorded in the EU (European Commission 2015, 30–6). At the 2013 election parties that can indisputably be characterized as populist—according to the criteria of Mudde and Kaltwasser (2013) and Müller (2016)—won more than half of the votes cast. Worse, one quarter of the electorate chose not to vote, in a country where until the 1980s turnout exceeded 90 per cent.

The new political elites again sought remedy and refuge in institutional reform. But their efforts were erratic, and often failed to convince their constituents. In 2006, and again in 2016, wide-ranging and partly similar revisions of the constitution were adopted by parliament but rejected in popular referenda. In 2005 the electoral system was again radically changed, to adopt a proportional system corrected by a variable and potentially very large majority bonus, which gave voters *no* say in the selection of their representatives (Regalia 2015). This highly idiosyncratic model was contrary to the constitution, however, and was revised in 2015. But the revision too was struck down by the constitutional court, primarily because it had retained a disproportionate bonus. As a result, Italy now has a de facto largely proportional system, which allows voters to select only about half of their representatives; the rest are chosen by party leaderships and are automatically elected. Another reform might therefore be adopted ahead of the election scheduled for early 2018.

The problem, we shall argue, is that over the past four decades political parties and public authorities progressively lost the capacity and the incentive to listen to society, collect its demands and ideas, and respond to its needs. And while they became ever less capable of organizing the country's moral and intellectual resources, a system of adverse selection set in, which increasingly kept the most talented and public-spirited citizens away from public office and active political participation. Thus a void opened between the political system and its constituents, in which the intermediate bodies that ought to link them together lie idle or are used for partisan or even personal objectives, often contrary to the public interest. Whence those illegitimate majority bonuses and automatically assigned seats, one of whose aims was precisely to insulate the political system from its constituents. Cause and effect of that widening void, this defensive strategy was but a manifestation of the problem, however: it is the void itself that still makes it hard for citizens to organize, demand more responsive government, enforce political accountability, and thereby restore a more efficient system of incentives. Opinion surveys suggest that citizens have not just revoked their trust in the political system, in fact, but feel also abused, frustrated, disillusioned, tired, disoriented, and 'alone' (Demos 2014, 3).

For the same reasons the rupture of 1992–4 failed to strengthen also the supremacy of the law. Grave scandals dotted almost each of the past two dozen years, during which the indicators of the diffusion of corruption registered a markedly worsening trend (see Figure 9.2). But if protests were vehement and sustained initially, they have gradually become rarer and more subdued, and seemingly confined to the private sphere, as though citizens have come to accept, resignedly, that illegality is a physiological feature of the manner in which their society is organized. This apparent loss of the capacity to demonstrate indignation is concerning, and might share some traits with the 'adaptive preferences' of the deprived that Sen discusses (1999, 62–3; 2009, 282–4). But its factual roots are in full view.

Illegality

For about 20 of the past 40 years, in fact, Italy has been governed by politicians who committed serious crimes while they were serving the republic.

In 2013 the longest-serving prime minister—Silvio Berlusconi, in office for over 9 years between 1994 and 2011—was sentenced to 4 years for tax fraud. Bettino Craxi—in office for three and a half years, in the 1980s—received two sentences for an aggregate of 10 years, one for corruption and one for accepting illegal financial contributions to his party. For the latter crime Arnaldo Forlani—in office for almost 1 year, in the 1980s—was sentenced to two years and four months. Giulio Andreotti—seven times prime minister, between 1972 and 1992, for about seven and half years overall, and twenty-seven times minister, the first time in 1954 (Di Michele 2008, 353)—was found guilty of having abetted the Sicilian mafia up to the spring of 1980. The supreme court writes of his 'authentic, stable, and friendly availability . . . to the *mafiosi*'.[3]

Unlike other rich and mature democracies, therefore, Italy was often governed by criminals. Unlike most developing countries Italy convicted them, however, albeit at the cost of a Manichaean polarization of society.

These four prime ministers were not only criminals, of course. They were, or still are, genuine politicians, who can be credited for having advanced policies beneficial to the country. But what distinguishes them most starkly from the statesmen of comparable nations is that they committed serious crimes while in office. Their offences, moreover, epitomize Italy's main problems on this front. The indicators we mentioned earlier now place it among the most corrupt countries in the EU, next to Bulgaria, Greece, and Romania. Tax evasion is between two and three times as high as in Britain, France, or Germany (Schneider and Enste 2013; Buhen and Schneider 2016). And in parts of the southern regions of Calabria, Campania, and Sicily, which host one fifth of the nation's population, the writ of the state is challenged by organized crime. The coexistence, at such scale, of these three criminal phenomena is unique to Italy in the developed world.

Four decades ago the writer Italo Calvino published in one of the country's main newspapers a short allegory, the *Apologue of honesty in the country of the corrupt* (1980), which begins thus:

> There once was a country founded on illegality. Not that laws lacked; and politics was based on principles that everyone more or less claimed to share. But the system, articulated into many power centres, required virtually limitless financial resources . . . and people could obtain them only illicitly, namely by asking for them from those who had them, in exchange for illicit favours. And those with money to trade for favours had usually gained it through favours that they had received previously; the resultant economic system was circular, in a way, and not without a certain harmony.

In hindsight, the interpretation that the financial needs of its many 'centres of power', presumably political, were the hinge on which Italy's 'system' turned

---

[3] Cited by Di Michele (2008, 354). Andreotti was not convicted, however, because when the crime was ascertained it was already time-barred, and for the period after the spring of 1980 the evidence was judged insufficient (Paoli 2015, 673).

is questionable, as it focuses on only one side of the exchange. But Calvino was prescient about the gravity of the problem and allegory allowed him to illustrate limpidly how politics and the economy were bound together by a logic, in which illegality was not an exception but an instrumental component of an 'harmonious' whole.

A Sketch of Our Interpretation

In such a country it would seem arbitrary to view political and economic inefficiencies in isolation from illegality. But how can these disparate problems be composed into an interpretation of Italy's decline? Most long predate the 1990s, moreover, and prevented neither the post-war economic miracle nor the slower but nonetheless sustained growth that the country generated until the early 1990s. Why would they have become obstacles to development only then?

We shall argue that those constraints became more binding because they fetter growth less in a far-from-frontier economy than in a more advanced one. Its approach to the productivity frontier required the country to shift to a fresh growth model, based more on endogenous innovation. The shift was only partial. The reason ultimately lies in the manner in which power is distributed in Italy, and in the degree to which it is exposed to competition and constrained by the rule of law. Innovation-led growth is a dialectical, conflictual phenomenon: a process of Schumpeterian 'creative destruction', by which new innovations continuously dissipate the rents generated by earlier ones and uproot entrenched positions, economic and political. The country's 'social order'—the allocation of power and its contestability, as we shall define it in Chapter 2—limited and still limits this process, and at the same time sustains those disparate institutional inefficiencies, which are the intermediate causes of decline.

Our main claim, in other words, is that Italy has not yet completed its transition from an illiberal, hierarchical society, as it still was in 1945, to an open, liberal democracy governed by the rule of law and served by an economy driven by competition and innovation. The establishment of a constitutional democracy, in 1946–8, was but the beginning of that transition. In the 1960s and 1970s its vicissitudes were often dramatic, but the transition was not reversed. It remains incomplete because parts of Italian society feared and still fear the effects of creative destruction on their rents and established positions, and have retained enough power to limit the opening up of the political system, which could usher in greater competition and innovation. Innovation and competition naturally exist in present-day Italy, but not in a degree sufficient to appreciably and sustainably raise living standards.

In a democracy such an obstacle to democratic and material progress ought to be removed through the majority principle. This has not yet happened for two main reasons. One is that the manner in which Italian society is organized makes it difficult for reforms to be demanded, discussed, adopted, and then enforced. The other is that wide segments of society support the status quo, despite its inefficiency, because a pervasive system of particularistic inclusion, built over several decades, grants them privileges valuable enough to align their (narrow) self-interest to that of the main beneficiaries of the status quo, namely large parts of the country's political and economic elites. And once the logic of particularistic inclusion has prevailed over that of universal opportunities it becomes self-sustaining, and is particularly hard to displace if deliberate reform is hampered.

Hence Borromini's helix-like staircase on the cover, which alludes to the spiral that locks the country into this equilibrium. The latter arose much less by design than for the gradual sedimentation of often independent but closely related causes. And although it is inefficient it persists because the vicious circles it aliments are pervasive and consistent among each other. This is what prevents too many firms from blossoming like those described by Giunta and Rossi (2017, ch. 5). This constrains the potential of the many and diverse vital forces, which two persuasive and widely read analyses saw in Italian society (Ginsborg 2001; Emmott 2012).

We shall argue, to conclude, that those institutional inefficiencies are more homogenous across the country than the often profound differences between the richer North and the poorer South might suggest, for the latter can equally be inscribed into an equilibrium in which one set of distortions feeds on the other. In the South, therefore, one finds both the most visible manifestations of the nation's problems, interspersed with remarkable examples of economic or civic vitality, and its largest reservoir of underused resources.

Outline of the Book

Describing the sequence of our arguments might make this sketch clearer. After an introductory chapter, which documents Italy's decline and reviews the main interpretations it received, Chapter 2 discusses the literature on *institutions* and *social orders*. These studies can explain, for instance, why in Italy laws sometimes are just 'bits of paper stuck up on a street corner', as Manzoni put it.

Chapter 3 integrates this literature with that on the *collective action problem*, the origin and change of *social norms*, the role of *trust*, *civicness*, and *culture*, and the political economy of *ideas*. These studies shall help us understand why, lacking universalistic protections and opportunities, parts of Italian society organized themselves into 'little oligarchies', as in XVII-century Lombardy, but also how innovative ideas can change that equilibrium.

Chapter 4 illustrates the manner in which we sought to blend this admittedly vast body of literature.[4] It does so through a simplified example, which relies also on some of the most basic insights of game theory. Its purpose is, at once, to summarize the conceptual framework of our inquiry, offer a first approximation of our interpretation, and serve as a lens to retrace in Italy's recent history the roots of its present predicament.

For it will already have become apparent that the country's decline is best approached from a historical perspective. Chapters 5–9 review the fifteen decades that run between the political unification of the peninsula, sanctioned in 1861, and the present day. The analysis is cursory until the end of Fascism, when Italy's transition began, and then more detailed. Not uniformly so, however, because we pause mainly on the few junctures that seem to have been critical in shaping the country's social order and institutions. These chapters are not a summary of its history, therefore, but merely a diachronic exposition of our interpretation. And as what we seek to explain is Italy's current decline, not its admirable secular development, we shall use colours that are often somewhat darker than the country would arguably deserve.

The penultimate section of Chapter 9 closes the circle opened in Chapter 1 and prepares the conclusions.

The Reasons for This Book

Demonstrating this interpretation conclusively is beyond our means, as we said. Even articulating it imposed a perilous route, for at every turn we shall risk arbitrary generalizations, excessive simplifications, anachronistic parallels, omissions. We judged it worthwhile to try because all too often the discussion about Italy's malaise is segmented into sectorial analyses, which tend to lead to equally segmented policy remedies. But if, as we think, the foundations of the house are weak, then inspecting and repairing the cracks that regularly appear in its walls will not suffice. Should we succeed in establishing that our line of analysis is fruitful, therefore, despite its weaknesses this book might be a useful contribution to the debate.

No other large industrialized democracy has yet been studied from that perspective, moreover, and the experiment seemed interesting. For instance, the literature reviewed in Chapter 2 maintains that countries can hardly

---

[4] Readers familiar with that literature, or uninterested in it, may therefore skip Chapters 2 and 3 without loss for the intelligibility of the rest of the book; both might nonetheless find some interest in the last section of Chapter 2 and the last two sections of Chapter 3.

change their politico-economic equilibrium without either a miscalculation of their ruling elites, an exogenous shock, a historical accident, or a combination of these factors. The reason might be that such theories arose in fields—economic history and development studies—that tend to focus on other types of society. We hope to show, conversely, that in contemporary Italy reform can happen also through a combination of collective action, sustained by the country's efficient institutions, innovative ideas, and *endogenously* generated shocks to the extant equilibrium, provoked by those same efficient institutions. The argument is not too dissimilar from that by which Akerlof and Shiller (2015) explain how civil society could overcome undesirable equilibria created by market forces. If sustained by a credible programme, organized collective action could drive the evolution of the country's social order through a succession of shifts from the existing equilibrium to fairer and more efficient ones, in a gradual but self-reinforcing process, for each shift would strengthen the credibility of the programme, change citizens' expectations, and thus lower the obstacles to the next shift.

We shall also suggest that the binary taxonomy—'limited-access' and 'open-access' social orders—proposed by North et al. (2009) might veil the importance of the transition phase, which can be long and seems most interesting from a theoretical perspective. Italy's began in 1943–8, if not in the 1910s or even the 1900s, continues to this day, and has produced a wealth of illustrations of the problems discussed by that literature.

Invisible Facts and Petrifying Ones

Drawing on his own direct experience in the army's general staff, in *L'étrange defaite* Marc Bloch investigates the causes of France's collapse in May 1940. 'We just suffered an incredible defeat... whatever one might think about the deeper causes of the disaster, the proximate one was... the incapacity of the command', he writes ([1946] 1990, 55).

The 'incapacity of the command' is a tempting explanation also for Italy's malaise, and is often invoked. Empirical research persuasively documents the decline and present weakness of the country's elites, as we shall see in Chapter 9. Just as in the case of inter-war France, however, one can scarcely account for the inadequacy of many of Italy's political and business leaders without considering the reasons why society chose, supported, and often hailed them. Reasons that are sometimes not very honourable, as Bloch demonstrates, and which we shall try to investigate with the same probity as the great historian, if not with the same rigour.

What led prominent politicians to cooperate with organized crime, for instance, is the fact that the latter is a significant force in Italian society. We are far from suggesting that the Sicilian mafia dictated policy to Andreotti, for example, who led governments that stewarded the republic out of a very dramatic juncture, in 1976–9, and passed far-sighted reforms, in 1990–1. But their proximity is hardly omissible: the fact that links have existed between the executive power and organizations whose power rests on the private use of violence calls for an explication. So does the persistence, at such high levels, of corruption and tax evasion, which are all too often explained away by invoking the nation's 'culture'.

Yet the politico-economic literature on Italy tends to leave criminality to specialist studies or works on current affairs, whose interpretations are seldom useful. One reason for this neglect might be the ingrained conviction that in advanced societies illegality and organized crime are aberrations, or at least quantitatively marginal phenomena, rather than organic features of the social order. Another reason might be the invisibility of what is too visible, as Michel Foucault writes in the epigraph. A third is suggested by the novelist Carlo Emilio Gadda, namely 'the desire, legitimate, "not to hear certain obscenities", which is proper to some well-bred gentlemen' ([1967] 1990, 35).[5] Gadda, a gentleman of braver stock, wrote these words near the end of Fascism. In the same vein, three decades later Pasolini (1975) said that one cannot look at Italy's real conditions without remaining 'petrified'. Four decades since that 'desire' remains 'legitimate', arguably. But in the epigraph Gadda warns us also that if it falls prey to it the nation shall not be able to begin the 'transition from madness to a life of reason', which it would again seem to need.

---

[5] Our translation, as uncertain as Gadda's prose is peculiar, of his 'disiderio, legitimo, di "non udire certe sconcezze" che è proprio d'alcuni galantomini bene educati'.

1

Introduction: Italy's Decline, the Existing Interpretations, and Our Hypothesis

The Gravity of Italy's Decline – Interpretations of Italy's Decline: the Main Questions – Secular Weaknesses, the End of Convergence, and Four Shocks – Sisyphus's Reforms: the Adjustment to Changed Conditions – The Empirical Studies and their Conclusions – The Open Questions and Our Interpretation

The Gravity of Italy's Decline

This chapter reviews the main studies that investigated Italy's decline and contrasts their interpretations with ours. But we ought to justify the use of that charged word first, 'decline', which lacks a received definition in the economic or historical literature. The reason we invoke lies in the evolution of 'total factor productivity' (see Box 1.1), which in advanced economies is the critical proximate determinant of long-term growth.

After seven harsh years, in late 2014 the Italian economy returned to growth. The end of this worrying recession, the longest among the country's peers and the deepest in its peace-time history, allowed the International Monetary Fund (IMF) to devote less attention to its immediate consequences than to its causes (IMF 2015a, 5–6):

> [p]otential growth estimates are low, at about ½ percent, [and] have been revised dramatically over the past 8 years, suggesting the crisis has had a lasting effect on labor, capital, and [TFP] . . . Potential growth in Italy declined significantly already [before 2008] and then further during the crisis. A drop in TFP growth accounts for most of the decline prior to the crisis.

Box 1.1 GROWTH THEORY, TFP, AND 'CREATIVE DESTRUCTION'

In neoclassical theory economic growth flows from the accumulation of capital, which depends, in turn, on the rate at which an economy builds up its capital stock—through investment, financed by savings—and the rate at which that stock depreciates (see, e.g., Aghion and Howitt 2009, ch. 1). So, assuming that the labour force remains constant, growth occurs if the investment rate exceeds the depreciation rate: then the capital stock increases and allows the production of more goods and services.

This model, first proposed by Solow (1956), assumes that capital yields diminishing returns: namely, that the marginal productivity of capital—the additional output of goods and services for each additional unit of capital—will eventually decline to naught. Only technological or organizational progress can counterbalance this dynamic, by increasing the productivity of capital and labour. In this model productivity is an exogenous parameter, however, which Solow's equations do not explain.

This parameter is usually called 'total factor productivity' (TFP), or the 'Solow residual'. It accounts for the portion of growth that is not explained by the accumulation of capital (e.g., Aghion and Howitt 2009, ch. 5). Often defined as an economy's 'disembodied' technological and organizational progress, to distinguish it from that which is already embodied in capital goods, it roughly measures an economy's capacity to innovate its products and production processes and raise the efficiency of the allocation of capital and labour. An economy's overall (or labour) productivity is measured by ratios that express its output as a function of a unit of measure of labour (GDP per worker, often 'full-time equivalent worker', or GDP per hour worked). TFP can be derived from them by subtracting the contribution of capital accumulation, for the greater is the amount of capital used by each worker the greater is their productivity (albeit, as we said, with diminishing returns). TFP is a 'better measure of productivity', therefore (Aghion and Howitt 2009, 106). Especially in advanced industrialized economies, which already underwent structural change and rely on ample stocks of capital and a well-trained workforce, the innovation that TFP measures is the main (proximate) determinant of long-term growth.

Subsequent theories have sought to account also for technological and organizational progress, building models in which TFP growth is endogenous. Namely, models in which the rate at which this indicator rises or falls is made dependent upon the characteristics of an economy and the broader environment in which it is set (e.g., Aghion and Howitt 2009, chs. 2, 3, and 4). These theories develop, not confute, the neoclassical model: next to capital accumulation, they include also innovation as a driver of growth.

Among them, following the methodology suggested by Rodrik (2015) we chose to rely upon the 'Schumpeterian' theory (Aghion and Howitt 2006; Aghion et al. 2008; Aghion et al. 2014; Aghion and Akcigit 2017). Its distinctive trait is that it posits that economic growth is a dialectic, conflictual process of 'creative destruction', in which past innovations are displaced by fresh ones. The main reason why this theory provides a useful framework for discussing Italy's decline is that, as Aghion and Howitt (2009, 17) write, it is 'well suited to analyze how a country's growth performance will vary with its proximity to the technological frontier... to what extent the country will tend to converge to that frontier, and what kinds of policy changes are needed to sustain convergence as the country approaches the frontier'. These, as we hinted in the Preface, are precisely the problems that Italy faced during its secular approach to the techno-logical and productivity frontier. And therein lay the political conflicts that are implicit in creative destruction, which by displacing past innovations dissipates also the rents that they generated. As we shall see, in fact, since the early 1960s the discussion of the policy and institutional changes that the country needed to sustain its convergence to the frontier largely coincided with the contest about the openness of Italy's social order and the permissible degree of creative destruction, political and economic: a conflict which involved ideas but also violence.

This passage captures well the starting point of our inquiry. The principal proximate cause of the country's downturn is the dynamic of TFP, which 'fell a cumulative 7.5 per cent since Italy adopted the euro in 1998' (IMF 2015b, 4).

This fall is an anomaly, an 'outlier' among Italy's peers (Broadberry et al. 2013, 217). In 2015 and 2016 TFP did return to positive growth, but at rates far lower than in the main Eurozone economies (IMF 2017, fig. 1). Indeed, despite the depth of the country's recession and a macroeconomic context—low nominal exchange rates, interest rates, and oil prices, and exceptional monetary easing by the European Central Bank (ECB)—that was unusually favourable, in 2015–6 the real growth rate (0.8 per cent per year: IMF 2017, 4) was about half the Eurozone average, and seems to have been mostly due to the combination of those factors with a supportive fiscal policy (Banca d'Italia 2016, 49–52; IMF 2017), which in turn relied on waivers or flexible interpretations of EU rules. Despite the acceleration observed in the first quarter of 2017, in fact, the latest projections of the IMF (2017, 11) nonetheless still foresee a growth path—about 1 per cent on average in 2018–19—which would not lift the country's output back to its pre-crisis level before the mid-2020s, as we said.

To fully appreciate Italy's predicament a longer-term view is necessary, however, for its productivity problem predates not just the Great Recession but also the adoption of the euro (Broadberry et al. 2013). Figure 1.1 lays out the performance of the country and its peers measured against the evolution of TFP in the productivity leader, the USA. These curves thus depict not the levels of technological and organizational progress achieved by these economies but their convergence to a moving target, which roughly coincides with the world's technological and productivity frontier. What should be remarked, therefore, is less Italy's performance relative to the USA's than its comparison with the convergence trajectories of its peers.

Post-war reconstruction was relatively rapid in Italy, as we shall see. Thanks to a 'strong recovery' of TFP already during the last years of the 1940s (Broadberry et al. 2013, 214), in the following decade the country set off from a level higher than either of its wartime allies, Germany and Japan. Hence its convergence was about as rapid as theirs, and faster than its other peers. Only France, like Italy, reached and then exceeded the TFP level of the

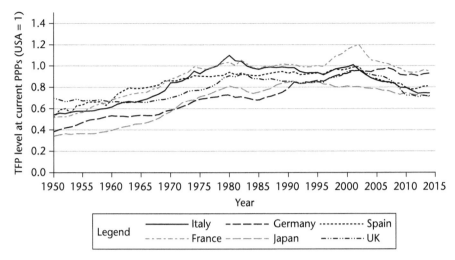

Figure 1.1 Comparative TFP Performances, 1950–2014
Source: Penn World Table

USA, in the late 1970s. But Italy's peak was higher, in 1980. Then a reversal occurred. If until 1980 the country had never ceased converging on the frontier, often at higher rates than its peers, since then it began to diverge, followed by Britain, at first, and later also by others, in a dynamic that accelerated at the turn of the century.

Figure 1.2 emphasizes this reversal, to portray it in starker contrast, by taking Italy's peak as the benchmark year and showing each country's subsequent performance relative to the level that they had reached then (the level, it bears repeating, of their convergence on the frontier).

Italy's singular trajectory speaks of a decline that is both relative, compared to other advanced economies, and absolute, compared to its own past performance. Of course, until recently the country suffered no sustained decline in the level of TFP. But the level of the world's technological and productivity frontier also rose, and what matters, especially in a context marked by deepening globalization, is an economy's capacity to remain at or near it. Its divergence from the frontier, after a remarkable process of convergence, suggests that Italy is gradually losing that capacity. Indeed, speaking not of TFP but of per capita GDP growth, Vecchi (2017, fig. 7.8 and 289) draws from the comparison between the country's 1861–2013 performance and that of the current member states of the OECD and of the whole world the conclusion that Italy's is 'a decline that is only relative, for now.'

The debate about the more general slowdown of productivity in the Western world brought up also an argument, which suggests that Figures 1.1 and 1.2 might even underestimate Italy's decline. One plausible critique addressed

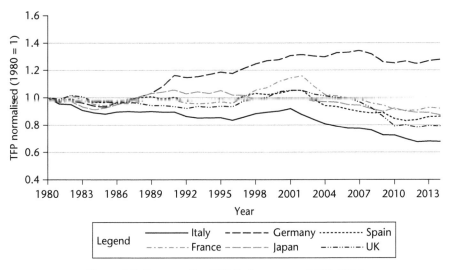

Figure 1.2 Comparative TFP Performances, 1980–2014
Source: Penn World Table

at the empirical basis for the supply-side version of the secular-stagnation hypothesis (e.g., Gordon 2015) contends that national accounts tend to lag structural change in the economy (e.g., Coyle 2014), and therefore underrate the productivity improvements already brought about by the 'revolution' in information and communication technologies (ICT). Whatever its size, which is disputed, this phenomenon must affect all advanced economies, and should *ex hypothesi* be more pronounced where change has been deeper. Consequently, as the ICT revolution has left a less profound mark in the structure of the Italian economy than in those to which we compared it (Barbiellini Amidei et al. 2013), we can safely assume that Figures 1.1 and 1.2 indicate but the lower bound of the gap that progressively opened between Italy and its peers.

The gravity of this unusual technological and organizational regress is confirmed by a closer analysis. For the rise of the share of services in the economy is not the only culprit: while after 1973 labour productivity growth 'collapsed' in that sector (Broadberry et al. 2013, 195), by then the dominant one, after 1993 it declined significantly in manufacturing too, in a downturn that has not yet been reversed (Calligaris et al. 2016; Pinelli et al. 2016).

More importantly, it was mainly TFP that drove Italy's progress towards prosperity. Figure 1.3 demonstrates it by displaying the respective contributions of population growth, capital accumulation, and TFP growth to aggregate economic growth (as they result from a standard growth-accounting exercise). It covers the past seven decades, during which Italy transformed itself from a still largely agrarian economy into an advanced industrialized one, and offers two alternative periodizations: the received one (Figure 1.3b), adopted by the literature discussed in this chapter, and that used in Chapters 7–9 (Figure 1.3a), which splits the Golden Age into two halves and emphasizes Italy's 1980 peak (for its justification see the first section of Chapter 7).

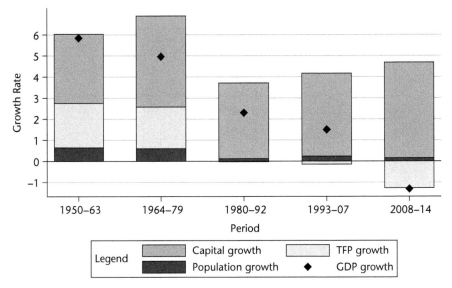

Figure 1.3a TFP Contribution to GDP Growth, 1950–2014
Source: Penn World Tables

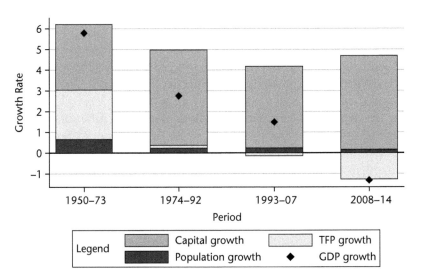

Figure 1.3b TFP Contribution to GDP Growth, 1950–2014
Source: Penn World Tables

Both graphs illustrate the downturn of TFP growth and a parallel rise in the relative weight of the contribution of capital accumulation. Compared to the orthodox periodization, Figure 1.3a highlights an acceleration of TFP during the Golden Age and suggests that the reversal occurred at the beginning of the 1980s, about one decade earlier than the moment emphasized by the literature reviewed here, when the trajectory of Italy's convergence to the frontier began to diverge from that of its peers, as shown by Figures 1.1 and 1.2.[1]

We shall return to this reversal in Chapter 9. For now it suffices to note that the contribution of TFP was high and rising while the scope for catch-up growth—through structural change and technology transfer—was greatest; hence it fell. The interpretation we shall discuss presently posits that as its convergence to the frontier progressed, and the potential for catch-up correspondingly diminished, Italy's development ought gradually to have relied more on endogenous technological and organizational progress: the declining contribution of TFP over the past three or four decades suggests that the shift between these two growth models was insufficient.

The effects were compensated by sustained capital accumulation, supported also by growing public expenditure, and by a slow but steady rise of the participation of the working-age population in the labour market (see Tables 9.1–9.3). While its capacity to combine capital and labour efficiently was falling, in other words, Italy lifted its growth rate by throwing more of them into production. But this strategy is unsustainable in the long term, as we said in the Preface, and even before the Great Recession it anyway alleviated only very modestly the effects of the downturn of TFP.

During the first decades after the war rapid growth greatly improved—and, in a virtuous circle, benefited from the improvement of—living standards, economic equality, and life expectancy, which approached the highest levels recorded in the world (Brandolini and Vecchi 2013; Vecchi 2017, ch. 3). The decline of TFP growth, first, and then the stagnation of labour productivity eventually broke that virtuous circle. The early 1990s thus marked a 'turning point' also for the nation's wellbeing, opening a phase of 'persistently high

---

[1] The evidence shown in Figure 1.3 differs from that provided by Broadberry et al. (2013). As we often rely upon this study of Italy's long-term (1861–2010) productivity performance, and upon others—those collected in Toniolo (2013a)—that refer to its findings, it seems necessary to provide a justification for that difference. It stems from the choice of data and methodology. In both cases, their approach—set out at pp. 210–16—is more sophisticated. Unlike them, in particular, we did not net out the housing sector (whose contribution to the growth potential is 'negligible', they explain: p. 213): for this and other reasons, compared to their estimates Figure 1.3 understates the relative weight of TFP. Their main findings (p. 214, fig. 7.4, and table 7.6) are that in 1951–73 capital and TFP provided contributions to aggregate growth of 1.7 and 3.3 percentage points, respectively; in 1973–93 their contributions declined, respectively, to 0.9 and 1.2 percentage points; in 1993–2010 they further declined, respectively, to 0.6 and 0.3 percentage points. In their analysis, therefore, it is only in this last period that the contribution of capital grew larger than that of TFP.

inequality and increasing sense of vulnerability' (Brandolini and Vecchi 2013, 248; see also Vecchi 2017, 287 *passim*). Now, after the global financial crisis and Italy's long recession, average real disposable income is a few percentage points lower than it was in 1995, whereas in France, Germany, and Spain it is about 25 points higher (IMF 2017, 4).

Italy faces a difficult challenge, therefore. Unless its technological and organizational progress resumes it is unclear how a parallel decline in living standards can be averted. This might lead to social dislocations, in turn, which are likely to add pressure on a parliamentary democracy that already suffers from widespread discredit (Vassallo 2015), populism (Passarelli 2015), and the personalization of politics (Pasquino 2014), faces a increasingly volatile elect-orate (Mershon 2015), and rests on a weak and fragmented party system (Cotta 2015), which appears to be evolving towards a potentially unstable and unpredictable tri-polar structure (Hopkin 2015). The moment seems dangerous, as we said.

Interpretations of Italy's Decline: the Main Questions

The literature that began investigating the causes of the nation's unusually low growth drew on a fairly uniform set of factors (de Cecco 2000; Ciocca 2003, 2007; Nardozzi 2004; Toniolo and Visco 2004; Boeri et al. 2005; Barca 2006; Rossi 2007). They include weak competition in the domestic product markets; inefficient financial intermediation, narrow capital markets, and an anaemic market for corporate control; low corporate governance standards; an inefficient labour market; public services of low quality and an inefficient public administration; low expenditure in research and development; low human capital and an inadequate education system; low trust, civicness, or social capital; and the deep regional divide.

These factors and their multiple interactions can explain why in Italy firms on average grow and innovate less than the country's peers. But both are long-standing traits of the Italian economy, and most of the underlying weaknesses 'show an incredible secular persistence' (Toniolo 2013b, 31). So any account of the causes of Italy's decline must explain also why such constraints to growth appear to have become more binding since the 1980s or the early 1990s.

Furthermore, those weaknesses were the target of the veritable flood of reforms—of the factor and product markets, of many realms of the public sector, and of essential structures of the state itself (see Barca 2006, 48)—that governments poured on the country during the 1990s and the early 2000s. They largely stemmed from the analysis we just outlined, and were spurred by the effort to accede to the EMU from the outset and adjust the structure of the economy to the ensuing loss of monetary autonomy. The reforms achieved only the first objective, however (Italy adopted the euro on 1 January 1999). In particular, the enactment of a modern competition law, three decades after it was first proposed, appears to have had modest effects on the intensity of competition (see Gigliobianco and Toniolo 2017), suggesting that the reluctance to accept the challenge of the open market—the primary defect of Italian capitalism, according to several authors (e.g., Caili 1996, Ciocca 2007; Cavazzuti 2017)—has deep and resistant roots. Hence a second question is why the reform of the institutions undergirding vast areas of both the private and the public sector failed to remove, or appreciably relax, those secular constraints.

The early studies considered both questions, and further progress was made by subsequent research (e.g., Toniolo 2013a; Gigliobianco and Toniolo 2017; Giunta and Rossi 2017). But only the first question received a satisfactory treatment, which we shall review presently. On the second one that literature has followed a line of argument that led it to the doorstep of a discussion of the *political* constraints to growth, but has not crossed that line, nor have political scientists sought to link organically their own analyses to the causes of Italy's economic malaise. So the question of why those reforms have often failed remains largely unanswered. This was no obstacle to unearthing the proximate or intermediate *economic* causes of the stagnation of productivity: but it did limit academia's ability to propose workable remedies to it, including because those that were suggested often implied yet more reforms.

Secular Weaknesses, the End of Convergence, and Four Shocks

Summarizing the results of a vast research project organized by the Bank of Italy, Toniolo (2013b) approaches the question of Italy's decline from a long historical perspective. He first notes, drawing on Gerschenkron (1962, 72–89), that between the 1890s and the early 1990s 'the narrative of Italy's economic development can be framed in the catching-up paradigm: one of Europe's "peripheral" countries converging to the "core"' (Toniolo 2013b, 9). Convergence saw the country growing faster than the early industrializers for about one century and was essentially completed in the mid-1990s, when Italy's labour productivity—in terms of output per hour worked—equalled that of its European peers and reached about 90 per cent of the level recorded by the world's productivity leader, the USA. Henceforth the country began to diverge, Toniolo (2013b, 28) argues, because it 'seems to have somehow lost its "social capacity for growth"'.[2]

---

[2] This expression, owed to Abramovitz (1986), encompasses a country's technical competence and its political and economic institutions (on which, see Chapter 2).

He contends that after the early 1990s the long-standing weaknesses of the Italian economy became binding constraints to growth because four exogenous shocks—the ICT revolution, intensified globalization, the rise of China and India, the adoption of the euro[3]—had radically changed the external environment, as well as because the country's growth model was no longer appropriate to an economy that had reached the proximity of the productivity frontier. On this last point, Toniolo (2013b, 31–2) explains that

> the very success of long-run convergence has altered the conditions that make its continuation possible. Once a country (almost) closes the productivity gap with the most advanced countries [through structural change and technology transfer], other growth factors become crucial: apt institutions (in the broad sense), research, human capital, and physical and intangible infrastructure.

Italy's failure to adjust to a transformed international environment and to its own evolution thus explains the decline of the past two decades, during which those shocks, which could have been growth opportunities, worked as 'fetters' instead.

This interpretation would equally follow from the literature we discuss in Chapter 2, and it relies, among others, upon the analysis of Barbiellini Amidei et al. (2013), who take the narrower but crucial perspective of Italy's long-run performance in technological innovation. They observe a roughly parallel decline in Italy's capacity to either absorb and creatively adapt superior foreign technology or generate technological advances domestically, a trend which 'seem[s] to have been directly associated with the dismal productivity growth' of the past two decades (p. 414). In a variegated picture, two discontinuities in long-term trends are worth mentioning here. One is that while investment in research and development (R&D) was comparatively low ever since the war, after the 1990s the 'considerable gap between Italy and the other main industrialized countries widened' (p. 413, fig. 14.13): a gap that is also of a qualitative nature, for if 'the 1960s and 1970s were characterized by R&D growth in sectors at the technologic frontier', including electronics and nuclear power, 'since the 1980s there has been a relative fall in research activity in high-technology industries and an intensification in intermediate technologic industries'. The other discontinuity, even more worrying, is that since the turn of the century also the import of foreign patents and other forms of disembodied technology has declined, in the absence of any sign that the capacity to generate technological innovation domestically has correspondingly increased. While the purchase of licences grew 'dramatically' during the economic miracle and was a 'crucial input'—relative, in particular, to domestic R&D—of firms' innovative efforts also beyond the Golden Age, it has

---

[3] Politically, this was an endogenous shock: see Chapter 9.

recently dropped back to the level of the early 1960s (0.20 per cent of GDP), well below the peak of 1978 (0.35 per cent of GDP), when Italy was the main importer of disembodied technology within the OECD, on par with Germany (pp. 396–7, fig. 14.9). In their conclusions Barbiellini Amidei et al. (2013, 414) speak of the 'decay' of Italy's innovative system, especially in the sectors of the digital revolution. In a changed world, it appears a shadow of the innovative system that Italy built half a century ago.

As to the proximate reasons for Italy's loss of its 'social capacity for growth', Toniolo (2013b) highlights both the declining average size and productivity of firms observed since the late 1980s—and especially the weakening and down-sizing of large firms, which had been and remain systemically important (Amatori et al. 2013; Onida et al. 2013)—and the large stock of public debt, which drove up both interest rates and the tax burden and often led to cuts in research and infrastructure investment (Balassone et al. 2013).[4] Following Di Nino et al. (2013), he views the overvaluation of the real exchange rate less as a cause than as a symptom of Italy's 'disease'. And he finally turns to the country's secular weaknesses. Among them, he uses the example of human capital to illustrate the argument we have just summarized (2013b, 33):

> [t]o simplify a complex issue: to successfully import and adapt foreign technology Italy needed a good pool of highly trained engineers and a workforce with basic education and skills acquired in agriculture, construction, or craftsmanship. It was well endowed with both. Close to the frontier, in a globalized world, low human capital is a barrier to the diffusion of ICT, to endogenous innovation, and to the adoption of state-the-art production processes.

This is why Italy largely 'missed the chance to exploit the ICT revolution, the present era's "general purpose technology," to increase productivity' (Toniolo 2013b, 32). The other reason that Toniolo quotes—excessive and inadequate regulation, which hindered the spread of ICT—leads us to the second question we posed.

Sisyphus's Reforms: the Adjustment to Changed Conditions

Besides achieving membership of EMU since the outset, as we said, the reforms enacted since the early 1990s were intended to adjust the structure of the economy, at once, to the completion of its convergence to the core of the

---

[4] Both Toniolo (2013b) and Balassone et al. (2013) quote also the argument—whose empirical and theoretical foundations were later carefully scrutinized, as part of the 2010–14 debate about fiscal austerity, and found partly wanting (e.g., Blyth 2013)—that a debt-to-GDP ratio greater than 90 per cent is likely to reduce growth.

Western world, and to the parallel transformation of the external environment. Toniolo contends that the adjustment proved inadequate because the implementation of the reforms 'met with grassroots resistance that rendered them often incomplete, ill-applied, and distorted', as well as because 'at the turn of the century the reform drive ran out of steam' (2013b, 31). Similar assessments may be found in the earlier and later literature (e.g., Ciocca 2007; Rossi 2007; Gigliobianco and Toniolo 2017).

To explain this resistance to institutional reform Toniolo (2013b) quotes the conclusions of Crafts and Magnani (2013), who invoke three reasons which, from converging perspectives, lead the discussion on the doorstep of politics. First, they claim that the ideological cleavage that divided society and the party system after World War II produced conflict or stalemate rather than reform: and when the divide gradually subsided, in the course of the 1980s, Italy saw the proliferation of rent-seeking interest groups, which prevented the stabilization of public finances, in particular, and were further strengthened by the collapse of the Cold War-era party system, as a result of the rupture of 1992–4. Second, Crafts and Magnani (2013, 104; our emphasis) observe a 'structural problem in the implementation of change because of a lack of political leadership in reforming the Public Administration', which stifled in particular the supply-side reforms that the private sector needed, and they suggest, in the same vein, that the reason may lie in 'the increasing influence of interest groups which *invade* both the Public Administration *and* the polity'.

Crafts and Magnani assimilate these groups to the distributional coalitions depicted by Olson (1965, 1982). Boltho (2013) appears to share this interpretation, but adds that the evidence supporting it is not very strong because empirical studies are lacking—Olson's theory 'did not attract much interest' in Italy, he explains (p. 110)—as well as because the power of trade unions—the 'major culprits of Olsonian institutional sclerosis', he argues, together with monopolies and oligopolies—has 'clearly shrunk' over the past two decades (p. 123). But other interest groups may have filled the void: in the next chapters we shall consider this possibility.

Finally, Crafts and Magnani (2013) maintain that the overall design of the country's political institutions hindered substantial policy decisions. They refer in particular to the literature that links economic performance to the characteristics of the electoral system (Persson and Tabellini 2003). If the strictly proportional electoral law in force until 1993 was widely blamed for Italy's unstable governments and relatively fragmented party system, the shift to majority rule, first, and then, in 2005, to a hybrid electoral law brought only moderate improvements: Crafts and Magnani conclude that, as we already suggested in the Preface, institutional engineering seems insufficient to raise the political system's capacity to implement structural economic reforms.

This analysis implies that the path is blocked at an earlier turn than that which retains the attention of those authors (e.g., Manasse 2013; Felice 2015, 359) and international organizations (e.g., IMF 2015a, 2017) that advocate further reforms, often more radical ones.[5] It points, rather, to the possible political causes of Italy's decline.

Toniolo takes one step in that direction in an earlier study (2012), which opens under a dark shadow. History, he reminds us, witnessed several cases of absolute economic decline, such as Belle Époque Argentina, post-war Soviet Union, Venice. Decline is often inconspicuously slow initially, Toniolo explains, and may go unremarked until a shock unveils it. It generally follows from cultural, social, and institutional sclerosis. But innovation is opposed by those (Olsonian) groups whose power and wealth would be threatened by it, and whose opposition is at once symptom and proximate cause of decline. Decline is reversible, Toniolo (2012, 15) writes, but

> cannot be fought by a small political, much less intellectual, elite. The reaction must be wide ['choral', he writes] because it implies the renewal of individual and collective ways of acting and thinking. What elites can do is to issue warnings, propose solutions, and mobilize a broad consensus around them. This is the noble and irreplaceable task of politics.

Echoing the earlier literature (e.g., Ciocca 2007; Rossi 2007), however, he concludes that although the consensus on what reforms Italy would now need is wide, they nonetheless appear to be 'politically impossible'. Events proved him mostly right. The question that we shall try to address is why.

The Empirical Studies and their Conclusions

If one accepts the main tenets of the interpretation that we have just outlined, the comparatively small size and conservative inclination of Italy's firms are both manifestations of the country's failure to adjust its growth model to a radically changed international environment and its own proximity to the productivity frontier, and proximate causes of its decline relative to its peers. Firm-level and sector-level data are thus rich fields of research to test this reading and explore the channels linking causes to effects.

This evidence is widely used in the essays from which we drew that interpretation (Toniolo 2013a). Next to them a vast empirical literature exists, recently summarized and developed by two thorough studies published by

---

[5] For example, three officials of the European Commission's directorate general for economic and financial affairs articulate a fairly extensive list of advisable reforms, simulate their impact, and conclude that the potential benefits are such that they 'leave no room for complacency' in the reform effort (Pinelli et al. 2016, 6).

the European Commission (Calligaris et al. 2016; Pinelli et al. 2016). The general approach of this literature often differs from that taken by Toniolo (2013a), which neither of those two studies relies upon. To highlight this difference, however, a more useful guide is the analysis of Pellegrino and Zingales (2014). For they test in rapid succession the main interpretations of the trends shown in Figures 1.1–1.3, and use reliable, rich, and relatively ample micro-level data covering the 1995–2006 period, which allows them to isolate the structural causes of Italy's decline from the effects of the Great Recession.

Their conclusions are clear-cut. Pellegrino and Zingales rule out all four most prominent explanations for the stagnation of Italy's productivity. The small average size of firms and their concentration in low value-added, labour-intensive sectors; the low flexibility of the labour market; the inefficiency of the public sector; and low human capital. They nevertheless find that competition from China, concentrated in those same sectors, has spurred less productivity growth in Italy than among its peers because its firms are smaller. But the decline of productivity is due almost entirely to the country's inability to exploit the ICT revolution, they conclude, ascribing it to poor management practices, which reward above all loyalty. Having remarked that 'there is something troubling about the way Italian managers are selected and rewarded',[6] Pellegrino and Zingales (2014, 24) end with this laconic assessment: 'familism and cronyism are the ultimate cause of the Italian disease'.

As we shall see, incidentally, one of these authors contributed also to research (Guiso et al. 2015) that attributes the different levels of civicness and inter-personal trust observed in present-day Italy—generally higher in the North and lower in the South—to a bifurcation that occurred in the twelfth century, which would have marked citizens' attitudes to political, economic, and social exchange.

The Open Questions and Our Interpretation

Neither Pellegrino and Zingales (2014) nor the empirical literature they build upon seem to consider the exhaustion of the catch-up growth paradigm that sustained Italy's convergence to the productivity frontier, however. Consequently, when they conclude that neither government inefficiency, low human capital, nor labour market distortions can explain the fall of TFP, because the variables employed to measure them do not show a comparable

---

[6] They find that '[e]ven after controlling for differences in firm size, the mean performance-oriented management index for Italian firms is about 0.8 standard deviations lower than the average for Austrian, French, German, Hungarian, Spanish, and British firms. Italy is also by far the lowest ranking country in [the fifteen-country sample from the EU database they used] in terms of the meritocracy index'.

decline, they neglect the possibility that after the beginning of the 1990s those factors gradually became (more) binding constraints to growth, not because they worsened but because the internal and external conditions had changed. This weakens their negative findings and reduces the explanatory power of their positive one, namely that as much as five sixths of Italy's productivity gap are explained by the relative rarity of meritocracy and performance-based management (2014, 24).

The analysis that underpins this conclusion is nonetheless persuasive, and quite consistent with the Schumpeterian growth theory that we take as our basic framework, which places firms and their incentives to innovate at the centre of the analysis. It is also cognate to the interpretation proposed by the literature we have reviewed earlier, which Crafts and Magnani (2013, 103; emphasis added) articulate thus:

> when [during the 1990s] the technological context started to change and required more product innovations, more ICT investments and corresponding changes in the organization of the production process, Italian firms got into increasing difficulties which still continue. The difficulty of achieving efficient allocations of entrepreneurial resources resulting from closed corporate governance structures centred on family-controlled and pyramidal groups proved to be a *major* competitive handicap in this context.

In essence, therefore, the contribution of this empirical literature was to isolate that causal channel among a handful of alternative ones, and measure its explanatory power. Other ones are discussed in Chapter 9, but the striking conclusions of Hassan and Ottaviano (2013) are worth noting at the outset:

> between 1995 and 2006 Italy invested more in sectors that experienced lower TFP growth [and currently] the TFP index in manufacturing is 5.77% lower than if productive resources were randomly allocated across firms.

These and similar findings (Calligaris et al. 2016) can be integrated with the interpretation according to which productivity has declined because the country's growth model was no longer appropriate to a close-to-frontier economy, and turned the four exogenous shocks that emerged in the 1990s into fetters to growth. In this perspective, resource misallocation and the low diffusion of the 'general purpose technology' of the current era, ICT, are at once effects of the country's failure to shift to a different growth strategy and proximate causes of decline. Poor management practices are one channel leading from that cause to that effect.

A channel that necessarily implies a longer and more elaborate causal chain, however, for unless one subscribes to the strong version of the cultural interpretation of Italy's secular weaknesses, 'familism and cronyism' cannot be 'the ultimate cause' of the fall of TFP. They are themselves in need of an explanation. Pellegrino and Zingales indicate one when they note (2014, 22) that in Italy 'the legal system is painfully slow and misappropriations by managers common', and suggest another one, when they use the family ownership of firms as a variable to interrogate the data. The literature we discussed earlier points to other ones: in Italy financial intermediation remains a 'petrified forest' (Toniolo 2013b, 31), and the market for corporate control inefficient (Crafts and Magnani 2013). But although this set of reasons can explain the character and persistence of the poor management practices of Italian firms, they too open further questions. Why did the efficiency of the courts not improve? Why are firms still disproportionately family-controlled, and, unlike in Germany, also predominantly family-managed? And why did sweeping reforms of company law, corporate governance, and capital markets—intended precisely to improve management practices and open up the market for corporate control—prove largely ineffective?

So the empirical literature leads us back to the questions raised by the interpretation we discussed earlier, according to which after the early 1990s Italy has lost its 'social capacity for growth'. But its focus on the choices of Italy's firms enriches such questions. For the switch to a new growth model implied change both in public policies and institutions, and in the practices and strategies of firms. Next to the failure of those reforms, therefore, stands the apparent conservative inclination of much of the private sector, which often preferred to compete on costs rather than on innovation (Daveri and Parisi 2010; Ciaccarone and Saltari 2015; Giunta and Rossi 2017). The two dynamics are intertwined, naturally, and suggest that systemic causes were at play, as the common finding—e.g., Hassan and Ottaviano (2013), Pellegrino and Zingales (2014), Calligaris et al. (2016)—that TFP growth declined in virtually all sectors and size classes would seem to confirm.

The reforms enacted since the early 1990s in fact aimed at some fundamental, deep-seated features of Italian capitalism. Not just the inefficiency and the size of the public sector, inherited by the mixed-economy model of the previous decades, but also an ownership structure largely based on family-controlled pyramidal groups even in the higher echelons of the private sector, and other features which make the country different from both 'varieties' of capitalism identified by the literature (Hall and Soskice 2001, 19–21), namely the bank-based 'coordinated market economy', exemplified by Germany and Japan, and the equity-based 'liberal market economy', exemplified by Britain and the USA. In other words, the vested interests that stunted such reforms acted to protect rents and established positions whose roots were equally deep.

These considerations suggested the lines of research we indicated in the Preface. What obstacles did the institutions, political and economic, and the social order that emerged from four decades of rapid catch-up growth pose to the adoption of a new growth model, once convergence was effectively completed? How could those institutions and that social order withstand the pressure for change that erupted after the crisis of 1992, and continues to this day? In other words, why was the public interest ignored, at that crucial juncture and a few other ones? What other interests imposed themselves on the political system, and how? Finally, the reforms that Italy needed and many of those it enacted would have benefited also the enlightened, long-term interests of many of the Olsonian groups that opposed them: why did they oppose them? What paradigm of rationality explains their strategies?

We must highlight, to conclude, that here we have not reviewed all interpretations of Italy's decline, much less all remedies proposed to reverse it.[7] Together with some lesser ones we omitted that which is arguably most prominent in the wider public debate, through the opinion pages of the *Corriere della Sera* (a wide-circulation centrist daily newspaper; for much of the past 100 years the '*Corriere*' has been Italy's most authoritative mass medium: see Ortoleva 1997b; Mancini 2015). This interpretation, propounded chiefly by Alberto Alesina and Francesco Giavazzi, argues that the main causes of the country's slow growth are the excessive size of the public sector, which crowds out private investment, and the interventionist inclination of economic policy, which distorts markets. We shall deal with it in the course of our discussion of the systemic nature of Italy's institutional inefficiencies, which emerge both in the private sector and in the public sector and show clear complementarities: our argument, in short, is that without remedying those institutional distortions shifting resources from one sector to the other is hardly a sufficient remedy.

---

[7] Most can be found in Magnani(II) (2013), a *Dictionnaire des idées reçues* written with less irony but greater detail than Flaubert's.

2

The Conceptual Framework: Growth, Institutions, and Social Orders

Long-Term Growth and Institutions – Convergence, Stages of Development, and 'Appropriate Institutions' – The Emergence and Persistence of Inefficient Institutions – The Primacy of Political Institutions and the Political Economy of Growth – Institutions: Definitions, Normative Theories, Controversies, and their Relevance – A Theory on Violence and Social Orders – The Subversion of the Formal Institutions, Transition, and Institutional Change

Long-Term Growth and Institutions

The subject matter of this book is the decline shown by Figures 1.1 and 1.2. So its point of departure must be the theories, sketched in Box 1.1, which explain economic growth. According to those theories over the long run economic growth depends on investment and innovation, which drive productivity growth.

Investment and innovation are the proximate causes of growth, however, not its deeper determinants. As North and Thomas put it (1973, 2), they 'are not causes of growth; they *are* growth'. So, what causes growth? What leads some countries to invest and innovate more than others? Four main answers have been given to these questions. Geography, and therefore climate, exposure to diseases, endowment of natural resources, and proximity to transport routes (e.g., Diamond 1997); trade and integration in international markets (e.g., Frankel and Romer 1999); culture, religion, and beliefs, following Max Weber's theory (e.g., Landes 1998); and institutions.

The latter hypothesis, owed to North and Thomas (1973), was developed by a growing literature, which holds that the quality of an economy's institutions is a first-order cause of its long-term growth and has greater impact on cross-country differences in economic performance than either geography, trade integration, or cultural traditions (e.g., North 1990, 1991, 1994, 2005; La Porta et al. 1998; Acemoglu et al. 2001, 2005; Glaeser et al. 2004; Rodrik et al. 2004; North et al. 2009; Acemoglu and Robinson 2012). This literature moves from the observation that neoclassical economic theory rests on extreme implicit assumptions about the role of the state, which is deemed to control violence, enforce rights, protect competition, and more generally ensure that economic exchange be effectively frictionless. Questioning these assumptions has stimulated research on the institutions that govern exchange and production, and has led lately to broader theories on social orders, the state, and the political economy of liberal democracy.

The scholar who re-founded this field of inquiry defined its object, 'institutions', as the rules of the game of a society, the framework within which political, social, and economic exchange occurs (North 1994, 360):

> [i]nstitutions are the humanly devised constraints that structure human interaction. They are made up of formal constraints (e.g., rules, laws, constitutions), informal constraints (e.g., norms of behavior, conventions, self-imposed codes of conduct), and their enforcement characteristics. Together they define the incentive structure of societies and specifically economies.

Among them, economists have primarily looked at the regulation of property rights, contracts, corporations, and markets, which structures the incentives of households and firms and thus influences the organization of production and exchange, the allocation of resources, the investment in capital and innovation, and the distribution of wealth. In their simplest form their conclusions seem intuitive, and can be traced back to Adam Smith's *Wealth of Nations*: if the right to property is not well-designed and effectively protected, if the contracts by which such rights are exchanged cannot predictably be enforced, and if the markets where such exchanges occur are not open to competition, there will be little incentive or opportunity to invest and innovate, resources will not be allocated to their most efficient use, markets will be smaller than they would otherwise be, and productivity and growth will remain below their potential. Inversely, societies whose economy is girded by institutions that effectively and predictably protect property rights, contracts, and competition are more likely to invest, innovate, and prosper.

Baumol's (1990) discussion of the allocation of entrepreneurial talent between alternative uses well illustrates this thesis. His argument (p. 918) is that the institutions 'that specify the relative payoffs to different entrepreneurial activities play a key role in determining whether entrepreneurship will be allocated in productive or unproductive directions': so, if a society's institutions were to change such that the returns of rent-seeking, tax evasion, or organized crime—all examples that Baumol uses—fell relative to industrial innovation, for example, then more entrepreneurs would prefer this activity over those socially undesirable ones, all other things being equal, and the economy's productivity would rise.

Hence the efficiency of institutions—quite apart from the question of their fairness—can be judged objectively, at least conceptually, depending on whether they favour investment and innovation. Several measures of the quality of institutions exist, designed on the basis of the results achieved by this line of research. Those we shall rely upon are the World Bank Institute's *Worldwide Governance Indicators* (Kaufmann et al. 2010), and, in the field of corporate governance standards, the World Economic Forum's *Global Competitiveness Reports*.

Italy's institutions generally receive low rankings, as we shall see, often far lower than the country's level of political and socio-economic development would lead one to expect. These measurements are to be taken with caution (see, e.g., Chang 2011a). But in the case of Italy they are both strikingly consistent among themselves—despite originating from different sources, data, and methodologies—and markedly distant from the country's peers. A plausible hypothesis, therefore, is that the country's decline is at least in part due to the defects of its institutions.

Convergence, Stages of Development, and 'Appropriate Institutions'

By reason of the influence that institutions exercise on the incentives to invest and innovate, growth theory, and especially its Schumpeterian version, has increasingly subsumed the main results of this literature into its own framework (e.g., Aghion and Howitt 2009, chs. 3, 4, 5, 7, and 11). Along the same rails, Gerschenkron's arguments (1962) that we evoked while discussing Italy's long-term performance were also developed into a more elaborate and empirically grounded theory of 'appropriate institutions' (Acemoglu et al. 2006; Aghion et al. 2014).

Gerschenkron's 'advantage of backwardness' (1962) is predicated upon technology diffusion. Comparatively backward countries, such as post-war Italy, can grow faster than more developed ones because if they adopt the more advanced technologies already employed by the latter they achieve technological and productivity progresses that are typically larger than those that can occur at the frontier. Backward economies can thus sustainably record faster productivity growth than more developed ones, in a process of 'convergence-led', or 'catch-up' growth, which continues until they reach the technological and productivity frontier: then convergence ends, productivity growth aligns with that of the frontier economies, and further accelerations depend on endogenously developed innovations improving on the frontier technologies.[1] Yet Gerschenkron noted that the policies and institutions that favour the importation, adaptation, and diffusion of foreign technologies are not necessarily capable of sustaining also endogenous innovation at the frontier: hence different institutions may be appropriate to different stages in the development of the same economy.

Acemoglu et al. (2006) have confirmed this argument by testing it on samples of advanced and backward economies through two measures of an economy's institutions: a measure of openness to international trade, developed by Frankel and Romer (1999), and a measure of the ease of entry of new firms in domestic markets (Djankov et al. 2002), which are significant determinants of the intensity of competition. Acemoglu and Robinson (2012) further developed this argument in a broader study, which we shall often draw upon. So as a country progresses towards the productivity frontier one would expect to see a parallel evolution in its institutions, to support the transition from a catch-up growth model to one based more on endogenous innovation.

In particular, institutions promoting competition appear to be especially important in contemporary close-to-frontier economies, in which the relationship between competition and growth—the subject of long debate (Aghion and Griffith 2005)—has been shown to be positive and fairly strong (Aghion and Howitt 2009, ch. 12; Aghion et al. 2014). Equally, the rule of law has been shown to ease firms' growth and innovation, creative destruction, and the reallocation of resources between less productive firms to more productive ones (see the last section of this chapter and Aghion et al. 2014, also for further references).

As we already noted, however, in Italy the rule of law is comparatively weak and the adoption of a modern competition policy was belated and proved relatively ineffective. In two crucial respects, therefore, the country's institutions might be inadequate to its stage of development. These institutional weaknesses may not have hindered growth during the first two or three decades after World War II: but as convergence proceeded, the impetus of structural change and technology import declined, and fresh sources of growth became necessary, they became increasingly more binding constraints.

---

[1] Of course, technology exchange would continue: there is no implication that all innovation must be endogenously generated.

The Emergence and Persistence of Inefficient Institutions

If institutions are so vital for growth and prosperity, however, why do inefficient ones emerge and persist? Why, in particular, are institutions that are no longer 'appropriate' not reformed?

Culture (Landes 1998), beliefs (Greif 1994, 2006), and legal traditions (La Porta et al. 1998; Djankov et al. 2003) certainly influence the shape of a society's institutions. But a more persuasive line of reasoning (Acemoglu et al. 2005; Acemoglu and Robinson 2006, 2012, 2013) moves from the observation that institutions are the product of the collective choices of a polity, and that they determine not just the allocation of resources but also the distribution of wealth and power (which we may define, very simply, as the ability to do or obtain what one wants in opposition to the intentions of others).

So, social groups holding political power will want to adopt, or retain, institutions that allow them to capture a disproportionate share of the resources and profits of an economy. Yet institutions of this kind are typically inefficient ones, such as regulations that allow firms to extract rents by limiting entry in the markets in which they are present. Consequently, in order to appropriate a larger share of wealth those groups must organize the economy—namely, design its institutions—in such a way that the overall wealth produced is smaller than it could otherwise be. Other social groups will oppose this, whether because they wish to receive a larger share themselves or because they care about aggregate growth, and the conflict between these two sets of interests will be solved depending on their relative political strength, and not only on the merits of their respective ideas as to the design of the institutions.

The political power of each group is determined not just by their strength within the authorities, agencies, and organizations where *de jure* political power resides, and by the prerogatives of the latter, but also by the availability of material resources—such as money to advertise their views, or to finance research supporting them—on which their *de facto* political power is based. The distribution of resources, in turn, depends on the institutions that organize the economy, namely the framework within which households and firms take economic decisions and the government makes economic policy.

Distinguishing between political and economic institutions, on one hand, and between *de jure* and *de facto* political power, on the other, clarifies the picture. If the future design of a polity's economic institutions is being discussed, the extant political institutions and the extant distribution of resources will influence the outcome of the debate: in the absence of constraints to its (*de jure* and *de facto*) political power the views of the dominant group or coalition will typically prevail, and the new economic institutions will reflect its preferences. Such institutions will determine the future performance of the economy and the future distribution of profits and resources: *ex hypothesi*, they will distribute to the elites a greater share than the previous economic institutions, and will therefore increase also their *de facto* political power. The elites will then be able to use it to reshape the political institutions too, in such a way as to increase also their *de jure* political power and further weaken the constraints to their economic dominance and *de facto* political power. So that at each round of the game elites can extract ever-larger shares of profits and resources, and further consolidate their political power.

It is thus that the dominant coalition can perpetuate, at once, its own power and the 'extractive' economic and political institutions on which it rests (Acemoglu and Robinson 2012, 335 *passim*). And as these institutions are typically inefficient—for elites cannot credibly commit to promote open economic competition and a vibrant system of political accountability, for instance, if their economic and political power ultimately depends on weakening them (Acemoglu 2003; Acemoglu and Robinson 2006)—the misallocation of the resources will also be perpetuated, to the detriment of the public interest.

More succinctly, in his Nobel lecture North (1994, 361) said that 'formal rules are created to serve the interests of those with the bargaining power to create new rules'. The preceding discussion is less pithy not just because our pen is more trembling than his, but also because it encompasses both the formal institutions, such as laws and constitutions, and the informal ones, such as social norms and conventions: for '[i]t is the admixture of formal rules, informal norms, and enforcement characteristics that shapes economic performance' (North 1994, 366). The question whether elites can influence also a society's informal institutions is dealt with in Chapter 3: but the hypothesis that they can ought to be borne in mind, as we turn to the literature that placed these interactions between economic and political dynamics at the centre of its attention.

The Primacy of Political Institutions and the Political Economy of Growth

While it is economic institutions that directly influence economic outcomes, therefore, the long-term performance of an economy may depend to a greater extent on the quality of its political institutions, whose openness is crucial. If they effectively constrain the elite's ability to reshape the economic institutions to its own advantage, and ensure that that power be contestable and the political system competitive and pluralistic, the emergence of inefficient institutions, both economic and political, will be less likely. Indeed, economists have often investigated the correlations between economic performance and institutions that are more usually associated with the health of a democracy, such as the accountability of governments and the role of the media (Besley and Burgess 2001, 2002), or the electoral systems and the form of government (Persson and Tabellini 2003; Acemoglu 2005).

More recent research has addressed directly the long-debated question whether democracy causes growth. Moving from the Schumpeterian paradigm we evoked earlier, Aghion et al. (2008) observed the long-run (1964–2003) performance of twenty-eight manufacturing sectors in 180 economies and compared it to a measure of the quality of their democracy (the *Polity IV* index). They found a positive correlation, dependent however on the proximity to the technological and productivity frontier: the nearer the frontier a manufacturing sector is, the stronger the positive effect of democracy (in the country of the sector in question) on its productivity: so growth is higher in more democratic countries when they are close to the technological frontier, but not also when they are distant from it.[2]

This literature largely belongs to the fields of development studies and economic history, and generally examines polities quite different from contemporary Italy. It is relevant also for our own purposes, however, because the theory of appropriate institutions applies at every stage of development, and especially when the push of convergence declines and an economy must switch to a growth strategy based more on endogenous innovation (Aghion et al. 2014). The creative destruction that such a transition implies will threaten those groups, economic and political, whose power and wealth are rooted in the catch-up model and are safeguarded by the institutions that sustained it: so these groups are likely to resist the transition, and if they command sufficient power they may delay or impede it (Acemoglu and Robinson 2012). This, indeed, is the hypothesis whose lineaments we sketched in Chapter 1, and shall develop later: the four decades of catch-up growth that Italy experienced after the end of World War II generated political and economic elites, which resisted reform as the country approached the productivity frontier, fearing a reduction of their power and rents. This idea was advanced already by Gerschenkron (1970), when he recognized that his earlier advantage-of-backwardness theory (1962) depends also on a political condition. He remarked, for instance, that the ruling elites of Austria-Hungary turned the state into an obstacle to economic development because they viewed industrialization, economic progress, and even the railways as threats to their power and potential carriers of revolution.

---

[2] Acemoglu et al. (2014) argue that democracy enhances growth also in backward economies. See also Sen's compelling arguments (1999, 36–40, 146–59; 2009, 345–8) on the 'constitutive and instrumental role' of individual freedoms and democracy for development.

These considerations, finally, may be relevant also at the other end of the development spectrum, for recent research identifies apparent oligarchic traits in the US democratic system. In particular, based on several indexes of 'material power', which may be roughly assimilated to the notion of *de facto* political power we used earlier, Winters and Page (2009, 740) suggest that through channels such as lobbying, opinion shaping, and election finance, 'an oligarchy may dominate certain narrowly defined but very important areas of policy making'. Gilens and Page (2014) tested a similar hypothesis by comparing survey data on policy preferences and actual policy choices during the 1981–2002 period, and confirmed it. The rise of an oligarchy is not per se inconsistent with democracy, Winters and Page (2009, 733) argue, and implies no conspiracy: elites need not explicitly coordinate their choices in order to exercise their power because '[t]he common material interests of the wealthy can be sufficient for that'.

This research has been criticized (e.g., Matthews 2016), and may have to be taken with caution. Even so, it is important to remark that it concerns only one aspect of the problem, for the data used by Gilens and Page (2014, 576) reflects the effects of elites' ability 'to shape policy outcomes on contested issues [and set] the agenda of issues that policy makers consider', but not also the effects of their ability to shape the preferences of the public, which is likely to be considerable (see, e.g., Rodrik 2014).

If so, however, oligarchy is not inconsistent with productivity growth either, as the US economy generally performed better than its more egalitarian European peers during the past three decades. This might be due to the fact that the US model—its financial markets and corporate governance practices, for instance—combines the interests of past and future innovators better than other ones, stimulating their cooperation. More interesting for our purposes is to note that these oligarchical traits have appeared in a democracy whose quality is generally ranked higher than Italy's: in the absence of comparable empirical studies on the country, therefore, this US literature may serve as a marker for the confines of a possible similar problem in the peninsula.

Institutions: Definitions, Normative Theories, Controversies, and their Relevance

Institutional economics is not without controversy. As the word is polysemic, the notion of 'institutions' itself is contested. North views them as rules, formal and informal, and their 'enforcement characteristics' (e.g., 1994). Others broaden its meaning so as to encompass also organizations and beliefs (e.g., Greif 1994, 2006). Organizations are often called 'institutions' in common parlance as well as in other fields of the social sciences. Organizations are created by, embody, shape, and respond to rules. They are naturally central to our discussion, as the next sections will illustrate, as is people's capacity to organize themselves into sustainable corporate bodies, such as banks or political parties, capable of undertaking credible commitments over the long term. Yet, precisely because of these interactions between institutions—as North defines them—and organizations, it seems preferable to keep them notionally separate.

Beliefs pose a more delicate question, for institutions-rules are certainly not the only factor that affects people's decisions. As the outcome of their choices depends also on how the world and other agents will respond to them, beliefs about how the world functions and expectations about the reactions of other agents will weigh on the evaluation of the costs and benefits of each available alternative—such as, for example, to either breach a commitment or comply with it—no less than the incentives generated by the prescriptions, rewards, and sanctions flowing from a polity's institutions (see Chapter 3 and Greif 2006). Indeed, both North (2005) and North et al. (2009) clarify that institutions do influence, and leverage upon, agents' cognitive beliefs and expectations: and changes in the formal institutions are intended precisely to alter, in some specific respect, the pre-existing beliefs and expectations of agents, so as to guide their choices, and will be implemented to the degree that they succeed in doing so (e.g., Basu 2015). In other words, the credibility of a rule—and consequently the degree of spontaneous, uncoerced compliance with it—depends not just on the rewards and sanctions it establishes, but also on one's expectations about whether the authorities will enforce it and whether other people too will comply with it. It depends, in North's terms, on the 'enforcement characteristics' of the rule and on the expectations and beliefs that agents have about them.

Incentives, beliefs, and expectations are not the only determinants of people's choices, finally, which reflect also the influence of culture, broadly understood, and of ideas, about one's interests and preferences as well as about fairness or justice (e.g., Sen 1999, 2009; Rodrik 2014; Mukand and Rodrik 2016).[3] But while Chapter 3 shall argue that rules, beliefs, ideas, and culture all influence each other and jointly shape people's choices, for the sake of clarity we shall nevertheless employ North's definition: institutions are rules, formal and informal, as actually enforced.

Simplicity suggests following also the practice of bundling several institutions into a composite one. We already mentioned 'openness to trade', which

---

[3] In a similar register, Chang (2011a, 489–90) argues that 'human beings are products of existing institutions, which are in turn a mixture of deliberate choices made by agents of yesteryears and the institutions that had existed prior to those agents and at least partially formed them', and that a country's choice of its own (formal) institutions may follow 'its own notion of rationality, efficiency and justice'.

is the sum total of the numerous 'micro' institutions governing the exchanges between an economy and the rest of the world. But even a notion as apparently anodyne as property rights—the central, and sometimes exclusive, object of study of much of the literature, Chang deplores (2011a, 485)—'is composed of an impossibly wide range of component institutions' such as land law, tax law, and inheritance law, for example. More importantly, Chang adds, concepts such as the 'rule of law', 'control of corruption', and the 'enforceability of contracts' do not just lump wide sets of underlying institutions together, but also identify their *function* rather than their *form*—such as the degree of independence of the judiciary, for example, which is a component of each of those 'macro' institutions. Yet, while bearing in mind that these notions are composite and shift the semantic focus from form to function, it nevertheless seems not just convenient but also legitimate to call them 'institutions' because they capture the concrete outcomes produced by the underlying formal ones, in keeping with North's argument that what matters for economic performance is much less the precise design of a 'micro' institution than its interactions with the other ones, formal and informal, and its enforcement characteristics. Empirical research for instance shows that while *formal* judicial independence does not have any impact on economic growth, an *actually* independent judiciary enhances it considerably (Feld and Voigt 2003), and that the actual—rather than merely formal—independence of prosecutors is a potent deterrent against government corruption (van Aaken et al. 2010). So focusing on form rather than function, and on micro rather than macro institutions, could blur the distinction between an institution's outward design and its concrete, actual character. The importance of this distinction is well illustrated by the evolution of Italy's judiciary, which, as we shall see, between 1948 and the 1980s moved from a condition of subservience to the executive power and the country's politico-economic elites, to one of actual and often confident independence. Under virtually unchanged formal rules, the informal ones and their enforcement characteristics had gradually evolved, leading to the emergence of a radically different micro institution (an *actually* independent judiciary) and a changed composite one (a stronger rule of law).

This example leads us to the more substantive controversies that traverse the field of institutional economics, which concern institutional change and the causal relationships between institutions and development. A critical essay by Chang (2011a), the sixteen responses to it (in the same issue of the same journal), and his reply to them (2011b) outline most of the contested points. The debate reaches also the theoretical and empirical underpinnings of the literature that we have reviewed, but focuses mainly on its normative implications—which in the last decade have often informed the policies of the IMF, the World Bank, and other development organizations. Chang is persuasive when he exposes the weakness of some of the prescriptions for developing countries, or criticizes their insufficient attention to the broader socio-economic context, the opportunity costs of institutional reform, and the complementarities between different institutions. Similar points are raised by North et al. (2009, 264–5) and Acemoglu and Robinson (2012, 446), who note that the adoption of 'model' institutions without regard to context may have limited or even perverse effects, as well as by Rodrik (2008), who indeed argues that the institutions adequate to a developing economy are often second-best ones.

This discussion is of limited relevance for our purposes, however, because we are interested mainly in the *pars destruens* of institutional economics. We shall employ this literature to illuminate the institutional roots of Italy's decline, and then argue that they are the main (intermediate) causes of it. We shall mostly concentrate on institutions whose importance is generally beyond dispute, moreover, such as the rule of law, political accountability, or the promotion of competition. And although some normative implications can be drawn from our analysis, Sen (2009) nonetheless demonstrates that to improve outcomes neither a complete theory of justice nor a theory of perfect institutions are needed: visible imperfections in a polity's institutions can be remedied also without them.

More relevant to our interests is Chang's observation (2002, 14–20; 2011a; 2011b) that the mainstream literature devotes insufficient attention to the possibility that causality may run in both directions: while good institutions do favour development, development may in turn stimulate, or even cause institutional improvements. In parallel, Chang (2011a, 489) persuasively criticizes both the 'extreme voluntarism' of part of the normative literature, for its belief that 'institutions can be changed very easily if there is a political will', and the 'fatalism' of what he calls the 'climate-culture school',[4] which holds that 'institutions are basically shaped by basically immutable factors, like climate, geography and culture'. He contends (2011a, 476), on the contrary, that

> [e]conomic development changes institutions through a number of channels.
> First, increased wealth due to growth may create higher demands for higher-
> quality institutions . . . Second, greater wealth also makes better institutions more
> affordable. Institutions are costly to establish and run, and the higher their quality
> the more 'expensive' they become . . . Third, economic development creates new
> agents of change, demanding new institutions.

North (e.g., 2005) recognizes the two-way causality between institutions and economic development, and thus also the possibility of endogenous institutional

---

[4] To which he (controversially) associates also Acemoglu et al. (2001, 2003).

reform (on which see Greif and Laitin 2004; Greif 2006, ch. 6 *passim*); and the evolution of Italy's judiciary between 1945 and the 1980s does indeed suggest that reverse causation was also at play. The argument is consonant with the theory of 'appropriate institutions', moreover, according to which an economy's technological and material progress creates the need and at least some demand for corresponding progress in its institutions. But the most convincing analysis of this question may be drawn from North et al. (2009), who broaden the horizon to the logic of the social orders in which institutions are embedded.

A Theory on Violence and Social Orders

The question of how institutions change is central to our interests. Because an economy's progression through the stages of its development requires institutional reform, according to the (Schumpeterian) growth theory we rely upon. And because any account of Italy's recent decline must explain also why the reforms enacted during the 1990s proved largely ineffective.

We already discussed how inefficient—or 'extractive', or 'inappropriate'—institutions can emerge and persist. North et al. (2009) enrich this analysis. They set the main findings of institutional economics as the foundation for an ambitious attempt to explain the various social orders that history has produced and the links between a polity's social order and its institutions. Articulated as a 'conceptual framework' to guide further research, this theory has already found significant empirical support (North et al. 2012; Gollwitzer Franke and Quintyn 2012) and is quite compatible with the main body of the literature reviewed thus far.

Violence is a notion that will recur frequently, because this theory moves from the observation that control of it is the primary function of social orders (North et al. 2009, 13–18). But what follows need not be read as a digression into matters of mere theoretical interest, because the Italian state does not have the Weberian monopoly of violence over the whole national territory. In parts of Calabria, Campania, and Sicily the use and the threat of violence by entrenched criminal organizations is accepted by significant segments of the population as a permanent organizing feature of society, in fact, and is often sought as a means to make unlawful pacts—such as corruption and vote buying, as we shall see in Chapter 7—immediately and predictably enforceable. The violence exercised by organized crime is thus legitimate, in a broad sense, and performs a function that makes it a direct, if parasitic, competitor of the state's law-enforcement function.

North et al. (2009) distinguish between three categories of social orders: primitive societies of hunter-gatherers; limited-access social orders; and open-access ones. The limited-access order arose between 5,000 to 10,000 years ago, on the emergence of agriculture, and it gave a hierarchical organization to the larger and more specialized groups that cultivation and irrigation required. At that juncture, the violence which prevailed in primitive societies was ended by granting special privileges to their more powerful members, which secured rents drawn from the increased output of the economy: as such rents would have declined or disappeared had endemic violence returned, because output would have fallen, the 'specialists in violence' to whom the rents were reserved could credibly commit to each other to restrain the use of force (North et al. 2009, 18–21, and 30 *passim*). This social order has dominated recorded human history and remains prevalent today, and is therefore also called the 'natural state' (North et al. 2009, 31). It organizes society through patronage networks, which guarantee to their adherents the protection of persons who hold military, political, economic, or religious power: the leaders of such networks make up the dominant coalition of society, tied together by a pact. What makes the pact possible and self-enforcing are such rents and the incentives they generate, without which violence would revert to being a rational choice. Rents, in turn, are created and protected by limiting access to valuable assets, resources, or activities (e.g., land, trade, education, voting), which are reserved for the elites, and by limiting ordinary citizens' ability to form organizations that could magnify their power and opportunities (e.g., militias, political parties, trade unions, joint stock companies).

Constraining political and economic competition is a necessary trait of the natural state, because rents must be permanent if order is to be maintained, and access must be limited in both spheres. Equally, the stability of this social order requires that the distribution of economic assets conform to, and support, the distribution of political and military power. This permits a 'double balance' to establish itself: a balance of privileges and rents among the military, political, economic, and other components of each of the factions that compose the dominant coalition, and a mirroring balance among such factions (North et al. 2009, 20, 42, and 259).[5]

By virtue of these features the natural state is a stable social order. But it is not static, for violence can erupt in the form of revolutions of the excluded, insurgencies of new elites, or conflicts within the dominant coalition about the distribution of rents: '[t]he dominant coalition holds together only if the balance of economic and political interests can be maintained' (North et al. 2009, 50). Natural states can thus be divided into fragile, basic, or mature ones, each displaying different degrees of economic efficiency and political stability. The spectrum is very broad, and encompasses Athens as well as Sparta and the European *ancien régimes* as well as the vast majority of contemporary

---

[5] On the mirroring balance and mutual support between extractive political and economic institutions, see Acemoglu and Robinson (2012, 335–403).

states. Outwardly, the differences among these examples outweigh their similarities: but in each case the social order rests on limits to competition, stable rents, patronage networks, and a pact among the members of the dominant coalition to restrain violence and share rents. Such coalitions may differ, equally, but must include at least the military, political, and economic elites. And the pacts that tie them together can be either informal or covert, as in tribal societies or contemporary imperfect democracies, or explicit and formalized, as in fourteenth-century Venice or sixteenth-century Genoa, for example.[6]

Unlike the natural state, the open-access social order grants to its citizens equal rights, protected by the rule of law, and allows them to enter political and economic competition as well as to form organizations, through which they can coordinate the pursuit of their aims and thereby amplify their power and influence: privileges are not protected by the state, and over time competition erodes those rents that arise out of political or economic success, in a Schumpeterian process of creative destruction (North et al. 2009, 15–16, 21–5, 110, and 260–2). Just as constraints to economic and political competition mutually reinforce each other in the natural state, so too in these societies open access to politics sustains open access to the economy, and vice versa. Hence the importance of the institutions and authorities that ensure that both systems remain open, such as the constitutional checks and balances and the rule of law, on one hand, and the judiciary and the regulators of the economy, on the other (North et al. 2009, 113, 138).

As competition and impersonally enforced rights organize social cooperation, open-access social orders are more inclusive and efficient than the natural state, and favour both economic and political development (North et al. 2009).[7] They are also stable, if the exercise of violence is centralized and placed under political control, because the authorities that hold the monopoly over the legitimate use of force are bound by the rule of law; the political and economic power of the elites that influence such authorities is exposed to competition and therefore contestable; and the possibility of coercing citizens beyond the established rules is constrained by the existence of freely formed political, economic, or other organizations, which can coordinate their reaction against the curtailment of their rights.

This social order emerged during the nineteenth century and did not expand much beyond Europe and a few of its older colonies. North et al. (2009, xii, 13, and 112) estimate that today only perhaps twenty-five nations

---

[6] See, e.g., Greif (2006, chs. 6 and 8), Acemoglu and Robinson (2012, 152–6), Toniolo (2012).
[7] Again, the analysis of this social order may usefully be compared with the discussion of the virtuous circle between inclusive political and economic institutions in Acemoglu and Robinson (2012, 302–34).

can be regarded as open-access societies, hosting about 15 per cent of the world's population.

An attempt to explain the logic of 'recorded human history' and organize it into a two-order taxonomy can seem perplexing. This theory is also quite recent, and its validity cannot be fully assessed without further testing and elaboration. Nonetheless, at its core lies a powerful and coherent synthesis of well-established results reached by economics and political science, which offers an especially persuasive framework for understanding the functioning of institutions and the conditions for institutional change, both radical and gradual. Within these more limited confines it therefore seems a reliable support for our inquiry.

The Subversion of the Formal Institutions, Transition, and Institutional Change

> *E se le leggi secondo gli accidenti in una città variano, non variano mai, o rade volte, gli ordini suoi: il che fa che le nuove leggi non bastano, perché gli ordini, che stanno saldi, le corrompono.*

> [And while a city's laws change according to its vicissitudes, never or rarely do its orders change: which implies that new laws will not suffice, for orders, which stand firm, will corrupt them.]

> (Machiavelli, *Discourses* I.3)

Both social orders are stable and self-sustaining. But the two equilibria are radically different. The open-access one is based on the centralization of the use of force, limited government, open competition, and equal rights, access to which is protected by the rule of law. The limited-access one guarantees stability through rents and patronage, conversely, buttressed by limits to competition. Two consequences particularly relevant for our discussion follow.

The first is that the same institutions function differently in the two social orders (North et al. 2009, 137–40). This phenomenon can be observed most starkly in those developing countries that have adopted formal institutions mirroring those of well-governed democracies. The reason is that such institutions have typically been 'corrupted', as the epigraph warns, or 'subverted' (North et al. 2009, 27–8 and 262–3; North 2005, 48 *passim*): through uneven enforcement and the influence of the pre-existing informal norms they have been altered and adapted to the logic of the limited-access social order. A sizeable gap may thus exist between a polity's formal, written institutions and its *actual* ones. In natural states the judiciary can hardly be impartial, in particular, for its logic implies both a structural bias in favour of the dominant coalition and its clients, and the use of law enforcement as an instrument to protect rents and strengthen patronage (so we may already advance the hypothesis that the Italian judiciary's progress from subservience to independence might reflect an evolution in the country's social order). Likewise, cartels are often formally proscribed but *de facto* tolerated, because competition would dissolve the rents on which the natural state is based (interestingly, as we already noted, in Italy the adoption of a modern competition law, in 1990, appears to have had little effect on the intensity of competition). Equally, in natural states government services and public goods are typically distributed according to who the recipients are, or to whom they are connected, for allocating them according to objective criteria would run counter to the logic of this social order: indeed, empirical research suggests that natural states 'cannot issue something as seemingly simple as a driver's license on an impersonal basis' (North et al. 2009, 11). Besides creating fertile ground for extracting rents through patronage and corruption, this increases the incentive for ordinary citizens to join those hierarchical patron-client networks, through which elites extend their control over society, limit electoral competition, and thereby also reduce their own political accountability.[8]

Such mutual influences, discussed in greater detail in Chapter 4, suggest also that a polity's set of institutions should be viewed as a *system*, in which the malfunctioning of one part affects the others. In natural states, in particular, elections typically do not guarantee 'citizen control of governments and officials' because political competition is generally restricted and the legislature is often unable to serve as a 'check on the executive' (North et al. 2009, 265, 267). This confirms the inherent limitations of analyses that concentrate on formal institutions alone, or, as already noted, of reform programmes that rely predominantly on constitutional engineering or on the precise design of 'micro' institutions: it implies that the focus of attention, for both descriptive and normative purposes, should rather be on the concrete performance of those horizontal 'macro' institutions that influence the functioning of the governance system taken as a whole, such as the rule of law, the constitutional checks and balances, the other constraints on the executive power, and the other sources of political accountability, such as the freedom of the media and citizens' capacity to act collectively.

The second consequence is that efforts to improve the institutions of limited-access societies tend to contradict the logic upon which that social order is based (North et al. 2009, 148 *passim*, 264–5). The dominant coalition will resist reforms that promote economic competition or strengthen the independence of the judiciary, for instance, because they threaten their power and

---

[8] This approach to the analysis of rents, patronage, and the elites' 'capture' of democratic politics can usefully be compared with Acemoglu and Robinson (2006) and Acemoglu et al. (2011).

rents (see also Acemoglu and Robinson 2006, 2012, 2013). But if such reforms succeed the incentives that had originally allowed society to contain violence would dissolve together with those rents (North et al. 2009, 264). Rents, as already noted, are the primary condition of stability in the natural state, for they make the pact among elites self-enforcing and stable: so even though reform would expand their economic and political opportunities, ordinary citizens too might withhold their support—as Machiavelli already noted[9]— because institutional change could threaten the peace and their own security. It follows that in the natural state accepting clientelism and corruption is often a rational strategy for ordinary citizens, which need not be explained by (often sweeping, as we shall see in Chapter 3) claims about culture or traditions. If reform is unviable, and if without reform citizenship rights are largely empty, citizens will exchange them for the favours that clientelism can guarantee: if a public good such as health or education services tends to be arbitrarily distributed, for example, it can be individually rational for ordinary citizens to pledge their loyalty to a faction of the elite in return for the particularistic provision of that service (which becomes, in effect, a private good), rather than to engage in a costly fight to enforce one's right to one's fair share of the public good. This, in essence, is the logic that drives the spiral discussed in Chapter 4.

Institutional change is an endogenous process, therefore, and deep, epochal reforms will hardly be feasible or effective without a parallel transition from a limited-access social order to an open-access one.[10] For if a polity remains on the same equilibrium the dominant coalition will either prevent the adoption of new formal institutions, or subvert and bend them to the logic of the extant equilibrium. Both North et al. (2009) and Acemoglu and Robinson (2012) argue that transition is an equally endogenous process, slow and non-linear: progress is neither necessary nor inevitable, and advances can always be reversed. They differ slightly on how transition can happen. We examine both approaches because the case of transition societies is that which interests us most, as Italy has progressively abandoned the limited-access social order, we shall argue, but has not yet fully shifted onto the open-access equilibrium.

Acemoglu and Robinson observe (2012, 455–62) that transitions occurred when pluralistic coalitions of non-elites were able to exploit 'critical junctures', that is, historical accidents which opened the opportunity to both constrain

---

[9] In the *Prince* (VI) he argues that changing 'orders'—*ordini* or *costituzioni* in the original—is 'the most difficult thing of all' by reason both of the opposition of those who profit from the old ones, and of the timidity of those who would benefit from change but are uncertain about the outcome (see also *Discourses* I.2). Likewise, the pre-eminence given by North et al. (2009) to the question of violence is strikingly reminiscent of Machiavelli's conclusion that only well-armed innovators succeed in changing 'orders'.

[10] The theory of endogenous institutional change outlined in Greif and Laitin (2004) and Greif (2006, ch. 6) focuses more on the evolution of individual (macro) institutions than on the institutional system and social order taken as a whole.

the power of the existing elite, or overturn it, and establish more inclusive political institutions, under whose aegis more inclusive economic institutions also emerged, which in turn strengthened political pluralism in a self-reinforcing virtuous circle. To set off this process, according to this reading, the 'empowerment' of a sufficiently broad segment of non-elite social forces is crucial.

Taking a different perspective, North et al. (2009) posit that transition must be compatible with the solution given by the natural state to the problem of violence, which is to pacify elites through rents. Hence transition is possible only if it proceeds through steps that are consistent with the immediate interests of the elite—which would otherwise prevent them or react violently—but are at the same time capable of opening up access to political and economic competition. And it will be sustainable only if violence can be constrained by other means than rents.

Natural states become ripe for transition when they can sustain 'impersonal exchange' (North et al. 2009, 25–7, 148 *passim*). The natural state is based on 'personal exchange', in which the two sides—two members of the elite, or a patron and a client—have a long-term relationship: in such societies what facilitates the enforcement of contracts, deters cheating, and fosters trust and cooperation is the fact that dealings are repeated, which allows the cheated party to retaliate. Impersonal exchange instead occurs outside of the restricted circle of the persons with whom one deals repeatedly, and by consequence it greatly increases opportunities, market size, specialization, and social welfare. But impersonal exchange is possible only if a credible form of third-party enforcement exists that can punish and deter cheating: what makes it viable is primarily the presence of courts, therefore, backed by the Weberian monopoly on violence and capable of protecting property rights and enforcing contracts. Such courts would typically first be available to elites only. But once impersonal exchange is possible among them, new entrants can be co-opted within their ranks and transition can begin.

Transition does not necessarily follow from reaching such a threshold, however, for elites comprise a small segment of the population and face a dilemma. Co-opting new members or classes of citizens makes the social order more resilient and improves economic outcomes, through economies of scale and specialization, but it can dilute the rents and especially the *de jure* and *de facto* political power of the original members. So transition begins when the dominant coalition judges that the benefits of enlargement outweigh the effects of dilution, or underestimates the latter: then a greater proportion of the population become citizens with equal rights, and the opening of the social order gathers strength (North et al. 2009, 190 *passim*).

The benefits of enlargement might be the prevention of a revolution. Acemoglu and Robinson (2006, 2012) note that democracy is typically granted by elites when ordinary citizens can credibly threaten an uprising, and would therefore not be appeased by concessions—such as larger provision of public goods—which, absent radical institutional change, can be revoked once the threat of revolution has abated. The establishment of democracy, the rule of law, and effective constraints on the executive power conversely allows the extant elites—and future ones—to credibly commit to respect the newly granted political and civic rights, and thus avert the revolution.

So, the capacity of non-elites to organize themselves—in political parties, for instance, including for the purpose of credibly threatening to revolt—plays a central role in the transition process delineated by North et al. (2009, 158–66, 194–213), and closely recalls the emphasis placed by Acemoglu and Robinson on the 'empowerment' of non-elites (2012, 455–62). The two approaches differ less than their language and lines of reasoning may suggest.

Italy's transition richly illustrates these theories. The alternative between democratization and repression is quite visible between the late 1890s and the early 1920s, for instance, and during the 1960s and 1970s we shall see both an expansion of citizens' equal rights and clear signs of the reversibility of transition. The Italian case will suggest also that the binary taxonomy of North et al. (2009) might be too rigid, however, and that, contrary to what Acemoglu and Robinson (2012) seem to posit, in a country in which inefficient and efficient institutions coexist—as is typically the case in the transition phase—change can stem also from *endogenously* generated shocks to the extant equilibrium.

3

The Conceptual Framework: Collective Action, Trust, Culture, and Ideas

Introduction: the Core of Our Conceptual Framework – The Collective Action Problem: the Common Good, Individual Rationality, and the Capacity of Citizens to Organize – The Consequences: 'Distributional Coalitions' and Institutional Sclerosis – Overcoming the Collective Action Problem: Laws and Social Norms – The Question of Compliance: Rational Choice, Beliefs, and Expectations – Social Norms: Origin and Change – Social Capital, Trust, and 'Civicness' – Trust, Good Government, and Development: the Question of Causality – A Critique of the Cultural Hypothesis – The Largely Independent Role of Ideas

Introduction: the Core of Our Conceptual Framework

In Chapter 2 we argued that over the long run economic growth depends primarily on institutions, whose evolution should follow and sustain a country's progress through the stages of its development. Institutions apt to support a backward economy's convergence to the productivity frontier—through structural change and the absorption of foreign, more advanced technology—may thus be no longer 'appropriate' once the frontier has been reached, and may depress growth by failing to stimulate the higher intensity of Schumpeterian creative destruction that at-the-frontier innovation requires.

Yet the synchrony between economic progress and institutional reform depends on political conditions, and can be broken. The character of a polity's institutions—efficient and 'inclusive', or inefficient and 'extractive'—is predominantly determined by its social order, in fact, which largely reflects the allocation of power. And as at any stage of development the extant allocation of power would be threatened by creative destruction, political and economic, the extant elites are likely to resist reform.

So we highlighted also the dynamics that can lead a polity to give itself inefficient formal institutions, or to retain ones that became inappropriate to its stage of development, as well as the reasons that explain how efficient formal institutions can be subverted and reform fail. Besides the interests and strategies of the dominant coalition, which typically seeks to preserve the social order on which its power rests, we highlighted in particular the logic that may lead society to acquiesce to the persistence of institutions detrimental to social welfare.

These are the foundations for the hypothesis that has already been sketched: namely, that Italy is declining because as it approached the productivity frontier its social order—which is in transition towards the 'open-access' equilibrium but still presents relatively more traits of the 'limited-access' one than its peers—often prevented or subverted the necessary institutional reforms.

If this hypothesis and its theoretical foundations seem unfit to explain the stagnation of a liberal constitutional democracy hosting Europe's second largest manufacturing sector, the reason may be that Chapter 2 has neglected three important issues: the role played by beliefs, expectations, culture, and ideas; how informal institutions—social norms, mainly—function and change; and what obstacles prevent citizens from collectively advancing their interest in reforming inefficient institutions and opening up the social order. The latter is a particularly salient question, because a society's capacity to organize in pursuit of its common interests is both a crucial variable for the transition from less to more open social orders (North et al. 2009) and for institutional reform (Acemoglu and Robinson 2012), and is the perspective from which the relevance of this literature for the analysis of Italy's problems is best visible.

The Collective Action Problem: the Common Good, Individual Rationality, and the Capacity of Citizens to Organize

Aristotle's *Politics* opens thus:

> [w]e see that every city-state is a community of some sort, and that every community is established for the sake of some good (for everyone performs every action for the sake of what he takes to be good).

If we read 'good' as 'common good', however, and assume that everyone pursues their own self-interest and acts rationally, this passage is vitiated by a fallacy of composition, because the common interest of the group may not coincide with the individual interest of its members. Although the establishment of the city-state would benefit all its prospective citizens, in fact, the rational pursuit of their self-interest will nevertheless prevent each of them from incurring costs to contribute to its establishment: for precisely because the *polis* is a public good, whose benefits would be enjoyed by all irrespective of whether or not they have contributed, each prospective citizen would have an interest to 'free ride' on the contributions of others: and it can readily be shown that in such circumstances no rational person would contribute. More precisely, the author who coined that expression (Olson 1965, 2) predicts that

> [u]nless the number of individuals in a group is quite small, or unless there is coercion or some other special device to make individuals act in their common interest, *rational, self-interested individuals will not act to achieve their common or group interests.*

Olson's logic is compelling, and was soon formalized in the language of game theory (Hardin 1971). The 'free rider' or 'collective action' problem that he identified is also unsettling, however, as it implies that societies may be locked into countless sub-optimal equilibria due to the impossibility of reconciling individual self-interested rationality with the common good.

And yet large *poleis* did emerge in Greece, and collective action leading to the creation or preservation of public goods is often observed beyond the narrow confines of Olson's 'zero contribution' prediction. The main reasons are two, according to the empirical and theoretical literature it spawned (reviewed by Ostrom 2000). First, social norms that favour cooperation—by leveraging on trust, reciprocity, and reputation—can allow rational, self-interested agents to overcome the free rider problem (Ostrom 1990, 2000). Second, collective action may respond also to motivations and values that trump—or shape the preferences that people maximize through—the strictly instrumental calculus considered by standard rational choice theory (Hirschman 1982, ch. 5; Sen 2009, ch. 8). In either case 'civicness' plays an important role, foreshadowed—to complete the classical example—by Pericles's funeral oration (Thucydides, II.40):

> [a]n Athenian citizen does not neglect the state because he takes care of his own household; and even those of us who are engaged in business have a very fair idea of politics. We alone regard a man who takes no interest in public affairs, not as a harmless, but as a useless character.

But before approaching these questions Olson's reasoning must detain us a little further, because, as Ostrom (2010, 156) noted, 'while empirical evidence generates some optimism that collective action can be achieved in some settings, the *problem* of collective action remains'.

This problem underlies also two issues very relevant to an analysis of Italy's decline, namely political passivity—or the preference of citizens for 'exit' or 'loyalty' over 'voice', in Hirschman's framework (1970)—and the weakening of the rule of law by reason of social tolerance for illegality—or, in North's language (1994), the distortion of formal institutions through lax or deviant enforcement. Both political accountability and the quality of the rule of law critically depend on costly actions—to monitor, assess, and remove or reward rulers (e.g., Persson and Tabellini 2000), and to report and sanction law-breakers (Akerlof 2015; Acemoglu and Jackson 2016)—by society at large, in fact, and both will be low if the collective action problem is pervasive.

More generally, this problem plays a central role in the dynamics that sustain inefficient social orders and institutions. For it can impede the open, reasoned debate about a polity's choices, which Sen (2009) views as central to both the notion of democracy as 'public reason' and the removal of injustice, and which can hardly take place in a representative democracy if political accountability does not align the interests of the citizenry with those of its elected officials, compelling the latter to seek the views and listen to the demands of their constituents (e.g., Rosanvallon 2015). And it can then distort the translation of a polity's choices into changes of the social reality through the implementation of its laws.

The Consequences: 'Distributional Coalitions' and Institutional Sclerosis

Olson's thesis (1965) rests on two main pillars. The first, already underlined, is that public goods—such as clean air or external security—cannot typically be denied to free riders. The second concerns the size of the groups that have an interest in creating or preserving public goods, and is summarized thus by Ostrom (2010, 157):

> Olson (1965) argued that as the size of a group increased, the probability of a group achieving a public good decreased . . . for two reasons. First, as group size increases, the noticeability of any single input to the provision of a public good declines. It is then easier for the individual to think that their own free riding will not be noticed and thus it will not affect the likelihood that the good will be provided. Second, coming to an internal agreement about coordinated strategies in larger groups involves higher transaction costs [i.e., monetary and opportunity costs borne to monitor contributions, sanction free riders, etc.]. Thus, a core theoretical hypothesis has been that the number of participants will likely reduce the probability of achieving any form of collective action or at least diminish the amount of joint benefits that could be achieved.

Elite theorists such as Gaetano Mosca and Vilfredo Pareto set out the reasons why organized minorities tend to prevail over non-organized majorities. Olson (1965) explains why some groups organize and some do not. He adds that large groups can solve the collective action problem if they offer to their potential[1] members some 'selective' incentives—such as the services and opportunities provided by trade unions and political parties, which are both valuable and can be denied to non-members, or non-contributing ones—that make it individually rational for them to organize. This condition rarely obtains, however, and the large groups that cannot so organize, such as consumers or taxpayers, will remain 'latent', 'forgotten' ones, consigned to 'suffer in silence' (Olson 1965, ch. VI.H).

From the observation that relatively small and homogeneous groups tend to have disproportionate power to assert their interests, Olson (1982) draws a broader theory of interest groups, which will illuminate also the protagonists of social orders and the dialectical process of institutional change. Olson posits that special interest groups—those that have solved their collective action problem—are costly to organize, but once organized are persistent and unlikely to dissolve even if their membership base declines or their original aims fade away. Over time, therefore, in a stable democracy they tend to accumulate. This congestion of organized special interests distorts a society's policies and political process, Olson argues, and weakens its dynamic forces.

Because of their small size, in fact, it is rational for special interest groups to promote policies that distribute to their members a disproportionate share of aggregate income without regard for the consequences on the efficiency of the allocation of an economy's resources. For as their own respective shares are anyway relatively small, the additional income gained by increasing their size is greater than the income lost due do the lower aggregate growth caused by the decline in economic efficiency. By reason of this structural incentive to engage in rent-seeking—which itself diverts resources from productive uses (e.g., Baumol 1990), and whose costs are typically shifted onto non-organized, 'latent' groups—Olson calls these groups 'distributional coalitions'. Their political influence will in the first instance be naturally directed at public resources, obtainable through government expenditure or transfers. But if the distributable portion of public revenue is insufficient to meet their demands they will typically aim at non-monetary benefits too, such as favourable regulation and measures restricting competition in the markets in which they are present.

Besides the direct harmful effects of such policies, Olson argues that the prevalence of distributional coalitions leads to 'institutional sclerosis', a

---

[1] Taking an *ex ante* perspective, consistent with the non-excludable character of public goods, Olson defines the size of groups in terms of their potential, not actual, numbers.

notion which both Toniolo's (2012) and Boltho's (2013) analyses of Italy's present predicament employ. In short, according to Olson distributional coalitions tend to minimize intra-group conflict in both politics and the economy, leading to intra-group collusion and weaker dynamic incentives more generally; the congestion of many coalitions with competing demands over scarce resources delays decision-making, and makes political consensus harder to reach; and, most interestingly from our perspective, '[d]istributional coalitions slow down a society's capacity to adopt new technologies and to reallocate resources in response to changing conditions, and thereby reduce the rate of economic growth' (Olson 1982, 74). For their incentives typically lead these coalitions to oppose the creative destruction brought about by innovation, which can challenge their material base, cohesiveness, organization, political power, and economic rents.[2]

Olson's can thus be seen also as an adaptation of Schumpeter's theory to the political domain. And it equally includes a specification of the conditions under which distributional coalitions' hold over a society can be relaxed, to allow *political* creative destruction. Olson (1982) first mentions exogenous shocks, such as defeat in war, which produce dislocations that can disrupt entrenched special interest groups. Writing near the peak of the German and Japanese economic miracles, in the early 1980s, he illustrates the argument by contrasting their impressive post-war performance—not also Italy's, regrettably—with the slower growth recorded by the (capitalist) victors, the USA and Britain, whose political and economic systems suffered less severe shocks. The parallel between this argument and the emphasis on 'critical junctures' in the theory of institutional change discussed in Chapter 2 is clear.

Beyond such events, Olson argues that distributional coalitions can be eclipsed by the emergence of organized groups, whose membership is large enough relative to the size of the economy that policies which harm the efficient allocation of resources would not be in their self-interest: groups, in other words, which tend to promote policies of redistribution and economic regulation that are compatible with allocative efficiency because, by reason of their large size, it would typically be irrational for them to pursue policies that increase their own share of aggregate income but at the same time diminish that same aggregate income. Olson calls them 'encompassing organizations', and points to broad-based political parties as examples, or nation-wide confederations of unions or business associations. Indeed, a plausible ideal-type of liberal democracy is a polity in which such organizations prevail over special interests.

---

[2] Collective action problems therefore exist also *within* distributional coalitions: a parallel can be made with cartels, for whose most efficient or innovative members it might become rational to end collusion and resume competition.

North (1983) finds the argument inconsistent with Olson's own logic (1965, 1982), which he shares, for if self-interested individual rationality prevents large groups from organizing it ought to follow that they shall not organize. North criticizes Olson (1982) also for neglecting the role of the state and its interactions with distributional coalitions, which he views as fundamental questions instead because the latter can use the former as an instrument of their power. This, indeed, seems to be the main thrust of North's critique, foreshadowing the theory developed in later work (leading up to North et al. 2009). The objection, which is persuasive, could therefore be reformulated thus: acting strategically, distributional coalitions will use the state, which they influence, to prevent the emergence of encompassing organizations: and until such influence persists the latter will arise only if elites allow the social order to open up, out of either deliberate choice or miscalculation, or else if an exogenous shock shakes the roots of the social order. This leads to pessimistic predictions for those polities that do not already have encompassing organizations, such as the typical nat-ural state, but suggests that the political conflict is open in those polities, such as post-war Italy, where the two categories of organizations coexist.

The rich parallels between Olson's work (1965, 1982) and the literature surveyed in Chapter 2 merit a few more remarks, to conclude. The institu-tional sclerosis that distributional coalitions produce mirrors the theory of '(in)appropriate' institutions, whose persistence harms development but pre-serves the growth model on which the material basis of the power of the extant distributional coalitions rests. The aims of the latter equally correspond to the logic of the limited-access social order, and, even more closely, to the objective function of inefficient, 'extractive' institutions, which manipulate the distribution of resources in ways that harm their efficient allocation, and which nonetheless persist because the collective action problem prevents ordinary citizens from having them changed. Mirror-like, one cardinal func-tion of efficient institutions is precisely that of relaxing the collective action problem, and the open-access social order is a polity in which this problem has largely been overcome. So the collective action problem and the capacity of ordinary citizens to organize are both the main link joining together the two literatures discussed here and in Chapter 2, and the ideal vehicle for crossing the line that divides the economic explanations for Italy's decline from the political ones.

Overcoming the Collective Action Problem: Laws and Social Norms

If Olson (1965) predicted that rational, self-interested agents would not contribute to a public good, Ostrom (1990, 2000) noted that social norms can induce them to cooperate. *Ex hypothesi*, therefore, norms capable of overcoming the collective action problem are ones that prescribe behaviour that is socially desirable but conflicts with the immediate self-interest of those to whom the norm addresses itself.[3] One clear example, considered by Ostrom (1990), concerns a category of public goods known as common-pool resources, such as forests and fisheries: their users have a common interest in avoiding excessive exploitation, which can deplete the resource, but typically have also a conflicting private interest in engaging in it: an interest which is necessarily denied, or at least constrained, by any norm seeking to protect the common resource.

Naturally, the function of solving such social dilemmas can be performed not only by social norms but also by formal institutions. By laws, ordinarily, which are explicit rules adopted—in a liberal democracy—after public discussion and deliberation, whereas social norms are the unintentional and unplanned outcome of human interaction, and which may remain unarticulated.[4] Ostrom (1990, 2000) and much of the related literature focus on social norms because they are mainly preoccupied with social dilemmas for which the polity has not designed a formal solution, and are interested in the conditions under which society spontaneously generates norms capable of solving them. But assuming this functional identity of laws and social norms casts the question of the interactions between formal and informal institutions into clearer light.

Ostrom (1990) shows that where social norms favouring both cooperation and the monitoring and sanctioning of violations exist, the excessive exploitation of common-pool resources is often averted. Monitoring and sanctioning are critical precisely because the cooperation rule demands behaviour that conflicts with one's immediate self-interest. So two categories of rules can be delineated, among both laws and social norms: a primary one specifying the required conduct, and a secondary one setting forth the sanctions for the breach of former. Herein lies a second structural difference between (primary) social norms and laws, for the latter rely firstly on the state for the monitoring of violations and the enforcement of sanctions, whereas the former rely on society's capacity and willingness to notice rule-breaking and punish it with sanctions, such as social discredit or ostracism, whose effectiveness equally depends on social variables.

---

[3] Social norms thus differ from conventions or customs, which coordinate choices in respect of which people tend to be indifferent, such as dress codes.

[4] See, e.g., Akerlof and Snower (2016) on the role of 'narratives' to diffuse and explain social norms.

The Question of Compliance: Rational Choice, Beliefs, and Expectations

> ...*quid leges sine moribus / vanae proficiunt*...
> [...without customs to support them / laws are in vain...]

> (Horace, *Carmina* III.24)

> *Perché, così come gli buoni costumi, per mantenersi, hanno bisogno delle leggi; così le leggi, per osservarsi, hanno bisogno de' buoni costumi.*
> [For, just as good customs need laws to persist, so too laws, to be observed, need good customs.]

> (Machiavelli, *Discourses* I.18)

As rules are assisted by sanctions, the question of compliance can in the first instance be framed as a cost-benefit calculation. The standard rational choice model (see Basu 2015, 7–10) predicts that the rule will be observed if, and only if, the sanction exceeds the benefits of pursuing the private interest that is denied or constrained by it: otherwise compliance would not be a strategy that maximizes one's utility, or preferences. Yet the sanction will enter this calculus as a function of the probability that it will be actually enforced: in this perspective, therefore, compliance with a rule depends on both the severity of the sanction assisting it, and on the agent's estimation of the probability that the breach will be observed and punished.[5]

It follows that in the case of social norms, rationality-based compliance will depend on one's expectations about society's willingness and capacity to monitor, detect, and sanction their violation.

To a lesser degree the same is true also for laws. This is Horace's argument, and before him Aristotle's.[6] The contemporary literature confirms it, upon the observation that the enforcement of laws relies not just on state agencies—whose budgets and possibilities are limited—but also on the cooperation of citizens and society: to spot and report law-breaking (Akerlof 2015; Acemoglu and Jackson 2016), and also to complement the legal sanctions with the discredit that frequently stigmatizes law-breakers. Social norms concerning either the compliance with laws in general or the observance of specific ones can therefore affect the actual level of compliance with them (Bénabou and Tirole 2011; Besley et al. 2015).

The effect is likely to be positive if a polity's laws and its social norms are aligned, as the epigraphs already suggested, negative if they are conflicting. Acemoglu and Jackson (2016, 2) articulate a model of these interactions, and

---

[5] Of course, a similar argument was used in 1764 by Cesare Beccaria as part of his seminal critique of the death penalty and cruel punishments.

[6] *Politics* II.8: 'a law derives all its strength from custom'.

find that 'when laws conflict with prevailing norms, there is less [private enforcement], which reduces the effectiveness of laws and encourages further law-breaking. As laws are broken by more people, [private enforcement] becomes even less likely, and law-breaking snowballs.' Similar conclusions are reached by Akerlof (2015), who focuses on anger instead, which leads citizens to report those who break the law. Anger ensues when the rule breached is legitimate—that is, when it elicits a sense of duty to comply with it—and the cost of compliance appears reasonable. But if the frequency of law-breaking increases, which Akerlof's model plausibly allows, the legitimacy of the rule declines, its violation appears more reasonable, the cost of compliance rises, relative to what the rest of society does, and anger weakens, setting in motion a dynamic that leads to an equilibrium in which law-breaking is pervasive.

This is one channel through which a polity's social order—which must, *ex hypothesi*, shape its social norms—bends incompatible formal institutions to make them consistent to its own logic. The other, of course, is biased, lax, or arbitrary enforcement by the state: but as under this respect post-war Italy witnessed significant improvements—thanks, as we noted, to the gradual emergence of an actual independent judiciary—this channel was probably less relevant than that we just discussed.

A different perspective on compliance with rules moves from the observation that one's normative beliefs and one's behaviour are generally strongly correlated.[7] Normative beliefs are views about what conduct is expected or proscribed in a given society, and provide a motivation to comply with the rule that is not immediately dependent on the risk of a sanction. This approach—relevant especially for social norms, which lack an explicit and official normative character—can be combined with the rational choice one: either because agents' normative beliefs affect their preferences, which the cost-benefit calculus then seeks to maximize, or because agents will consider both normative beliefs and the cost-benefit analysis in making their decision, differing among themselves on the weight attached to each of the two horns of the dilemma.

But even people who attach preponderant importance to their own normative beliefs—such that the latter either ordinarily trump the cost-benefit analysis, or are predominant in shaping their preferences—will generally choose to comply with a social norm only if they expect that others will follow it too.[8] Norms, in fact, are valued (also) because they are understood as being intended

---

[7] The introductory pages of the studies cited in the text offer brief surveys of the relevant political economy literature. On the social determinants of human behaviour more generally, see Hoff and Stiglitz (2016).

[8] Unless, that is, the norm is viewed as so fundamental to one's convictions, values, or (salient) identities that it must be followed regardless of what the rest of society does, as Kant's categorical imperative.

to govern the whole of society, or at least most of it, and solve its collective action problems: and an oft-disregarded norm largely ceases to perform this function. Norms are obeyed also in order to safeguard one's reputation of honesty or trustworthiness, moreover, which has both moral and economic value (Tirole 1996; Bénabou and Tirole 2011; Besley et al. 2015): this motivation too will necessarily weaken with regard to norms of whose transgression society appears to have become tolerant or indifferent. But if normative beliefs too are at least partly dependent on the behaviour of others, and thus also on one's expectations about it, they become vulnerable to similar spirals as those characteristic of the rational-choice approach to compliance.

To conclude, whether it stems from a cost-benefit calculus, from normative beliefs, or from both, the decision to comply with a rule, formal or informal, will to some degree depend upon one's expectations about the probability of incurring the sanctions specified for it, about the normative beliefs of others, and about the proportion of citizens who are likely to breach the rule or to be indifferent to rule-breaking. But as this is true for every member of society, also one's *cognitive* beliefs about the expectations and beliefs (normative and cognitive) of others will enter the calculus: because other agents too will choose whether to observe or breach the rule, and whether to excuse or sanction rule-breakers, based on their own expectations and beliefs about the same questions (see Basu 2015). As interactions are repeated, moreover, if expectations and beliefs (normative and cognitive) differ from reality the former will tend to change and adapt to the observed outcomes, leading potentially to pervasive lawlessness—as in the models of Akerlof (2015) and Acemoglu and Jackson (2016). This dynamic interdependence among compliance, cognitive and normative beliefs, and observed outcomes opens the possibility for self-fulfilling expectations, multiple equilibria, and shifts between different equilibria, to which we shall return in Chapter 4.

Social Norms: Origin and Change

> *E dove una cosa per se medesima sanza la legge opera bene, non è necessaria la legge; ma quando quella buona consuetudine manca, è subito la legge necessaria.*
>
> [And where without laws things work well, laws are unnecessary; but when that good custom is lacking, presently laws become necessary.]
>
> (Machiavelli, *Discourses* I.3)

Thus far we have reviewed the function that institutions perform in solving or relaxing the collective action problem, and their capacity of actually doing so: the conditions that elicit compliance with them, and thus determine what North calls their 'enforcement characteristics'. The dynamics governing the design and reform of formal institutions—laws—were discussed in Chapter 2. The same questions arise in respect of social norms.

The literature on their origin and on people's normative beliefs about them is roughly divided between a cultural-historical hypothesis—which focuses on the inter-generational transmission of norms and values within one's family, narrow social group, or cultural sphere—and a theory that emphasizes the socio-institutional context, broadly defined.[9] Ample empirical evidence showing that migrants generally adapt to the set of norms prevailing in the host country, but nonetheless retain traits of their own heritage of values and normative beliefs, indicates that both factors are at play (e.g., Helliwell et al. 2014), and shifts the debate onto the question of their relative importance. Notably, however, both Giavazzi et al. (2014) and Helliwell et al. (2014) find that migrants' views and normative beliefs about social trust and cooperation converge rapidly with the norms found in the host country, suggesting that the main determinant of the norms that matter the most from the perspective of solving social dilemmas is the socio-institutional environment.

Uncertainty about this question is no obstacle to gaining at least some understanding of how norms may change, at any rate, which for our purposes is more relevant. If inefficient social norms exist in present-day Italy, such as norms condoning tax evasion, for example, their origin is of less urgent interest than their effects and the possibility of changing them.

The question might seem misplaced, because social norms are the unplanned outcome of social interactions. Yet their function makes them interdependent with laws, as we just saw, and this may not only imply that social norms can frustrate the implementation of laws that conflict with them, as Akerlof (2015) and Acemoglu and Jackson (2016) demonstrate, but also that laws can change social norms. This, indeed, is the assumption implied by Machiavelli's passage cited in the epigraph: that when adequate social norms are lacking—when, that is, a society's system of informal norms is inadequate, taken as a whole—laws can direct society towards the desirable behaviour. The model formulated by Acemoglu and Jackson (2016) does in fact demonstrate also that laws which broadly accord with the extant social norms and are imposed gradually can succeed in changing the behaviour of citizens, leading to a change in social norms too. The interdependence posited by a later passage of the *Discourses* (I.18)—'just as good customs need laws to persist, so too laws, to be observed, need good customs'—is thus to be viewed not just as a static two-way relationship, as this language suggests, but also as a dynamic one: a society can change its own norms by deliberate political choice, if its laws satisfy those two conditions.

---

[9] For brief overviews, see the literature cited in the next section.

This interdependence raises the question of what shapes, at any given moment, the cognitive beliefs that are relevant for compliance, which include one's expectations about other agents' beliefs, expectations, and readiness to comply with a rule. In respect of this question, one literature—summarized and further developed by Acemoglu and Jackson (2015)—persuasively argues that prominent members of society—those whose actions are particularly visible, such as the elites, broadly understood—can influence citizens' expectations and change their priors based on past observed outcomes (past experience, in short). In particular, the model they construct shows (p. 3) that 'prominent agents can counter the power of history by exploiting their visibility to change the prevailing social norm from [low to high cooperation]'.

Like laws, to conclude, norms guide behaviour. Yet changes in behaviour can change or eclipse them, precisely because they are intended to govern social exchange. What this literature demonstrates is that changes in behaviour capable of changing norms can be determined also by the deliberate choices of either the polity, through a new (carefully designed) law, or of its most visible members, through their (credible) actions.[10] The channel is the interdependence of citizens' expectations with each other and with observed reality: once the initial resistance of the norm against the change in behaviour begins to be overcome, the expectations of rational agents will both change and incorporate the anticipation that the expectations of others will change too, accelerating the process.

This logic arguably underpins the findings of recent empirical research on tax evasion in Italy. Filippin et al. (2013, 22) find evidence that, beyond its direct effect of raising the costs of tax evasion, stricter tax enforcement strengthens also 'tax morale', namely one's intrinsic motivation to pay taxes; and they suggest a reading of this causal effect—a change in taxpayers' behaviour—which involves precisely the interaction between formal and informal institutions and their enforcement characteristics: stricter enforcement 'can be interpreted as a restatement of the society's [norms]'. In our analysis, behind the word 'restatement' lies the logic we just discussed.

Social Capital, Trust, and 'Civicness'

The nucleus of any norm of cooperation is inter-personal trust. Its importance for social exchange and economic development has long been recognized.

---

[10] That this should be possible is arguably a direct implication of the assumptions based on which polities legislate, for laws and social norms depend on each other in eliciting society's compliance and the latter can frustrate conflicting laws or too innovative ones: hence a legislator must be able to change social norms too, at least over the long term. See also Bénabou and Tirole (2011, 17–26) on the 'expressive function' of laws.

The economic effects of the ability of people to trust each other are 'incalculable', Mill ([1848] 2008) wrote, and Arrow (1972, 357) explained that

> [v]irtually every commercial transaction has within itself an element of trust, certainly any transaction conducted over a period of time. It can be plausibly argued that much of the economic backwardness in the world can be explained by the lack of mutual confidence.

It seems equally plausible that underlying the singular diffusion in Italy of corruption, tax evasion, and organized crime are pervasive collective action problems, which might in turn arise out of a relative 'lack of mutual confidence'. The literature on 'social capital', which investigates the origins and effects of social trust, can therefore assist our inquiry.

That notion is even more polysemic than that of 'institutions', however, has been given a plethora of different definitions, and encompasses heterogeneous phenomena. The scholar who re-founded this field of research (Putnam 1993, 1995, 2000), and whose work drove its remarkable flourishing in the past two decades, defines (1995, 65) social capital as those 'features of social organization such as networks, norms, and social trust that facilitate coordination and cooperation for mutual benefit'.

Putnam (1993) employed this notion to study the performance of regional government in Italy. He used a measure of social capital based primarily on the density and vibrancy of associational life among citizens, and their levels of trust and 'civicness'. The latter can broadly be interpreted as civic virtue in the classical republican sense, as used in Thucydides and Machiavelli's *Discourses* (public engagement, sense of duty, and respect for the rules, formal and informal), whereas the emphasis on associations mirrors Tocqueville's. Putnam found that despite having near-identical formal institutions, all established at the same time, in 1970, regional government was considerably less efficient and transparent in regions with lower social capital (mostly in the South) than in those with higher levels of it (mostly in the Centre-North). Although we shall criticize Putnam's interpretation of it, this correlation is clear, well-established, and quite relevant for our analysis.

A related literature finds a strong positive correlation also between social capital and economic performance (e.g., Fukuyama 2000), and explains, following Mill and Arrow, that high levels of trust—which increase also the moral and economic value of one's social reputation—make informal bonds and commitments more credible, reduce the need for (costlier) formal contracts and sanctions, and lower transaction costs more generally. One such cost is that of monitoring and ensuring compliance with the rules that govern the relationships among a firm's shareholders, directors, and managers, for instance, which features prominently in Pellegrino and Zingales (2014): thus low social capital can at least partly explain the 'familism and cronyism' to which they ascribe Italy's decline.

Yet trust, reciprocity, and norms of cooperation can nurture also phenomena such as social exclusion, organized crime, or the rise of a fascist party (Satyanath et al. 2013). For these reasons Sen (2004, 41) argues that 'it may be a mistake to treat "social capital" as a general purpose asset (as capital is, in general, taken to be), rather than as an asset for some relations and a liability for others'. Hoff and Stiglitz (2016) similarly observe that

> a disturbing implication of the social capital literature is that essentially any Pareto-efficient equilibrium can be supported, including equilibria entailing the exploitation of one group . . . Discriminatory equilibria can persist unless there is an exogenous intervention.

The question chiefly concerns what Fukuyama (2000, 4) calls the 'radius of trust', namely the circle of people among whom mutual trust is established and norms of cooperation emerge. In this perspective, Putnam (2000) delineates two types of social capital: a 'bonding' one, rooted in networks of people with homogeneous backgrounds and socio-demographic characteristics, and a 'bridging' one, underpinned by wider, more encompassing networks, in respect of which what matters is less the intensity of the inter-personal relationships than their number. This dichotomy is largely coextensive with that between generalized trust, which extends to any other member of society, and particularized trust, whose scope is limited to people known to the agent or to members of the same narrower social group: these two forms of trust, in turn, are correlated with the prevalence in the relevant society of either universalistic or particularistic values (de Blasio et al. 2014; Paccagnella and Sestito 2014). In sum, therefore, wide networks and generalized trust may compose an explicitly positive notion of social capital, which some authors (e.g., Guiso and Pinotti 2013; Guiso et al. 2015) call 'civic capital', evoking the notion of 'civic culture'—'a set of beliefs, attitudes, norms, perceptions and the like, that support participation'—used by Almond and Verba (1963, 178).

The literature on social capital thus contributes to the analysis of institutions, social orders, and development by casting its light on the links among norms of cooperation, trust and civicness, and the scope and density of the networks within which social reputation acquires its value.[11] In particular, the parallel between the two couples of generalized and particularized trust, on one hand, and personal and impersonal exchange, on the other, is clear. North et al. (2009) argue that making impersonal exchange possible—which requires a system of third-party enforcement of rules, formal and informal,

---

[11] It is less clear whether it is useful to distinguish between trust and civicness per se and the social norms based on them.

credible enough to ensure widespread compliance—is a necessary condition for limited-access social orders to evolve into open-access ones: societies where impersonal exchange cannot be sustained will therefore rely predominantly on particularized trust, which emerges in narrow 'bonding' circles such as the patronage networks typical of the limited-access order. Hence the argument, already advanced, that the social order—and therefore the allocation of power—largely determines the character of a polity's social norms, as well as the level and scope of the values and practices of trust that undergird them. This, however, is not the position of most of the social capital literature. The discussion must therefore turn to the question of how civicness and generalized trust, underpinned by 'bridging' networks, can sediment and condense into credible and effective norms of cooperation sustained by normative beliefs.

Trust, Good Government, and Development: the Question of Causality

Putnam (2000) acknowledges that the question of causality—whether social capital causes good government, is caused by it, or both—is the most difficult one. The issue is significant, for the levels of social capital do change: indeed, Putnam himself studied (1995, 2000) its 'strange disappearance' in the USA over the space of a few decades, following a decrease in the active membership of certain associations. This author holds (2000, 23) that social capital has 'forceful, even quantifiable effects on many different aspects of our lives', including on the quality and integrity of government (1993).

Another literature contends that causality runs also, or predominantly, in the opposite direction, from government and its policies to trust and social capital, through channels that are all relevant for an analysis of contemporary Italy. One is education, in respect of which Putnam (2000) too posits a two-way relationship: education is critical for the creation and maintenance of social capital, an important outcome of which is, in turn, greater educational attainment. The other channels are the quality of government and public regulation, and inequality.

Rothstein (2005) inverts the relationship formulated by Putnam. If public officials are corrupt, he argues, citizens will expect less honesty and trustworthiness in their peers and become less honest and trusting themselves, whereas effective and impartial government—especially by the agencies directly in contact with citizens, according to Rothstein and Stolle (2008)—enhances social trust. The argument is consistent with the findings of Acemoglu and Jackson (2016), according to whom laws that succeed in changing behaviour change social norms too. And it finds indirect support in Aghion et al. (2010), who estimate a negative relationship between trust and the regulation of market entry, and especially in Pinotti (2012), who builds a model upon the hypothesis that the level of regulation in an economy is an equilibrium outcome determined primarily by the level of social trust, and finds supporting empirical evidence.

On the second question, the empirical literature—reviewed by Barone and Mocetti (2014)—had long identified a negative correlation between economic inequality and social trust, which emerges also from research on Italy (de Blasio and Nuzzo 2012). But until recently the evidence on the direction of causality seemed inconclusive. Alesina and La Ferrara (2002) suggested that income inequality has a causal influence on 'civic capital', and Rothstein and Uslaner (2005) formulated the hypothesis that universal or near-universal social policies, such as those typical of Scandinavian countries, lead to a more equal distribution of wealth, which strengthens social solidarity, which, in turn, sustains generalized trust. Barone and Mocetti (2014) have broadly confirmed these views: relying on country-level panel data, they found strong evidence that among developed countries income inequality does significantly and negatively affect generalized trust. Indeed, the notion that inequality is inimical to republican government—which rests on, and sustains civic virtue—is present already in Machiavelli's *Discourses* and in Tocqueville, and is retained by contemporary literature (see Winters and Page 2009; Gilens and Page 2014), which underlines also that, besides technological innovation and globalization, a society's institutions and policies have decisive influence on the levels of income and wealth inequality (Stiglitz 2012; Piketty [2013] 2014, chs. 13–15; see also Milanović 2016, however, who argues that the effects of technological innovation, globalization, and institutions or policies can hardly be disentangled).

To introduce the discussion of the role of culture and ideas, therefore, a plausible hypothesis is that there is at least a two-way causal relationship between trust, civicness, and social capital, on one hand, and the quality of government and the character of public policy and institutions, on the other; that the influence that the latter exercise on trust and civicness dominates the reverse effect; and that inequality—relevant here as an outcome of policies and institutions—harms generalized trust, probably through its effects on social cohesion and social solidarity.

A Critique of the Cultural Hypothesis

> *Italians are particularly unreligious and corrupted.*
>
> (Jacob Burckhardt, 1860)

> *L'uomo del Guicciardini* vivit, immo in Senatum venit, *e lo incontri ad ogni passo.*

(Guicciardini-like [i.e., particularistic-minded] types still exist, even come
in the Senate, and one meets them all the time.)

(Francesco de Sanctis, 1869)

Contrary to the literature reviewed thus far, one school of thought, which
is quite popular both in Italy and in analyses of the country, holds that a
society's culture has significant and independent causal effects on its development. The author we mentioned in Chapter 2 to exemplify this position,
Landes (1998, 516), sums it up neatly when he writes that 'if we learn anything from the history of economic development, it is that culture makes all
the difference'. This literature is quite varied—compare this study with Collier
(2016), for instance—on both the causal chain and the effects, and if 'social
capital' and 'institutions' are polysemic words 'culture' has an even richer list
of definitions, reflecting also that variety. The authors of a comprehensive
review of the literature on the transmission of those cultural traits that appear
most relevant for economic development, Bisin and Verdier (2011, 341), use a
notion that is broad enough to encompass much of that literature but sufficiently precise to distinguish it from other ones: 'we define culture to represent
those components of preferences, social norms, and ideological attitudes
which "depend upon the capacity for learning and transmitting knowledge
to succeeding generations"'.

Defined thus, there is no doubt that culture matters for development. Not
just to explain its process (e.g., Greif 1994; Tabellini 2010), but also to set its
aims. This oft-neglected point is emphasized by Sen (2004, 39; emphasis
added), who argues that the 'freedom and opportunity for cultural activities
are among the basic freedoms the enhancement of which can be seen to be
constitutive of development'.

Rather, the objection raised by the literature we rely upon concerns the
scale and especially the independence of the effects of culture on development, and it is based on the theoretical and empirical arguments summarized
in Chapter 2 (e.g., Acemoglu et al. 2001), to conclude that institutions and
the social order underpinning them, not culture, are the main determinants
of long-term growth. Criticism of the cultural-historical thesis is not unique
to the institutionalist school, at any rate, and is expressed with rare clarity by
Sen (2004, 38):

There is some evidence ... that in the anxiety to take adequate note of the role
of culture, there is sometimes a temptation to take rather formulaic and simplistic views of the impact of culture on the process of development. For
example, there seem to be many supporters of the belief—held explicitly or
by implication—that the fates of countries are effectively sealed by the nature
of their respective cultures. This would be not only a heroic oversimplification,

but it would also entail some assignment of hopelessness to countries that are seen as having the 'wrong' kind of culture. This is not just politically and ethically repulsive, but more immediately, it is, I would argue, also epistemic nonsense.

Sen concludes (2004, 49) that 'attempts to view culture as a singular, stationary and independent source of [or hindrance to] development have not—and could not have—worked', because cultures are polymorphic, have no fixed or even recognizable borders, endlessly influence each other, and change. Drawing on nineteenth-century Western literary, anthropological, moralist, and travel writings, for instance, Chang (2008, 184–5) shows that

> [a] century ago, the Japanese were [viewed as] lazy rather than hardworking; excessively independent-minded ... rather than loyal 'worker ants'; emotional rather than inscrutable; light-hearted rather than serious; living for today instead of considering the future ... A century and half ago, the Germans were [viewed as] indolent rather than efficient; individualistic rather than co-operative; emotional rather than rational; stupid rather than clever; dishonest and thieving rather than law-abiding; easy-going rather than disciplined.

A particularly strong version of the cultural-historical theory is found in Putnam's study of regional government in Italy (1993). As we said, Putnam shows a clear correlation between the civicness of Italy's regions and the integrity and effectiveness of their governments, which on average are markedly lower in the South. He infers that civicness causes superior government performance, and formulates the hypothesis that Italy's deep regional divide is due to a bifurcation that began about nine centuries ago. As the power of the Holy Roman Empire began to wane, the North and most of the Centre of Italy saw the rise of numerous city-states, the communes, whereas the Normans who took control of much of the South in the twelfth century established a relatively centralized autocratic state there, later consolidated by Friedrich II. Putnam argues that unlike this monarchy, whose latest incarnation was the Kingdom of the Two Sicilies that fell in 1860–1, the medieval communes fostered civic virtues that persist to this day. The vicissitudes of the peninsula between the high middle ages and the late 1980s, which were varied, are not considered.

These arguments sparked much debate in Italy, not least for their arresting policy implications. They are contradicted frontally but not explicitly by the literature we rely upon, which quotes Putnam more on the role of trust and social capital than on their origin. But they have been convincingly confuted, both theoretically and empirically (see, e.g., Tarrow 1996; Golden 2003, 194; Trigilia 2012, 94–101). In particular, using different time periods and variables than Putnam's, and arguably more plausible ones, Seravalli (1999) obtains different results, which suggest that the quality of government and institutions, the level of civicness, and the rate of economic growth are linked by two-way relationships, and that the influence exercised by the quality of government over civicness dominates the reverse.

We must nevertheless return to Putnam's arguments because the cultural-historical hypothesis remains present in public discourse—with damaging effects, as this literally disarming theory naturally leads to fatalism—and the scientific debate continues.[12] Two recent contributions clarify and extend the causal chain that Putnam suggested (Guiso et al. 2015), and employ it to explain the gap in political participation between the North and the South (Guiso and Pinotti 2013). The arguments are similar, and more articulately illustrated in the later study.

Guiso et al. (2015) enrich Putnam's analysis in three main respects. First, they compare differences in medieval political regimes and present-day civicness within a more homogenous set than his, which excludes the South and covers only the communes. Second, they compare them according to how independent they were, from both the empire and other city-states, and how long their independence lasted, neither of which Putnam considered. Their results show that the present-day level of civicness is higher in those cities that were independent communes, an effect which is greater the more independent they were and the longer the period of independence was. Third, Guiso et al. (2015, 30) suggest an explanation for this persistence, which they identify in a stronger collective sentiment of 'self-efficacy'—measured based on a survey of attitudes of schoolchildren—due to a city's history of independence:

> [i]f self-efficacy is a measure of an individual's perception of the impact of his effort, people with stronger self-efficacy beliefs should contribute more to the public good because they think that their impact is greater. Psychology research seems to support this prediction [references follow]. Therefore, in communities with above average self-efficacy, the level of civic behavior should be higher. While we cannot test causality, we can at least test whether there is a correlation between self-efficacy beliefs and today's civic capital... Our measure of self-efficacy is positively and significantly correlated with the level of civic capital.

---

[12] The public debate is bred less by Putnam's theory, admittedly, than by popularizations of Max Weber's on the role of protestant ethics in the development of capitalism. More interesting is the last sentence of an authoritative and widely read general history of Italy (Ginsborg 2001, 324), which, albeit couched in general terms, ascribes its failures also to 'the culture of its families'. These words are part of a call for greater civic virtue and political engagement, both much needed; but their implicit premiss is that the country's 'culture' is an *independent* obstacle to democratic development: indeed, elsewhere (p. 314) this author cites the 'deep-lying tendency in Italian political culture, clearly of Catholic origin, towards pardoning and forgetting' as one cause of the failure to purge the state from either Fascists, in the 1940s, or corruption, in the 1990s.

The correlation is positive on two measures of civic capital, but modest in one case,[13] and negative on the third. Even leaving the objections of Box 3.1 aside, therefore, the ambiguity of these results makes them a remarkably weak basis for explaining the persistence of a collective sentiment over several lively centuries. To remain on the plane of the history of ideas, for instance, during the period considered by Guiso et al. (2015) the Purgatory was 'invented', allowing Roman Christianity to reconcile the rise of credit with the proscription of usury (Le Goff 1979, 52: 'the birth of Purgatory is also the dawn of banking'), and near the end of it a veritable rupture occurred, which led to Humanism and then the Renaissance (e.g., Garin [1965] 1993).

Above all, Guiso et al. (2015) do not overcome the objections of the earlier literature, and in particular those raised in Seravalli's analysis (1999)—which they do not cite. By their nature, the statistical techniques that they employed yield results whose cognitive value depends critically on the quality of the variables used. Using other variables than Putnam's, and certainly no less plausible ones, Seravalli obtains results which contradict his interpretation: as the variables used by Guiso et al. are far closer to Putnam's than to Seravalli's, his confutation of the latter may safely be extended also to the former.

There is no clear evidence, therefore, to suggest that the comparatively low level of civicness observed in southern Italy is due to very distant—and therefore hardly superable—causes. As we have argued, conversely, this phenomeon, just like the 'amoral familism' unveiled by Banfield (1958) in a rural village of the South and the 'parochialism' that Almond and Verba (1963) observe in the whole country, or the corruption and particularism that the epigraphs of this section stigmatize,[14] are all, in varying degree, at once effects of inefficient institutions, inadequate public services, illegality, poverty, inequality, political distrust and cynicism, and low political accountability, as well as proximate causes of the persistence of the latter, underlying which are Italy's social order and the obstacles it raises to the collective action of citizens. Chapter 4 shall provide a simplified example of these interactions.

---

[13] A one standard deviation increase in self-efficacy is associated with an increase in civicness equal to 5 per cent of the sample mean.

[14] Both polemically, it must be underlined: De Sanctis hoped that with national unity, then just achieved, the spirit of the Risorgimento would eclipse the moral weaknesses exemplified by *l'uomo del Guicciardini*. Nowadays such judgements are often issued self-indulgingly, conversely, to explain why *così fan tutti*, or to argue that fighting or even hoping for greater civicness is in vain: an example, particularly reprehensible for its sexist overtones, is a recent op-ed in the *Corriere* by a former editor-in-chief of the newspaper (Ostellino 2011).

Box 3.1 CIVICNESS, COMMUNES, AND TYRANNY: DANTE
AND LORENZETTI

Besides the confutations we already discussed, the causal chain that Guiso et al. (2015) lay out seems also intrinsically questionable and internally contradictory. Both objections concern the assumption, which is central to their thesis, that communes fostered civicness because (p. 9) they were governed under the 'principle that power originated from the people and was to be exercised in the people's name'.

First, it can be said that power originated from a group plausibly definable as 'the people', and was exercised in its name, only for an often brief period in the life of a commune, which typically evolved from an oligarchic regime ruled by a relatively narrow aristocratic-mercantile elite, and later by contracted foreign rulers or judges; to a more broad-based *commune populi*, often existing in parallel to the oligarchic structures of power; to a more stable form of oligarchy, as in Genoa and Venice, or to autocracy (*signoria*).

Second, the results of Guiso et al. (2015) show that in the present day civicness is comparatively *high* in those cities whose medieval communes arose as republican polities but later fell under the autocratic leadership of a *signore*, a lord or tyrant, and became *signorie*. Their explanation of this apparent paradox is that these principalities anyway retained republican forms and statutes. Yet this is often equally true of those communes which either lost political independence, because they were conquered or subjugated by another commune, or originally lacked full autonomy, because they were allied to the emperor: in their results both sets of non-independent communes show comparatively *low* civicness today. Hence the contradiction, for in this case what matters seems to be the reality of power whereas in the case of the *signorie* it would be its forms.

But even aside from this contradiction, the argument based on the maintenance of the republican forms directly replicates the propaganda of the *signori*, who described, and depicted, their own government as the 'comune in signoria' (Boucheron 2013, 134). The difference between the forms and the substance of power was clear to Ambrogio Lorenzetti, conversely, who in 1338-9 painted his celebrated allegories of good and bad government precisely to defend before the eyes of Siena's citizens the republican ideal from the lures—the pacification of factional struggles, chiefly—of the *signoria* (Boucheron 2013). It was equally clear to Dante (who, having served the Florentine commune, after the coup of 1301 lived the rest of his life in exile). One of the charges of his invective against Italy, written around 1310, is that its cities were 'full of tyrants' (*Purgatorio* VI.124–5). A few years later, however, he accepted the protection of one of them, Cangrande della Scala, *signore* of Verona. Thus, in the letter by which he dedicated the *Commedia* to him, Dante felt the need to explain a choice so antithetical to his republican political culture (*Epistulae* XIII.2).[15] Notably, one of his arguments is that, assisted by intellectuals, an enlightened *signore* can 'correct the mistakes' of the people, which 'lacks judgement'.

These considerations deprive the variable of the length of independence, which is critical in Guiso et al. (2015), of much of its value, and call into question also the very equation between a city's history as a commune and its present-day level of civicness. Especially as other interpretations of the twelfth-century bifurcation between communes

---

[15] The attribution of the letter is fairly well established, especially in respect of this part.

and centralized territorial autocracy appear possible. Friedrich II is sometimes credited with having built the first modern state, moreover, and according to Acemoglu and Robinson (2012) political centralization—which communes could achieve, but seldom sustain, only within often narrow territorial limits—is a precondition for the emergence of efficient institutions.

The Largely Independent Role of Ideas

Tutti sanno con Orazio, che le leggi senza i costumi non bastano, e da altra parte che i costumi dipendono e sono determinati e fondati principalmente e garantiti dalle opinioni.

[Everyone knows, after Horace, that laws without customs shall not suffice, and that, on the other hand, customs depend from, are determined and founded primarily on, and are guaranteed by, opinions.]

(Giacomo Leopardi, 1824)

Commenting on Olson's (1965) zero-contribution prediction, Hirschman (1982, 80–1) observes that 'people who have experienced a great deal of disappointment in their search for happiness through private consumption [can be led by this] to participate massively in public actions'. This disappointment may have to grow above some threshold before it conquers people's expectations or delusions about their earlier choices, Hirschman adds, but when the tipping point is reached there is a

sort of 'rebound effect' [which] can explain many choices. It makes for an exaggeration of the benefits and an underestimate of the costs of the [public] action that provides a counterpoint to the action that has been taken previously and has turned sour [such that] a good portion of the so-called puzzle of collective action and participation in public affairs disappears when the rebound effect is taken into account.

Though undemonstrated, this 'rebound effect' does have the ring of truth. And even though it offers only a partial solution for the collective action problem, it can easily be incorporated into that theory: as Hirschman explains, in fact, in the circumstances he describes the act of participating in collective action may be so intrinsically gratifying that citizens view it as a benefit rather than as a cost, as rational-choice theory would otherwise assume. In other words, the rebound effect is an abrupt change of one's understanding of one's self-interest or preferences, which, once changed, are then pursued with the same rationality that previously led citizens not to contribute to collective action, or to prefer 'exit' or 'loyalty' over 'voice' (Hirschman 1970). This sudden switch occurs on a plane that we have largely ignored thus far, that of ideas.

Ideas are the subject matter of a recent literature, which aims to integrate them into the standard political economy models based on vested interests and rational choice. For example, the analysis of the oligarchic traits of the US political system that we have discussed in Chapter 2 (Gilens and Page 2014) explicitly neglects precisely that channel of elites' influence over policy choices, whose vehicle are ideas rather than the persuasion of policy-makers: namely, their ability to shape the preferences of the public. This is not a harmless exclusion, because, as Rodrik (2014, 192) notes, 'powerful interests rarely get their way in a democracy by nakedly arguing for their own self-interest. Instead, they seek legitimacy for their arguments by saying these policies are in the public interest.'

Rodrik moves from the observation (p. 191) that in the political sphere 'each of the three components of the optimization problem—preferences, constraints, and choice variables—rely on an implicit set of ideas'. Ideas directly determine one's preferences, which depend on what one seeks in life and which of one's several identities—gender, class, profession—are most salient in respect of a given choice, as well as one's views about how the world works, which guide one's choices about how to pursue such preferences and interests. Widespread changes in these sets of ideas can bring about deep political reform, as the example of the rebound effect suggested. Yet Rodrik remarks (p. 206) that 'reform often happens not when vested interests are defeated, but when different strategies are used to pursue those interests, or when interests themselves are redefined', and devotes the core of his analysis to the former question. Standard political economy models explain redistribution from non-elites to the elites, he observes, but do not explain inefficiency, for innovative ideas can point elites towards more efficient ways to satisfy the same interests.

This argument calls into question one *fil rouge* that runs through this chapter and Chapter 2, and surfaced also in Chapter 1, namely the notion that elites will oppose innovation and reform if they foresee that the effects will lead to a reallocation of power or their replacement by a fresh elite: if they fear the 'political replacement effect' of efficiency-enhancing reforms, in the words of Acemoglu and Robinson (2006), who remark also (2013) that much policy advice goes unheeded, or leads to perverse consequences, precisely because it neglects that political constraint. Citing this last study as an example, Rodrik (2014) objects that vested interests should not be taken as a given, but rather as an obstacle which ideas can overcome: if innovative policies are proposed that both improve efficiency and minimize the political replacement effect, the equilibrium on which a politico-economic system rests can be brought closer to the efficiency frontier with the consent of the extant elites.

This approach may be unappealing to those who aim for radical, epochal political change, or wish to see elites or distributional coalitions defeated in open battle. Yet it mirrors Sen's (2009) persuasive argument that even in the absence of consensus on the requirements of justice, reasoned public debate nonetheless can, and should, yield partial agreements on the removal of well-identified injustices. And it opens promising perspectives. For if, despite their diverging ultimate aims, elites and non-elites can nonetheless agree on some efficiency-improving new policies, around such partial agreements those broad-based pluralist coalitions can begin to coalesce, which are critical for achieving deep and sustainable institutional reform.

Rodrik (2014) then draws a parallel between technological innovation and policy innovation, both of which are partly endogenous and partly dependent on idiosyncratic factors, such as serendipity, creativity, or leadership. And he discusses those sources of innovative ideas that lend themselves to systematic analysis: trial and error and learning-by-doing, unplanned policy experimentation arising along the margins of existing policies (China's two-track pricing policy is one example, which had far-reaching consequences), crises, policy emulation, and, most interestingly, political entrepreneurship. 'Inefficiency creates opportunities for political entrepreneurship. As long as there are unexploited efficiency gains to be had, political agents have *some* incentive to [search for innovative ideas]', Rodrik notes (2014, 202).

On this basis, Mukand and Rodrik (2016) articulate a rational-choice model in which political entrepreneurs engage in 'worldview politics', in divisive and exclusionary 'identity politics', or in both, so as to achieve political or policy change. Their model incorporates both interests and ideas, and specifies the vehicles—narratives, 'memes'—through which political entrepreneurs and their allied think tanks and partisan media convey new ideas to the public, in competition with each other. The main results of the model concern the complementarities between worldview and identity politics. But Mukand and Rodrik (2016, 33) draw from it also the suggestion of an empirical criterion to distinguish between ideas and interests, and a broader conclusion:

> any behavior that is predictable on the basis of preference characteristics or worldviews that are salient ex ante [i.e., before an episode of political entrepreneurship] can be attributed to 'interests'. Behavior that is the result of ex post shifts in preferences or worldviews, brought about by [a political entrepreneur's] memes and narratives, can be attributed in turn to ideational politics…Interests are determined by identities and worldviews that are salient ex ante. Ideas possibly intervene to transform these ex post. A broader implication of our framework, therefore, is that today's ideas become tomorrow's interests. In the very short run, it is all about interests. In the long run, it is all ideas.

This study, its authors stress, is still in 'very preliminary' form. Yet the more prudent and certainly persuasive conclusions reached by Rodrik (2014, 206)—that '[w]hat the economist typically treats as immutable self-interest is too often an artifact of ideas about who we are, how the world works, and what actions are available'—already demonstrate (p. 205) that 'for all the emphasis placed on them in contemporary models of political economy, vested interests play a considerably less-determining role than appears at first sight'.

These conclusions are critical for our inquiry, because ideas are not as trapped into a society's politico-economic equilibrium as its institutions, culture, and levels of material and civic development are. Stemming also from idiosyncratic sources such as entrepreneurship, ideas are only partly endogenous to the social order, which can influence less the conception of innovative ones than either their dissemination or, through Gramscian cultural-political 'hegemony', their status in the eyes of public opinion. While remaining within the framework of the political economy models discussed thus far, therefore, we may nonetheless posit that ideas can be the catalyst for sustainable institutional reform, especially in societies, like Italy, that are in transition between the limited-access social order and the open-access one.

4

Vicious Circles and Multiple Equilibria: The Spiral

An Illustration: Public Services, Taxation, Corruption, and Political Accountability – The Public Interest, Individual Interests, and Multiple Equilibria – A Sketch of Italy's Problems – Institutions, Trust, Civicness, and Their Co-Evolution; Preferences and Ideas

Tutto deve essere logico, tutto si deve capire, nella storia come nella testa degli uomini: ma tra l'una e l'altra resta un salto, una zona buia dove le ragioni collettive si fanno ragioni individuali.

[Everything must be logical, everything must be understood, both in history and in men's minds: but a gap remains between one and the other, a dark area where collective reasons become individual reasons.]

(Italo Calvino, 1947)

An Illustration: Public Services, Taxation, Corruption, and Political Accountability

To introduce the next chapters it may be useful to sketch out the theories discussed in the previous two. Both to illustrate the manner in which we sought to integrate them with each other, and to draw up the hypothesis that Chapters 5–9 shall seek to demonstrate.[1] For this illustration we use a

---

[1] This chapter draws also on the following more specialized or empirical literature, which is grouped here for mere reasons of convenience. On corruption, Glaeser et al. (1996), Rose-Ackerman (2006), and Persson et al. (2013), who explicitly couch it as collective action problem, and Golden and Mahdavi (2015). On the links between corruption and political life, Clausen et al. (2011), who demonstrate that corruption lowers confidence in public authorities, and Stockemer et al. (2013)

simplified example of the interactions between citizens, politicians, and the state that are centred on the provision of the goods and services that society expects the authorities to provide. Its purpose is to show how clientelism, corruption, tax evasion, and low political accountability can spread, reinforce each other, and crystallize into a stable and persistent equilibrium.

Those interactions, set in the context of a contemporary Western democracy, involve two exchanges. One is that between the provision of such goods and services and the payment of taxes. We assume that such goods and services can be distributed either to all citizens in an equal and impartial fashion (we shall call them 'public services'), as the law requires, or to selected citizens only, in a targeted, particularized manner ('private services'). A budget constraint limits the sum total of services, private or public, which the state can distribute to society. Citizens too act under a budget constraint. They can evade their obligation to pay taxes, to improve their living standards by purchasing more goods or services on the market, but incur the risk of penalties greater than the gain.

The other exchange is that between the value of the public services provided to citizens, relative to the taxes they pay, and their political choices. Of course citizens often differ in their preferences as to the quantity and nature of the public services that the state should provide and the corresponding level and form of taxation, but we focus on the equivalence between public services distributed and taxes paid, in respect of which citizens can be assumed to have uniform preferences: all other things being equal, they will support politicians who are expected to guarantee that equivalence and oppose those who are not.

We examine a case in which this equivalence is broken. At first the whole public budget is distributed in the form of public services, all citizens pay their taxes, and the two flows are judged as equivalent. But an exogenous inefficiency arises in the distribution of services, which absorbs part of the original budget and therefore reduces the public services distributed, such that each citizen will receive a value that is lower than the taxes paid.

Citizens then have two options. One is to continue paying taxes, and in parallel exercise pressure on politicians—through actions, which we now assume to be costly, such as informing themselves, voting, writing petitions, demonstrating—to demand that the equivalence be restored through policy innovation, which we assume to be possible over the medium term but

and Sundström and Stockemer (2015), who discuss its sometimes ambivalent effects on voter turnout. On clientelism, Schefter (1977), Carey and Shugart (1995), Stolfi and Hallerberg (2016), who analyse also, or only, Italy, and Keefer and Vlaicu (2007). On political selection, Besley (2005). On tax evasion, Besley et al. (2015), who discuss and empirically test the role and persistence of social norms in sustaining either compliance or delinquency, and, among the studies that focus also, or mostly, on Italy, Galbiati and Zanella (2012), Chiarini et al. (2013), and Zhang et al. (2016).

uncertain in the short term. The other option is to resort to private remedies: evading taxes, at least in a measure sufficient to purchase on the market the portion of public services that the state did not deliver; bribing politicians, either to receive private services or to avoid the penalties attached to tax evasion; or a combination of the two. Politicians, in turn, must choose between accepting these bribes and the clientelistic political support that accompanies them, and staking their political survival only on the (uncertain) search for policies that may redress the balance between taxes and public services. Naturally, corruption too entails a risk of sanctions for both sides of the exchange.

In respect of these choices we assume that there are two types of politicians and citizens. There are politicians who always prefer to provide public services and eschew corruption irrespective of any other consideration ('public-spirited politicians'), and politicians who can choose to accept bribes, tolerate tax evasion, and provide private services if the benefits are greater than the costs ('opportunistic politicians'). Likewise, there are citizens who always prefer to receive public services, pay taxes, actively exercise their political rights, and oppose opportunistic politicians irrespective of any other consideration ('public-spirited citizens'), and citizens who decide on each of these questions depending on a cost-benefit calculation ('opportunistic citizens'). We assume that opportunistic politicians and citizens value civic virtues too, but unlike public-spirited ones they are ready to disregard their public duties when the benefits of doing so exceed the costs by more than a certain margin, which we may conceive of as the moral cost of deviating from one's values and normative beliefs: so we can imagine a continuum, between opportunists who will breach their public duties only if the net benefit of doing so is very large, whose stance is in practice very close to that of the public-spirited, and those ready to act opportunistically also for very small benefits. All members of society know that there are citizens and politicians of both types but nobody knows either what type other persons are or what their threshold is, such that, all other things being equal, unless their misdeeds are uncovered opportunistic politicians have the same chances to gain votes as public-spirited ones: bribes and clientelistic support can thus give them a distinct advantage over public-spirited politicians.

Society's response to the exogenous reduction of the public goods distributed will depend on its size. If it is large enough to lead at least one opportunistic citizen and one opportunistic politician to conclude that it is in their interest to breach their public duties, then some taxes will be evaded, some private services will be provided, and at least one clientelistic relationship will be established. By consequence, the budget available for the next distribution of public services will be further reduced. And as the balance between the taxes demanded by the state and the public services offered by it will further deteriorate, at the next round of the game the benefits of disregarding one's public duties will correspondingly rise: so more opportunistic citizens and politicians will breach them, with the same consequences. The speed of this dynamic shall accelerate, moreover, because the more people engage in tax evasion and corruption the lower is the risk of being caught, and therefore the higher the net benefit of such choices (e.g., Çule and Fulton 2009), as well as because progressive reductions of the public services distributed will signal to society that growing numbers of opportunists are engaging in tax evasion, corruption, and clientelism, leading others to bring forward their own reaction (namely, to act opportunistically before their own threshold has been reached, anticipating that it shall soon be).

If opportunists rationally pursue their short-term individual interests, therefore, after a sufficiently large initial reduction of the public budget a spiral will ensue, as a result of which society will reach a fresh equilibrium when only public-spirited citizens will continue to pay taxes, only public-spirited politicians will eschew corruption and clientelism, and opportunistic politicians will have largely prevailed over them. Besides its distributional consequences, which can be significant but we do not now consider, the shift to this equilibrium will have made society poorer, because pervasive tax evasion and corruption typically harm the efficient allocation of resources, because the state's capacity to provide critical public goods (e.g., security) may be reduced, as well as because the prevalence of opportunistic politicians—who are less exposed to political accountability than public-spirited ones by virtue of their loyal clientelistic bases and greater funds to spend on propaganda—is likely to damage the quality of public policy.

This equilibrium could prove persistent, for over time the spread of opportunistic behaviour may affect not just citizens' cognitive beliefs—their expectations as to how their immediate counterparts and society at large will respond to either opportunistic or public-spirited behaviour—but also their normative ones, which will gradually align to observed reality. As we argued in Chapter 3, in fact, if opportunistic behaviour rises, civicness, generalized trust, the legitimacy of laws, anger at their transgression, and citizens' contribution to their enforcement are all likely to decline. By consequence, the normative beliefs of some public-spirited citizens may equally change, turning them into opportunists (which allows this convenient but artificial bipartition to largely fade away). Further stages of the vicious circle may therefore ensue, leading to even lower equilibria.[2]

---

[2] Equilibria, that is, in which only Kantians—see note 8 of Chapter 3—behave public-spiritedly. The limit is lawlessness, as in Athens during the plague of 429 BC: '[f]ear of gods or law of man there was none to restrain [men]' (Thucydides II.53).

If so, was opportunistic behaviour a rational response to the exogenous shock from which we started? And under what conditions can society prevent this destructive spiral, as contemporary Western democracies generally do? We start from the first question, which is relevant also from the opportunists' perspective because the happiest of them is he who is the only one, and vice versa. Keeping one's 'covenants' may well be just, Hobbes's fool effectively says (*Leviathan* XV.4), but if all keep theirs and thereby end the war of all against all, why would it not be rational for me to breach mine? Society's only tax evader would likewise enjoy an effectively undiminished amount of public services and could spend his whole budget—minus the bribe paid to purchase impunity—to improve his living standard.

The Public Interest, Individual Interests, and Multiple Equilibria

Underlying this example is a collective action problem comparable to those discussed in Chapter 3. Similar social dilemmas have frequently been examined by the literature, often through the lens of game theory (e.g., Bidner and Francois 2013; Basu 2015; Svolik 2015), which helps clarifying their logic.

The dilemma lies in the fact that the good equilibrium is desirable for all, such that in a referendum all members of society would vote for it (Sen 1967), but opportunistic behaviour, which can set off the descent to the bad equilibrium, may nonetheless be in one's individual interest. The critical question is whether or not opportunistic behaviour is *always*—that is, irrespective of what the rest of society does—in one's interest. The latter must be defined, however, and to address the question which closes the previous section we may define it as one's enlightened interest: namely, one's objective long-term interest, taking into account the likelihood and foreseeable effects of the downward spiral.

If opportunistic behaviour is always in one's interest, which is the defining feature of the game known as the 'prisoners' dilemma', then the standard rational-choice model based on cost-benefit analysis predicts that public-spirited behaviour will derive only from compulsion, through adequate laws and consistent enforcement (motivated by society's interest in preserving, or achieving, the good equilibrium).[3] In our example, compulsion could take the form of raising the penalties for tax evasion and corruption, raising the probability that such crimes are discovered and punished, or a combination of the two. Yet, as Basu (2015) shows, effective compulsion presupposes that law-enforcers will act public-spiritedly, which cannot be assumed because

---

[3] Strategies such as 'conditional cooperation' or 'generous tit-for-tat' have nonetheless been shown to be capable of sustaining long-lasting cooperation.

they are part of the same society that may be caught in the spiral, and may themselves choose to act opportunistically. In our example, moreover, opportunistic politicians will gradually prevail over public-spirited ones, and are unlikely to favour effective law enforcement. Basu persuasively argues that the solution to such social dilemmas may lie in the realm of beliefs, normative and cognitive (and in an evolution of the theory of 'focal points' advanced by Schelling 1980).

The logic changes if opportunistic behaviour is *not* always in one's interest. Public-spirited behaviour may well be in one's interest when everybody else— or, more realistically, the vast majority of society—acts public-spiritedly, as in the case of the common-pool resources mentioned in Chapter 3, which can be destroyed by excessive exploitation. If so, one's choices will depend on one's expectations about what others will do. This is the 'assurance game', which has more than one equilibrium. Namely, if opportunists expect public-spirited behaviour from the rest of society they will act public-spiritedly, and society will rest on the good equilibrium; if they do not they will not, and society will descend to the bad equilibrium. To avert this outcome compulsion is unnecessary, strictly speaking, as it is sufficient to coordinate society's expectations and choices: as Ostrom (1990, 2000) noted, social norms favouring cooperation and reciprocity do often solve collective action problems of this kind. Yet the coordination device must not just be credible *ex ante*, to guide opportunists' choices, but also effective *ex post*, to generate the benefits expected from their public-spirited behaviour, for otherwise those who chose to pay taxes and eschew corruption in the expectation that the rest of society would have acted likewise will lose out—they will receive less public services than their cost-benefit calculus projected, and will end up with less value than if they had acted opportunistically—and at the next round of the game they are likely to reverse their choices, setting the downward spiral in motion.

It is in this sense that we said, in Chapter 2, that it can be individually rational for ordinary citizens to accept clientelism and petty corruption, despite their social consequences.

Two implications ought to be noted. First, if public-spirited behaviour is in one's interest when the vast majority of society—and not necessarily everybody—acts public-spiritedly, then the spiral will not be set off until opportunistic behaviour spreads beyond a tipping point, which coincides with the reverse of that 'vast majority'. Second, a return (or rise) to the good equilibrium is nonetheless possible because public-spirited reciprocated cooperation always remains a rational strategy, if it is sustained by society's expectations. But the virtuous circle too will depend on reaching a tipping point, which may or may not be the same as that which sets the vicious circle in motion.

Whether a society's choices are driven by the logic of the prisoners' dilemma or by that of the assurance game thus depends on an assessment of its members' (enlightened) interests. This, in turn, depends on the likelihood and foreseeable effects of the downward spiral, which determine the costs of the shift from the good equilibrium to the lower one. Yet, the trigger of the spiral is the individual interest itself. Also on this plane multiple equilibria are therefore possible, which further complicates the analysis. Under fairly realistic assumptions, however, it can be conjectured that both logics are at play in contemporary Western societies (which do indeed resort to both compulsion and coordination to avert the descent to the bad equilibrium). The reason lies in the different political and economic power and opportunities of different strata of the population. For at least part of the elite, in fact, opportunistic behaviour may be in one's individual interest even if the descent to a lower equilibrium causes a large deadweight loss to society. If the law-enforcement system is weak enough, for instance, as it is likely to be in the bad equilibrium, grand corruption—that affecting significant procurement or regulatory decisions of the state—may yield large enough net benefits to both sides of the exchange. This is unlikely to be true for most other citizens, conversely, because they have far lesser scope for evading taxes and typically no opportunity to engage in anything other than petty corruption.

This difference flows directly from the logic of North et al. (2009), for thanks to the rents that they can draw from it, elites typically prefer the limited-access social order to the open-access one, despite the inefficiencies it entails. This may remain true in societies that are in transition between the two social orders, such as the France of the Third Republic or post-war Germany, Japan, and Italy, because the elite may have retained enough political and economic power to ignore or subvert the new formal institutions. If so, the rule of law is likely to be weak, for a wide gap would separate a society's formal institutions (the written laws) from its actual ones (the manner in which laws and norms are actually enforced); and grand corruption is precisely one form that the elites' rents will take during the transition phase, when equality of rights and opportunities is legislated for, unlike in a limited-access society, but the allocation of power allows it to be transgressed with impunity, unlike in an open-access society.

It can thus be argued that at least in transition societies the (enlightened) individual interest of most citizens typically coincides with the general interest, whereas that of elites does not. This does not imply that all elites are opportunists, but just that those who are can generally gain from opportunistic behaviour benefits greater than their share of the efficiency gains forsaken by reason of the failure to shift decisively to the open-access order (or, in our example, their share of the losses caused by the descent to the low equilibrium).

It follows also that opportunists among the elite have an interest in minimizing opportunistic behaviour among ordinary citizens, for this raises their net gains. So they will favour the establishment of a two-tier system, in which opportunistic behaviour benefits from widespread impunity among elites but is dealt with rigorously among ordinary citizens (or at least rigorously enough to avoid reaching the tipping point). Again, the two-tier system is typical of the limited-access order, which does not grant equal rights to ordinary citizens, and it may persist in a formally democratic transition society as a deviation from the universalism of the new laws. Impunity must not be visible, however, not just because of the obvious reasons but also to avert a breakdown of coordination—namely, of public-spirited reciprocated cooperation—among ordinary citizens. The argument is the same as that discussed in Chapter 3, according to which the visible actions of its prominent members influence a society's expectations: if ordinary citizens see that opportunistic behaviour is prevalent among elites they may cease expecting public-spiritedness from their peers and consequently begin to act opportunistically. Hence a veil must hide the two-tiered system. In this setting hypocrisy is the homage that the old allocation of power pays to the new formal institutions, and it serves to insulate the dynamic that prevails among elites from that which prevails in the rest of society. Yet the more marked the two-tier system is, the more its traits will transpire from behind the veil. As we shall see, during the 1980s the diffusion of tax evasion and corruption appears to have accelerated significantly in Italy. One reason might be precisely that the veil shielding grand corruption and tax evasion had then begun to be pierced, thanks chiefly to the work of an increasingly independent judiciary: yet, as its investigations neither significantly reduced impunity nor improved public ethics, society is likely to have adapted its behaviour to that observed among elites.

The rise or return to the good equilibrium can be impeded by other vicious circles running in parallel to the main one, moreover, equally sustained by the progressive alignment of citizens' normative and cognitive beliefs to the prevalence of opportunistic behaviour.

One was identified by Tirole (1996), through a model of the interactions between the level of corruption in a society and the collective reputation enjoyed by its politicians in circumstances in which, as in our example, citizens ignore the type of each politician. Tirole shows that a reputation for integrity is hard to rebuild once it has been shattered, and that a general suspicion of corruption, which taints all politicians, lowers their incentives to be honest and thus fuels a vicious circle, which, he adds (p. 11), is unlikely to be broken by a temporary anti-corruption campaign, however tough it may be. As we shall see, this logic may contribute to explaining the persistence of corruption in Italy after the 1992–4 Clean Hands investigations.

A second reason why it may be hard to escape the bad equilibrium is illustrated by Hoff and Stiglitz (2008), in a model of the conditions under which a society can 'exit the lawless state'. We just defined the rule of law as the gap that may separate a polity's formal institutions from its actual ones:

more vigorously, but equivalently, they define it as what 'stops the few from stealing from the many' (p. 1474). They assume that to establish—strengthen, in the case that interests us—the rule of law, society must also 'recapture' at least part of what had previously been stolen: this is not just a requirement of fairness or law but also of logic, for a society cannot *credibly* commit itself not to recapture any ill gotten wealth once the rule of law has prevailed. On this basis, they show that even minimal recapture may delay or impede the establishment of the rule of law, also when this is in the long-term interest of all members of society. Lawlessness, in other words, can endogenously perpetuate itself.

This may not be so if the proceeds of corruption, tax evasion, and other forms of illegality can be safely invested abroad, beyond the reach of the state's recapture demand. Then opportunists might accept the strengthening of the rule of law in their home state, where their economic activities are located, on account of the efficiency gains it entails.[4] As we shall see, a similar logic was probably at play during at least one significant episode of capital flight in post-war Italy.

As we argued in Chapter 2, to conclude, the channels through which the bad equilibrium harms growth are a society's *actual* institutions. We discuss this link at the end of the chapter, but some of its features are worth mentioning here because they seem particularly relevant for Italy, to which we are about to turn. The literature, recently reviewed by the IMF (2016, 5), shows that although it is difficult to establish empirically a direct causal relationship between corruption and growth, the former 'has significant negative effects on key channels that affect growth': among them, in particular, are the efficient allocation of resources, firms' propensity to invest and innovate, the quality of public goods, and the efficiency of taxation. Taking a broader definition of corruption, a related channel is explored by Acemoglu (1995), who shows how the reward structure that determines the allocation of entrepreneurial talent—as in Baumol (1990)—is at least partly endogenous, as it is shaped by an economy's institutions, and is potentially characterized by multiple equilibria: for an increase in rent-seeking can raise the rewards of this activity relative to those of more productive ones, and thereby further skew the allocation of talent towards it. Thus a society locked in a weak-rule-of-law equilibrium is likely to see more entrepreneurs engage in rent-seeking, tax evasion, and organized crime—Baumol's examples, as we noted—than better regulated ones, with the effect of both lowering its productivity and reinforcing that equilibrium.

---

[4] This reasoning does not hold if opportunists do not wish to eschew their 'stealing' strategies: on the contrary, the possibility of placing their wealth offshore will *lower* their incentive to establish the rule of law in their own state (to protect their assets).

More recently, Aghion et al. (2016) and Bobbio (2016) designed similar Schumpeterian growth models to assess, respectively, the effects on growth of corruption—through its repercussions on the quality of the public goods financed by taxation—and of tax evasion. The former apply the model to US data, and find that 'taxation's marginal impact for growth depends sharply on local corruption': it is positive where corruption is low, negative in 'states with very high levels of corruption and taxes' (Aghion et al. 2016, 2–3). The other study concerns Italy, and was published by its central bank. Bobbio (2016, 5) moves from the assumption, empirically grounded, that 'small firms are less likely to be monitored by the tax enforcement authority than large firms, other things equal'. On this basis, the model shows (p. 28) not just that 'small firms spend less on innovation and remain small so as to [avoid the] cost of tax regularization associated with growth', but also that their cost advantage

> results in unfair competition, lowering the incentives to innovate for all firms. Both these channels depress the innovative activity of incumbent firms in the economy. As a result there is less selection in equilibrium and the economy is populated by [a] higher fraction of small, less productive and less innovative firms than it would be in the absence of tax evasion, further reducing the aggregate growth rate [and] potentially triggering a vicious cycle where the growth process brakes down [*sic*] and incumbent firms stop innovating.[5]

Corruption, tax evasion, and the vicious circles that they may generate can thus contribute to explaining the persistence of several of the weaknesses mentioned in Chapter 1: firms' comparatively low average size and propensity to grow and innovate, in particular, and low reallocation. Of equal interest, this model, Acemoglu's (1995), and Baumol's (1990) theory all imply that the socially desirable route to profits may at least in part be alternative to—and crowded out by—less virtuous ones, such as rent-seeking and tax evasion.[6] The reasons are diverse—small size lowering the risk of tax enforcement, in one case; the scarcity of entrepreneurial talent, in the other two—but the effects equivalent, similarly sensitive to the quality of the rule of law, and potentially self-propagating. The same logic might be retraced elsewhere: in selecting a firm's optimal corporate governance standards, for instance, including because paying bribes and evading taxes often requires falsifying the firm's accounts.

---

[5] The counterfactual evidence suggests (p. 28) that over the 1995–2006 period 'enforcing taxes would have increased the long-run growth rate from 0.9 to 1.1%'.

[6] An analogy can also be drawn with a trait of Italian academia discussed by Gambetta (2009, 43 *passim*), who argues that where promotions are based less on merit than on loyalty displaying incompetence credibly signals one's reliability to the other participants of the (informal) selection system, which is based on reciprocity: this, he suggests, can explain why where such system prevails its most influential organizers are often professors who produce poor research 'and do not try to hide their weakness'.

A Sketch of Italy's Problems

The example that opened this chapter and the considerations that followed it were meant also as a first approximation to the political economy of Italy's current problems. Tax evasion and corruption are widespread, in fact, and political accountability and the quality of public services relatively low, even though this state of affairs is neither in the general interest nor, we may safely conjecture, in the enlightened individual interest of most citizens. So that example can shed some light on how this equilibrium works and why it persists, despite its unfairness and inefficiency; not on how it emerged, though, as the example relied on a fiction—the exogenous reduction of the public budget—to set the spiral in motion. We can nonetheless use it to retrace in Italy's history the signs of the emergence, evolution, and adaptation of the main drivers of the spiral. This analysis is conducted in the following chapters. To serve as a useful guide for them, however, that example ought to be integrated in four main respects.

First, similar social dilemmas exist also in the private sector. Entrepreneurs need households' capital to create and develop their firms, and especially equity capital, reliance on which tends to be positively correlated with firms' growth and innovation. They thus share an interest in operating in an environment in which good corporate governance standards minimize the cost of equity capital and maximize its availability. But they may have an interest in falsifying their firm's accounts, to evade taxes or pay bribes, or in engaging in other predatory practices by which, for instance, minority shareholders are deprived of part of their share of profits. The logic of this trade-off is akin to our example, and also in this case it may correspond to either the assurance game or the prisoners' dilemma, depending on whether opportunistic behaviour is always in one's individual interest. For instance, entrepreneurs and majority or controlling shareholders whose firms have relatively low growth prospects—whether because of firm-specific problems or because their sector is stagnant—may judge that predatory practices yield benefits that are greater than those afforded by a more efficient market for equity capital, especially if they can count also on collusion with the public authorities to protect themselves from competition (through, for instance, procurement corruption, arbitrary subsidies, or anti-competitive regulation, all observable in both pre-war and post-war Italy).

Downward spirals in the private and the public sector may thus be linked and mutually reinforcing. But the reverse is equally true, as also in the private sector the existence of multiple equilibria implies that the downward spiral can be reversed. It is unlikely, conversely, that a vicious circle in one sector may for long run alongside a virtuous circle in the other one. Indeed, the theories reviewed in Chapter 2 persuasively argue that in a stable equilibrium access must be limited in both politics and the economy, such that the power and rents of a society's political and economic elites may be balanced (North et al. 2009), and that a society's political and economic institutions tend to be either both efficient and 'inclusive' or both inefficient and 'extractive' (Acemoglu and Robinson 2012).

Second, the implicit correspondence between public-spiritedness and public-spirited behaviour may not always hold. In particular, the interactions among clientelism, corruption, and the provision of private services are rarely as simple as we fashion them. More realistically, clientelism and the provision of private services can concern also wide categories of citizens, to whom the government lawfully reserves a preferential treatment—to the detriment, necessarily, of more universalistic welfare policies—in the expectation (also) of winning their political support. As we shall see, both during Fascism and in republican Italy farmers, retailers, civil servants, and other categories were the recipients of preferential regulation and welfare policies. Public-spirited citizens may respond positively to this tactic while being convinced that their conduct will not harm the means by which society avoids the descent to the bad equilibrium. But this may well be the effect, for the link with corruption and the degradation of public policies remains: also this corporatist form of clientelism lowers politicians' incentive to win votes based on the quality of their political programme and the coherence with it of the choices made when in power, gives them an advantage over more public-spirited politicians, and thus weakens their political accountability. This creates political rents, in turn, which can be monetized also through corruption, grand or petty.

Seen from another perspective, moreover, corporatist clientelism can strengthen, or even stimulate the rise of the distributional coalitions that Olson (1982) discusses.[7] Besides their direct effect on the distribution of public resources, distributional coalitions are socially undesirable solutions to the collective action problem, as we saw, because they tend to harm the efficiency of regulation, segment society, and weaken its dynamic forces.

Third, politics naturally concerns not only the equivalence between taxes paid and public services received but also the level and nature of both, as we said, and countless other issues relevant to citizens' interests. Nor is the politics that appeals to their ideas limited to 'worldview politics', as Mukand and Rodrik (2016, 2) call it, which revolves around the efficacy of policy, for it hosts also what is known as 'identity politics', which seeks to make one of citizens' perceived identities—class, creed, ethnicity, nationality—salient. Thus, in the making of citizens' political choices, the questions on which our

---

[7] In Olson (1982) the process leading to the formation of a distributional coalition begins among its members: as we shall see in Chapters 6 and 7, in Italy politicians may often have played a role in initiating it.

example focuses may well be eclipsed by other motivations. Indeed, identity politics that is not based on class can lead people to vote irrespective of, if not even against, their objective economic interests.

During the Cold War the presence in Italy of what for long was Western Europe's largest communist party widened the scope for this phenomenon. Its effects were magnified by the fact that the mass-media market was, and remains, highly concentrated and dominated by publishers controlled either by the government or by large businesses whose main activity was not publishing, which tended to use their mass media also as bargaining cards in negotiations with the government (Ortoleva 1997a, 1997b; Gundle 2015; Mancini 2015), deepening the collusion between public authorities and private interests.

Fourth, in the regions where it is present organized crime can raise the benefits of opportunistic behaviour. Through its ability to credibly threaten the use of violence it can make corruption exchanges and cartels more enforceable and secure, by dissuading cheating and whistleblowing, and through its control of parts of the national territory it can also better organize political clientelism, and make this exchange enforceable as well. These functions may explain why apparently archaic phenomena such as the Sicilian mafia and similar organizations in Calabria and Campania persist to this day.

These four factors add to the complexity of the picture but do not harm its coherence, for each either replicates the logic of the initial example or reinforces it. A plausible hypothesis, therefore, is that the compulsion and coordination devices—the laws and social norms—that Italian society employed to first achieve and then safeguard the good equilibrium are defective, relative to its peers'.

Institutions, Trust, Civicness, and Their Co-Evolution; Preferences and Ideas

Laws, social norms, and their enforcement characteristics are what we defined as institutions, namely the rules that, by shaping people's incentives, govern social, economic, and political exchange. In Chapter 3 we concluded that laws critically depend on social norms to be implemented, but that the latter—that is, the cognitive and normative beliefs that generate them—can be changed by carefully designed laws, which succeed in guiding society's behaviour, as well as by the credible actions of its most visible members, often its elites. In both cases, the channel is the interdependence of citizens' expectations with each other and with observed reality: if society's behaviour changes, social norms change too.

We noted also that social norms favouring public-spirited reciprocated cooperation are typically underpinned by high levels of civicness and generalized inter-personal trust, and we concluded that there is a two-way causal relationship between these features of a society, on one hand, and the character of its institutions, on the other, and that the influence that the latter exercise on trust and civicness dominates the reverse effect. This last conclusion was based less on empirical evidence than on theoretical arguments, however, and may have to be taken with caution (besides the self-evident observation that if its laws favour opportunistic behaviour and are coherently enforced a society will hardly escape the bad equilibrium). More important was the confutation, which we regard as solid, of the theories arguing that the levels of trust and civicness are effectively permanent traits of a society, susceptible to change only over several generations or even centuries. Conversely, civicness, trust, social norms, laws, their enforcement characteristics, and social behaviour all co-evolve, albeit at different speeds, and if laws are consistently enforced they can guide this process, under the conditions we just highlighted.

Laws 'are created to serve the interests of those with the bargaining power to create [them]', North said (1994, 361). In other words, they are the product of the allocation of power in a society, its social order. The latter, in turn, is the product of a society's history, just like its social norms and its levels of trust and civicness. It is for this reason that new laws that run counter to the logic of the extant social order, such as an attempt to improve governance after a fleeting change in the parliamentary majority, often remain ink on paper (see Basu 2015). Low trust and civicness are not *independent* obstacles to their implementation, but tools by which the extant social order safeguards itself. If the latter changes, the former can change too.

Yet it is precisely in the context of the transition from the limited-access order to the open access one that the mutual influences among the various determinants of social behaviour appear most complex. New laws then are no longer just the stroke of a progressive legislator's pen, but the embodiment of the ends and ideals of a revolution or regime change. Yet the forces that drove change and the laws that they wrote will inevitably face the inheritance of the old regime: norms, customs, a culture, and entrenched positions which, sustained by the forces of inertia, can delay, obstruct, or even frustrate the transition. This is the challenge that Italy faced after 1943–8, when a democratic republic rose from the ruins of the Fascist dictatorship and the Savoy monarchy. It may be pictured as the uncertainty of the citizen who enters the office where for two decades a Fascist bureaucrat used to trade favours in exchange for devotion to the regime and *baksheesh* to himself, and must decide whether to act likewise with the new man sitting behind the desk, or else invoke her newly acquired citizenship rights. The epigraph to this chapter is the thinking of the political commissar of a communist partisan unit in the Maritime Alps, a student of medicine, whom Calvino describes, on the eve of a battle, as he reflects precisely on what choices people will make after the war: whether, to reformulate his question, the 'collective reasons' that underpinned the new republic would have been credible enough to become 'individual reasons'.

This leads us to the role of ideas. As we argued at the end of Chapter 3, relying primarily on Rodrik (2014), they are the determinant of social behaviour that is most independent of the other ones and of the extant social order. They can change one's preferences, in the first place, and for instance turn opportunists into public-spirited citizens (or, more realistically, raise the threshold after which they are willing to act opportunistically). But even when all other determinants of social behaviour are aligned in making opportunism rational, such that also in an assurance-game context cooperation fails, ideas can nonetheless unearth one's *latent* preferences—i.e., public-spirited reciprocated cooperation—from below one's *revealed* ones, for they can change the perception of both one's interests and the ways to satisfy them. The challenge, of course, is that the new ideas must persuade people to act *as if* all other determinants of social behaviour were *not* so aligned. Unless Hirschman's 'rebound effect' (1982) or similar phenomena occur, therefore, persuasive ideas may not suffice. To bring a society to behave *as if* public-spiritedness were rational, the expectation that by this such behaviour will actually become rational must be realistic. This presupposes an organization, to develop and disseminate the new ideas and build a credible political programme upon them. It is also from this perspective that we shall analyse both the critical years of 1943–53, when Italy's transition began, and two subsequent attempts at comprehensive reform, in the early 1960s and in the second half of the 1990s.

5

Italy's Social Order between Unification and Fascism

Social Order and Elites in the Nineteenth Century – Italy's Late Industrialization and the Policies of the Giolittian Era – World War I, Fascism, and the Rise of the State-Entrepreneur – The Liberal Elites and Fascism: the Regression of Italy's Social Order

truth, whose mother is history, rival of time, storehouse of deeds, witness for the past, example and counsel for the present, and warning for the future.

(Cervantes, *Quixote* I.9)

Social Order and Elites in the Nineteenth Century

The result of long-sedimented political and economic inefficiencies, Italy's recent decline is best approached from a historical perspective. This chapter offers a rapid overview of the 'liberal' (1861–1922) and Fascist (1922–43) epochs, drawn mainly from Mack Smith (1997), Ciocca (2007), James and O'Rourke (2013), and Felice (2015). Chapter 6 examines in greater detail the years between the end of Fascism and the early 1950s, during which the country became a democratic republic, readied for full industrialization, and began its transition from the limited-access social order to the open-access one. Chapters 7, 8, and 9 follow this transition up to the present day. Conceived as a prelude to the following four, this chapter prepares them by retracing the evolution of the country's social order up to the beginning of that transition.

In each case the lens are the theories outlined in Chapters 2 and 3 and summarized in Chapter 4. The focus is set on the few junctures that proved critical in shaping the country's social order and institutions. And the aim is to highlight the evolution of those factors that most contribute to explaining the inefficiencies of the current politico-economic system. This and the following chapters are not intended to offer a comprehensive summary of the country's history, therefore. We take the luxury of digging deeper where the events appear most interesting from the vantage point of our interpretation, conversely, or when it has some aspiration to originality, and of being cursory where we have nothing to add to the prevailing ones. For the same reasons, it bears repeating, these chapters are painted in often darker colours than Italy's remarkable secular development, material and moral, would otherwise have merited. While we frequently consider the power, interests, and ideas of the main actors, finally, it ought to be underlined that we have eschewed the question of whether, or under what conditions, different outcomes would have been possible at the junctures we focus upon.

Unified in 1861, after thirteen centuries of political fragmentation, Italy rested on weak unifying political, economic, or cultural factors. The six states that Piedmont merged under the crown of the House of Savoy—the Kingdom of the Two Sicilies, the Pontifical monarchy, and the small principalities and Habsburg dominions of the Centre-North—were heterogeneous. They traded less among each other than with the rest of the world. Only part of their elites supported unification. And the politico-intellectual movement advocating it—the Risorgimento ('resurgence')—did not reach much beyond the upper classes, also because perhaps only 2.5 per cent of the peninsula's inhabitants spoke the Italian language, besides the regional vernacular (De Mauro 1970, 34–43 and 342–5). By comparison, it can safely be assumed that in the German Reich, unified one decade later, the majority—probably the vast majority—of the population could speak standard German (*Hochdeutsch*), and, at a basic level, could also write it.[1]

Another revealing detail is that the repression of 'brigandage'—in effect a long (1861–5) rebellion, chiefly against the North's annexation of the South—caused more casualties than the army's losses during the wars fought against the Austrian Empire over Lombardy and the erstwhile Venetian state. Brigandage was less widespread in Sicily. In the west of the island the temporary decline of state authority that followed unification instead saw groups of mafiosi—a word whose first recorded use dates from those years—providing protection services

---

[1] We owe this assessment to Paul Rössler, who suggests that the reason why the Germanistic literature (e.g., Mattheier 2000, 1959) does not offer estimates comparable to De Mauro's is precisely that linguistic unification was not nearly as acute a problem as in Italy. Italian was still mostly a literary language, in fact, less spoken than written or read; up to 1859 Piedmont's parliament transacted its business in French, for instance, and it is with these words that on the day of the country's unification (17 March 1861) its first Prime Minister, Count Cavour, celebrated the event in a letter to another Piedmontese statesman: 'Dès ce jour, l'Italie affirme hautement en face du monde sa propre existence' (quoted by Eco 2011, 1).

to the owners of citrus groves and sulphur mines, both sources of profitable exports (Gambetta 1993; Bandiera 2003; Lupo [1996] 2009).

The upper classes of the unified state nonetheless shared the interest of keeping the extant allocation of power intact. They set aside the democratic, republican, and federalist ideas present in the Risorgimento (Cardoza 2015). The electoral franchise was limited to 1.9 per cent of the population (Guiso and Pinotti 2013, 309). And the extension to the whole country of Piedmont's moderately liberal 1848 constitution scarcely opened up the semi-feudal social order of the South, as Tomasi di Lampedusa's *The Leopard* ([1958] 2007) famously illustrates.[2] Commenting on the electoral fraud that tainted the plebiscite by which Sicily chose to join the new state, incidentally, the novelist (p. 113) advances an argument proximate to our critique of the cultural interpretation:

> a great deal of the slackness and acquiescence for which the people of the South were to be criticized during the next decades was due to the stupid annulment of the first expression of liberty ever offered to them.

The Pope and the Church remained hostile to the monarchy that had conquered their state, however, and proscribed the participation of their flock in political life. Until this dictate—the so-called *non expedit*—was relaxed and then lifted, in the tense aftermath of World War I, the liberal elites faced an 'anti-systemic' opposition which included also Catholics, besides republicans, democrats, socialists, and anarchists (Salvadori 2013). The challenge that this posed to the construction of a popular base for the new state casts the remark often attributed to the Piedmontese statesman Massimo d'Azeglio—'We have made Italy. Now we have to make Italians'—into clearer light.

This disjunction between the state and its constituents, or between the 'legal country' and the 'real country' (Urbinati 2015, 538), will prove a persisting trait of the Italian state (Cassese 2014), just like the comparative weakness of its ruling class (Salvadori 2013), which to this day appears 'unable to exercise hegemony' (Newell 2015, 13). These interpretations partly draw on Gramsci's ([1929–35] 2011), who argued that at the roots of these phenomena lay the landowning elites' reluctance to involve the masses in the Risorgimento, as the Jacobins had done, fearing that they would demand land reform. The extant social order was thus preserved, but the liberal elites failed to extend their cultural-political hegemony over the nation.

In 1861 the material foundations of the 'lumière' that Braudel (1989 [1994]) celebrates had long faded, eroded since the height of the sixteenth

---

[2] Tancredi: '[i]f we want things to stay as they are, things will have to change' (p. 28); the prince: 'all will be the same though all will be changed' (p. 33). Both lines were retained in Luchino Visconti's 1963 film.

century—when Italians still enjoyed the highest average per capita income in Europe—by the rise of the Atlantic trade and the political influence of foreign powers, among other causes. Unified Italy had a backward, overpopulated, capital-scarce economy, poor in infrastructure and lacking both the main ingredients of industrialization, coal and iron ore. Per capita income was roughly half that of Britain, then the productivity leader, and two thirds that of France.

Unification favoured the integration of the peninsula's regional markets and strengthened the incentive to industrialize in order to raise the nation's standing in both the European exchequer and the competition for colonies. But in the context of the first globalization, already under way in the 1860s, the liberal policies favoured by the dominant and export-generating agrarian sector did not assist the expansion of manufacturing. Nor did the liberal elites rely on education to raise the economy's production potential, as Japan did after the Meiji Restoration. At unification a universal system of free and compulsory education assured two years of schooling, later increased to three and then to five, but until 1911 its financing was left to municipalities, which lacked the necessary resources: in 1901 the illiteracy rate was still 48.5 per cent, considerably higher than in Britain, France, or Germany (De Mauro 1970; Bertola and Sestito 2013). 'When they will all have become learned, who will plough our lands?' Manzoni's irony (Belgiojoso [1848] 1977, 20) on an acquaintance's plan to educate the peasants of her Lombard estates dates from the 1840s, but stems from a conservative approach that persisted well beyond those years. For most of the century and a half since unification the policies of Italy's elites were characterized by a comparative neglect for universal education (De Mauro 1970, 2014), in fact, which made this the 'gloomiest chapter' of the country's social history (Vecchi 2017, 206).

In the second half of the 1870s the homogenous landowning elite that had unified the country was replaced in government by a more diverse faction of the same liberal grouping, the *Sinistra* ('Left'), which adopted a more protectionist trade policy and an activist industrial policy. This was not an unusual response to the challenges of industrialization and intensified international competition, and reflected the political alliance—Italy's 'historic bloc', in Gramsci's terms ([1929–35] 2011)—between southern landowners and notables and the rising industrial and financial sectors of the North, henceforth the pillar of the dominant coalition. Industrial policy was conducted mainly through discretionary measures, however, and especially after 1887 trade policy favoured relatively mature sectors (mainly steel-making and textiles) over emerging and more technologically advanced ones, such as engineering and machine-making, and land-intensive agricultural productions (wheat, in the South) over labour-intensive ones, more appropriate for Italy's comparatively ample workforce and scarce natural resources. Under these policies manufacturing expanded and some larger firms arose, but the country grew at a slower rate than Europe's early industrializers.

Though dampened by growing emigration, during the 1880s social tensions intensified. The response of the *Sinistra* blended repression with an attempt to strengthen the national sentiment of the masses, by rallying them behind the irredentist cause of Trento and Trieste, still in Austrian hands, and the effort to establish Italy as a great power. This policy largely failed, also because after a crushing defeat at Adowa in 1896, at the hands of the Ethiopian army, Italy became the first European power to lose a colonial war. During the late 1890s demonstrations grew more frequent and repression harsher. On 8 May 1898 the army used artillery in the streets of Milan, killing approximately 100 demonstrators.

In this epoch, finally, greater and more discretionary government intervention in the economy coincided with a marked deterioration of public ethics. In 1882 the electorate was widened to 6.9 per cent of the population (Felice 2015, 126), and the parliamentary representation of the upper middle class—a *bourgeoisie* of notables and professionals far more than of entrepreneurs—correspondingly increased. Their absorption into the contests and shifting alliances of the competing factions of the liberal elites saw the rise of the parliamentary practices that became known as *trasformismo* (a 'prototypical Italian trait' still observed nowadays: Valbruzzi 2015, 27); practices, such as the trading of parliamentary votes or the co-optation of single parliamentarians, often accompanied by the manipulation of the electoral process, which generally lacked transparency and encouraged political clientelism. In this context, as the theories summarized in Chapter 4 would predict, the relationship between the authorities and the economic elites gradually morphed into collusion. Ciocca (2007, 117–8) writes that there 'spread among Italian capitalists the [thought] that profits could more easily be gained by colluding with public powers while shifting losses onto workers, consumers, and finally the public budget'. The degeneration of public ethics was conspicuously revealed in 1892-3 by the bribery and financial fraud scandal centred on a (private) bank of issue, the Banca Romana, which implicated also Prime Minister Giovanni Giolitti, who temporarily fled abroad (Galante Garrone 1996).

In this context also the influence of the Sicilian mafia grew. At the turn of the century the head of police in Palermo (quoted by Lupo [1996] 2009, 17) remarked that prominent mafiosi

> are under the protection of senators, members of parliament, and other influential figures who protect and defend them, only to be protected and defended by them in turn.

In the region of Naples another constellation of criminal groups, the camorra, likewise translated its control over parts of the urban area into political influence. Unlike the mafia, however, its influence was exercised relatively more at the local level, over both the electoral process, through large-scale clientelism, and the choices of the administration (Bevilacqua 2005, 69–73). In both regions these early forms of organized crime thus appear to have adapted themselves to the politico-economic equilibrium of the new state, which, correspondingly, was relatively tolerant towards them.

Italy's Late Industrialization and the Policies of the Giolittian Era

Economic growth accelerated sustainably only after the late 1890s, driven by the forces of convergence discussed in Chapter 1 (Toniolo 2013b). By then Italy's per capita income had dropped to 38 per cent of Britain's, but by 1913 it had risen back to 54 per cent, about the same level as in 1861. Among other causes, the acceleration was favoured by policies that increased competitive pressures on firms and by an attempt to at least reduce the collusion that characterized the earlier decades: the governments of this period, led mostly by Giolitti, fought monopolies and restrictive practices, nationalized some sectors (the railways, most notably), took a stance of neutrality in the conflict between capital and labour, made the economy more open to the international markets, and maintained stable exchange rates (Ciocca 2007). Recent research does indeed suggest that during the Giolittian era competition became intenser and stimulated growth (Giordano and Zollino 2017). Productivity growth accelerated remarkably, in both industry and services (2.5 and 2.2 per cent per year, respectively, in the 1901–11 period: Broadberry et al. 2013, 193).

In the sectors of the second industrial revolution a first nucleus of large firms emerged, which gave a decisive contribution to growth. Since the early 1890s they could increasingly rely on the water of the peninsula's mountains—Italy's 'white coal'—as a source of energy, and among the fastest-growing sectors were the electrical and electro-mechanical ones: 'at a time when electrification was the world's new "general purpose technology"', thanks to sustained invest-ment, imports of both equipment and disembodied technology, adequate legislation, and well-trained engineers, Italy soon placed itself on the frontier in the hydro-electric industry (Toniolo 2013b, 16 and 18; Barbiellini Amidei et al. 2013, 381).

Among the firms that established an enduring advantage in their respective sectors were Ansaldo (steel-making and engineering), Falck, Piombino, and Terni (steel-making), Fiat (automobiles), Pirelli (cables and tires), and a rather concentrated oligopoly in electricity generation and distribution led by Edison, the so-called *elettrici*. Arising from a mass of micro or small family firms, these first larger ones responded to the capital scarcity and relative backwardness of Italian capitalism with corporate governance practices—pyramidal control chains, cross shareholdings, interlocking directorates—that ensured stability of control with relatively limited equity-capital investment and wove tight links among them, reinforcing their dominant positions. The 'osmosis' between smaller and larger firms—by which profitable innovations developed by the former are given large-scale application by the latter—was limited, however (Ciocca 2007; 2012, 13).

Industrialization was favoured also by an institutional reform provoked by the banking crisis amidst which the Banca Romana scandal arose, which led to the rise of German-style 'universal' or 'mixed' banks, often backed by foreign capital. This model drew finance and industry closer together, dampening competition and creative destruction, but proved appropriate to the needs of a capital-scarce economy at the outset of large-scale industrialization. As the theories discussed in Chapter 2 would predict, however, without reform this institution became inadequate once that stage of development was passed. The ever-tighter relationship between banks and industry, founded also on the corporate governance practices we just mentioned, fused with the parallel collusion between the public and the private sphere and eventually became symbiotic, building up risks that the industry and banking crises of the inter-war period will expose.

Industrialization was concentrated in the North and especially in the Genoa-Milan-Turin triangle, which in 1911 produced 55 per cent of value added (Toniolo 2013b, 16). The regional divide widened: between the late 1890s and 1915 GDP per capita in the South declined, as a percentage of per capita GDP in the Centre-North, from close to 90 to less than 75 per cent (Iuzzolino et al. 2013). And emigration from the South accelerated steeply (Gomellini and Ó Gráda 2013).

In a comparative perspective, however, Italy's late industrialization appears to have been 'unusually "benevolent" toward the lower classes' (Toniolo 2013b, 16). Life expectancy grew, the incidence of child labour fell sharply, and between 1901 and 1921 income inequality declined (Brandolini and Vecchi 2013; Vecchi 2017, chs. 3 and 7). Also the illiteracy rate dropped, to about 27 per cent in 1921, but the national average hid an almost six-fold disparity between the South and the North-West (Bertola and Sestito 2013; Vecchi 2017, ch. 5).

With industrialization arose a larger urban working class. Among manufacturing workers in the North-West, salaried peasants in the wider North, and sharecroppers in the Centre mutual-aid societies, cooperatives, trade union membership, and support for the Partito socialista italiano (PSI[3]) grew. In 1913 Socialist candidates obtained a little less than one fifth of the vote. During the

---

[3] This and other parties changed their name during their history, some more than once: we use the names most commonly used during the republican period.

Giolittian era the liberal elites' response shifted from repression to an attempt to widen the popular base of the state. Besides taking a position of neutrality between capital and labour, which saw real wages rise with productivity, they prolonged and better financed compulsory free education, in 1912–13 they extended the electoral franchise to almost all adult males,[4] and they sought to associate in the management of the state also the moderate wings of the anti-systemic forces, Catholics first and Socialists later.

This operation was conducted through the practices of *trasformismo*, as Gramsci already noted (quoted by Valbruzzi 2015, 29), which could serve both the 'molecular' co-option of the rising *bourgeois* by the *Sinistra*, in the 1880s and 1890s, as well as the more ambitious operation attempted by the Giolittian liberals. Indeed, co-option was the vehicle of change of a 'blocked' political system (Salvadori 2013), which saw no rotation in power but the alternation of different factions of the same liberal elites: facing an anti-systemic opposition and masses whose loyalty the state had not stably acquired, they contemplated only repression or co-option as a strategic response. This interpretation mirrors the theories illustrated in Chapter 2: the dominant coalition of a limited-access social order would co-opt non-elites to stabilize the equilibrium, not to change it, and those it co-opted would henceforth act likewise. Equally, the collusion between public powers and private interests is but a reflection of the fact that the dominant coalition of a limited-access social order typically includes also the economic elites. None of these features was unique to Italy, of course, but the lack of rotation in government suggests that the limits to competition, both political and economic, were more stringent than where power did change hands, as in contemporary France (North et al. 2009, 219–27). More interesting to note is that after the turn of the century the *political* elites did not just launch a more inclusive co-option strategy than their predecessors, but also displayed greater autonomy from the *economic* elites, who indeed judged, disapprovingly, that the Giolittian liberals were giving 'full political citizenship' to workers and peasants (Banti 1996, 323). This suggests that the country was then moving closer to the transition to the open-access social order.

World War I, Fascism, and the Rise of the State-Entrepreneur

Italy entered World War I in May 1915, when its unprecedented destructive character was already becoming apparent. The decision was taken after a divisive debate. Among those urging the government to join the hostilities, contrary to Giolitti's advice, were most of northern industry and finance. They

---

[4] Compared to 1909 the electorate grew from 2.9 to 8.4 million, or from 8 to 23 per cent of the population (Ciocca 2012, 23).

expected to profit from the war economy, and influenced the public debate through the *Corriere* and other newspapers they controlled. Indeed, during the war 'the steel, shipbuilding, engineering, and chemical industries—all heavily subsidized—underwent rapid expansion', and the electrical sector received high investment (Toniolo 2013b, 18). The profits, size, and market power of Italy's large firms and their financiers, the main universal banks, all rose steeply. Ciocca (2007, 183) comments that in those few years 'the higher echelons of Italian capitalism' took shape, comprising the firms we mentioned earlier and a few other ones, and their 'oligopolistic strategies' consolidated.

After the *débâcle* of Caporetto, in late 1917, the imminent risk of being defeated by Austria-Hungary sparked a choral and ultimately successful effort to defend the country. This strengthened the national identity. But the war had also raised the cohesion, confidence, and political agency of the lower classes, as elsewhere in Europe, and had tested Italy's social order, revealing its fragility. At the outset there was no *union sacrée* between government and oppositions. During the conflict a disproportionate[5] number of soldiers were court-martialled, and its aftermath, marked by soaring inflation and unemployment, rather resembled that of a defeated nation (Chabod [1950] 1961).

At the 1919 election the PSI, in which maximalists had prevailed over the reformist wing, obtained the highest share of the vote (32.2 per cent), a dozen points ahead of the newly founded Catholic party. In 1920 the trade unions represented 3.3 million members, in a population of 36 million: two thirds belonged to the PSI-led Confederazione generale italiana del lavoro (CGIL), and the rest to a Catholic confederation that was hardly less radical in supporting salaried peasants' demands for land redistribution (Chabod [1950] 1961, 35 and 46). The 'red' years of 1919–20 witnessed widespread demonstrations and a potentially revolutionary wave of factory occupations in the North-West, in whose wake divergences over the Socialists' strategy provoked a split from which the Partito comunista italiano (PCI) arose, with a Leninist manifesto (and Gramsci among its leaders). The Giolittian liberals succeeded in restoring order peacefully, and renewed the attempt to bring also the Socialists into the government. The PSI again refused, but in 1919–21 workers nevertheless obtained a partial confiscation of the war profits and real wage increases—50 per cent in the manufacturing sector—that significantly altered the balance between capital and labour in the distribution of national income.

In parallel, however, the government was challenged also by movements of nationalists and war veterans, drawn mostly from a *petite bourgeoisie* that felt squeezed between workers and elites. Among them, notable for its violence,

---

[5] Four hundred thousand soldiers were tried and 170,000 convicted: by comparison, the losses were 650,000 (Ciocca 2007, 165).

was the Fascist movement. In May 1921 it won only 0.4 per cent of the vote (Socialists and Communists obtained 24.7 and 4.6 per cent, respectively), but it enjoyed the tolerance of the authorities and the financial support of the economic elites of the Centre-North, which had borne most of the workers' and the Marxists' pressure: although by then the revolutionary threat had subsided, Chabod ([1950] 1961, 52–3) notes that 'fear can also be retrospective'. This was especially true of the landowners of the Po valley, Emilia Romagna, and Tuscany, where Fascist violence was harshest (and communist support would be strongest over the subsequent seven decades).

In October 1922 the Fascists staged a show of force, the 'March on Rome', which the army could have suppressed with ease. The King invited their leader to form a new government instead, in coalition with liberals and Catholics. The industrialists' confederation (Confindustria) hailed Mussolini's cabinet, which was also welcomed, albeit with greater caution, by the *Corriere* and, on its pages, by the liberal economist Luigi Einaudi (Banti 1996, 365–6 quotes them). Divided, revolutionary, and therefore also isolated, the Left offered feeble resistance to the liberal elites' reactionary turn. The government it produced curtailed political rights and civil liberties, repressed Marxists and trade unionists, largely reversed labour's gains in the distribution of national income, and interrupted the decline in income inequality (Brandolini and Vecchi 2013).

Fascism hardened into an autocracy in 1925, after a crisis sparked by outright election fraud and the assassination of a prominent Socialist parliamentarian. Mussolini had lost the support of most Catholics, many liberals, and the *Corriere*, but had retained that of the Crown, the army, and the economic elites. The regime jailed or murdered several of its relatively few active opponents, such as Gramsci and the radical democrat Piero Gobetti. It rapidly expanded its own popular base, through means—the creation of a genuine mass party, increased welfare spending, the expansion of the civil service—that opened the state to the wider middle classes. And in 1929 a pact signed with the Vatican, to settle differences dating back from Italy's conquest of Rome in 1870, brought also the Church closer to the regime: welcoming this agreement, Pius XI famously hailed the dictator as the 'man of Providence'.

Fascism did fight the mafia, whose activities challenged its authority and the state's monopoly on violence, but it achieved short-lived results because its repression policy targeted the mafia's foot soldiers rather than the political and economic roots of its influence, which were closely intertwined with the hierarchical power relations of the Sicilian agrarian economy (see Lupo [1996] 2009). Nor did the regime fight bribery, which proliferated (Galante Garrone 1996; Mack Smith 1997). A contemporary observer (Calamandrei [1947] 2004, 235–6) argued that political corruption was a physiological and necessary 'component of [Fascism's] system', for the solidarity of those engaged in the exchange—each vulnerable to the blackmail of the other and of the 'tyrant' (Calamandrei cites La Boétie here)—was a 'guarantee of stability' for the regime, which made it also 'distrustful' towards officials who preserved their integrity.

The collusion between public powers and private interests equally intensified. The vicissitudes of a financial transparency measure—the requirement that companies' shares be issued in registered rather than bearer form—are revealing. Adopted by Giolitti in 1920, it was repealed by Mussolini ten days after he took office (Banti 1996, 351 and 366). He decided to re-instate it in 1941, increasingly frustrated with the country's elites ('the worst Italians'), but it took six months and the dictator's 'obscure threats' to revolutionize property rights to overcome the 'furious' opposition of Giuseppe Volpi, member of the electrical oligopoly, former finance minister (1925–8), president of Confindustria (1934–43), and, as such, member of the Grand Council of Fascism, formally the regime's highest decision-making body (Ciano 1990, 537, 539, and 600).[6] Giolitti had adopted this measure for fiscal reasons, and Ciano (1990, 628) is quite candid on the autocracy's tolerance for tax evasion. But bearer shares were an instrument also for the opaque practices then frequent in Italy's stock exchanges, of whose capitalization the *elettrici* represented a large share: indeed, during Fascism Confindustria also successfully resisted other measures that could have made the capital markets more transparent and efficient, such as tighter regulation of the prevailing corporate governance practices—those, as we said, which allowed firms to be stably controlled with relatively limited equity capital and favoured collusion among them—and the introduction of minority shareholders' liability claims against managers and directors (Marchetti 2011; Siciliano 2011). Fascism thus seems to reveal several traits of the 'bad' equilibrium discussed in Chapter 4, even though the parallel is only partly possible as our example concerned a democratic polity.

The regime subjected the labour market to its political control, moreover, favoured the formation of cartels and dominant positions in the product markets, pursued an industrial policy based on the discretionary concession of subsidies and regulatory privileges, and progressively closed the economy to foreign competition (in an international context, admittedly, of growing protectionism). Overall, Fascism considerably reduced competitive pressures on firms (Gigliobianco and Toniolo 2017; Giordano and Zollino 2017), which recorded high average profits but contributed less to productivity than in the previous or subsequent decades.

---

[6] Emma Stone, who won the Best Actress award at the 2016 Venice film festival, received the 'Volpi Cup'. Fascism created the festival as part of its propaganda policy, and honoured Volpi, a self-made man, also with the earldom of Misurata (Misrata), in Libya, where as governor he oversaw the brutal repression of an insurgency in the 1920s.

Aggregate labour productivity and TFP growth both slowed down, in fact, especially during the years of the Great Depression that followed the crisis of 1929. The best performance was recorded by the public utilities sector, but one reason is that the gains from past investments and innovations in hydro-electric power were reaped with a lag (Broadberry et al. 2013, 193–4).

Other choices of the regime reveal a degree of ambivalence, however. In particular, its decision to take direct control of the high end of both the banking and the manufacturing sectors attests to low trust in the entrepreneurial capacity of Italy's capitalists.[7] These nationalizations were provoked by the banking crisis of the early 1930s. Unlike other universal banks in Austria or Germany, the Italian ones did not collapse because of illiquidity: they became insolvent instead, primarily because they owned large manufacturing shareholdings acquired during the rescue, in the 1920s, of many of the firms—including Ansaldo, Piombino, Terni, and Edison—that had vastly increased their capacity during World War I, and struggled to adjust to the peace-time economy. But by 1932 Italy's two main banks also owned most of their own share capital, through the opaque corporate governance practices mentioned earlier (Ciocca 2014, 32–3, 39–40). The regime nationalized them and their assets, and shed the universal-bank model by rigidly separating banks from industry and short-term from longer-term credit. As Fascism equally mistrusted the public administration, this operation was conducted through ad hoc agencies (*enti pubblici*) wholly autonomous from the ministerial hierarchies: the 'Istituto per la ricostruzione industriale' (IRI), a holding entity in whose portfolio the nationalized businesses were placed (Ciocca 2014); and the 'Istituto mobiliare italiano' (IMI), in charge of providing medium- and long-term credit to industry. By 1937 IRI controlled about a quarter of Italy's share capital, including most of the capital-intensive, high-technology segments of manufacturing, and IMI and IRI's banks dominated financial intermediation. IRI's managers were expected to act like private-sector ones and reported directly to the political leadership, which largely respected their autonomy.

The nationalizations were meant to be temporary. But the private sector could initially re-absorb only the smaller or less risky assets, such as Edison, and Fascism anyway eventually judged the *enti pubblici* a superior arrangement for mobilizing the country's resources, allocating them efficiently, managing heavy industry, and preparing the economy for the projected war effort. The mixed-economy model of post-war Italy has its roots in these choices.

The first aggression, the brutal conquest of Ethiopia in 1935–6, brought international sanctions. The regime responded with intensified autarky, a

---

[7] This is hardly surprising from the perspective of Baumol's (1990) thesis, as during Fascism rent-seeking can be presumed to have yielded relatively high returns.

damaging policy for a resource-poor transformation economy. Also for this reason it was a rather weak army that entered World War II, after a prudent wait. War was declared on 10 June 1940, four days before the German army took Paris; attacking from the ridge of the Alps, over the two weeks that elapsed before the armistice was signed, the army scarcely entered French territory. The ineptitude of this dishonourable aggression is vividly narrated by Revelli (2003), then an officer of the alpine troops and later a partisan commander on the same mountains. A string of military defeats followed, until the regime fell.

The Liberal Elites and Fascism: the Regression of Italy's Social Order

Turning Gobetti's interpretation—'the autobiography of the nation'—on its head, the intellectual leader of the liberal elites, the philosopher Benedetto Croce, claimed that Fascism had been a parenthesis in Italy's history, likened to the invasion of the Hyksos.[8] The interpretation of Fascism is a vexed question. Yet it seems well established that Mussolini's *rise* to power was the elites' response to the forces that animated the revolutionary pressures of 1919–20 and won a considerable increase of labour's share in national income. Far from being a parenthesis or aberration, Fascism was the dominant coalition's response to a grave threat to the extant social order.

Italy's weak economic and political institutions made it difficult for the elites and their (maximalist) challengers to agree a credible and sustainable settlement, in fact, for each could have reneged on their commitments once the crisis had passed (see, e.g., Acemoglu et al. 2015). The 1848 constitution was flexible, *octroyée*, and therefore reversible (Cassese 2014, 329), in particular, making any political or economic concession equally reversible once the balance of power would change. In this context, in 1921–2 the components of the dominant coalition that preferred a reactionary response—the Crown, the army, the bureaucracy, landowners, especially in the Centre-North, and northern industry and finance—prevailed over those, like Giolitti, who had sought to open the state to the lower classes. Yet once that strategy was chosen also Croce, the Giolittian liberals, and the Catholic party went along with it, at least until Fascism hardened into an autocracy. Facing a grave risk, therefore, the dominant coalition remained united and co-opted the Fascists, and when it split, in 1924–5, the reactionary wing prevailed.

---

[8] Obscure warriors from the East, the Hyksos stormed Egypt, ruled it for two centuries, and vanished without trace. Gobetti's more honest interpretation shares some traits with the cultural hypothesis criticized in Chapter 3.

The regime's pre-war policies largely vindicated these choices. The liberal elites may well have lost control over the autocracy as it moved towards war. Influenced by its political strategies, also the regime's earlier monetary and trade policies may have had greater autonomy from the economic elites than at least part of them desired. But Fascism's approach to the conflicts between capital and labour, producers and consumers, incumbent firms and new entrants consistently favoured the economic elites' short-term interests: it severely reduced real wages, cartelized the economy, and shifted most of the costs of autarky onto workers and consumers.

Fascism adopted anticompetitive regulations in the retail, craftsmanship, and professional service sectors too, to the benefit of its popular base. But to blunt the effects of its economic policies on the *petite bourgeoisie* it also allowed clientelism and petty corruption to rise in the public sector (Galante Garrone 1996; Mack Smith 1997). These phenomena thus appear to have been a component of the regime's policy equilibrium, like violence and propaganda, and they suggest the existence, next to the distributional coalitions of the economic elites, of comparable forms of collusion within the middle classes too. Also in this respect, Fascism resembles the bad equilibrium discussed in Chapter 4.

In sum, between unification and World War II Italy evolved from a more open to a more closed limited-access social order—from a constitutional monarchy based on very limited suffrage and still bearing traits of the *ancien régime*, which gradually became more liberal and broad-based, to a *soi-disant* totalitarian dictatorship. The popular base of the state widened significantly and sustainably only during Fascism, but the composition of the dominant coalition changed less than the turn to autocracy suggests, and the logic of its strategy remained constant: repression, whose symbolic peak was the use of artillery in Milan in 1898, or co-option, which during the Giolittian period arguably approached a strategy of democratization (Ciocca 2007). What changed dramatically in 1925, once repression became a permanent strategy, was the means by which the dominant coalition assured the loyalty of the social groups excluded from power, whose consensus it did not have: the forms of mass coercion and persuasion that Fascism employed have no precedents in the liberal epoch.

It is worth noting, finally, that over these eight decades the Italian state failed to either reduce the regional divide—which widened considerably during the regime: in 1939 GDP per capita in the South was about 55 per cent of GDP per capita in the Centre-North, down from 75 per cent in 1915 (Iuzzolino et al. 2013)—or to fully assert its own monopoly on violence, whether in the parts of Sicily where the mafia was rooted or in the areas of Campania and Calabria where the camorra and lesser, less organized criminal groups acted. For all the regime's modernism and nationalism, moreover, after an

91

acceleration during the Giolittian period the spread of literacy, the rise of schooling, and the linguistic unification of the country all slowed down during Fascism (De Mauro 2014). The data of the 1951 census in fact depict an 'educationally underdeveloped country' (p. 20): the average years of schooling were three, or about one, two, and three less than in France, Germany, and Britain, respectively (p. 24); only 30.6 per cent of the population had completed primary education, only 10.2 per cent had pursued its studies beyond that level, and 12.9 per cent qualified themselves as entirely illiterate (table 2).

6

The Formation of the Republican Institutions

The Resistance and the Birth of the Republic – A Sketch of the Post-War Period: the Contest over Italy's Social Order – The Emergence of the Post-War Political Cleavages and Alignments (1944–1947) – A Constitutional Compromise Written Behind a Rawlsian Veil of Ignorance – The Consolidation of Italy's Democracy and its Ideological Fractures (1948–1953) – Continuity and the Subversion of the New Political Institutions – Collective Action in the Agrarian South – Reconstruction and the Economic Institutions – The Nature of Italy's Democracy and the Character of its Institutions in the 1950s

The Resistance and the Birth of the Republic

A few days after the Allies landed in Sicily and bombed Rome for the first time, between 24 and 25 July 1943 a palace coup led by the Crown and the higher ranks of the army ousted Mussolini. A period of duplicity and uncertainty followed. The new military regime proclaimed its loyalty to the alliance with Berlin and fired upon demonstrations that demanded peace, besides bread and basic freedoms, but it opened secret negotiations with the enemy. Unopposed, the German army was meanwhile taking commanding positions across the peninsula. When the Allies prevailed over their procrastination and announced the armistice, on 8 September, in a famous act of cowardice the King and his generals fled Rome for the South, leaving no orders for the army. The state fell into German hands with hardly a shot fired. Carrying weapons that the territorial command had declined to use, and left in deserted barracks, on the evening of 11 September twelve men were climbing a ridge south-west of Cuneo, where they set up the first headquarters of what was to become an effective partisan unit, *Italia libera* (Revelli 2003).

In the following two years Italy was the theatre of three interwoven wars (Pavone [1994] 2013): a liberation war, conducted by the Allies and the few formations of their belated co-belligerent, the so-called Kingdom of the South, and, north of the frontline, by the largest resistance movement in Western Europe (100,000 fighters, before their ranks swelled in the spring of 1945, more than one third of whom died: Ginsborg 1990, 70); a civil war, between the latter and the Fascist puppet state set up in the German-occupied territories; and a class war, hoped for and partly prepared by Marxist partisans but never really waged. These wars ended on 25 April 1945, when the resistance liberated the cities of the North several days before the Allied army reached them.

Italy suffered considerably less war damage than either Germany or Japan (Boltho 2013). Yet in 1945 GDP was half the pre-war peak, in 1939 (Toniolo 2013b, 20), and hunger returned, 'on a large scale' (Vecchi 2017, 4). The resistance, a unique example of collective action in the nation's history (Chabod [1950] 1961), had raised its morale and prepared it for reconstruction. But it had involved only part of the peninsula and only a minority of its population. Already in May 1945 the poet Eugenio Montale saw 'the danger...that Italians will not be able to draw the lesson from the catastrophe that has befallen them'.[1]

Between 1946 and 1947 Italy became a republic and gave itself a democratic constitution, which also promised to its citizens equal economic opportunities. But underneath these new institutions lay a less open and inclusive social order, which soon dampened, distorted, or subverted them. A gap thus opened between Italy's formal institutions and its actual ones (those, as we said, that actually shape people's incentives in respect of their political and economic choices). This chapter and the next ones follow the evolution of this chasm, which was the cause of lasting inefficiencies. But the first question is why the gap could open at all, for the events of 1943–5 had upset the extant social order and forces that in the main aimed at opening it up had prevailed decisively.

A Sketch of the Post-War Period: the Contest over Italy's Social Order

According to Acemoglu and Robinson (2012) deep and sustainable institutional reform is possible when an exogenous shock, such as defeat in war,

---

[1] Quoted by Crainz (2016, 6).

allows a broad-based pluralist coalition to replace the former elites. The theory of transition advanced by North et al. (2009) is not too dissimilar, as we remarked. The trauma of war was undoubtedly severe, and the anti-fascist coalition broad-based and pluralist. But the divisions that traversed it, and especially that separating Marxists from other forces, deepened soon after the joint effort of the resistance ended, under the shadow of the impending Cold War, and opened a fracture that broke the coalition irremediably.

In the same vein, Olson (1982) argued that the shock of defeat eclipsed the pre-war distributional coalitions in Germany and Japan. Later research suggests that the effect may have been weaker and less long-lasting than Olson maintained, but confirms that it did open 'a window of opportunity for radical changes in institutional set-ups' (Boltho 2013, 110). Comparable research on Italy is lacking, as we said, but the historical evidence indicates that while that window was open the country's pre-war elites commanded greater political influence than their peers in Germany and Japan. The most obvious reason is that, unlike them, Italy brought down the regime that had attacked the Allies, switched sides, and fought against the German army from the liberated South and in the occupied North, leading the victors to treat it less harshly. The constitution was not imposed by them, in particular, and Italy was allowed to judge its own war criminals. This may well have been 'a curse in disguise . . . a missed opportunity for a more radical institutional change', as Toniolo (2013b, 35) writes. But other reasons were eminently endogenous. One is highlighted by Hobsbawm (1994, 128), who contrasts Fascism—'openly a regime in the interests of the old ruling class'—with Nazism, which by subjugating and eventually crushing Germany's landowning and military elites indirectly facilitated the rise of the post-war *bourgeois* democracy. Unharmed by Fascism, inversely, Italy's pre-war elites retained enough power to bring the regime down before the country's collapse, and could thus manage that critical phase and give themselves both the time to regroup and the chance to find new alliances (see Ginsborg 1990). The divisions that split the anti-fascist coalition then widened the space in which conservative interests could assert themselves.

Herein one might find an explanation for the strategy of the King's military regime between July and September 1943, incidentally. Their choices made the peninsula a battleground for two years, during which Italy suffered about half of the casualties and two thirds of the material damage sustained during the war (Ciocca 2007, 226). Some of these losses might have been avoided had the government switched sides rapidly enough to stem the German occupation of the country and then defend it on the Alpine border: to do so, however, the King's regime needed the anti-fascists' assistance, to purge the army of Fascists and mobilize the masses' support, and would therefore have increased their influence over the post-war settlement. Salvadori (2013, 101–2) plausibly argues that it is for this reason that the pre-war elites eschewed this strategy. Their choice was largely vindicated, at any rate, for the only component of the old dominant coalition that could not save itself was the Crown.

The post-war political and economic institutions were the result of the confrontations and negotiations among three main fronts, therefore: Marxists; the other anti-fascist forces; and the pre-war elites. The cleavage separating the former from the other two proved deeper than that traced by anti-fascism, for both ideological incompatibility and the domestic political repercussions of the Cold War. It influenced less the contest over the design of the new institutions than the parallel ones over the openness of Italy's social order and the political support of the masses.

The features of what became the hinge of the 1948–92 political system, the Christian Democrat Party (Democrazia cristiana, DC), are a good metaphor for the outcome of these contests. Founded in 1942 by liberal-period politicians and anti-fascist Catholic democrats, several of whom fought in the resistance, by 1948 it had become a catch-all, inter-class mass party, which hosted much of the pre-war economic elites and the formerly fascist middle classes next to the Catholic masses, and benefited from the open support of the Vatican and Washington (Agosti 2015; Baldini 2015; Pombeni 2015). For example, the industrialist who had battled with Mussolini on financial transparency, Volpi, supported the DC (Ginsborg 1990, 55). In other words, although the anti-fascist coalition had succeeded in approving a progressive constitution, under the pressure of the power that conservative interests had managed to preserve Italy's social order was opened up far less than its formal institutions were, and the governance system that the republic inherited from the regime—which rested also on the particularistic use of public power and widespread corruption—was not decisively uprooted. This is the origin of the gap mentioned earlier, which has alternatingly narrowed and widened during the following decades and persists to this day.

The social order that emerged was one in transition between the two equilibria—limited access and open access—described by North et al. (2009). These authors posit a neat distinction between the two categories. Italy's transition, which has not been linear and equally continues to this day, confirms their argument that progress towards the open-access social order is always reversible, but it suggests that the two equilibria are separated by a continuum instead, in which societies exhibit features of both, variously combined. We leave these questions for later, however, to look more closely at the contests over the post-war social order, which, shaken by the events of 1943–5, was still malleable.

Although we do not delve into whether different outcomes would have been possible, as we said, two observations may nonetheless be useful. First, the next sections show that it was mainly the DC's choices that contributed to the institutional inefficiencies we focus upon. While reviewing them, however, it should nevertheless be borne in mind that those choices also eased the inclusion of the fascist middle classes into democratic politics, allowed the country to be pacified rapidly, facilitated its equally fast reconstruction, anchored it to the Western world, and either assisted or at least did not hinder Italy's remarkably rapid development in the following two decades. Some of these choices also relied on the PCI's support, moreover. Their most intransigent opponents were the PSI, rather, and above all the radical democrats—liberal-socialists, republicans, liberal-democrats—assembled in the Partito d'azione (PDA), to which most of the founders of *Italia libera* belonged (De Luna 2006). Second, those choices were certainly supported by the Allies, whose troops were stationed in Italy until late 1947, and especially by Washington. But their influence is sometimes exaggerated in Italian historiography (Pavone 1995). The primary interests of the USA concerned the international orientation, stability, and prosperity of the country, rather than the weight of conservative interests in the post-war allocation of power: this question was mostly determined by the alignments and relative power of the forces at play, and by choices ascribable to Italy's new political leadership (e.g., Ginsborg 1990; see also Chabod [1950] 1961).

The Emergence of the Post-War Political Cleavages and Alignments (1944–1947)

The resistance, the Kingdom of the South, and the Allies cooperated closely until the end of the fighting, but their post-war aims diverged (Ginsborg 1990; Crainz 2016). One cleavage separated the forces that favoured a return to the liberal state from those who aspired to more radical discontinuity. *Heri dicebamus*, 'just yesterday we were saying': both Croce and Einaudi used these words to suggest that, the 'parenthesis' of Fascism closed, the life of the liberal state could resume. Aligned on this position were the court and the army; the economic elites, which dominated the re-founded Liberal Party (Partito liberale italiano, PLI) but were increasingly represented also within the DC; the Vatican and the Church; and London, in whose sphere of influence Italy had been placed at Yalta. The opposite front included other voices among the Allies, especially in Washington, Communists, Socialists, the *azionisti* of the PDA, part of the DC, and a few progressive Liberals.

What came to be known as the 'wind of the North' blew mainly from Marxists and *azionisti*, therefore, who had shouldered the main burden of the resistance and had most of their support among the working classes and urban intellectuals of the Centre-North, where the partisans had fought and Fascist repression had been most violent in the 1920s. But even though they shared the immediate objective of democratization, their ultimate ends differed. While the *azionisti* and progressive Christian Democrats and Liberals wanted Italy to mature into an open, competitive, and possibly federal democracy founded on a market or mixed economy, the two Marxist parties aimed at the establishment of socialism. Realism, Moscow's prudent post-war international policy, and the choice of achieving that goal through democratic means, soon pushed it into a distant long term, where it eventually vanished; but the ideological fracture it opened was nevertheless deep.

Unburdened by quarrels of this nature, the conservative camp could count on the 'enormous force' of the bureaucracy (Chabod [1950] 1961, 141), which rapidly shifted its allegiance to the Crown's government once Rome was liberated, in June 1944, as well as on the silent support of the middle classes that had formed the popular base of Fascism, naturally averse to the radicalism of the resistance. In an implicit exchange for their support, the Kingdom of the South neither purged the civil service of Fascists, as the Allies had demanded (Pavone 1995, ch. 2), nor seriously attempted to enforce the mobilization orders it issued to raise the units that would join the Allies in liberating the country (Peli 2004, 228–32). Somewhat paradoxically, moreover, conservatives also benefited from the prestige and popular gratitude acquired by the papacy during 1943–4, when Pius XII stood as the *defensor urbis* in a city deserted by the secular power (Chabod [1950] 1961, 124). During the last dozen months of the hostilities, while the partisans' war was at its harshest, conservative interests could therefore lay down firm foundations for institutional and political continuity. Distant and concerned above all about the unity of the war effort, the anti-fascist coalition failed to stem this 'wind of the South'. In February 1945 the *azionista* Guido de Ruggiero observed that below the frontline Italy 'seemed less a rising democracy than a decaying dictatorship'.[2]

Nonetheless, after the war ended the anti-fascist coalition imposed a fresh government, which was headed by the military leader of the resistance, the *azionista* Ferruccio Parri. With no change in the governing coalition, however, six months later he was replaced by the leader of the Christian Democrats, Alcide De Gasperi. Parri's cabinet was felled by the party that more directly represented the pre-war elites, the PLI, with the support of a DC already hospitable to conservative interests (Ginsborg 1990). The demeanour of Parri and his ministerial clerks during the press conference in which he announced his resignation is splendidly described by the *azionista* Levi ([1950] 1951) as a metaphor of the incompatibility, moral and administrative, between the wind of the North and the forces of continuity. The novelist's assessment is

---

[2] Quoted by Crainz (2016, 6).

confirmed by the historiographical literature, which however also underlines Parri's own political inadequacy, the divisions among the *azionisti*, and the Communists' and Socialists' reluctance to oppose the rise to power of the party that seemed set to acquire the support of the Catholic masses (Ginsborg 1990; Crainz 2016). In the perspective we have taken, moreover, that incompatibility is but a reflection of the underlying contest over the character of Italy's future social order, which was far less clear-cut than the dramatic contrast between the vanquished just and the stolid bureaucrats suggests, for the same cleavage also traversed the DC, separating progressives from conservatives, and it did not prevent the adoption of an enlightened constitution in 1947.

On 2 June 1946 Italy held the first vote also open to women.[3] The nation chose to become a republic and elected a 556-member assembly to write the new constitution. The referendum unveiled another facet of the regional divide, as the South voted for the monarchy with majorities as wide as those with which the North opted for the republic. The election—held with a simple proportional representation system, which will be retained until 1993— revealed both the dominance of the anti-fascist coalition and a balanced distribution of the vote along the fault line that already divided it, as the DC won a slightly smaller share (35.2 per cent) than the Socialists (20.6) and Communists (18.9) combined, but the Republicans (Partito repubblicano italiano, PRI) obtained a share (4.3) equal to the margin. The rest of the vote went mostly to alliances representing the pre-war liberals or to a movement, ephemeral, which attracted the (mostly southern) middle classes that still rejected the DC's anti-fascism.

The PDA failed the challenge of mass-party politics. The *azionisti* had given a decisive military and political contribution to the resistance, second only to that of the Communists, but their party was divided and lacked grassroots capacity (Chabod [1950] 1961, himself partisan and *azionista*). It won 1.4 per cent of the vote and soon dissolved. Its valuable legacy was not lost, however, because during the next three decades the *azionisti* who remained politically active, mostly in the PSI and the PRI, will exercise considerable influence over the nation's political culture (Novelli 2000; De Luna 2006).

In May 1947 the DC excluded the Marxists from the government—which until the 1948 parliamentary elections also exercised the legislative function— and formed a fresh one, supported only by Liberals, Republicans, and the Social Democrats who had just left the PSI (Partito socialista democratico italiano, PSDI). A little earlier US President Truman had delivered the speech that conventionally marks the beginning of the Cold War, and the exclusion of the

---

[3] They had voted also in municipal elections held shortly before, which gave a first indication of the relative force of the main contenders (see Chabod, ch. II.1).

Marxists was desired by Washington and accepted by Moscow (Ginsborg 1990). The new cabinet also included technocrats like Einaudi, who joined the functions of central bank governor, budget minister, and deputy prime minister, and will achieve a rapid and crucial macroeconomic stabilization, as we shall see. As he prepared this operation, De Gasperi explained that it was no longer possible to govern Italy without the support 'of the natural organs of economic life, i.e. the financial institutions and the categories of the industrialists, employers, and workers'.[4] Omitted from the list of the DC's present and future allies among the pre-war economic elites are only the landowners and notables of the South.

The break-up of the coalition that had led the resistance portended the acute polarization of the following decades, whose domestic and international sources reinforced each other. But it did not hinder the cooperation of the anti-fascist parties in the economic and political reconstruction of the country. This was also true of the DC and the PCI, which shared the assessment that stability and national cohesion were necessary preconditions for it, and retained enough autonomy from Washington and Moscow to pursue a national policy (Agosti 2015; Pombeni 2015).

A Constitutional Compromise Written Behind a Rawlsian Veil of Ignorance

The writing of the constitution took one and a half years. Its text was approved by a very wide majority, 453 against 62, in late 1947. The first article defines Italy as a 'democratic Republic founded on labour', in which sovereignty 'belongs to the people' but must be exercised 'in the forms and within the limits' set by the constitution. The second article 'recognizes and guarantees the inviolable rights of man', which were thus placed before and above the republic, but demands of citizens the performance of the 'mandatory duties of political, economic and social solidarity'. Having laid down the classical principle of equality before the law, the third article (emphasis added) imposes upon the republic also the duty to

> remove those obstacles of an economic and social nature which, by limiting the actual freedom and equality of *citizens*, hinder the full development of the *human person* and the effective participation of all *workers* in the political, economic, and social organization of the country.

This passage well reflects the elevated compromise that was forged among the three main political cultures—liberal-republican ('citizens'), Christian (the

---

[4] Quoted by Agosti (2015, 348).

'human person'), and socialist ('workers')—represented in the assembly, despite the rising polarization of domestic politics and international relations and the poisons of the 'decaying dictatorship'.

The compromise was arrived at behind a Rawlsian 'veil of ignorance', for neither the Marxists nor the DC could safely count on winning power at the imminent parliamentary elections (Ginsborg 1990; Crainz 2016).[5] It is also for this reason, and not just because of the fresh memory of the rise of an autocratic regime from within the liberal order, that a relatively strong system of checks and balances and a comprehensive set of civil liberties were agreed. This compromise was written into a 'rigid' constitution, moreover, which prevails over incompatible laws, prior or subsequent, and whose amendments require special majorities and a special procedure, which may include a referendum. And the constitution was placed under the protection of a constitutional court, whose independence was not just proclaimed but carefully constructed.

The parliamentary form of government was chosen but power was studiously divided (see, generally, Jones and Pasquino 2015). The legislative function was assigned to two chambers, equal in their prerogatives but slightly different as to their electoral base, and popular referenda were allowed, albeit only to repeal laws. The government, headed by a *primus inter pares* in the council of ministers, was placed firmly below the parliament. The presidency of the republic was shaped as a neutral authority, but was given powers— nominating the prime minister and dissolving parliament—that can be decisive absent a cohesive parliamentary majority. Power was allocated across four layers of government, national, regional, provincial, and municipal. And the judiciary was granted a high degree of autonomy and independence, both external (from the other powers) and internal (to safeguard the independent judgement of junior magistrates and lower courts from the influence of higher ones). Crucially, these guarantees were extended also to the public prosecution, which was fashioned as a decentralized and largely non-hierarchical authority, harder to influence, and was assigned the duty—not the discretion, as is common where prosecutors depend on the justice ministry—to pursue all crimes it uncovered or learned about (Guarnieri 2015). Yet for two or three decades its formal independence was but a veil over the judiciary's subservience to the executive power and conservative interests,

---

[5] According to the political philosopher John Rawls, for institutions to be just they must be agreed by agents negotiating behind a veil of ignorance that prevents them from knowing what their position in respect of the choice to be made will be. Rawls's theory of justice is broader and has been criticized (e.g., Sen 2009), but that insight rests on firm foundations: if a polity's checks-and-balances system is agreed among parties that do not know whether they will be in government or in opposition, their agreement is likelier to be 'just'—or efficient, in the perspective that interests us most—than if they had known.

as we shall see, which served chiefly to shield them from accountability (Bruti Liberati 1997; Neppi Modona 1997; Guarnieri 2015).

The constitution left Italy's economic institutions undefined. It upholds private property and safeguards the freedom of enterprise, but allows legislation to direct it to 'social ends' (article 41). Consistent with this approach, which views social welfare as a limit rather than as a purpose of economic liberty (Barca 1997, 41), the constitution neglected both markets and competition, which are never mentioned.

The constitution set Italy firmly on the path of international cooperation and regional integration, political and economic. Article 11 'repudiates' war as a means for settling international controversies, enjoins the republic to promote peace and justice in international relations, and authorizes the 'limitations of sovereignty' that these objectives may require. It is also on this basis that the North Atlantic Treaty Organization (NATO) and especially the European Communities—Italy was a founding member of both—could serve as external anchors of stability and responsible government (Del Pero 2015; Della Sala 2015), albeit sometimes in tension with the democratic principle. In particular, NATO was one channel of the *political* limitation of sovereignty induced by the Cold War, and in Italy its clandestine 'stay behind' organization, named Gladio, 'glaive', which was set up to prepare the resistance after a possible Soviet invasion, appears to have also been given the task of obstructing the rise of the PCI, since at least the early 1950s (e.g., Ferraresi 1996).

On the vexed question of the relationships between the secular and the religious sphere, finally, against the opposition of Socialists and *azionisti* the PCI—which was concerned about national cohesion, as we said, but also feared antagonizing the Catholic masses ahead of the imminent parliamentary election (Ginsborg 1990)—acceded to the DC's request to elevate the 1929 pact between Italy and the Vatican to constitutional status. In it Fascism had agreed to 'concessions that no liberal government would ever have made' (Chabod [1950] 1961, 65): constitutionalizing them gravely dented the secularity of the state, and strengthened the basis for the Church's influence in the schools and over society at large (Cassese 2014, ch. 14; Melloni 2015; Teodori 2015).

The Consolidation of Italy's Democracy and its Ideological Fractures (1948–1953)

Political polarization reached its spectacular height in the campaign for the 18 April 1948 election (Pombeni 2015). The DC faced a 'Popular Front' uniting Communists and Socialists. Both sides employed religion or ideology as the main vehicle for political communication, obscuring policy issues. Both relied on mass membership bases (in a 45 million population, the PCI had 2.25 million members and the DC 1.2 million: Crainz 2016, 24). Both were aided by their foreign mentors and by organizations such as the trade unions and Confindustria. The Vatican, which initially had looked sceptically upon the DC on account of its progressive traits, lent to it both the Pontiff's voice and the campaigning capacity of the Church's pervasive network of parishes and of the 2 million members of a nationwide affiliated organization (Baldini 2015; Melloni 2015). The vote was portrayed as a choice between freedom and serfdom, equality and feudalism, stability and chaos, barbarism and civilization.

The margin of the DC's victory was wide: 48.5 per cent against the Popular Front's 31 per cent. A comparison with the results of the 1946 election shows that the Marxists lost hardly any support, besides the split of the Social Democrats: the result was determined by a slightly higher turnout (92.1 per cent, 3 points more than in 1946), and above all by the Christian Democrats' capacity to attract much of the electorate that previously had voted for the Liberals, Republicans, and other parties. In this, the Church's campaigning power and its call for the nation to unite under the aegis[6] of the main bulwark against communism carried 'enormous importance' (Chabod [1950] 1961, 166). After decades of distance and hostility to the Italian state the Vatican became a decisive political actor.

Although his party had gained an absolute majority of seats[7] in both chambers, De Gasperi joined Liberals (3.8 per cent), Republicans (2.5 per cent), and Social Democrats (7.1 per cent) into a centrist coalition. This choice cemented an enduring, if conflictual alliance between the Christian Democrats and these smaller parties, and relegated the extreme right—monarchists (2.8 per cent) and neo-fascists (2 per cent)—beyond a republican and anti-fascist *cordon sanitaire* (Ignazi 2015). During the legislature that lasted from 1948 to 1953, De Gasperi led his composite party and this coalition by arbitrating ably between their progressive and conservative components (Agosti 2015; Pombeni 2015).

Despite its polarization, in the following years Italy's democracy consolidated (Ginsborg 1990; Pombeni 2015; Crainz 2016). In particular, shortly after the election the PCI resolutely quelled a wave of spontaneous armed revolts sparked by a failed attempt on the life of its leader, confirming a loyalty to the parliamentary republic that would never waver (Bellucci 2015); and in the following years De Gasperi equally resolutely resisted insistent conservative, clerical, and US pressure to outlaw the Communists, whom Pius XII excommunicated in

---

[6] The DC's symbol was a white shield bearing a red cross, the *scudo crociato*, resembling that of the Crusaders.
[7] We refer to elected seats. The Senate then still retained about 100 members appointed by the Crown in the preceding decades.

1949 (Melloni 2015). Ahead of the 1953 election the centrist coalition did impose a change in the electoral law, dubbed the 'swindle law' (Ginsborg 1990, 142), which aimed at granting to itself an artificially high parliamentary majority: but the threshold (the absolute majority of the votes cast) for winning the majority bonus (15 per cent of seats) was missed by very few votes, no serious electoral fraud was observed, all sides accepted the results, and the law was soon repealed (Regalia 2015). Equally importantly, the DC, the PCI, and, in lesser measure, the PSI, schooled millions of party members in the practice of democracy, and opened politics and the state to the vast segments of society that had hitherto been left at the margins of public life, such as women and the working classes (e.g., Ginsborg 1990). This work was often tinged by paternalism, due also to the low education of the masses (De Mauro 2014), and it reinforced political polarization, because it forged two deeply rooted subcultures and loyal electorates—Christian Democrat and Communist—that remained strong and stable well into the 1970s, but it cast the roots of democracy deep into Italian society.

The 1948 election gave rise to another 'blocked' political system (Salvadori 2013), however, which saw no rotation in government until the rupture of 1992–4 and effectively mirrored in domestic politics the frontline of the Cold War. With it arose also Italy's 'imperfect two-party system', or 'polarized pluralism', characterized by persistent moderate fragmentation around two dominant poles (Hopkin 2015; Mershon 2015).

In short, until 1992 the country was always ruled by DC-dominated governments and, but for a few years in the 1980s, DC prime ministers; in the 1960s the PSI joined the PSDI, PRI, and PLI[8] as a relatively stable ally of the Christian Democrats; the PCI was never in government, though it supported two DC-only cabinets in 1976–9, at a difficult juncture for the republic. Until the early 1970s its loyalty to Moscow and opposition to capitalism cast the PCI as an anti-systemic party, from both a domestic and an international perspective: but even after those two stances were effectively abandoned and the party fully became a catch-all one, it nevertheless remained relegated to permanent opposition (Bellucci 2015; Hellman 2015). The DC's share of the vote in national parliamentary elections gradually declined to 34.3 per cent (in 1987), the PCI's reached its peak at 34.4 per cent (in 1976, 4.3 points below the DC), and their combined share was always greater than 60 per cent until the 1990s (Mershon 2015, fig. 12.1). The numerical strength, strong sub-cultures, stable electorates, and political incompatibility of Italy's two competing political 'churches' left little space to either a social-democratic alternative or a liberal-democratic one (Conti 2015; Orsina 2015). This blocked political system

---

[8] Until the 1980s Liberals and Socialists were never in government together, however.

and its imperfectly polarized party system guaranteed stability, despite the frequent changes of government, but stunted the maturation of Italy's democracy.

The Marxists' ideology and international orientation thus set the defining fault line of Italy's Cold War political system, and distanced them also from those—liberal-democrats, republicans, liberal-socialists, social democrats, progressive Catholics—with whom concrete policy incompatibility was far lower than with conservative interests in either the DC or to its right. With comparable effects, similar fractures also separated reformist Marxists from maximalist or orthodox ones: the division was clearer among socialists first, then distanced them from the PCI, when the PSI joined the governing coalition, and eventually also came to light among the communists. These ideological cleavages were often mainly rhetorical, for maximalists also viewed socialism as a long-term goal and were anyway loyal to the parliamentary democracy, but were persistent all the same. Although they stimulated public debate, they arguably dissipated precious moral and intellectual energies, strengthened the conservative camp, and hindered the erection of efficient and inclusive institutions, both political and economic. They partly eclipsed what Mukand and Rodrik (2016) call worldview politics, which focuses on the efficacy of policy, and veiled the contest about the openness of Italy's republican social order: they hampered, more precisely, the pursuit of a fairer and more efficient politico-economic equilibrium than that inherited from Fascism, one based on intenser competition, lesser collusion between public powers and private interests, more universalistic public services, greater public integrity, and, with the advent of electoral democracy, also effective political accountability.

Damaging though they may have been, however, the ideological divisions of post-war Italy cannot be bemoaned. They stemmed from the history we have summarized—as Mack Smith (1997, 435) notes, in particular, 'one legacy of fascism was a polarization of society and the creation of a strong communist party'—and were reinforced by the war-like polarization of international relations. Yet they also involve a problem of interests and ideas, because through open, reasoned public debate the obstacle that those cleavages posed to the emergence of a reformist compromise could have been relaxed. Conservatives thus had an interest in maintaining ideological polarization at a high level. We return to these questions at the end of the chapter.

Continuity and the Subversion of the New Political Institutions

If electoral democracy took root rapidly, for a long time the constitution stood like a solitary flower in an expanse of continuity. In part, continuity was inertial. In part, the constitutional design to divide power was undermined by the effect of political polarization over the parliamentary model, for the strong nexus linking the electoral majority, the parliamentary majority, and the government overwhelmed the formal reciprocal independence of the legislative and the executive (Cassese 2014, 332–4), and likewise undermined the distinction between the public authorities and the dominant Christian Democrat party. But the subversion of the civil liberties and the checks and balances written into the constitution was also deliberate.

Conservative interests were laying down foundations for administrative and institutional continuity already in 1944, as we noted. But then they faced a cohesive anti-fascist coalition. Four years later the DC and much of those interests faced the Marxist front, conversely, in what both viewed as a decisive struggle over the social order and international orientation of the country. Having won power, they began to undermine the Rawlsian compromise of the constitution, aiming to weaken the constraints over the executive, keep power concentrated, and contrast an anti-systemic opposition (see Ginsborg 1990 and Pombeni 2015).

First, the DC and its allies prevented the adoption of legislation necessary to implement critical parts of the constitution. Most notably, they delayed the establishment of the regional layer of government until 1970, for Marxist victories were expected in the 'red' regions of Central Italy, where several Communist-led municipal administrations indeed arose; for two decades they equally blocked legislation regulating popular referenda; and they allowed the constitutional court to be set up only in 1956. During the formative years of the republic this crucial function was therefore left to the (unreformed) supreme court, which interpreted the most innovative parts of the constitution as unenforceable statements of intentions and routinely upheld Fascist or earlier legislation that ought to have been declared unconstitutional instead (Neppi Modona 1997).

Second, the centrist coalition chose not to adjust the instrument of the state, the public administration, to its new founding principles (Cassese 2014). Fascism inherited a French-like centralized and strictly hierarchical administration, which was liberal far less in its approach to the citizen than in the minimalist conception of the state that informed it. The regime added functions to it, made it more subservient, clientelistic, and corrupt, and increased its staff: but it lacked confidence in it, and for strategic tasks it relied on *enti pubblici* like IRI and IMI instead. Both this mistrust for the 'ordinary' public administration and the preference for bypassing rather than reforming it characterized the post-war period too (Piattoni 2015).

Linked to this approach was the choice not to purge the public sector and the economy from Fascists, as laws adopted in 1944–5 required. The purge was poorly implemented from the outset, as we already said, due to the opposition of the pre-war elites and the Catholic right (Acanfora 2015). It effectively ceased when De Gasperi became prime minister, in December 1945. On the contrary, his government removed all partisan leaders whom the resistance had appointed as prefects, with the Allies' consent, and after 1948 the DC-led interior ministry completed the de facto reverse purge by also dismissing many of the partisans who had entered the police (Pavone 1995, ch. 2). As a result, for at least two decades the republic was served by an administration predominantly staffed and led by officials who had served Fascism: officials who had not just pledged allegiance to it, as the law then required, but had also been trained in the practices and methods of a police state and had applied them for years. In particular, in 1960 all but two of Italy's prefects (64) and all officials (274) in the highest ranks of the police had served the regime (Ginsborg 1990, 92), and as late as 1968 the same was true for all judges of the supreme court (524) and for 70 per cent of the appeal court ones (Di Michele 2008, 27; Neppi Modona 1997). Even more strikingly, each of the four officials successively appointed by the interior ministry as head of the Rome police during the 1945–60 period had served in the notorious Fascist secret police (Di Michele 2008, 27). Similar figures later appeared in the milieus of Gladio and the secret services, involved, often together with neo-fascist terrorists, in clandestine operations aimed at influencing the nation's political choices (Ferraresi 1996; Cento Bull 2015; Conti 2017).

Already accustomed to subservience, and now spared of the purge that much of society demanded, the bureaucracy, the judiciary, and the security services became naturally docile to their tolerant new political masters (Piattoni 2015). The implicit exchange concerned especially the higher ranks, more comprom-ised with Fascism, but through the tight hierarchical structure of the adminis-tration it percolated to the lower ranks as well.

Having been spared the justice of the victors, moreover, Italy effectively declined to judge the crimes of Fascism (Ginsborg 1990; Pavone 1995, ch. 2). Upon a proposal by the minister of justice, who then was the PCI's leader, in 1946 the government issued a wide amnesty, which also covered torture (unless if inflicted with 'particular cruelty'). The courts, not purged, applied it liberally to Fascists, across the spectrum of their political, war, and ordinary crimes, but rigorously to partisans. Having reviewed a sample of these genuinely unsettling judgements, Pavone (1995, 139) wonders how the nation could have 'tolerated that justice be administered by judges capable of such aberrations'.[9]

The most prominent Fascist criminal, for instance, commander first of the aggression of France and then of the vicious anti-partisan war, was convicted on some counts in 1950. But his sentence was almost entirely condoned, in

---

[9] They understood the 'particular cruelty' criterion as a subjective one, for instance, and measured it on the reaction of the victim and the presumable beliefs of the torturer, leading to two simple alternative syllogisms: if the victim resisted and did not speak, the methods of torture used cannot have been particularly cruel; if the victim spoke torture can hardly have been particularly cruel either, because torturers generally do not use methods that, by their own standards, are crueller than the circumstances require.

1952 he joined the neo-fascist party, and during the campaign for the 1953 election he was publicly hugged by a junior cabinet member, Andreotti, then a rising figure in the DC's right wing and particularly close to the Vatican. To illustrate this pattern of impunity and continuity, Conti (2017) reviews the careers of a dozen (presumed) Fascist war criminals, from both the army and the repression agencies; accused by either the Allies or the nations that Italy had occupied, they were neither extradited nor charged and became prefects, army generals, heads of the secret service, parliamentarians, ministers.

Coherently with these choices, the nation declined to examine its fascist past as rigorously as both the Bonn republic and reunified Germany eventually did, allowing also the false popular perception that Italy was blameless for the Holocaust to persist (e.g., Collotti 2003). The moral and historical value of the resistance indirectly assisted collective oblivion, paradoxically, to the benefit of those who in 1943–5 had either sat on the fence or fought against the partisans.

When their democracy arose, to conclude, Italians were scarred by three decades of war and repression, deeply divided between North and South, relatively uneducated, and quite unaware of their new civil liberties. In February 1945 de Ruggiero wrote that 'the daily experience [during Fascism] of seeing dishonesty not just unpunished but triumphant' had left a 'genuine ethical disorientation' among them, which clemency for the regime's crimes can hardly have repaired.[10] To irradiate its principles across such a society, the constitution needed a cohesive political leadership and a civil service animated by a strong *souffle républicain*. On the contrary, the centrist coalitions' partisan use of both public power and the administration gravely distorted Italy's new political institutions. This was perhaps most evident in the field of public order, which involves delicate trade-offs between different human rights, political freedoms, and civil liberties. Relying on authoritarian legislation left in place by the supreme court, and on equally pliant criminal courts, the DC-led interior ministry followed harsh policies: in the 1948–50 period alone the police killed 62 demonstrating workers, wounded 3,126, and arrested 92,169 (Di Michele 2008, 55).

Collective Action in the Agrarian South

Three of the victims were a man, a young woman, and a boy of a village in Calabria, Melissa, shot in the back by the police as they evicted the peasants who had unlawfully occupied part of a large estate, on the morning of 29 October 1949 (Ginsborg 1990, 124). We turn to the causes of this famous incident to illustrate the challenges that conservative interests nonetheless

---

[10] Quoted by Crainz (2016, 6).

faced during the contests over the post-war social order, as well as the metamorphosis that Italy's elites underwent under the mediation of the DC. The picture of those years was more varied than our summary or de Ruggiero's desolate remarks may have suggested.

In 1944 the Crown's government approved reforms—known as the 'Gullo decrees', by the name of the Communist agriculture minister who proposed them and pushed their implementation—that shook the vertical power relations of the agrarian South (Tarrow 1967; Rossi Doria 1983; Ginsborg 1990, ch. 4; Bevilacqua 2005, 133–8). The main one was an institutional reform, which affected the property rights regime: it legalized the occupation of idle land in large estates, then frequent. The right to occupy land was reserved to cooperatives, however, which led the peasants to organize, assisted by the ministry and the trade unions, and prevented conflicts about the distribution of the occupiable plots from interfering with the strategic objective of changing the allocation of land. This sparked an episode of collective action without precedent in the history of the South, which saw destitute and illiterate families—those for whom Banfield (1958) will coin the expression 'amoral familism'—shedding their immediate self-interest to appropriate land for themselves in favour of the collective pursuit, through the cooperatives, of a common interest that the state's laws had recognized. In other words, this institution overcame the collective action problem—the peasants' low generalized trust and capacity to organize—that underlies their secular oscillation between long periods of quietism and explosions of unrest, and gave rise to a direct attempt to change the social order of the South: for in a predominantly agrarian economy founded on land-intensive crops and salaried labourers, altering the allocation of land, albeit by occupation and not expropriation, means altering the allocation of power. The occupations peaked in 1946–7 and spread support for the left and the trade unions.

The political significance of this episode is attested by the backlash it elicited, a long succession of murders and intimidations of trade unionists and leftist activists, mostly unpunished but, in Sicily, often attributed to the mafia. The wave of violence culminated in the attack on peasant families perpetrated by bandits hired by the mafia on 1 May 1947 in Portella della Ginestra, near Palermo, shortly after the Marxists won the highest share of the vote in the Sicilian local elections (Ginsborg 1990, 62–3 and 111–12; Lupo [1996] 2009, 191–2). The automatic fire lasted fifteen minutes and left eleven dead, four of whom were children, and sixty-five wounded, five of whom died of their wounds.[11] Recent empirical research suggests that at least in Sicily this strategy

---

[11] Forty years later Stajano (1997) proved that also shells or grenades had hit the victims. After an X-ray exam, in 1997 one of them learnt that the object lying next to her heart was not a bullet but a small piece of shrapnel. In 1947 she was nine years old.

proved effective in curbing the rise of the left, which between the 1947 local elections and the national vote of 18 April 1948 lost almost one third of its electoral support (Alesina et al. 2016).

Violence did not quell the peasants' demands, however. The DC's policies did (Ginsborg 1990, ch. 4). The party initially chose to protect the status quo. In 1946, still allied with the Marxist parties, it managed to replace minister Gullo with a DC southern landowner, Antonio Segni, who revised the reform, limiting the legal basis for the occupations, and helped bring the peasants' movement to an end before the 1948 election. But the peasants' agitation soared again the next year, in mostly peaceful but, by then, often illegal forms, and spread to salaried peasants in the North-East. The government's response, in Melissa and elsewhere, provoked scandal across the nation and widened the movement, until in 1950 the DC changed its policy. Its leftist wing pressed for land reform. Already in 1946 De Gasperi had declared himself in favour of it, aiming also to strengthen a critical component of the DC's electorate, the farmers, whose association (Coldiretti) was closely tied to the party. But the opposition of the landowners in the DC and especially the PLI prevented the reform. By early 1950 the DC's leftists were also supported by Washington, however, which was averse to absentee landowners and shared De Gasperi's objective of widening the farming class to stem Marxist advances in the agrarian sector, as well as by Confindustria, which feared that continued clashes between the peasants and the police would upset the social peace. The DC formed a fresh governing coalition without the Liberals, and in the second half of 1950 the reform was adopted.

The expropriated land was insufficient and of low quality, however, and was divided up into small plots (700,000 hectares for 120,000 families: Ginsborg 1990, 130). Rather than on cooperatives, moreover, the reform relied on ad hoc public agencies to provide housing, credit, irrigation, and other services to the recipients of the plots. The peasants thus became small farmers whose livelihood largely depended on the aid of agencies, which the DC soon captured (Ginsborg 1990, 136; Barca 1997, 29). By the end of the 1940s Coldiretti—the main mediation channel between the farmers the public administration and the DC—represented 800,000 families, and twice as many in the mid 1950s (Crainz 2016, 61).

Ginsborg (1990, 139) comments that the reform 'broke for ever those attempts at aggregation and cooperation [which] had been the inspiration behind peasant agitation from 1944 to 1950'. It emarginated the 'values of solidarity, of self-sacrifice and egalitarianism' that sustained the peasant movement, as well as its 'attempts to overcome familism and distrust'. More, it 'determined the values of contemporary southern life': it 'dealt a mortal blow' to the old elites, but supplanted them with local politicians who acted as mediators between the farmers and the subsidy-providing public agencies. In other words, with this reform the DC changed the allocation of power by replacing control over land with control over government aid as its main instrument, and it led peasants to abandon the collective pursuit of their common long-term interest for the pursuit of their narrow individual ones, through the exchange between clientelistic political support and the particularistic distribution of public resources. Although clientelism long pre-dates this episode, as we saw, the character of the patron-client relationship that became typical of the South in republican Italy took shape then. The model was replicated in other regions and sectors, as public expenditure rose, laying down one important foundation for the vicious circle we hypothesized in Chapter 4.

Nonetheless, this was the only major structural reform of the two decades between the end of Fascism and the early 1960s, and the peasants' movement that provoked it was also a major cause for the adoption, for the first time since unification, of systematic policies for the development of the South (discussed in Chapter 7). Moreover, by replacing the old power structure, which still bore traits of the feudal system, with one based on political mediation, the land reform arguably opened up the social order of those regions, for the new form of patronage, based as it was on mutually beneficial exchange (Crainz 2016, 71–2), was at least more contestable than that which preceded it.

More importantly, whatever its limits the land reform was provoked by a remarkable episode of collective action. Most interesting is the earliest phase, before the *institutional* reform of 1944 was revised, during which between 150,000 and 200,000 hectares of land were lawfully occupied by cooperatives representing about as many peasants (Tarrow 1967; Rossi Doria 1983). This poses the question of why that institutional reform succeeded, unlike many subsequent ones, and what its success implies for an interpretation of the South's or Italy's politico-economic problems.

The 1944 reform appears to have overcome the peasants' collective action problem because it responded to a genuine need; it was well-crafted (crucially, it required the formation of cooperatives); the PCI-led agriculture ministry actively supported its implementation; it relied on effective intermediate organizations (the trade unions); and, until 1946, it enjoyed enough political support to both elicit the peasants' trust and withstand the reaction of those whose rents it endangered. After 1946, conversely, when the new institution was revised, the government turned against it, and only the Marxists remained to support it, the peasants' movement first declined, then resurfaced in less orderly and lawful forms, and eventually suffered a political defeat 'of historic proportions' (Ginsborg 1990, 139). Political consensus and the backing of the law thus appear to have been decisive in sustaining the peasants' collective action. This episode therefore suggests that even in a forbidding environment, characterized by a secular tradition of peasant submission and the mafia's power of intimidation, a credible reform programme relying on broad-based consensus and effective organizations can gain the citizens' trust, spread public-spirited reciprocated cooperation, and achieve significant results. The latter proved temporary and partial, of course, but proof of their significance, it bears repeating, is that large-scale violence was also used to reverse them. On the causes of the comparatively low civicness of the South, therefore, this episode supports much less the interpretation offered by Putnam (1993) and Guiso and Pinotti (2015)—neither of whom mention the peasants' movement—than that advanced in Chapters 3 and 4, or indeed Lampedusa's ([1958] 2007, 113). Not their own culture but the balance of power obstructed the peasants' attempt to change the agrarian South.

Yet, until the social movements of the late 1960s no comparable episode of collective action was observed. Three reasons can contribute to explaining why. First, this episode was based on an institutional reform, a law, and between May 1947 and the early 1960s similar projects lacked a parliamentary majority to support them. Collective action could have also relied on existing institutions, of course, such as the constitutional principles that the centrist coalitions deliberately subverted, or could have pressed the latter to enact reforms. So a second reason may lie in the PCI's moderate, parliamentarist strategy during that decade, which aimed at reaching agreements with the DC on individual reforms, on one hand, and, on the other, at increasing the party's membership base and electoral support (Agosti 2015; Bellucci 2015). As a result, Ginsborg (1990, 83) writes, 'the most powerful weapon in the hands of the left, working-class militancy, was virtually discarded in the major political battles of the time'. The PCI exercised considerable influence over the trade unions, moreover, then assembled into a unitary nation-wide confederation, the CGIL (Regini 2015): having the Communists eschewed the route of mass militancy, other potential challengers of conservative interests lacked a comparable capacity to mobilize citizens.

The land reform well displays the DC's role, finally. In the blocked political system that we have described, which lasted until the rupture of 1992–4, functions that properly belonged to either parliament or government were insensibly transferred to the composite party that permanently dominated both, which came to serve as the locus where the competing pressures over the main policy choices were composed into compromises. As we saw, in fact, the land reform was the result of a half decade-long process of mediation and negotiation among the DC's own different souls (progressive, centrist, and conservative), as well as among the different interests the party was tied to (landowners, farmers, Washington, and Confindustria, in this case), which was conducted under the constraints posed by the consolidation of electoral democracy, by the presence of a large opposition, and, in this instance, also by the decreasing social tolerance for harsh repression policies. The republican economic institutions, to which we now turn, emerged from a similar process, arbitrated by and largely played out within the DC. The complexity of this form of policy-making increased further when, in the late 1950s, organized factions arose in the party.

Reconstruction and the Economic Institutions

Reconstruction was fast, faster than in either Germany or Japan (Boltho 2013). If in 1945 GDP was half the level of the pre-war peak, in 1939, by 1949 it exceeded it by 10 per cent (Toniolo 2013b, 20). Productivity and especially TFP growth accelerated rapidly after 1945, having fallen across all sectors during the conflict (Broadberry et al. 2013).

Underpinned by wide political consensus, reconstruction was largely left to market forces and completed by an early macroeconomic stabilization (Barca 1997; Ciocca 2007; Crafts and Magnani 2013), earlier than in either Germany or Japan (Boltho 2013). In 1945–6, while the Marxist parties were still in government, entrepreneurs reacquired control of their factories—which the resistance had protected from the retreating German army and entrusted to committees it appointed—and a wave of redundancies eased the transition from the war economy. In 1946 Italy was admitted into the Bretton Woods system, and under Einaudi's leadership in 1947 monetary policy was decisively tightened—after high inflation had reduced the (domestically held) public debt from 108 per cent of GDP in 1943 to 40 per cent in 1946 (Ciocca 2007, 235)—and the country's foreign exchange reserves reconstructed. The Marshall Plan contributed less for its size—lower than 2 per cent of GDP in 1948–52, or 0.5 points below the average in the recipient countries—than 'for easing the "dollar gap" for import of raw materials and US technology, and for lessening the distributional costs of monetary stabilization' (Toniolo 2013b, 20). It of course also contributed to anchoring Italy to the Western bloc.

The economic institutions, left undefined by the constitution, were shaped by choices taken during these years (e.g., Barca 1997). Like reconstruction itself, these choices did not follow an explicit plan but were the result of discrete compromises mediated by the DC. They gave rise to an equilibrium, which underpinned a long decade of very rapid and stable growth and the country's full industrialization. We now consider the compromises that forged this equilibrium, leaving for Chapter 7 the question of why the institutions that descended from it were appropriate to the needs of the country's development.

Besides early macroeconomic stabilization and participation in the Bretton Woods system, the main features of that equilibrium were the choices to progressively open the economy to international competition, to leave the product, labour, and capital markets essentially unreformed, to preserve IRI's dominant role in heavy industry and financial intermediation, and not to reform the 'ordinary' public administration.

We already mentioned the political rationale for the latter choice but can now better explain it. Having decided not to reform the domestic markets and to rely instead on IRI's direct intervention to guide and accelerate development, the state did not need an efficient public administration: it lacked a sufficiently strong incentive to address the deep-seated inefficiencies of a complex instrument whose role, in essence, was not to regulate the economy but merely to 'compensate' the adverse social and economic effects of the unreformed markets (Barca 1997, 24–9). Hence, in particular, the persistence of a subsidy- and exemptions-based discretionary industrial policy and of similar policies directed at the middle classes and the civil service itself. Hence, by consequence, a three-phase vicious circle: the inefficiency of the public administration discouraged more ambitious and results-oriented policies, their eschewal further lowered the incentive to reform the administration, which derived from it a stronger incentive to be docile to the ruling parties and their political interests. This vicious circle, in turn, spun in resonance with the broader one—running between particularistic public expenditure and political clientelism—discussed in the preceding section. Both, finally, lowered political accountability and formed a favourable context for the collusion between public powers and private interests—collusion which had flourished during both Fascism and the last quarter of the nineteenth century, albeit in different contexts, and which was now also underpinned by the centrist coalitions' and the economic elites' converging interest in averting the rise to power of the Marxists.

The choice not to reform the domestic markets was balanced by the other features of the post-war settlement. The perspective we take is that of the evolution of the competitive pressures faced by firms, and especially the dominant ones (e.g., Fiat, Pirelli, Edison, Falck). And, in the absence of markets reform, following Ciocca (2007) we look chiefly at how the macroeconomic determinants of the intensity of competition, actual or potential, changed in respect of the conditions that obtained during Fascism.

Openness to the international markets and price and exchange rate stability certainly increased competitive pressure on firms, and indeed 'were seen by the leading economic authorities [including Einaudi] as useful steps to foster competition and to weaken the industrial oligopolistic groups' (Crafts and Magnani 2013, 77). The same is true for the choice to retain IRI, which competed directly with private firms in some sectors, such as steel-making and electricity generation, and whose banks were vigilant providers of finance to the private sector (Ciocca 2007, 2014; Battilossi et al. 2013). Competitive pressures grew also by reason of the mere onset of democracy, for although the Marxists were relegated to opposition and the centrist coalitions were quite hospitable to conservative interests, they nonetheless included forces that prevented the government from colluding with the economic elites to the extent observed during Fascism: the left wing of the DC aimed at full employment and advocated the establishment of the welfare state and direct public intervention in the economy (Barca 1997, 17–18), for instance, and De Gasperi himself shared with the left and the *azionisti* the purpose, albeit vague, of 'fighting monopolies' (Ciocca 2007, 231–2). Indeed, the decisions to retain IRI and open the economy to international competition were 'fundamental political choice[s], upheld even in the face of resistance from powerful economic lobbies, the same that from 1925 onward had advocated autarky' (Toniolo 2013b, 20).

Considering the influence that such 'lobbies' had retained, it is hard to overstate the significance of these two choices. Both will prove crucial ingredients of the country's rapid growth, as we shall see, and among their determinants was a 'good dose of mistrust—resulting from ideology and the experience of the 1930s—of the ability of private enterprise to generate adequate capital accumulation, technology, and productivity growth' (Toniolo 2013b, 21; see also Ciocca 2014).

Among the economic elites the positions were diversified, however. Barca (1997, 18–20) identifies a 'conservative' group—the *elettrici*, the steel-makers, and the cement producers, chiefly—and some 'innovators': firms in more labour-intensive sectors, such as Fiat, which had promising growth prospects and ambitious development plans. The latter supported the decision to retain IRI, in particular, and especially its plan to build three large state-of-the-art full-cycle steel mills, from which they expected good-quality intermediate products at internationally competitive prices. Dominated by conservatives, Confindustria opposed the plan instead, aiming to protect the less efficient, scrap metal-based mills run by Falck and the other private steel-makers (Ciocca 2014, 119). The three mills were built, and, again, gave a crucial contribution to Italy's economic progress (Barca 1997; Ciocca 2014, 139–43).

Innovators and conservatives nonetheless shared a preference for 'a "subsidy-providing" state over a "regulating" one' (Barca 1997, 20), and in particular opposed the reform of the product, capital, and labour markets. This is the feature of the post-war settlement that more closely reflects their interests. It both revealed and strengthened the political influence of Italy's main firms, and allowed them to face intensifying international competition while being relatively sheltered from domestic sources of competitive pressure (Carli 1996; Cavazzuti 2017).

Barca (1997, 12–23) shows that, with the exception of liberals like Einaudi and some former *azionisti*, the political forces of the time probably underestimated this question, as they had done while writing the constitution. The long-term objective of nationalizing some sectors—only one will be, in 1962—overshadowed that of promoting competition across all domestic markets: coupled with the expectation that IRI's capacity to compete with the dominant firms would have been a viable substitute, this approach led them not to follow Britain—and, a decade later, Germany—in adopting an explicit competition policy and establishing a competition authority. Equally, the fact that the financial system was bank-oriented and that 'practically the entire system of financial intermediation [was] in public hands' may have led them to underrate the importance of regulating the capital markets, which is another important source of competitive pressure on firms: as a result, 'corporate governance structures remained closed' (Crafts and Magnani 2013, 77), the opaque practices—such as pyramidal groups and cross shareholdings—inherited from the liberal and Fascist epochs persisted, and '[t]he stock market stayed thin, oligopolistic, and vulnerable to the speculative forays of a handful of raiders' (Toniolo 2013b, 21). Not even the innovators pressed for capital-market or corporate-governance reform, because they counted on financing their investment plans primarily through profits, which they projected to be high thanks to rapid growth and low wages (Barca 1997, 18).

This brings us to another critical feature of the post-war settlement, namely the decision not to regulate the labour market. It was taken because both Confindustria and the Marxists and the trade unions preferred to leave industrial relations to the raw bargaining power of the two sides, rather than to a more structured negotiation process (Magnani 1997). Italy thus approached its full industrialization lacking institutions comparable to those that in Germany and other Western economies would underpin the 'corporatist social contract which allowed a cooperative equilibrium in which wage restraint was rewarded by high investment which benefited both firms and their workers in the long run' (Crafts and Magnani 2013, 79). We return to this question in Chapter 7, for in the early 1960s similar institutions were proposed.

The land reform, to conclude, the only major structural reform of the 1950s, was the result of an isolated episode of collective action, as we saw, which the DC employed to widen the farmers' class and consolidate its support among them. A similar rationale underpins the decision to retain the fascist anticompetitive legislation in the retail, craftsmanship, and professional services sectors, to the benefit of other components of the DC's electorate.

Continuity thus prevailed in the economic institutions, with the exception, decisive, of the opening of an autarkic economy to international trade and competition. Unlike in the case of the formal political institutions, by consequence, there was no equivalent gap between *formal* institutions and *actual* ones. The origin of that gap was the anti-fascist coalition's failure to alter Italy's social order as radically as the formal political institutions. Coupled with the weakness and incoherence of the progressives' reform ideas, especially on the regulation of markets and the promotion of competition, the same reason explains why the economic institutions were not reformed. If the leap forward embodied by the constitution fell short of its ambitions, in other words, in the economic sphere it was not even attempted.

Chapter 7 reviews the effects of this combination of distorted political institutions and unreformed economic ones. Here we draw from it some observations on the quality of Italy's democracy in its first decades, to corroborate the thesis that the post-war years merely began the country's transition from a limited-access social order to an open-access one.

The Nature of Italy's Democracy and the Character of its Institutions in the 1950s

Electoral democracy consolidated rapidly, we have noted. But the rule of law remained weak, in two main respects (see Cassese 2014). First, Italy's legal system was itself internally contradictory, because the centrist coalitions adjusted neither the pre-existing legislation nor the public administration to the constitution, and the judiciary routinely upheld and applied laws that conflicted with it (or tolerated their breach, as we shall see, when this was convenient). Second, the judiciary was both partial to the centrist majorities and the economic elites allied to them, and was shielded from accountability by reason of the strong constitutional safeguards for its independence. So it served neither as an effective constraint on the executive power, nor as an impartial administrator of justice for society at large. Episodes such as those of Melissa suggest that not just civil liberties, but also the right to life was weakly protected.

We already argued that these features were due also to the polarization of political competition and the anti-systemic character of the opposition, and not just to the amphibious nature of Italy's social order, which combined features of both the limited-access social order and of the open-access one. The model by which Mukand and Rodrik (2015) explain how liberal democracy can emerge and be sustained helps us to combine those two perspectives. The notion of 'liberal democracy' they use and the concept of 'open-access social order' in North et al. (2009) are largely coextensive, in fact, enough to allow the two theories to be usefully juxtaposed.

Mukand and Rodrik (2015, 2) posit a neat taxonomy of democratic regimes:

> [e]lectoral democracies, which constitute the majority of present-day democracies, protect property and political rights, but not civil rights. Liberal democracies protect all three sets of rights. [The] main distinctive feature of a liberal regime

[therefore are] the restraints placed on those in power to prevent discrimination against minorities and ensure equal treatment [i.e.] non-discrimination in the provision of public goods such as justice, security, education and health.

Historically, they argue (p. 3), the rise of democracy 'was typically the result of a quid pro quo between the elites and the mobilized masses': the former acceded to popular demands that the franchise be extended, and the masses 'accepted limits on their ability to expropriate property holders. In short, electoral rights were exchanged for property rights.' Yet, next to the class divide there may be another cleavage in society, based on either identity (ethnic, religious, etc.) or ideology, which divides the masses into a majority and a minority. In such circumstances, their model suggests (p. 3) that a political settlement will emerge, whose defining characteristic is that

it excludes the main beneficiary of civil rights—the dispossessed minorities—from the bargaining table. These minorities have neither resources (like the elite) nor numbers (like the majority) behind them. So they do not have something to bring to the table, and cannot make any credible threats. The political logic of democratization dictates the provision of property and political rights, but not civil rights [because providing them] is costly to the majority and largely unnecessary for the elite (who can pay for their own collective goods by extracting a surplus from the masses). Therefore the political settlement is one that favors electoral democracy over liberal democracy.

Compared to North et al. (2009), this model privileges the viewpoint of the interests and ideologies of the protagonists of society's main cleavages over that of the allocation of power between them. Yet under both perspectives the crucial question is how the polity can sustainably guarantee equal treatment in circumstances in which, as Mukand and Rodrik (2015, 4) put it, '[b]y discriminating against the minority, the majority can enjoy more public goods for itself'. In their view, the question depends on whether the class divide and the identity or ideology divide are aligned: liberal democracy is more likely to arise if they are *not* aligned, because the elites will share the minority's interest in seeing equal treatment guaranteed.

Their model fits the Italian case very well. The masses, represented by the anti-fascist coalition, and the pre-war elites exchanged electoral rights (universal suffrage was granted and election manipulation abandoned) for property rights (the Fascist-era profits were not confiscated and the markets were not reformed). The masses soon divided along an ideological cleavage, however, in respect of which the majority and the elites stood on the same side. This alignment allowed the majority to place the governments it elected under weak constraints (e.g., a subservient judiciary), to appropriate a disproportionate share of public goods (e.g., through the discretionary provision of subsidies), and to subvert or deny the formally established civil rights (e.g., in the public order sector).

Neither the model's categories nor Italy's case are clear-cut, naturally. Some rule of law and some civil rights are compatible with electoral democracy (Mukand and Rodrik 2015, 7), just like features of the open-access social order typically coexist with features of the limited access one in a transition society. Our argument is that in the 1950s the rule of law, the constraints over the executive power, and civil liberties were too weak for the country to be seen as a liberal democracy: the real constraints over the centrist political majorities were electoral democracy, on one hand, and, on the other, the opposition's numerical strength, cohesion, and organized grassroots base. What stands out are the formal political institutions: the constitution, which does in fact appear like a leap forward. We explain it with the cohesion, values, and ideas of the anti-fascist coalition, and with the 'veil of ignorance' that allowed the future majority and minority to negotiate the constitutional compromise without knowing whether they would be in government or in opposition. But when the veil was lifted, on the strength of the underlying social order the majority subverted that compromise.

This model can be combined with those summarized in Chapter 4, finally, because political polarization was another obstacle to the rise of the 'good' equilibrium. As long as the class divide and the cleavage traced by Marxism remained aligned, in fact, the rule of law and the constraints over the executive power were likely to remain weak. The damage produced by Italy's defining ideological rift will thus appear clearer, as well as the conservatives' interest in perpetuating it. This is precisely what emerges from the minutes of the council of ministers held on 7 December 1959, during which a DC minister said that 'to survive we need a Cold-War situation'.[12] The centrist coalitions could hardly determine the intensity of the international confrontation, but they could certainly hinder the open public debate through which, as we have argued, the obstacle that ideology posed to the emergence of a reformist compromise could have been relaxed. As we shall see, in fact, the most ambitious reformist programme of republican Italy arose during a period of *détente* in international relations, and to fight it the reactionary wing of the conservative front resorted also to threatening a coup d'état.

A self-reinforcing vicious circle could have set in, by which political polarization would weaken both the rule of law and its future credibility, which would further heighten polarization, and so on until either autocracy or revolution follows (see, e.g., Acemoglu et al. 2015). Italy avoided this fate, in

---

[12] Quoted by Crainz (2016, 67).

part because the opposition was strong and loyal to the democratic principle, in part because the governing majority included wise statesmen. But that logic—by which every weakening of the rule of law only increases the extant majority's incentive to exclude the opposition from power—can contribute to explaining the recurrent political use of violence and of the threat of it during the 1960s and 1970s: the clandestine operations we already mentioned, and the coups d'état and the 'strategy of tension' we shall discuss in Chapter 7.

If the rule of law was so weak that one segment of the ruling class could resort to such strategies, moreover, a dynamic similar to that revealed by Hoff and Stiglitz (2008) is likely to have been at play. The impossibility of shielding stolen assets from recapture once the rule of law has been established can impede its establishment, they argue, if this depends also on the choices of those who were engaged in predation. If we read 'political violence' and 'criminal sanctions' where they write 'stealing' and 'recapture', and consider that those presumably implicated included high officials—the head of state, in one case—and segments of the security services, the logic does not change. Indeed, in respect of many of those episodes of political violence justice has not been done (e.g., Cento Bull 2015). Scandalous though it may seem, impunity for grave political crimes is less a problem per se than a manifestation of Italy's graver and deeper ones.

To introduce Chapter 7, we conclude with an observation about one other consequence of political polarization and the weak rule of law. In an essay published while the constitution was being written, the *azionista* Calamandrei ([1947] 2004, 248–9) noted that as political competition intensified, the signs also emerged that party interests were beginning to trump public ethics. With deliberate hyperbole, he stigmatized the apparent rise of a norm whereby 'stealing millions' for one's party is legitimate: in a silent parliament, forty-five years later a leading politician who had actually stolen billions invoked precisely that norm to defend himself and accuse his peers of having done the same (Rhodes 2015, 312).[13] We do not refer to political corruption often in the first part of Chapter 7 because until the mid 1970s reliable information about it is sparse. We know for instance that 'corruption was rife since the outset at Eras', the Sicilian land-reform public agency (Ginsborg 1990, 136), but lack empirical studies covering those decades. Yet it seems plausible to assume that political corruption did not rise all of a sudden in the second half of the 1970s but rather underwent a more gradual expansion, which went unremarked because the judiciary, the law enforcement system, the broadcast media, and the main newspapers—except those

---

[13] The politician was Craxi, later convicted for corruption (see Preface).

owned by the opposition—were either subservient to the political authorities or controlled by the economic elites (Ortoleva 1997a and 1997b; Gundle 2015; Mancini 2015). Democracy certainly reduced the tight collusion between the public and the private sphere that obtained during Fascism, as we said, but did not eliminate its worst manifestations.

7

The 'Economic Miracle' and an Ambitious Reform Programme

Overview and Periodization – The 'Economic Miracle' and Full Employment (1950–1963) – The Juncture of 1962–1964 and the Defeat of an Ambitious Reform Programme – A Battle of Ideas – The Political Influence of Organized Crime

Overview and Periodization

Under the political and economic institutions that we have just described Italian society underwent the most rapid and profound transformation of its history, propelled by productivity growth. Between the early 1950s and 1963, a period known as the 'economic miracle', industry became the dominant sector, national income doubled, and affluence began to spread beyond the upper classes. Despite their weaknesses, those institutions allowed the country to exploit the vast potential for catch-up growth that was offered by its own backwardness and a favourable international environment. Once the forces of convergence began to fade, however, and society grew richer and more sophisticated, those institutions insensibly became a hindrance to development and productivity growth progressively slowed down.

The interpretation that we have already begun to articulate is that institutional reform was impeded by the idiosyncratic social order that took shape between 1943 and the early 1950s. So we shall seek to highlight both the essential continuity of that social order, suspended in an as yet unaccomplished transition, and the signs of the onset and persistence of the vicious circles discussed in Chapter 4, which are at once manifestations of that social order, buttresses of its stability, obstacles to reform, and sources of the diverse inefficiencies that now constrain Italy's material and democratic progress.

The country stood at a critical juncture by the end of the economic miracle, in 1962–4, when a vast reform programme was thoroughly defeated. Reform having been eschewed, during the late 1960s and the 1970s the country's social order was severely tested. Growth decelerated, the international environment became less benign, inflation soared, citizens' demands rose, social tensions broke out, and political violence was often a daily occurrence in Italy's main cities. The country's elites responded to these challenges less by expanding the opportunities available to all, which would have exposed them to greater political and economic competition, than by granting selective protections to the social groups that had either the size to attract them or the bargaining power to exact them. The social order became more inclusive but its logic was not altered. That form of co-option, through which particularistic privileges were traded against political support, gave impetus to the proliferation of distributional coalitions, raised inflation, and set the main spiral hypothesized in Chapter 4 in motion. This policy assured enough social consensus to allow the country to overcome the tensions of the 1970s, which were mostly endogenous, but dampened the dynamic forces of society and hampered the shift from a convergence-driven model of development to one based on innovation.

The political and economic crisis of 1992–4 shook a nation indulged by a decade of social peace, lower inflation, comfortable growth, and widening affluence, which does not appear to have remarked either the downturn of TFP (Figure 1.3a) or Italy's incipient divergence from its peers' approach to the productivity frontier (Figures 1.1 and 1.2). The economic crisis erupted when the two sources of growth that had compensated the waning of convergence—namely, the vitality of the country's small- and medium-sized enterprises (SMEs) and industrial districts, and an expansionary fiscal policy financed by debt—exhausted their possibilities. The political crisis broke out when judicial investigations unveiled the depth of the corruption that the vicious circles enfolding much of society had generated. The spectacle was properly obscene, for the precise traits of the degeneration of the *arcana imperii* were twice removed from the public scene, and popular indignation profound. At first the urgency of deep economic and political change seemed set to impose itself. But the social order weathered the double crisis. Compelling though they were, the reasons for change were not condensed into a credible reform programme, and by 1994 the preexisting equilibrium was largely restored. The reforms of the second half of the decade were to a great extent subverted, and for long further ones were impeded. Yet as the economy did not find fresh sources of growth decline began, and began to lay the seeds for the insecurity and distrust that opinion polls now record.

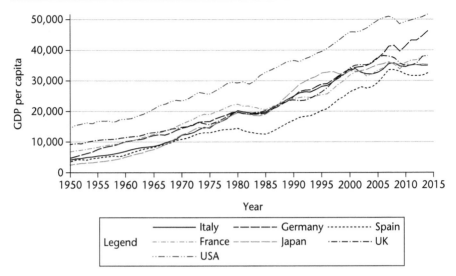

Figure 7.1 Comparative Per Capita GDP Levels, 1950–2014
Source: Penn World Table

The periodization reflected by this chapter and the next two differs from those most commonly used (illustrated, respectively, in Figures 1.3a and 1.3b). Within a framework of progressively rising globalization, the seven decades covered by these chapters were marked by two major discontinuities: the end of the Bretton Woods system and the first oil shock, which in 1971–3 brought the Golden Age to an end and opened a period of slower growth and higher inflation; and the financial crisis of 2007–8, which sealed the period of macro-economic stability often described as the 'Great Moderation' and pushed the Western world into the Great Recession, within which Europe's own crisis arose. Italy fully partook in these developments, as Figure 7.1 shows. Yet our emphasis is placed on two junctures of the country's own history, 1962–4 and 1992–4, which from the vantage point of our interpretation appear to have been critical, and, between them, on the passage between the turbulent 1970s and the so-called 'missed opportunity' of the 1980s. Though heterodox, therefore, this periodization orders the narration in a manner better suited to the illustration of our arguments.

The 'Economic Miracle' and Full Employment (1950–1963)

During the Golden Age, Western Europe and Japan steadily converged towards the productivity leader, the USA (see Figure 1.1), and recorded the highest growth rates of their history. Italy shared in these trends, and in its essential traits its development model mirrors that of its peers. Growth was fuelled by structural change, as agriculture shed capital and labour, by high rates of investment, and by the absorption of superior US technology, and it benefited from a benign international environment, as world trade rose rapidly, thanks to the progressive reduction of trade costs and protectionist barriers, and the Bretton Woods system of pegged exchange rates promoted financial and macroeconomic stability.

Like Germany and Japan, during the Golden Age Italy too outperformed the rest of Western Europe. The higher growth rates of the three defeated powers mostly reflect the greater potential for catch-up that was implicit in their relative backwardness (Boltho 2013, fig. 4.1). Yet, between the early 1950s and 1963, Italy's growth model 'delivered extraordinary results . . . even by the standards of the time' (Crafts and Magnani 2013, 82). Table 7.1 presents the main variables.

Until 1963 real growth was high, stable, and driven predominantly by TFP, which rose at the fastest rates in Italian history and accounted for about half of aggregate growth (Figure 1.3a).[1] Productivity growth reflected not just the efficiency gains and composition effect flowing from structural change, and especially from the shift of masses of workers from agriculture to manufacturing, but also rapid improvements within each sector, including agriculture: structural change accounted for less than one quarter of overall productivity growth, the rest being within-sector growth (Broadberry et al. 2013, fig. 7.3).

Table 7.1 Selected Macroeconomic Indicators, 1950–1963

Year	GDP Growth[a]	Per-Capita GDP Growth[a]	Total Investment (%GDP)[a]	Labour Productivity Growth[a]	TFP Growth[a]	Inflation (CPI)[b]	Debt-to-GDP Ratio[c]
1950	–	–	20.3	–	–	–	29.5
1951	8.7	8.0	22.1	6.7	5.5	–	29.9
1952	4.3	3.8	22.7	2.3	1.2	–	31.6
1953	6.2	5.5	23.8	4.1	2.7	–	32.5
1954	4.1	3.4	24.6	2.1	0.6	–	34.9
1955	5.3	4.6	27.0	3.3	1.4	–	33.9
1956	4.1	3.5	27.8	2.1	0.3	3.4	32.92
1957	3.8	3.2	28.9	3.1	0.8	1.3	32.1
1958	4.7	4.1	28.5	4.2	1.8	2.9	32.0
1959	6.5	5.8	29.2	5.3	3.1	–0.5	33.1
1960	8.2	7.4	30.6	8.0	5.0	2.3	31.4
1961	8.3	7.6	30.3	8.5	5.0	2.0	30.0
1962	6.1	5.5	29.8	8.9	4.5	4.7	29.0
1963	5.5	4.8	30.3	8.1	3.8	7.4	27.2

Note: [a] Source: Penn World Table. [b] Source: OECD. [c] Source: IMF.

---

[1] More than half, according to Broadberry et al. (2013): on this difference, see note 1 of Chapter 1.

Indeed, next to the import of technology, both disembodied and incorporated in capital goods, also R&D expenditures grew, from an estimated 0.2 per cent of GDP in the mid 1950s to about 0.6 per cent at the peak of the economic miracle (Barbiellini Amidei et al. 2013, 400–1 and fig. 14.13; only half of this volume of expenditure came from the business sector, however, compared to an average of 60 per cent among Italy's peers). The highest productivity growth rates were recorded in the fast-expanding manufacturing sector, which benefited also from the rising economies of scale realized by Italy's large or growing firms, which introduced mass-production technologies and organization models: both established firms, like Fiat and IRI's manufacturers, and newer and highly innovating ones like Olivetti (Onida et al. 2013, 425–7), as well as the first mid-sized producers of consumer durables. Their response to the competitive pressures and profit opportunities brought about by the post-war settlement was 'formidable' (Ciocca 2007, 239).

So we return briefly to the main features of the post-war settlement, to discuss its contribution to these 'extraordinary results'. It is well established that the choice to progressively integrate the economy into European and world markets—which became irreversible when Italy and the other five founding states signed the Treaty of Rome, in 1957, and created the European Common Market—was decisive. After two decades of autarky and war, it opened new outlets to the country's manufacturers and gave them both the stimulus and the means—respectively, exposure to external competition, and access to more advanced technologies, machinery, production processes, management practices, and products to import, adapt, or imitate—to grow in scale and efficiency. Equally important was the choice to preserve IRI's dominant presence in heavy industry and financial intermediation, which also had important spill-over effects in the private sector. IRI's firms invested heavily in innovation, absorbed and diffused foreign technology and management practices, upgraded the transport and telecommunications infrastructure, and guaranteed to Italy's manufacturers critical intermediate products—the steel produced by the new state-of-the-art mills we already mentioned, in particular—at internationally competitive prices (Ciocca 2014). In parallel, since 1953 a state-owned oil-and-gas conglomerate broadly mirroring IRI's model, the Ente Nazionale Idrocarburi (ENI), met increasing shares of the rapidly expanding domestic demand for energy at equally competitive prices (Berta 2015; Castronovo 2015).

The choice to leave the domestic capital, labour, and product markets unreformed did not constrain growth in these years. The intensity of product-market competition remained low in this period, recent research finds, but firms' persisting market power also reflected innovation rents and was anyway attenuated by external openness (see Gigliobianco and Toniolo 2017). IRI itself proved to be an efficient mechanism for allocating resources, moreover, and in the private sector the exceptionally high rates of investment were funded far less by debt or equity financing than by firms' own profits. Low competition in the product markets assisted this form of accumulation. But corporate profits were high—37 per cent of value added, the highest level observed during the republican period (Ciocca 2007, 241)—primarily because wages rose much more slowly than productivity, owing to the absence of institutions promoting coordinated wage negotiations during years in which structural change made the supply of labour effectively unlimited in the industrial sector.

Nor did the persistence of much authoritarian pre-war legislation dampen the dynamism of society. Internal migration offers a revealing example. During this decade some 10 million Italians changed their place of residence, mostly moving to urban areas, and about 1 million migrated from the rural South to the cities of the North-West and their suburbs, seeking employment in their Fordist factories or around them (Ginsborg 1990, 435–9; Ciocca 2007, 282). This epochal flow, which continued throughout the following decade, embodies a large part of the structural change that underpinned Italy's leap towards full industrialization. Yet until 1961, when it was finally repealed, it occurred in breach of a Fascist-era law against urbanization (Ginsborg 1990, 218–19). The government's preference for tolerating the transgression of this measure rather than repealing it is another instance of what we said in Chapter 6 about the weakness of the rule of law, and well illustrates its effects. For that law turned a few millions of citizens into illegal internal migrants and aggravated their exposure to the exploitation of employers and landlords, which was pervasive (Crainz 2016, 88–9): to picture the personal dramas that they often suffered, illustrated by Luchino Visconti's 1960 film *Rocco and his Brothers*, it suffices to consider that in 1955 only about one third of the population could express themselves in Italian (and only 18 per cent spoke it habitually: De Mauro 2014, table 7). In part, therefore, the poor working and living conditions that they suffered, which contributed to the accumulation of the social tensions that erupted at the end of the 1960s, were a direct effect of the persisting limited-access features of Italy's social order. By contrast, although during those years Germany and Japan faced much larger migration flows—which included the millions of refugees uprooted by the war and the new borders, or expelled from formerly occupied territories—they nonetheless managed to integrate them 'smoothly' into their cities and labour markets (Boltho 2013, 116).

The centrist coalitions supported this growth model chiefly by guaranteeing political and macroeconomic stability. Fiscal policy was orthodox, monetary policy accommodating, the exchange rate stable, and banking supervision effective (Ciocca 2007; Crafts and Magnani 2013). Besides this, the governments of this period largely left the country's development to market forces and to IRI's, the central bank's, and ENI's managers. Competent and dedicated, they had been selected by the exacting challenges of war and reconstruction and were far-sightedly protected from undue external interference by De Gasperi's DC (Barca and Trento 1997; Ciocca 2014; Castronovo 2015).

Two parallel processes characterized domestic politics during these years. One led to the co-option of the Socialists into the governing majority, and is discussed in the next section. The other concerns the evolution of the DC and its centrist coalitions. Under a new leadership, after 1953 the party increasingly sought to emancipate itself from Confindustria and the Vatican by strengthening its own organization and widening its electoral base (Baldini 2015; Cotta 2015; Pombeni 2015). This effort was only partly successful. The Church retained considerable influence over the party and its electorate (Acanfora 2015; Melloni 2015). And, as Berta (2015, 482) writes, '[t]he "interweaving"—or, some would say, collusion—between the leading economic groups and the political class [remained] a constitutive element of the Italian Republic'. In the context of a blocked political system, moreover, this effort became intertwined with growing competition between the DC and its coalition partners, as well as among the party's increasingly organized internal factions. Intra-coalition and especially intra-party competition tended to overshadow the pursuit of the general interest, and often turned policy-making into a process of mediation between parties or factions and special interest groups, large or minute. In part, therefore, the locus of politics insensibly shifted from the open debate in parliament towards the negotiations within the DC, if not even within its majoritarian centrist faction, the *dorotei*, which was founded in 1959 and 'dominated' party politics for the subsequent decade (Baldini 2015, 176). All this harmed the transparency of policy-making, bred the incipient degradation of politics into mere management of power, *gestione del potere*, and raised the returns of clientelistic practices, which the tight political control over the public administration already allowed.

The management of the subsidies programme ancillary to the 1950 land reform provides an example. A broader and more illustrative one concerns welfare policy. While the centrist coalitions neglected the social demands brought up by large-scale migration and urbanization, in fact, they chose to extend the coverage of the pension system to wide categories of the self-employed: retailers, craftsmen, and farmers. The aim was political and partisan, for the three social groups were part of the DC's core electorate, but the consequences for the evolution of welfare policy were profound and long-lasting, because other categories soon began demanding similar treatment. Thus arose two distinctive and enduring traits of Italy's welfare state, two of its 'original sins' (Ferrera et al. 2012). One—which need not detain us here, except as another sign of the inefficiency of the public administration—is its disproportionate emphasis on pensions and monetary transfers. The other is its 'fragmented development' (Ferrera and Jessoula 2015, 507), which over the following decades generated 'a true "labyrinth" of categorical privileges which has very few comparative counterparts'. Particularistic or corporatist policies nurture demands of the same nature, in fact, and both stimulate the proliferation of Olsonian distributional coalitions. Coupled with the disregard for the needs created by society's transformation, which called for universalistic policies instead, the granting of those pension schemes set this dynamic in motion.

The signs of the spiral conjectured in Chapter 4 are thus beginning to emerge. One is precisely the exchange between political support and the selective use of public power and resources, at the level of either groups (e.g., the pensions and anti-competitive regulation enjoyed by retailers) or individuals (e.g., the farmers' subsidies). These exchanges were part of the great war, the struggle against Marxism and its Italian representatives, as well as of the small war, the contests and rivalries within the centrist coalitions, amongst the DC's own factions, and within the *dorotei*. They were part of political competition, therefore, but at the same time they limited it, because they tended to shift its objective from the acquisition of that form of support which always has 'voice' as an alterative, in Hirschman's (1970) terms, to the acquisition of a more silent and stable 'loyalty', underpinned by selective privileges. Consequently, they also limited the centrist coalition's and the DC's accountability to society at large. In turn, the collusion between public powers and private interests linked this political elite to the economic one, which equally benefited from low competitive pressures in domestic markets that parliament had left unreformed, and controlled the newspapers that could most effectively have invoked the centrist coalition's political accountability (Ortoleva 1997a and 1997b; Mancini 2015).

Republican Italy had inherited from the liberal and Fascist epochs both this form of collusion and a long practice of clientelism, corporatist and individual. Yet continuity lay only in the function of these phenomena, which is to limit political and economic competition so as to generate or protect rents. There was much less continuity in their forms, which in the 1950s were shaped by the need to sway the masses from the temptations of the socialist idea in circumstances in which, unlike before, suffrage was universal and the vote free. Thus corporatist clientelism aimed at social and political inclusion on a much larger scale than during Fascism, and collusion was lesser (for after 1943 the social order had been opened up, if less than Marxists and *azionisti* desired).

Besides the land reform of 1950, the only major initiative of the centrist coalitions was a systematic policy for accelerating the development of the South, the first in the country's history. It was motivated by the objective, common to the land reform, of absorbing the social tensions that traversed the agrarian sector of those regions. But it stemmed also from the conviction that their development was central to the progress of the country as a whole, and could not be left to market forces alone (Iuzzolino et al. 2013). This policy was entrusted to the Cassa del Mezzogiorno, like IRI an ad hoc autonomous agency, and benefited also from the loans and support of the World Bank. It was based on the 'principle of additionality', which will inform also EU cohesion policy: the principle, namely, that the investments it brought were to be in addition to the South's own share of ordinary national capital expenditure (Crafts and Magnani 2013, 78). It was first centred on infrastructure, irrigation, and land reclamation projects, and in 1957 it shifted towards the construction of a manufacturing base, chiefly through the investments of IRI and large private firms in large capital-intensive industrial 'poles'. Combined with the effects of migration and structural change, this policy allowed the most backward regions of the country to grow at rates very close to those of the most industrialized ones. In this period the South steadily reduced its income gap, for the first time since unification, and supported the development of the North-West by offering to its manufacturers a growing market and increasing economies of scale. This regional development policy thus was an important ingredient of the national growth model sketched earlier (Crafts and Magnani 2013).

Two intrinsic weaknesses of that model are worth noting, however. The first is that the decisive contribution that IRI, the Cassa del Mezzogiorno, and ENI gave to the country's development was in large part due to the fact that their managers were both competent and free from political interference (Iuzzolino et al. 2013). This was the result of the accidents of history and the enlightened choices of De Gasperi's DC, however, which *chose* not to influence those agencies, not of the institutions governing their autonomy and the selection and oversight of their managers, which were either lacking or inadequate (Barca 1997). This inherently fragile arrangement, which in the case of IRI dated back from Fascism, broke down in the course of the 1960s (Barca and Trento 1997; Crafts and Magnani 2013; Ciocca 2014). Though inspired also by an explicit interventionist strategy, the decline of the managerial independence of those critical agencies went roughly in parallel with the degradation of politics and the rise of clientelism, and was their most immediately damaging effect.

The second, deeper weakness is that the unlimited supply of labour was a critical condition for that growth model, but a naturally transitory one. The equilibrium based on low wages, high profits, and high investment rates was upset in the early 1960s, in fact, when the economy approached and probably reached full employment, at least in the North-West, and witnessed the first significant wage push since the early 1920s. Nominal wages rose by 12 per cent in 1962, upon an unprecedented wave of strikes, and by 18 per cent in 1963, when the unemployment rate fell to its historical minimum, 3.9 per cent (Ciocca 2007, 240 and 258; Toniolo 2013b, 23).

In those same years the governing coalition prepared to co-opt the Socialists, on the basis of a reform programme that included proposals aimed precisely at establishing a more cooperative wage-bargaining system. These developments brought the country to a delicate passage.

The Juncture of 1962–1964 and the Defeat of an Ambitious Reform Programme

The polarization of international relations abated somewhat after the Korean War ended and Stalin died, in 1953. Three years later the Soviet intervention in Hungary accelerated the distancing of Italy's Socialists, who condemned it, from the PCI. In this context, during the second half of the 1950s progressives in the DC engaged with liberal-democrats, republicans, liberal-socialists, and Socialists in a discussion on economic and social reforms. The work, led in large part by former *azionisti*, was underpinned by scientific research and punctuated by a succession of important conferences and public debates.

After an attempt to shift the ruling coalition to the right failed dramatically, in the summer of 1960, the Christian Democrats took those discussions as the basis for including the PSI in the governing majority, to widen its popular base and isolate the Communists. Once the Vatican's and Washington's initial opposition to this policy was dropped, in early 1962 Aldo Moro, the leader of the DC, persuaded a still reluctant party to implement it. In June 1962 also Fiat, then the leading private industrial group, publicly 'endorsed' it (Berta 2015, 480).

By then a vast reform programme had been articulated, arguably the most ambitious in Italy's history (Magnani 2016, 8), certainly in its post-war history (e.g., Craveri 2016). It aimed at directing a greater share of the resources generated by rapid growth towards public uses, in the welfare, health, education, and infrastructure sectors, and at remedying the main structural problems of the economy, prominent among which again was the North-South divide (see La Malfa 1962). In contrast with much of the practice of the centrist coalitions the programme was informed by a genuinely universalistic approach, including in the critical field of social insurance (Ferrera et al. 2012, 234 *passim* and 303 *passim*). Though markedly dirigiste, as it aimed at directly orienting both consumption and investment, it included far-sighted and liberal proposals on competition policy, corporate governance, and the regulation of financial markets (Marchetti 1997), which addressed problems that had been identified since at least the 1900s, as we saw. Written as the wage push of 1962–3 began,

131

moreover, the programme also foresaw a form of 'incomes policy': a policy, as Crafts and Magnani (2013, 81) describe it, which was intended to ensure

> the sustainability of growth by preserving competitiveness and by keeping inflationary pressures under control [through] an attempt to render industrial relations less adversarial by involving unions in discussions about the compatibility of wage dynamics with macroeconomic objectives and to pave the way for a coordinated market economy.

On the basis of this programme the Socialists gave parliamentary support to a DC-only cabinet in 1962, as the Liberals moved into opposition, and entered the government in late 1963. During these two years the electricity sector was nationalized, despite the stiff resistance of the *elettrici*, the judiciary and other professions were opened to women, and an important reform of secondary education was adopted, which raised the compulsory years of schooling to eight and postponed to the eighth grade the choice between the vocational track and the academic one (Bertola and Sestito 2013, 253–5).

But the rest of the programme was passed on unimplemented from one cabinet to the next for the rest of the decade (Barca 1997; Crafts and Magnani 2013; Favretto 2015). The country thus faced the waning of structural change and the progressive erosion of the potential for convergence with institutions that had proven appropriate for catch-up growth, but were unlikely to be adequate to support its transition to a development model fitter to an industrial economy.

The prospects of the reforms certainly suffered from a sudden worsening of the economic climate. In 1963 the central bank resolutely tightened monetary policy, to counter inflationary pressures driven by the wage push, a widening current account deficit, and widespread fears of currency devaluation; the latter were alimented by vast and often illegal exports of capital, sparked, in turn, by plans to raise the taxation of capital income,[2] by worries about further nationalizations, and, more generally, by the leftward turn of the governing majority and its reform programme (Ciocca 2007, 259 and 262; Crafts and Magnani 2013, 81).[3] The economy slowed down, as a result, and unemployment rose. Particularly marked was the decline in investment. Borrowing the Marxian notion, Salvati (1984, 89 *passim*) described it as an 'investment strike': between the 1958–63 and 1964–73 periods the yearly growth rate of fixed investments dropped from 11 per cent to 5 per cent, nearly twice as

---

[2] In striking continuity with the liberal and Fascist epochs, the regime of registered shares was again fought upon (Craveri 2016, 178–9): the question was settled only in 1977 (Siciliano 2011, 27).

[3] Crafts and Magnani (2013, 81) add that the limited sophistication of the Italian financial markets contributes to explaining the capital outflows. Also this cause can be viewed as endogenous, however.

much as the decline of consumption in percentage terms, and contributed to rising outflows of both labour and capital (Ciocca 2007, 265).

'Evading taxes and taking the money to Switzerland: this was the behaviour of a large part of the bourgeoisie' in those years (Carli 1996, 263). This remark appears in the memoirs of the then governor of the central bank, Guido Carli, a liberal economist who after a long governorship (1960–75) served as president of Confindustria (1976–80), DC senator, and treasury minister (1989–92). He was severely critical of the dirigisme of the reformists' programme, and is often described as the intelligent guardian of the interests of free enterprise and private capital in Italy's mixed economy (e.g., Ginsborg 1990; Ciocca 2007; Rossi 2007). The 'extremely severe' criminal provisions soon adopted to stem the drainage of capital were ignored, Carli writes, and that 'behaviour' continued until the mid 1970s. Later estimates covering the period between 1959 and 1990, when capital controls were lifted, do indeed suggest that irregular outflows of capital were particularly sustained until at least 1972 (Committeri 1999, tables 3 and 4). It was, Carli comments, 'genuine desertion' on the part of the Italian bourgeoisie. Yet their response to the events of 1962–3 appears consistent with the logic of the country's social order. We take this perspective to discuss the defeat of the reformists.

In part their programme was unrealistic, based as it was on the expectation that the growth rates of the 1958–63 'boom' years would have continued, and the wide set of institutional reforms it foresaw was hardly compatible with the inefficiency of the public administration (Crafts and Magnani 2013). Yet not all reforms were equally sensitive to the programme's macroeconomic assumptions, and over one decade their design and sequencing could have been adjusted. This is especially true of *institutional* reforms such as those concerning the regulation of product and factor markets. These failed primarily because they met the impervious resistance of conservative interests, in circumstances in which the country's polarization and ideological cleavages—dividing socialists from other progressives, and orthodox Marxists, socialist or communist, from reformist ones—constrained the reformists' capacity to form a wider alliance behind their proposals. After some initial overtures the PCI gave no support to them, mindful also that the political objective of isolating it had been superimposed upon the reformists' work, and deprived them of the push that popular mobilization could have imparted to their programme. Within the DC the dominant centrist faction was tepid and the right-wing contrary. The former, the *dorotei*, were averse to the radicalism of the reforms and presumably calculated that their universalistic orientation would have limited the scope for the clientelistic practices on which their electoral support and membership base increasingly depended. The latter joined the Liberals—who had gained votes in the 1963 election, mostly at the expense of the DC (Ginsborg 1990, 348)—in giving voice to the objections of Confindustria and other conservative interests. Few of the conditions that had determined the success of the 1944 Gullo decrees were thus in place, to support far more ambitious reforms.

In part, the conservatives' opposition can be explained by the dirigisme of the programme (see Carli 1996). In part, it reflected a defence of rents, political and economic (Barca 1997; Crafts and Magnani 2013). But neither reason can fully explain why not even the innovators among Italy's firms—such as Fiat, in particular, which had endorsed the inclusion of the Socialists into the governing coalition—stood in support at least of those institutional reforms, which would have opened greater opportunities to them by making the product markets more competitive and the capital markets deeper and more efficient. On the contrary, the nationalization of their most conservative peers, the electrical oligopoly, was an implicit quid pro quo against the shelving precisely of proposals to promote competition across the economy. And once the mergers and transformations of the *elettrici*'s cash-rich firms drastically reduced its list, the stock exchange, unreformed and already small and inefficient, became a mere instrument for 'predation' (Carli 1996, 298). So it remained for the following two decades (e.g., Cavazzuti 2016; Magnani 2016, ch. 3).

The rationale of the economic elites' joint opposition to the reforms lies in the weakness of Italy's political institutions, we suggest, and in the logic of the 'political replacement effect' discussed in Chapter 3. Combined with the rise of labour's bargaining power, signalled by the wage push of 1962–3, and with the parallel leftward turn of the governing majority, in fact, the implementation of the reforms—policy and institutional ones—would have diluted the political and economic power of Italy's industrialists. This entailed risks, for the weakness of the rule of law and the checks-and-balances system, hitherto employed against the social and political opponents of the centrist coalitions, could have been turned against them. Risks that were magnified, not reduced, by the fact that the reformist front was relatively small, ideologically divided, and pressed from the left by a large anti-systemic opposition, the PCI, which could have taken advantage of the changed balance of power to superimpose its own aims over those of the reformists. The response of the political and economic elites therefore stemmed directly from the distortions of the country's political institutions: by failing to reassure them about the future protection of their rights and interests, such distortions were probably decisive in turning also innovating entrepreneurs against the reforms. At a time when long-term growth was expected to remain on the levels of the previous decade, in fact, the reduction of profits and of capital's share in national income that the reforms were likely to bring, to the benefit of labour and consumers, are unlikely to have been paramount. More important was the change in the allocation of power that the reforms could be expected to produce, the political replacement effect. Herein lie also the roots of the collusion between political and economic elites, joined in the defence of the extant social order, and the reasons why the main body of the DC, its centrist allies, and the economic elites all opposed the reformists' programme once its short-term objective—the absorption of the Socialists into the governing majority—had been achieved.

It is not surprising, therefore, that the stiff criminal provision adopted after 1963 to stem the outflow of capital proved as ineffective as the succession of ever harsher and shriller laws—the Spanish governor's *grida*, literally 'shouts'—in Manzoni's passage reproduced in the Preface, which did nothing but 'demonstrat[e] the impotence of their authors'. It was not impotence, though, but collusion. Not just because the political elite controlled the public administration and still influenced the judiciary, but also because the reform programme remained on the agenda for the whole decade and the reformists persisted in pushing it. The 'investment strike' and the related export of the excess savings was thus at once a strategy to limit the feared consequences of the reformists' victory, which remained possible, and a means to make it less likely, through the effects of capital drainage on the balance of payments, most immediately, and on employment. So, the conservative rump of the ruling coalition—the DC's *dorotei* and right-wing factions and the Liberals, chiefly—would not have been able to stem the illegal transfers to Switzerland without at the same time blunting an effective instrument to hold the reforms at bay.[4] The fact that they were allowed to be ignored suggests that those criminal sanctions were but symbolic measures, taken to assuage the ruling coalition's reformists and especially its new component, the Socialists (whose long-term aim, it bears repeating, then still was the establishment of socialism).

The outflows of 1963 nonetheless seem to stand out, as the literature cited earlier implied. Though such phenomena naturally escape precise measurement, the available estimates (see Committeri 1999, tables 3 and 4) suggest that the acceleration in irregular capital exports of that year exceeded the variations observed throughout the decades while capital controls were in force. This indicates that Italy's conservatives viewed the reformists' victory as both possible and of potentially far-reaching consequences, and attests that 1962–4 was indeed a critical juncture. Much of the country's elites defended the social order from institutional changes that could have eased creative destruction, and thereby challenged their political and economic rents: in so

---

[4] No conspiracy is implied, therefore: as we noted in Chapter 2, the convergence of interests is a sufficient explanation. Mirror-like, the private papers of a prominent conservative, Cesare Merzagora, reveal his conviction that the exported capitals would have been repatriated had the conservative front prevailed (reproduced in Franzinelli and Giacone 2013, 480–2, esp. 481).

doing, however, they lowered the country's growth prospects—as the theories discussed in Chapters 1–3 would predict—and arguably also dealt a blow to the very idea that meaningful reform was possible (see Magnani 2016, ch. 1).

A Battle of Ideas

> *dans les Coups d'État, on voit plus tôt tomber le tonnerre qu'on ne l'a entendu gronder dans les nuées.*
>
> [in coups d'état, one sees the lightning strike before one has heard its rumble in the clouds.]
>
> (Gabriel Naudé, 1639)

In essence, we have ascribed the failure of the reforms to vested interests. Yet in Chapters 3 and 4 we argued, following Rodrik (2014), that ideas can overcome or at least relax that obstacle. And we just noted that the reformists' programme was the product of serious and wide discussions, and included also proposals that could appeal to the enlightened interest of many of their eventual opponents. So why did the decade-long debate on the reforms not lead them to revise their worldviews and preferences?

One reason is that neither the reformists, the conservatives, nor the Communists were sufficiently aware that the forces of convergence were beginning to wane and that a fresh compact among capital, labour, and the state would soon be needed to give the country a more sustainable growth model. High long-term growth rates were commonly expected, as we said, and the growing need for institutions more appropriate to the stage of development that the country had reached was not sufficiently widely appreciated: thus neither of the two large poles at least one of which the reformists had to persuade, conservatives and Communists, looked much beyond their immediate self-interest or pre-existing ideological postulates, and the debate on the reforms mostly took the form of a non-cooperative struggle (see Barca 1997; Favretto 2015). The failure of the proposal for an incomes policy, which deprived Italy of a cooperative system of industrial relations comparable to those of Germany and Japan (Boltho 2013), appears indicative. Entrepreneurs preferred to slow down investment and regain the bargaining power that they had 'ruthlessly' exploited against labour during the 1950s; the Communists and the trade unions remained prey of their 'weak' reform culture (Magnani 1997; Crafts and Magnani 2013, 79–82), and counted rather on a reversal of fortunes in the balance of power between workers and employers. Lacking a correct, and therefore also broadly common analysis of the challenge that the Italian economy then faced, neither side had reason to revise its worldviews and reassess its preferences and interests.

The second reason is that the force of innovative ideas is greater where collective decisions are taken in open, reasoned, public discussion, and the political institutions we described in Chapter 6 were far from guaranteeing such conditions. The *political* debate on the reforms was quite unlike the *policy* debate that prepared their articulation. To illustrate the forms that it took under Italy's weak institutions we turn to the events that surrounded the formation of the second centre-left cabinet, in July 1964.

The first, led by Moro, had fallen on a peripheral question, and he prepared to resume the premiership. In the wider public arena the debate revolved mostly around a reform of land-use and urban-planning policy, which was intended to redistribute the vast rents[5] appropriated by landowners and real-estate developers (Oliva 1997), stem the degradation[6] of Italy's cities and landscapes (Benevolo 2012), and fight illegal construction (Berdini 2010). Relying on the *Corriere* and other newspapers, conservatives painted this reform as a 'second nationalization' and a threat also for the property rights of the middle classes (Ginsborg 1990, 271 *passim*). The President of the Republic—Segni, the DC landowner who as agriculture minister in 1946–8 contributed to bringing the southern peasants' collective action to an end—resolutely opposed the reform, and wrote arguably inappropriate letters to Moro against it (reproduced in Franzinelli and Giacone 2013).

The conservatives' aim was to block or empty it, weaken the rest of the reformists' programme, and avert the risk that the PSI would leave the coalition and rejoin a strengthened PCI in opposition, reawakening spectres that had been laid to rest in 1948. This meant persuading the Socialists to accept a watered-down programme for the new government. They accepted. One reason for their choice was a grave threat to the constitutional order.

While the talks were on-going, in mid July the main protagonists became aware that in consultation with President Segni the commander of the militarized police force, the Carabinieri, readied to launch a coup d'état. This was unveiled only two years later, in 1966–7, by investigative journalists. Yet already then, in articles published on the party's newspaper, the Socialist leader explained that what had led them to accept the pallid programme of Moro's new executive was the threat of an authoritarian turn. 'All of a sudden', he wrote on 26 July, political parties and the parliament realized that they could be 'overcome', 'swept aside' ('scavalcati': reproduced in Franzinelli and Giacone 2013, 601). Writing in his diary, ten days earlier he had drawn a

---

[5] Notably, construction is the subsector that recorded the lowest productivity growth during the Golden Age (0.5 per cent per year: Broadberry et al. 2013, 195): those rents can therefore be assumed to have represented a relatively large share of profits in the broader real-estate business.

[6] A degradation narrated by Calvino in his novel *La speculazione edilizia*, written in 1956–7, and shown, cruelly, by Francesco Rosi's 1963 film on Naples, *Le mani sulla città*.

parallel with the situation of September–October 1922 (p. 550), when conservatives and the Crown pondered the fascist solution.

What emerged about the plan suggests that it was serious, well rehearsed, and similar to that of the Greek coup of 1967, which was successful (Ferraresi 1996, 78; Franzinelli 2014). Code-named 'Piano Solo', it foresaw the takeover of government and party offices and media and telecommunications installations throughout the country and the deportation of 731 likely opponents.[7] Both Washington and Confindustria were informed. Unlike the former, the latter appears to have encouraged the plan (Ferraresi 1996, 80, note 22; Franzinelli 2014).

Yet there was no baroque lightning or thunder but just 'sabre rattling', as the Socialist leader put it in his memoirs (quoted by Favretto 2015, 278). The reasons why Piano Solo was not activated are not well established (see Franzinelli 2014). On 1 July 1960 the overwhelming popular response to a grave political provocation in Genoa by the neo-fascist party—encouraged by the formation, that spring, of the first and only (until 1994) government relying on their votes—saw the demonstrators effectively in control of the city, spread to other cities, and led the DC to hurriedly change the cabinet and, as we said, abandon that political formula (Ginsborg 1990, 256–8). In this Genoa and the other industrial cities of the North were not fully representative of the country, arguably: but the strength and the width of anti-fascist sentiment that those events revealed suggests that a coup d'état would have met stiff resistance. The plotters anyway appear to have viewed it as an *extrema ratio* (Franzinelli 2014), and may well have judged—correctly, in hindsight— that sabre rattling was sufficient.

What matters from our perspective is that the threat certainly helped the wider conservative front achieve its political objective (Ferraresi 1996, 74–83; Gotor 2011, 510–13; Franzinelli 2014; Favretto 2015, 278). It was not decisive, most probably, because the reasons we already discussed seem sufficient to explain the failure of the reform programme. But the consequences were broader, because not even after it was unveiled was Piano Solo officially condemned—on the contrary, state secrecy was invoked to minimize disclosure—or the plotters punished. The latent threat of the use of large-scale violence by organs of the state thus persisted, casting its shadow on political life. Italy was never inflicted a coup, of course, but one reason may well be that both opposition and ruling parties adjusted their strategies to the threat.[8]

---

[7] The list might be incomplete; another 157,000 personal files were also available, covering the whole spectrum of society, illegally collected by the intelligence service in previous years, often updating Fascist-period files (Ferraresi 1996, 76).

[8] Commissione parlamentare (1984, 100) and Ferraresi (1996, 121–3) make a similar argument in respect of a later—and apparently less serious—coup, that which was launched and almost immediately called off in the night of 7 December 1970.

The government that in 1967–8 invoked state secrecy on Piano Solo was led by Moro, arguably a political victim of the coup, probably instrumental in averting it, and certainly opposed by Segni, possibly the main culprit (Franzinelli 2014). Yet the two were part of the same party and the same dominant coalition, and in those years Moro acted in a highly polarized electoral democracy with weak institutions and escalating social tensions: exposing a plot led by the head of state and the head of the Carabinieri—erstwhile head of the military secret services, and, one year after the coup, promoted army head by the very Moro government that had been formed in July 1964—posed considerable risks to political stability and the DC's own hold on power. Moro's personal integrity is widely recognized, as is the orientation of his main choices towards the strengthening of Italy's democracy (e.g., Bernardi 2015). Yet in those circumstances he acted fully within the logic of the extant social order. As we suggested in Chapter 4, drawing on Hoff and Stiglitz (2008), where the rule of law is weak elites' political crime typically cannot be punished, which in turn perpetuates the weakness of the rule of law: and this logic is so cogent that even one of the most far-sighted politicians of his generation bowed to it.

Indeed, after these facts 'the Intelligence Service became a prime *political* actor, one that would not shy before illegal, even criminal actions in order to foster its own or its associates' political ends' (Ferraresi 1996, 82). As Cento Bull (2015, 659) writes, in fact, a convincing interpretation of at least the first phase of the wave of extreme-right terrorism that began in 1969

> postulates that neo-fascist groups started to theorize the need for organized violence as a prelude to [Piano Solo, and later as] part of a wider 'Strategy of Tension', devised in collaboration with sectors of the army, the secret services, and Freemasonry, and possibly backed by international forces opposed to the formation of center-left governments in Italy after 1963 and fearful of the social movements of the late 1960s [which aimed at] curbing the activities of [such] movements and/or sending a clear warning to the [PCI].

Set off by a hardly radical reform of land-use and town-planning policy, the events of the summer of 1964 show how wide the gap separating Italy's formal institutions from its actual ones was. Disfigured by five more decades of ill-regulated construction (Benevolo 2012), many of the peninsula's coasts, valleys, and cities silently bespeak that.

The Political Influence of Organized Crime

Before resuming our narration, we pause briefly on the evolution of organized crime during the first two decades after the war. Even though the authorities still tended to deny its danger or even its existence, during those years the Sicilian mafia adapted itself to the development of the country and grew in influence (Lupo [1996] 2009; Paoli 2015). It became more urbanized, and employed its military power to draw profits also from construction and real-estate development. Of the two DC politicians who alternated each other as mayor and public works secretary of Palermo over the 1954–64 decade, while the city was defaced, one was a member of the mafia and the other appeared very close to it (Lupo [1996] 2009, 15–16, 214, and 258–62; Ginsborg 2001, 203–5; Paoli 2015, 673). The latter in 1968 became Andreotti's informal representative in Sicily, and acted in this capacity for the whole period, up to 1980, in respect of which his mentor was found guilty of abetting the mafia. Unlike Andreotti he was not tried, because the organization killed him, in 1992, most probably for having failed to honour his commitments (Lupo [1996] 2009, 261–2). This is precisely the comment—'[w]hen agreements are struck they have to be kept'—he had made in 1980 about another prominent Sicilian Christian Democrat killed by the mafia (quoted by Ginsborg 2001, 206).

It is well established that organized crime at the same time exploits democratic freedoms and, by its actions, 'mortifies' them (Allum and Siebert 2003, 5), and that the trait that most distinguishes organizations such as the Sicilian mafia from other forms of crime is their ability to employ violence to control parts of the national territory and thereby influence also politics, at both the local and the central level (e.g., Armao 2003). We have mentioned the mafia's links with high politics in the liberal epoch, as well as the reluctance of Fascism to sever those ties. The proximity between the mafia and segments of the DC and other conservative parties during the republican period is equally well documented (e.g., Paoli 2015). Recent empirical research has brought quantitative evidence in support of this analysis, which assists us in placing organized crime within the picture we are drawing.

De Feo and De Luca (2013) document the mafia's ability to use territorial control to orient the political choices of citizens. They examine the results of all national elections in the 1946–92 period, and find that in the Sicilian municipalities where, based on police data, the mafia's presence was strongest, support for the DC was distinctly higher than in other municipalities, especially at times when the party was most exposed to the electoral competition of the PCI. In particular, they find (p. 28) that between 1958 and 1983, when the Communists' share of the vote edged progressively closer to that of the Christian Democrats, 'a drop of the gap between DC and PCI in the rest of Italy by one percentage point implies an average increase of DC vote share by almost 0.8 percentage points' in the municipalities most infested by the mafia: when the reduction of that gap was largest (17 percentage points), 'the presence of the mafia increased the share of the votes gained by the DC by about 13 percentage points on average'. The mafia's support for the DC, never estimated before, thus appears to have been quite valuable. In line with much historiographical literature, moreover, De Feo and De Luca (2013, 5) provide econometric evidence suggesting that in exchange for those votes the mafia received support in expanding its activities in the construction sector.

Alesina et al. (2016) address the related question of how the mafia influenced politics. They examine the frequency of political homicides in Sicily during the 1945–2013 period, and measure it against both the electoral results and the frequency with which parliamentarians elected in the island mentioned the mafia in their parliamentary speeches. First, they note (pp. 2–3) that political homicides were abnormally high during the twelve months before and after each election (respectively, three and two times higher than the average number of political homicides per month), and they find that rises of political violence were correlated with declines in the electoral support for the DC's left-wing adversaries: 'an additional homicide during the electoral period brings, on average, a 3 percentage point decrease in the vote share of the Left'. Second, they note that left-wing Sicilian parliamentarians were twice as likely to mention the mafia in their speeches than their colleagues of other parties (which suggests that this variable indirectly indicates pressure for fighting organize crime: indeed, as we just said, in the 1950s and 1960s the authorities were often loth to even acknowledge its existence). Alesina et al. (2016) then measure the two sets of data against each other, and estimate (p. 3) that 'one additional political homicide during the electoral period lowers the probability that a given MP appointed in Sicily mentions the Mafia at least once over the following legislature by 4 percentage points—on a baseline probability of 10 percent'. Political violence thus appears to have allowed the mafia to both strengthen its political allies and protect itself, by favouring the election of politicians who lack either attention for its activities or the will to oppose them.

Next to political clientelism and the collusion between public powers and private interests, therefore, also this other component of the spiral sketched in Chapter 4 was already present during the 1950s and 1960s. Like them, also organized crime adapted itself to the conditions of those years, marked by rapid growth and urbanization and acute political polarization. Growth and urbanization offered profit opportunities, which were largely dependent on the benevolence of public power, however; polarization added to the reasons that since the turn of the nineteenth century had brought politics and the mafia close to each other. The conditions were therefore present for these ties to continue, as in exchange for tolerance for its own criminal and business activities the mafia could offer valuable electoral support and political violence. The effects of the exchange made it self-reinforcing, moreover, for two main reasons. First, it provided rising gains to both sides and exposed each to the blackmail of the other, such that neither side could sever those ties without risking adverse consequences (loss of turnover, for the mafia, and retribution for the politician). Second, the mafia's electoral support and political violence served the same function as clientelism, corporatist and individual, namely to increase the votes of the DC and its allies and lower their political accountability: the political benefits that the latter drew from the exchange indirectly insulated it from the pressure of society's demands, therefore, and thus offset, at least in part, the electoral and reputational cost of being perceived as close to the mafia or tolerant towards it.

For similar reasons the mafia also established links with segments of the economic elites of the island or active there (Paoli 2015), which in turn were closely tied to the political elites. This further increased the mafia's entrenchment in society and the difficulty of fighting it (La Spina 2014).

It is from this perspective that we shall henceforth look at the mafia, as well as from that of its ability to serve as the enforcer of illegal pacts, such as cartels and corruption (Gambetta 1993; Lodato and Scarpinato 2008; Varese 2014). We shall leave its commoner sources of profits aside, conversely, such as smuggling or drug trafficking, except to note their geographical expansion. We shall neglect also the criminal organizations rooted in Campania and Calabria, camorra and 'ndrangheta (on which quantitative research such as that we just cited is lacking, incidentally). The three differ in both structure and historical evolution, and the mafia, more organized and centralized, cannot be taken as fully representative of Italian organized crime. Yet what we just said about it is in large degree valid also for the other two. In particular, also the Neapolitan camorra—more fluid and less centralized than either the mafia or the (contemporary) 'ndrangheta—is judged to have had links with politics already in the period we are now discussing (Paoli 2015).

8

Continuity and Instability: The Spiral Sets In

Social Tensions, Macroeconomic Instability, Political Violence, and Selective Inclusion – A Decline in Political Polarization and the Evolution of the PCI – A 'Metastasis of the Institutions' and a Revelation of Their Distortions – Counterpoises: 'Democratic Citizens', the Judiciary, the Bank of Italy

Social Tensions, Macroeconomic Instability, Political Violence, and Selective Inclusion

Between the Economic Miracle and the Outburst of Tension

In the second half of the 1960s growth was sustained but slower than during the economic miracle, as Table 8.1 shows, due also to the declining impetus of structural change. While the agony of the reform programme unfolded, the Socialists were absorbed into the governing majority. They gradually began to partake in the nepotism that plagued the public administration and began to touch also the autonomous agencies. The disequilibria and social demands that had motivated the reformists' programme persisted, however, and the Communist opposition strengthened.

After the monetary tightening of 1963 firms responded relatively weakly to the opportunities offered by re-established wage moderation and macroeconomic stability. Convergence progressed, as Table 8.1 shows, but compared to the previous years private investment decelerated, as we saw, and the contribution of TFP to aggregate growth marginally declined: in these years labour productivity growth derived in large measure from the rationalization of the production process, after a decade of very fast accumulation of fixed capital (Broadberry et al. 2013; Crafts and Magnani 2013). And although foreign technology continued to spread through imitation, reverse engineering, and adaptation, and the steep rise of investment in R&D proceeded without discontinuity, its level as a share of GDP—0.6 per cent on average—remained comparatively

Table 8.1 Selected Macroeconomic Indicators, 1964–1979

Year	GDP Growth[a]	Per-Capita GDP Growth[a]	Total Investment (% GDP)[a]	Labour Productivity Growth[a]	TFP Growth[a]	Inflation (CPI)[b]	Debt-to-GDP Ratio[c]
1964	2.7	1.9	27.3	3.4	0.7	5.9	27.2
1965	3.3	2.6	24.6	8.9	4.6	4.5	28.4
1966	6.0	5.3	24.3	6.8	4.2	2.3	33.4
1967	7.1	6.4	25.1	4.5	3.0	3.7	33.3
1968	6.6	6.0	24.6	7.0	4.3	1.3	35.8
1969	6.0	5.4	26.1	6.9	3.8	2.7	36.5
1970	12.6	11.8	31.5	13.2	9.0	5.0	37.1
1971	1.8	1.1	28.6	4.4	−0.1	4.8	41.9
1972	3.7	3.0	28.1	4.9	1.1	5.7	47.7
1973	7.1	6.4	30.2	6.6	3.4	10.8	50.6
1974	5.5	4.8	31.9	5.7	2.4	19.2	50.2
1975	−2.1	−2.6	25.4	−1.3	−4.1	16.9	56.6
1976	7.1	6.6	27.6	6.2	3.9	16.6	56.2
1977	2.6	2.1	25.0	4.1	1.0	17.1	55.2
1978	3.2	2.9	24.3	3.4	1.0	12.1	59.4
1979	6.0	5.6	25.0	5.0	3.0	14.8	58.2

Note: [a] Source: Penn World Table. [b] Source: OECD. [c] Source: IMF.

low, as we said: two thirds less than in Germany, where R&D expenditure grew at an even higher rate (Barbiellini Amidei et al. 2013, fig. 14.13; Boltho 2013). Industrialization continued apace, nonetheless, the country's share in the world trade in manufactures rose steadily, and until 1972 the economy generated current account surpluses close, on average, to 2 per cent of GDP (Ciocca 2007, 261).

But besides products Italy was also exporting capital and workers, pushed abroad by the deceleration of investment and the rise of unemployment. Such drainage of resources that could have been used to develop the country was without logic, Carli argues, who blames it on the economic elites' defence of their *peculio*, their 'stuff' (1996, 304–6). The interpretation we advanced earlier is consistent with his. What is worth adding is that to a large extent this defensive strategy—containing investment, to regain bargaining power with labour, and exporting the resulting excess savings—was made possible by gains in labour productivity achieved through higher rates of utilization of the installed capacity and more intensive work schedules (Barca 1997; Crafts and Magnani 2013). In other words, having successfully defended the extant allocation of power from the challenges of 1962–4, the economic elites coherently exploited it by raising the effort demanded of the workforce, which then still enjoyed relatively weak individual and collective protections (Vesan 2015). This equilibrium, at once offspring and buttress of the country's social order, broke down at the end of the decade, when long-accumulated demands and unmet needs found an outlet.

Italy's Long 1968 and its Aftermath

In Italy student demonstrations began well before May 1968. The literature identifies a 'cycle of protest', which ran from the mid 1960s to the mid 1970s (Tarrow 1989; Della Porta 2015). One of its manifestos was a book published in 1967 by the priest and educator Lorenzo Milani, *Letter to a Teacher*, which denounced the persisting classism of the education system—despite the progressive reform of 1962 (Bertola and Sestito 2013, 255–6)—and called for political participation. From the schools and the universities, the agitation against what was perceived as an archaic and authoritarian organization of society spread widely and fused with long-breeding discontent among workers, especially in the North-West. It drew also on Italy's peculiar tradition of revolutionary Marxism, which had flourished in 'a people of the most vivid imagination, idealistic yearnings and unconsoled injuries' (Drake 2003, ix)—injuries dating as far back as the Fascist violence of 1921–2, or even the courts martial of the Great War, which conservatives left unhealed after their victory in 1964.

Workers' mobilization 'assumed much more radical and ideologically charged forms than those traditionally envisaged by the unions', and often overstepped them (Regini 2015, 530). It reached its peak in the autumn of 1969, Italy's 'hot autumn', when it took an intensity unseen since the red years of 1919–20, and remained high during much of the 1970s. The drastic shift in bargaining power from capital to labour caused 'a huge and persistent wage shock' (Crafts and Magnani 2013, 82).

France, Germany, and the wider Western world witnessed similar phenomena in those years. But Italy's were comparatively severe. In particular, Boltho (2013, 115 and table 4.5) remarks that in Germany, where industrial relations were governed by institutions promoting cooperative bargaining, 'wage increases were not accompanied by the wave of strikes that were an integral part of [Italy's hot autumn], nor did they bring about lasting changes in labor market regulation': in 1969–70 Italy lost about 170 times more working days per employee than Germany did (table 4.5), in fact, and in 1970 it passed a relatively rigid law on the protection of workers' rights and union activity in the workplace.

So the Italian economy had already been weakened when the end of the Bretton Woods system and the first oil shock lowered growth and raised instability throughout the Western world, in 1971–3. Equally, the country's comparatively high inflation rates throughout the 1970s reflect also the eminently domestic causes of the greater difficulties that it faced in adjusting to the changed international environment.

These internal and external dislocations were compounded by the epidemic of political violence that began in 1969, arguably the worst in Western Europe for either intensity or duration, separatist struggles aside. The last significant episode dates back from 1987. Until then 491 deaths, 1,181 injuries, and 14,591 politically motivated acts of violence on persons or property have been counted (Cento Bull and Cooke 2013, 13).

In the afternoon of 12 December 1969 a bomb exploded in the main hall of a bank in the centre of Milan, within sight of the flèche of the cathedral. It killed seventeen people and wounded eighty-eight: mostly farmers, as the bank specialized in that sector. The head of the Milan police—who during the Fascist regime commanded the confinement centre for political prisoners on the island of Ventotene[1]—immediately blamed the anarchists (Ginsborg 1990, 333). The *Corriere* and most other media embraced this interpretation. It seemed implausible, though, and harmed the credibility of the authorities. It stood in stark contrast to the display of civic fortitude during the funerals, in the cathedral and the vast square before it, entirely full.[2] The courts eventually established that the bomb was a false-flag operation, planted by neo-fascists who for years benefited from the assistance of members of the secret services to evade justice (Ferraresi 1996; Cento Bull 2015); in 2005 the material perpetrators were conclusively identified, even though they could not be convicted because they had been acquitted in an earlier trial (Cento Bull and Cooke 2013, 2–3). Preceded by a few lesser episodes, this bombing marked the beginning of the strategy of tension we already mentioned. It aimed, at the very least, at preventing the cycle of protest that began two years earlier from pushing the political equilibrium towards the left, and it lasted until 1974 (later bombing attacks seem to belong less to that strategy than to straightforward extreme-right terrorism: Cento Bull 2015). It marked also its peak, though. At the funeral citizens filled the square to stand as guardians also of the constitution, before authorities whose republican loyalty was not beyond doubt (the public cover-up of Piano Solo had taken place a mere two years before). They were protected by a thick cordon of blue-collar workers, in turn, who had walked to the city in their thousands from the northern industrial suburbs. This response, akin in spirit to Genoa's in July 1960, is likely to have been read also as a signal of the limitations of the strategy of inducing political moderation by way of provoking fear.

One year later a coup d'état was launched, by other neo-fascists, but suddenly stopped. Preparations for two other ones emerged, in 1973 and 1974. Based on what has emerged about them, none was as serious as that of 1964 nor benefited from comparably high political support. Yet both involved

---

[1] There two inmates, Altiero Spinelli and Ernesto Rossi, in 1941 wrote (on cigarette paper) their celebrated manifesto for a federal Europe.

[2] We owe these impressions to Corrado Stajano, then present, and to a documentary he co-authored (*La forza della democrazia*, 1977).

segments of the army and the secret services, like the strategy of tension, and probably aimed at similar purposes (Ferraresi 1996, ch. 6; Cento Bull 2015). This is the conclusion also of the widely respected report (Commissione parlamentare 1984, ch. III.2) of a parliamentary inquiry on the masonic lodge Propaganda 2 (P2), which during the second half of the 1970s grew into 'one of the most secretive, sinister, and all encompassing power centers in the country' (Ferraresi 1996, 120). Among the members of this organization, on which we shall soon return, were fifty army and police generals, the heads of Italy's three intelligence services, and several security agents involved or credibly implicated in those coups, in the strategy of tension, and in several episodes of neo-fascist terrorism (including the bombing attacks of 1974–84, which killed more than 100 citizens).

The third component of this wave of violence, better-known and longer-lasting, is left-wing terrorism, exemplified by the Red Brigades that in 1978 kidnapped Moro, still a chief protagonist of political life, held him for seven weeks, and killed him. Unlike the extreme-right one, this form of terrorism targeted individual victims: business managers, public officials, journalists. Often progressive ones, perversely, whom their murderers viewed as the humane face of the 'system' on which they had declared war. The acutest phase of red terrorism was 1977–80. A convincing interpretation (see Cento Bull 2015) links its origins to the cycle of protest that began in the late 1960s: as it began to wane, circa 1973, street violence escalated, police repression intensified, semi-clandestine extreme-left organizations emerged, and some adopted terrorism as the main form of political struggle. They seeped into Italy's peculiar tradition of revolutionary Marxism (Drake 2003), on which they built the remarkable ideological dogmatism that informs their writings.

In varying degrees, therefore, each component of this epidemic of violence was a response to the challenges brought about by the vast social and labour movements that rose against the unequal and illiberal traits of the country's social order. Although stemming from often diverging strategies, equally, each of these three strands of violence had the effect of constraining the political space available to those movements and diverting civic activism from the critique of the status quo to the defence of the republic. This, indeed, appears to have been one objective of both the strategy of tension and some instances of wilful negligence by the authorities in confronting the terrorist threat, red and black.[3]

---

[3] These points are not fully settled in the literature, which often laments the limitations of the available primary sources: see Cento Bull (2015). Significant uncertainties remain also on Moro's kidnapping and murder (e.g., Gotor 2011).

Policies of Particularistic Inclusion

Having eschewed reform, the political elites responded to the challenges of the 1970s with a policy that Toniolo (2013b, 24) describes as 'a series of off-the-cuff measures...adopted to expand welfare provisions and provide indiscriminate subsidies to firms'. The rise of social expenditure was particularly fast—from 17.4 to 22.6 per cent of GDP, a level higher than Britain's and close to France's (Ferrera and Jessoula 2015, 506)—between 1970 and 1975, when social conflict was most acute. To finance it, however, the governments of this period abandoned the orthodox stance of the preceding decades and resorted to issuing debt and monetizing much of it: they found it 'politically more viable to let public debt, inflation, and the fiscal drag do the job of finding a new though unstable macroeconomic equilibrium' (Crafts and Magnani 2013, 89). With fiscal pressure roughly constant—a tax reform adopted in 1973–4 did eventually raise revenue, but was undermined by persisting tax evasion—public debt grew far higher and faster than in Italy's peers, as Figures 8.1 and 8.2 show.

Again, the rationale of this response can better be gauged from the distortions it induced in Italy's welfare state (Ferrera et al. 2012). With the major exception of the establishment of a national and universalistic health service, which in 1978 replaced a plethora of separate professional insurance funds, both 'original sins' of the welfare system aggravated. Its functional emphasis on pensions grew: reforms passed in 1968–9 under the pressure of the vast workers' mobilization mentioned earlier provided for a high replacement rate and very generous eligibility requirements, which contributed to 'an astonishingly high implicit tax on working after the age of 60' and correspondingly high levels of inactivity

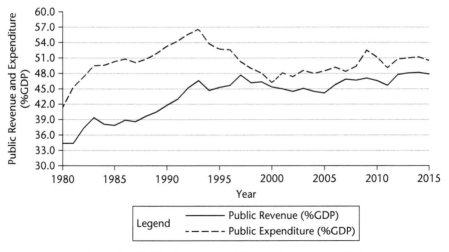

Figure 8.1 Public Revenue and Expenditure, 1980–2015
Source: ISTAT time series

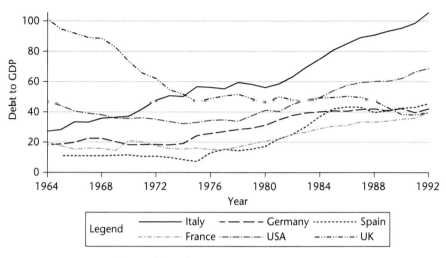

Figure 8.2 Debt-to-GDP Ratio, 1964–1992
Source: IMF

among those aged fifty-five or more (Crafts and Magnani 2013, 84). And the 'distributive distortion' of the social insurance system deepened, mainly along the 'cleavage [that] opposed workers located in the core sectors of the (industrial) labor market [and] those located in the more peripheral sectors (semi-regular and unemployed)' (Ferrera and Jessoula 2015, 507). The logic of group-level clientelistic co-option that informed these choices was particularly visible in the public sector. In sum, after the proposals for universalistic reform advanced in 1962–4 were defeated, the trend of particularistic inclusion that began in the late 1950s continued: the only real difference with the policies of those quieter times is one of scale.

Besides the more general inefficiency of the public administration, moreover, the execution of welfare policies suffered also from a particularly low level of 'legality' (Ferrera and Jessoula 2015, 508):

> [e]specially in some sectors and areas, the degree of compliance with the rules disciplining the access to benefits and the payment of contributions remained very low, not only on the side of the various clienteles of social programs, but also on the side of public authorities. This syndrome assumed inordinate proportions in the sector of disability pensions, which became the privileged currency of an extended clientelistic market: between 1960 and 1980 the total number of disability pensions rose almost five times, and in 1974 (following an expansive reform) it came to surpass the total number of old age pensions—an unparalleled record in the [OECD] area.

The same 'clientelistic', 'micro-distributive' logic also informed labour market policies (Vesan 2015, 491): '[m]easures such as public works, unemployment benefits, or employment incentives [were] often... diverted by political parties in order to gain consensus at a national or local level'.

In its broad outline the response of Italy's political elites seems clear. They set aside the universalistic aspirations of the 1962–4 reformist programme. With the support or acquiescence of the economic elites, they sought to make the social order more inclusive, and therefore more resilient, but did so by co-opting more social groups into it, albeit in the lower ranks: rather than enhancing the equal protection and opportunities of all citizens, as society increasingly demanded, they preferred to acquire much-needed consensus by exchanging it with selective privileges and protections. During the 1950s and 1960s these had been granted to the core of the DC's and its allies' electorate. After 1968 they were extended to more and wider categories, including those that had taken to the streets: the employees of the main industrial sectors, most notably, among whom the left and labour militancy had their base. The weakness of the rule of law then affected the implementation of these policies and widened the scope for political clientelism, exemplified by those spurious disability pensions.

This policy permeated also the regional layer of government, established in 1970. Except in the 'red' regions of the Centre, where the Communists won power and often proved to be as competent administrators as their mayors had generally been, the regions' elected and administrative authorities replicated the practices of the central ones and largely debased their own autonomy, which was the rationale for their creation (Putnam 1993; Cotta 2015; Piattoni 2015). The regions' spending powers, chiefly in the health care and social assistance sectors, were governed by fiscal arrangements that favoured irresponsibility, moreover, as their budgets were funded disproportionately by transfers from the centre. And fiscal irresponsibility further fuelled clientelism, in both its minute, often illegal forms and its large-scale ones, targeted to whole cities or provinces.

Again, particularistic policy nurtured particularistic demands. The mass protests or even riots that erupted in a dozen towns and cities of the South between 1969 and 1974 illustrate the dynamic well, as they were sparked by either unmet demands or the perception that the clientelistic exchange was unfair, or had been broken (Ginsborg 1990, 338–40). The worst revolt was Reggio Calabria's, in 1970–71, motivated by the decision to place the headquarters of the regional government in another city. Led by the DC mayor and neo-fascist agitators, it was a genuine rebellion, which lasted for months and was quelled not by the army—which repeatedly deployed tanks to break the barricades, and suffered several casualties—but by Rome's promise to place in the city some offices of the regional government, and to have IRI build a large steel mill nearby.

IRI's Decline and the Response of the Private Sector
to the Challenges of the 1970s

IRI's managers were opposed to this decision (Ciocca 2014, 223). It was taken because by then the agency had lost the autonomy it enjoyed during the economic miracle. The governments of the 1970s increasingly used it and the Cassa del Mezzogiorno as instruments for the policy of particularistic inclusion that we have just described, harming both their efficiency in allocating resources and their broader contribution to the country's development (Barca and Trento 1997; Crafts and Magnani 2013; Ciocca 2014). In their disorderly effort to acquire partisan consensus and, at once, buttress the equilibrium that social tensions were threatening, the political elites effectively sacrificed two agencies that had proven decisive in developing the country.

The special development policy for the South thus relied increasingly less on capital investment and more on current transfers to firms and households, often mediated by local politicians, and gradually lost its character of 'additionality'; in parallel, the Cassa del Mezzogiorno was pervaded by clientelistic practices (Cannari et al. 2010; Felice 2013; Iuzzolino et al. 2013; Davis 2015). The convergence of the South came to an end, circa 1973, and has not resumed since (Trigilia 2012; Crafts and Magnani 2013; Toniolo 2013b).

Mirror-like, IRI lowered its investments in the capital-intensive and high-technology sectors it dominated, and diverted growing financial resources to more labour-intensive sectors, politically driven investments, and the rescue of failing inefficient private firms (often merely to preserve employment, and sometimes bailing out shareholders at inflated prices): its role as a channel for the diffusion of technological and organizational innovation declined and aggregate investment in high-technology sectors—in which IRI's weight was disproportionate to its share of manufacturing output—decelerated (Barca and Trento 1997; Ciocca 2014). IRI's firms and ENI's too became increasingly vulnerable to clientelism, both large-scale and minute.

We turn, finally, to the private sector's response to the challenges of this decade. The broader background is characterized, as we said, by the progressively diminishing potential for catch-up growth, the decline of Fordism, and a markedly more challenging international environment compared to the Golden Age. Italy's economic institutions were effectively unchanged, moreover. If they had successfully presided over an epochal wave of structural change, they were increasingly less appropriate to the growing needs of resource reallocation and creative destruction within the manufacturing and services sectors: the reason, predicted by the logic explored in Chapters 2 and 3, is that by limiting *political* creative destruction Italy's political institutions had impeded the reform of the economic ones too, most notably in 1962–4, and had thereby constrained the country's growth potential. In this context, Ciocca (2007, 303) writes that although the rise of costs had reduced the private sector's profits

> reallocation was delayed, also by those manufacturing firms which were exposed to international competition. The shifting of resources towards innovative productions, research and development, and human capital was slow in both large and small firms. Profitability was at least in part regained, but through routes other than the virtuous strategy of labour and especially capital mobility: namely, through state subsidies, tax avoidance and evasion, the decentralization of production towards smaller firms, economic informality and illegal labour, collusion among producers and other restrictive practices, support from friendly banks, often mediated by politics. The last defence of profits was inflation. The loss of competitiveness was circumscribed through currency devaluation.

The only trait that we would add to this picture concerns innovation (Barbiellini Amidei et al. 2013, figs. 14.9, 14.12, and 14.13). During the 1970s imports of foreign disembodied technology essentially stagnated and investment in R&D—which had risen very rapidly throughout the Golden Age, as we said—dropped, if marginally. In Germany and Japan—where they had risen even faster—they merely decelerated, conversely. This, arguably, is the clearest sign that the reaction of Italy's private sector was an eminently defensive one: certainly induced by the severity of the domestic challenges, but probably counselled also by collusion with the political power—on which more later—and the incentives discussed in Chapter 4.

Competitive pressures on firms remained relatively low (Gigliobianco and Toniolo 2017), and their macroeconomic determinants weakened, in a dynamic perspective (Ciocca 2007). Average firm size declined, more than in Italy's peers, and both TFP and labour productivity growth decelerated: not just in the services sector—where productivity 'collapsed', as we said, if heterogeneously across subsectors (Broadberry et al. 2013, 195)—but also among the larger firms that had driven the rapid rise of productivity during the Golden Age (Crafts and Magnani 2013).

Industrial Districts

Increasingly, growth was sustained by agglomerations of micro, small and medium-sized enterprises organized into a growing number of 'industrial districts' (Arrighetti and Seravalli 1997; Brusco and Paba 1997; de Cecco 2013, 152–3). This production arrangement was based on the horizontal informal integration of numerous firms, allowing a high degree of flexibility, and it combined efficient cooperation with vigorous competition. Later identified as 'one of the most peculiar and successful Italian institutions'

(Toniolo 2013b, 22), districts generally specialized in one or a small set of traditional or medium-technology products, and showed high export capacity. They recorded high growth rates throughout the 1980s, hence suffered increasingly stiff competition from emerging markets, but nonetheless generated many of contemporary Italy's most successful and celebrated firms, including its so-called 'pocket multinationals' (Amatori et al. 2013, 480 *passim*; Giunta and Rossi 2017).

From our perspective industrial districts are interesting mostly for the comparison they suggest with the rest of the private sector, and especially with larger firms. For districts critically relied on eminently informal and localized institutions (Arrighetti and Seravalli 1997). Besides widespread regulatory and tax evasion, they relied on generalized inter-personal trust of comparatively high intensity but limited geographical radius, often relying on long local traditions of social cohesion (Brusco and Paba 1997), which effectively allowed the component firms to insulate themselves from the inefficiency of the 'national' institutions. And they relied also on the support of the local authorities, which in most cases were the comparatively efficient and accountable ones of north-eastern and especially central Italy (Putnam 1993).

Districts thus informally built and exploited at the local level some of the efficient institutions that lacked at the national level. They flourished not thanks to the country's economic institutions but largely despite them. Their success, in other words, demonstrates how under Italy's weak *political* institutions the solution to the problems posed by inadequate regulation often was not reform but private contravention and public tolerance.[4] A pragmatic and often effective solution in the short term, but a precarious and particularistic one, which segmented society and dampened the demand for reform and political accountability.

Collusion and Corruption

More relevant from our perspective was the evolution of large firms, which then were and thereafter remained of systemic importance (e.g., Toniolo 2013b, 30). In the 1970s their defensive response closely mirrored that of those same political elites whose support they sought and plentifully obtained. This also reflected an objective convergence of interests, as firms could leverage on the government's reluctance to see redundancies rise in a period of acute social tension, and on its readiness to delay or cushion

---

[4] In 1996 the author worked on a plan to float the lead firm of a North-Eastern district on the stock exchange. It was abandoned because the organization of production—mostly outsourced to dozens of small workers' cooperatives—was incompatible with the labour laws, then arguably too rigid, and could not be changed without severely reducing the firm's (and, in part, the district's) flexibility and profitability.

them—in the absence of universalistic remedies—through state-funded income-support schemes. But collusion deepened. As Berta (2015, 479–80) writes, in this period 'the marriage of convenience between the system of government and Italian big business . . . was heavily relied upon, with a steep increase of state aid to industry . . . In this respect the trajectory of Fiat is emblematic [for the benefits it drew] from its links with politics and with state institutions.'

Besides lowering the incentives for the reallocation of capital and labour, this policy is also likely to have raised the rewards of rent-seeking relative to those of productive entrepreneurship (see Baumol 1990; Acemoglu 1995). Concretely, the ability to attract subsidies or persuade IRI to rescue one's firm probably rose in value relative to the capacity to face the challenges of those years through technological and organizational innovation.

That marriage of convenience had a hidden face, moreover. Clear light was first shed on it in 1974, and provoked scandal. In Genoa three magistrates found that oil companies, domestic and foreign, had for years paid the governing parties in exchange for favourable regulation. The exchange was systematic: both the level of the payments (often 5 per cent of the gain secured by each legislative or administrative measure) and their distribution (about 50 per cent to the DC, 25 to the PSI, and 25 to the smaller parties) were pre-defined (Crainz 2003, 490–1). In response to the scandal a law providing for the public financing of political parties was hurriedly adopted, to lower their incentive to seek such forms of funding and reduce the economic elites' influence on them. But the law also retroactively downgraded the gravity of the crimes, and the parliamentary committee competent for deciding whether the judiciary could be authorized to try Andreotti and the other five ministers involved eventually denied the request.[5]

One year later a US Senate enquiry unveiled that Lockheed had paid bribes in several Western countries, to sell its airplanes. Three Italian ministers were implicated, two Christian Democrats and one Social Democrat. Moro publicly defended his party, parliament allowed two ministers to be tried, and in 1977 one received a mild sentence.

Another element of the spiral that we are retracing was already in place, therefore, in a form which suggests that its roots were already deep. Indeed, it is then that from the pages of the *Corriere* Pasolini (1975) demanded that *all* Christian Democrat leaders be submitted to a public trial, that which Moro equally famously refused to countenance. Indeed, although the party-financing

[5] This immunity was intended to shield parliamentarians from politically motivated charges. Initially it chiefly protected opposition legislators from charges related to their political activities, but since the early 1970s it protected mostly governing party ones, usually from corruption or economic crime charges (see Chang et al. 2010). Often misused, it was repealed in 1993 (see Chapter 9).

system it introduced was relatively reasonable, the 1974 law will soon prove to have been an ineffective remedy for corruption (Rhodes 2015). Four years later, for example, the oil sector was again shaken by a similar scandal.

A Decline in Political Polarization and the Evolution of the PCI

The second half of the 1970s was marked by a rapprochement between the PCI, increasingly distant from Moscow, and the DC (Hellman 2015). At the 1976 election the Communist vote reached its zenith (34.4 per cent) and its distance from the DC's its nadir (4.3 per cent).[6] The terrorist threat was then at its gravest and macroeconomic instability still high. In this context, both dangerous and favourable, a long-prepared PCI strategy to accept the burden of a coalition with the party representing the Catholic masses—to widen the popular base of the republic and reform it—and Moro's parallel objective of sharing some responsibility of government with the permanent opposition party—to strengthen the state and prepare the ground for future alternations in government, which he viewed as crucial for the maturation of Italy's democracy—came to fruition (Bernardi 2015).

As at the time of the absorption of the Socialists into the governing coalition, in 1962, Moro had to overcome the opposition of the DC's right wing, the Church, and Washington. Like in 1962, the Communists joined the parliamentary majority but not the cabinet. This coalition of 'national solidarity' supported two DC-only executives, in office between August 1976 and March 1979. The delicate balancing that made them possible led the premiership to be entrusted to a representative of the party's conservatives, Andreotti (who was then still abetting the Sicilian mafia, and whose faction was already suspected of entertaining links with it: Varsori 2015, 380). The two cabinets were almost identical. One succeeded the other because the Communists insisted on acceding to ministerial posts: they obtained Andreotti's resignation, sought to reassure Washington, but met its veto (Hellman 2015, 287–8). The confidence vote for the second cabinet was scheduled for the morning of 16 March 1978. The Red Brigades kidnapped Moro en route to the parliament.

The national-solidarity coalition was not prepared by discussions comparable in either breadth or depth to those that had preceded the reform programme of 1962–4, especially on the Christian Democrats' side, and its policy objectives were anyway overshadowed by the pressure of terrorism and the imperative of defeating it. Even Moro's openness to progressive reform, ever

[6] We refer to national elections: in the regional elections of 1975 the PCI had lowered the distance to just 2 per cent, with a nationwide share of 33 per cent, and in the European elections of 1984 it will outstrip the DC (33.32 and 33.02 per cent) for the first and only time in their history.

rarer among Christian Democrats after the early 1960s (Baldini 2015), was veiled by his political objective of taming the PCI through a manoeuvre of large-scale *trasformismo* (Hellman 2015, 287), akin to that which had eventually digested the PSI—but introduced it also to patronage politics and, as we saw, grand corruption.

This grand coalition did strengthen the republic, during its most dramatic years. It could also sustain policies that stemmed the rise of both inflation and public debt (Rossi 2007; Crafts and Magnani 2013), as Table 8.1 documented, even though the earlier industrial policy based on discretionary and often ill-allocated subsidies continued. But the only major structural reform was the already mentioned 1978 health-care law, whose universalism starkly contrasted with prior DC policy. It received inadequate implementation, however, and failed to stem the clientelism and corruption that had risen under the previous approach (Ginsborg 1990, 392). A moderately ambitious law on land use and urban planning—the reform on which the battle had been fiercest in 1964—was even more thoroughly sabotaged by the public administration and, more interestingly, also by its constituents: Ginsborg (1990, 391) explains that even outside of itself, in civil society, 'the state lacked nearly all the necessary instruments, both cultural and material, to enforce its laws'. A sweeping comment, taken alone, but one which rests on a careful analysis of Italian society and converges with our own reading, for by necessity the logic of the spiral generated by the country's social order imposed itself also on citizens.

The same reasons explain why in 1977–9 Communists acquired their own share of posts and partisan control in the public broadcaster, the state-owned banking system, and other national public or quasi-public bodies (Ginsborg 1990, 388). They evidently calculated that taking control themselves of parts of the public sector was a more effective strategy to counter the DC's pervasive occupation of it than insisting for greater separation between politics and the management of Italy's mixed economy. Again, this might have been a wise choice in the circumstances of those years, like Moro's cover-up of the 1964 coup, but it remained fully within the logic of an increasingly distorted governance system and exposed the party to the concomitant risks. Already in 1973, in fact, the minutes of the PCI's central committee (quoted by Crainz 2003, 495–8) recorded worried remarks about signs of unscrupulous practices and even corruption within the party's peripheral ranks. The phenomenon was novel, for in the cities and regions that they administered Communists had hitherto generally excelled for their integrity as well as for their performance (Putnam 1993; Bellucci 2015). It was also limited and scarcely visible, such that when the corruption scandals of 1974–5 broke out the PCI could nonetheless plausibly claim to be the one party whose hands were 'clean'. But in the second half of the decade the PCI's vulnerability to unethical practices increased, despite its leadership's concerns about them.

On 9 May 1978 Moro's corpse was found, in a car that the Red Brigades had symbolically parked very near the Roman headquarters of the two coalition partners. He had been the architect and main driver of the coalition on the DC's side: the PCI had lost its main interlocutor, in a political strategy whose results were anyway lesser than it expected (Bellucci 2015, 189–90).[7] In early 1979 the party again moved to enter the cabinet and eventually forced early elections, held in June. Compared with the results of 1976, the DC lost a mere 0.4 percentage points: the PCI lost 4 nationally and 9 in a traditional strong-hold, the Turin suburb where Fiat had its main factory. This was a stiff defeat in Italy's finely balanced political system (see Mershon 2015). The party moved back into opposition, upon the strategy of joining up with the PSI in a 'left-wing alternative' to the DC's regained dominance (Hellman 2015, 292–3). It suffered an even graver political defeat in October 1980, when a drawn-out strike at that same factory, explicitly supported by the party, was called off days after tens of thousands of white-collar workers marched silently across Turin demanding regular production to resume (Ginsborg 1990, 407). Hampered by this and other setbacks the PCI's new strategy will bear no fruit, also because throughout the 1980s the Socialists aimed chiefly at altering the power- and rent-sharing agreement with the DC in their favour (Bull 2015).

The slow decline of the PCI's electoral support and membership base continued until 1991, when the party changed its name and suffered a large split. In parallel, however, its electoral appeal progressively expanded beyond the confines of its traditional political subculture, and the party fully became a catch-all one (Bellucci 2015). In an only apparent paradox, as we shall see, this evolution was however accompanied by a recrudescence of anti-communism and political polarization.

The 1979 vote marked also a small but noticeable drop in electoral participation. Having hovered around 93 per cent for about three decades, turnout fell to 90.6 per cent. This was the beginning of a steady decline, which does not yet appear to have ended.

A 'Metastasis of the Institutions' and a Revelation of Their Distortions

During the second half of the 1970s, while the challenge of red terrorism was at its peak and the two mass parties cooperated in defending the republic, a

---

[7] Ginsborg (1990, 400–1) qualifies as 'extraordinary' the Communist leader's admission—in May 1979—that the party had been 'lenient' and sometimes 'ingenuous' in dealing with the DC. This criticism—espoused, among others, by Crainz (2003)—might underestimate the fact that in deciding whether to accept the undoubtedly dangerous embrace with the DC, the PCI may have weighed also the threat that the republic faced.

less visible threat was eroding its foundations. Its locus was the P2, the Masonic lodge we already mentioned in connection with the strategy of tension and neo-fascist terrorism (Commissione parlamentare 1984; Colombo 1996; Ferraresi 1996, ch. 6; Ginsborg 2001, 144–8). We turn to this organization to illustrate the depth then reached by the spiral. It offers a limited vantage point, because its field of activity was confined to the public authorities and the higher echelons of society. But its nature and function indirectly reveal both the progress and the persisting vulnerability of the country's drawn-out transition from the limited-access social order to the open-access one.

The two Milanese judges who discovered the P2's hidden power, in March 1981, found a list of 962 members, possibly incomplete, its political programme, and twenty-one sealed envelopes, which contained incriminating evidence implicating several prominent members of the country's political and economic elites. In the P2's hands were also the 157,000 personal files that had been collated by the intelligence agency led by one protagonist of the coup threat of 1964 (Ferraresi 1996, 120–1).

Besides dozens of army and police generals and secret agents, as we said, its members included two sitting ministers, the leader of the Social Democrats, more than forty parliamentarians (out of about 900), and numerous senior judges, journalists, publishers, financiers, bankers, industrialists, entrepreneurs (one was Berlusconi[8]). Its programme, adamantly anti-communist, had presumably been drafted in 1975: namely, right after the first large corruption scandals and the remarkable rise of the PCI in the regional elections of that year. Most of its members joined the P2 in 1977 or thereafter: namely, soon after the PCI's 1976 electoral success and the formation of the first national-solidarity coalition.

Two early and prominent members, on whom we shall return, were Roberto Calvi (Paoli 1995) and Michele Sindona (Magnani 2016). Both bankers to the Vatican, both closely linked to the Sicilian mafia, on one hand, and to governing parties, on the other, both protagonists of large banking failures, both died violently. In 1982 Calvi was found hanging under Blackfriars Bridge, in London. In 1986 Sindona died of poison in prison, two days after having been convicted for the assassination of the liquidator of his bank. Unlike Calvi, Sindona probably committed suicide (see Magnani 2016, 139–40).

While it included also blander proposals, the P2's programme prefigured a form of guided or controlled democracy, softly authoritarian, to be achieved through infiltration, corruption, and persuasion. The list of its members does suggest a remarkable capacity to infiltrate both the military and civilian

---

[8] In 1990 he was found guilty of having testified falsely about his membership, but benefited from an amnesty (Lane 2004, 88).

authorities and the country's elites; in 1977 the lodge did acquire control of the *Corriere*, chiefly through Calvi's Banco Ambrosiano, then Italy's second largest private lender; and the P2 did in particular finance the conservative faction of the national judges' association, presumably to influence it. But besides its considerable financial means, at the roots of the P2's power was primarily the blackmail potential of the twenty one envelopes and 157,000 secret-service files.

The latter reveal a predictable but remarkable degree of continuity among reactionary circles. The P2's programme however suggests that by 1975 at least part of them had shifted away from strategies based on coup threats or indiscriminate terrorist attacks—in which the P2 was nonetheless heavily implicated (Ferraresi 1996, 120–7), as we said—to ones apter to a situation changed by the DC-PCI coalition, by the incipient rise of the judiciary's independence, and by the progress made by Italy's transition. As we shall see presently, in fact, society had matured, tempered also by the terrorist threat, and democracy strengthened.

Having documented its varied, reiterated, and partly successful attempts to influence the nation's political and economic life, a parliamentary commission of inquiry concluded that the P2 was a 'metastasis of the institutions' and a grave and direct threat to popular sovereignty (Commissione parlamentare 1984, 155; the word 'institutions' is used here in its commoner sense, equivalent to 'public authorities'). On this basis, the lodge was dissolved by an act of parliament.

Yet its power and pervasive infiltration had been discovered after several years of activity, and then only by accident (Colombo 1996, 47–8). As we shall see, moreover, on the judicial plane the P2 and its members enjoyed effective impunity: in essence, the only reaction of the state was a careful inquiry and the publication of a detailed and still widely appreciated report, which made the nation fully aware of the danger of the lodge. Of course, once revealed the P2's power had been drastically reduced. As the report persuasively writes, however, the lodge was an 'instrument', in the service mainly of interests— never conclusively identified—that stood above or outside of it (Commissione parlamentare 1984, 153–4).[9] Disclosure eclipsed the instrument but not the possibility that its components would be agglomerated again: primarily because impunity had indirectly shielded also the source of the P2's power of blackmail, namely the illegal practices of the country's elites, evidence of which the lodge possessed. This is not to say that the P2 could be easily

---

[9] The P2 is often viewed also as a channel through which foreign interests sought to influence domestic politics in an Atlanticist direction. While plausible, this interpretation remains unproven. From our viewpoint, at any rate, the gravity of the threat posed by the P2 and the character of the authorities' reaction to it matter more than the origins, domestic or external, of its strategies and motivations.

recreated under a different guise. On the contrary, the large-scale anti-mafia and anti-corruption investigations of the following decades identified no comparable organization, and presumably had one existed it would likewise have been uncovered. The point, rather, is that the state proved unable to eradicate the deeper roots of the threat it had faced. '[I]mpunity was an organized institution, and had roots that the [laws] did not touch': Manzoni's words, cited in the Preface, remained to a large extent valid; the reason, as we repeatedly noted, is that where the rule of law is weak the crimes of the elite are typically left unpunished. In this case it was a sizeable minority of the country's establishment that had connived in a plan that threatened its democracy, and a presumably larger segment was vulnerable to the organization that embodied that plan. In line with the conclusions we reached in Chapter 6 on the quality of Italy's democracy, therefore, the reaction that its healthier forces opposed to the P2 was much less an institutional one, based on the rule of law, than a political one, namely disclosure and symbolic condemnation, which ultimately relied on society's readiness to protect its own political freedoms.

Similar conclusions can be drawn from the vicissitudes of both bankers of the P2, and especially from those of Sindona—which Magnani (2016) convincingly articulates into a politico-economic 'biography' of the 1970s. In his remarkable rise from tax lawyer to corporate raider to banker, in both Milan and New York, Sindona systematically exploited the weakness of Italy's corporate-governance and financial-markets regulations. But he also gravely breached them, including before he launched (circa 1971) operations that challenged part of the same economic elites that he had hitherto served. From having 'half of Italy'[10] backing him, Sindona eventually coalesced against himself most of the authorities and the economic establishment: unlike Andreotti, by 1977 even the P2 had effectively abandoned him, to rely more on Calvi.

The reaction against Sindona was not that of a rule-based system, however, nor was it due to his attempts at predation, quite common in Italy's financial markets, as we said. It responded to a perceived attempt at domination, conversely, and was based chiefly on the wide use of administrative discretion, on one hand, and on recourse to the financial power and broader influence of a wide and cohesive front of economic elites, on the other, organized around the (largely state-owned) merchant bank Mediobanca: the same power, influence, and cohesion that served as a barrier to entry protecting the higher ranks of Italian capitalism from outside competition. Also Sindona's US bank had failed, and the comparison between the reaction of the two countries is not, admittedly, overly unfavourable to Italy's authorities (Magnani 2016); in the

---

[10] Thus reads a worried August 1973 note (quoted by Stajano 1991, 72) that the treasury minister—former *azionista* and widely respected figure—sent to Carli, then still governor.

wake of Sindona's raids a modest but progressive reform of financial-markets regulation was also adopted (Marchetti 1997). Yet, the list of the approximately 500 creditors that had for long benefited from Sindona's services to evade taxes and regulation and export capital unlawfully—a list that had been drawn up upon his bank's bankruptcy, in September 1974—disappeared and has never resurfaced, and one reason why it could disappear is that Governor Carli refused to receive it (Stajano 1991, 87–8; Magnani 2016, 75–7). His refusal, arguably unwarranted, de facto secured the impunity of those creditors—prominent names, the fate of the list suggests—and allowed them also to be repaid like legitimate ones. As both Stajano (1991) and Magnani (2016) show, after his bankruptcy Sindona met firm intransigence on the rule of law and the primacy of the public interest primarily, if not exclusively, in the persons of the liquidator of his bank, Giorgio Ambrosoli, of Carli's successor as central bank governor, Paolo Baffi, and of his head of banking supervision, Mario Sarcinelli.

The idiosyncrasy of their intransigence is proven by the consequences. After three months of menacing leaks from Rome's judicial authorities, on 24 March 1979 the latter placed Baffi under investigation and arrested Sarcinelli, on charges that seemed and later proved to be 'entirely specious' (Magnani 2016, 107). After having threatened him for six months, on 11 July 1979 Sindona killed Ambrosoli, through a gunman of the Italo-American mafia.[11]

The judicial attack provoked scandal and concern also beyond Italy's borders, and the central bank closed ranks in support of the accused. The case was in the hands of magistrates, and concerned interests, that were viewed as close to the DC and especially to Andreotti, then prime minister (Magnani 2016, 101–10). In 2010 a jurist who then acted as Baffi's and Sarcinelli's counsel, and in 1987–92 was three times minister for the DC, revealed that he negotiated directly with Andreotti to persuade the magistrates to allow Sarcinelli to resume his functions at the central bank, where several executives were preparing to resign: Andreotti agreed, on account of the possible macroeconomic repercussions (Magnani 2016, 109–10), and instructed the magistrates accordingly, with a simple telephone call (Craveri 2016, 342–3). This suggests that the attack had been directed or at least supported by Andreotti or circles that he represented, and was withdrawn by reason of the—evidently unexpected— resistance it provoked and risks it entailed.

The punishment for Ambrosoli's intransigence was not equally remediable, as the victim had lucidly foreseen (Stajano 1991, 102–3 and 185 *passim*). But not even a symbolic gesture was made: the only public figure who attended his funeral was Baffi, besides several Milanese magistrates (Stajano 1991, 237).

---

[11] The P2 was discovered in the course of the investigation of this murder (Colombo 1996, 47–8).

The P2, to conclude, reveals that the transition of Italy's social order had progressed but remained nonetheless vulnerable. Reversing it was the lodge's objective, which would scarcely have attracted so much and such high-ranking support had the country's transition not progressed *and* been still vulnerable. Indeed, the membership of the P2 perfectly mirrors the definition of a limited-access social order's 'dominant coalition' in North et al. (2009), for it included the military, political, and economic elites, and linked them to the country's criminal ones: it was perhaps not the nucleus but certainly the image of the prospective dominant coalition of the softly authoritarian state that the P2's programme prefigured. It comprised only segments of those elites, though, and the programme failed; it was also the last forceful attempt at reversing Italy's transition, presumably precisely because it failed. What makes it especially interesting from our perspective is that the contest took place primarily in the space separating Italy's formal institutions from its actual ones, and therefore illuminated it: it showed how the country's (actual) political institutions were incapable of either preventing the formation of the P2 or eradicating its roots. If we understand the word in the sense in which we just used it, therefore, the P2 was much less a 'metastasis of the *institutions*', as the parliamentary inquiry concluded, than a manifestation, however conspicuous, of their weakness. This might be what Pasolini (1975) alluded to when he wrote that one cannot look at Italy's 'real' conditions without remaining 'petrified'. As befits its status, conversely, the parliamentary commission measured the P2 against the image of Italy's democracy that the constitution depicts, and eschewed that petrifying thesis.

One gloss is necessary, at the end of an account that may have seemed colouristic. Neither the P2, Sindona, Calvi, Ambrosoli's assassination, nor the 1979 attack on the Bank of Italy are mentioned in the essays collected in Toniolo (2013a). The other edited work that we frequently take as our reference (Jones and Pasquino 2015) does mention them but fails to highlight their significance for reconstructing the country's economic development. Neither work can be criticized for this, as they belong to disciplines—economic history and political science—whose boundaries do not always touch. But we hope to have shown that at least part of Italy's institutional inefficiencies germinated precisely in the no man's land between the two fields. It seems hard to appreciate those inefficiencies, or indeed the distance that then separated Italy from Britain, France, or Germany, without considering, for instance, that the person who led the national-solidarity governments that successfully stewarded the country through a period of high macroeconomic instability and unprecedented terrorist violence was at the same time abetting the mafia, was protecting a criminal banker tied to the Vatican, Italy's establishment, and the mafia, and was presumably also directing an unwarranted judicial attack on the central bank, only to back down, reasonably, when the consequences for the country risked escalating.

Having established that by the second half of the 1970s the vicious circles hypothesized in Chapter 4 were all running, we can now invert the perspective. From watching the spread of dark spots over the white sheet, we can turn to looking for bright colours in the dimming fresco. For next to those three intransigent civil servants other countervailing forces existed.

To appreciate their significance, by way of introduction it seems useful to recall our discussion of the weakness of democracy in post-war Italy, at the end of Chapter 6, which emphasized the cleavage traced by Marxism. More pragmatically than the literature we relied upon there, Linz and Stepan (1996, 15–16) describe a 'consolidated democracy' as a polity in which the democratic principle 'becomes routinized and deeply internalized in social, institutional, and even psychological life'. In such a democracy, more precisely, 'no significant political group seriously attempts to overthrow the democratic regime'; 'even in the face of severe political and economic crises, the overwhelming majority of the people believe that... political change must [proceed through] democratic procedures'; and 'all of the actors in the polity become habituated to the fact that political conflict within the state will be resolved according to established norms, and that violations of these norms are likely to be both ineffective and costly'. More than three decades after the war only the second of these conditions was fully met, mostly thanks to the work of Italy's three mass parties. Political violence was often threatened or used, in particular, was generally effective, and, with the exception of red terrorism, was typically left unpunished. This changed only in the course of the 1980s.

Counterpoises: 'Democratic Citizens', the Judiciary, the Bank of Italy

> *Lo Stato oggi consiste soprattutto nei cittadini democratici che non si arrendono, che non lasciano andare tutto alla malora.*

> [Today the State is made up above all of those democratic citizens who haven't given up, who won't let everything go to ruin.]

> (Italo Calvino, 11 May 1977)

'Democratic Citizens' and the Choices they Faced

Ginsborg (1990, 386) writes that after Moro's assassination 'Italian democracy was not just defended but strengthened'. Three reasons, which reinforced each other, are that the PCI and the trade unions were steadfast in defending the republic from red terrorism; the authorities largely eschewed recourse to extraordinary measures to fight it (see Cento Bull 2015); and citizens supported them. The epigraph is taken from an article published in the *Corriere* right after the trial of several Red Brigades leaders had to be postponed because, scared by their threats, many lawyers and jurors refused to serve. On the next day, on the same pages the writer Leonardo Sciascia retorted that he too would have refused, and added: '[s]aving democracy, defending freedom, not giving up ... are just words'.[12] So the alternative was stark, and uncivicness had distinguished advocates and much evidence to support it: but citizens by and large chose to trust the republic.

The fortitude displayed one decade earlier at the Milan funeral had not waned but spread. Economic growth, rising affluence and average schooling, and the progress of linguistic unification had changed Italian society.[13] The speed of economic transformation, much faster than the rise of schooling and literacy (Bertola and Sestito 2013, fig. 9.2; Vecchi 2017, ch. 5), may well have left Italians culturally more vulnerable than the British, the French, or the Germans; and the policy of particularistic inclusion did encourage the diffusion of what was already then described as 'protectionist individualism', namely the claim to be at once free from the state's interference and supported by it (Crainz 2003, 2016). Yet the roots of democracy had reached deep into society, thanks also to Italy's mass parties, and citizens had greater reason and moral resources to defend it. Sustained by the wind of Italy's long 1968, they demanded also laws allowing no-fault divorce, abortion, and contraception, and a reform of family law, hitherto governed by Fascist-era unequal rules. They obtained these and other reforms, such as that on the treatment of mental illnesses. They were often balanced reforms, moreover, because political parties still had the grassroots organization and the political culture to receive, filter, and coordinate the demands of the various segments of society, and then face a reasoned discussion about them before the eyes of public opinion: as in the case of the 1974 referendum against the new divorce law, most notably, a battle which the Church and the DC fought vehemently and lost decisively (Melloni 2015; Teodori 2015).

This analysis, finally, is not inconsistent with our earlier observation about the weakness of civil society in supporting the 1978 land-use reform. For it is both pragmatically and psychologically possible, we would argue, to be ready at once to defend the state from terrorism and one's rents from the state, if the incentives generated by the spiral into which the country was sinking so dictated.

---

[12] Quoted by Crainz (2016, 208–9).

[13] By 1974 about half of the population could speak Italian; this percentage rose above 90 per cent only in the 1990s, and reached 94.7 per cent in 2006 (De Mauro 2014, table 7).

The Evolution of the Presidency of the Republic

These developments were assisted by a change in the standing and function of the presidency of the republic. Suspected of involvement in the Lockheed scandal and accused of nepotism, in 1978 the head of state resigned (Pasquino 2015a, 86–7). Former leader of a minor DC faction, he had been elected with the decisive support of the neo-fascists: parliament replaced him with the Socialist Sandro Pertini, an early anti-fascist who served a long prison sentence because he refused to ask for Mussolini's pardon, was then confined in Ventotene, and in 1943–4 became a prominent leader of the resistance. His election took place shortly after Moro's assassination, and reflects the assessment that in such a difficult passage the state needed a more credible representative. Pertini 'became a very popular president and played a very incisive political role': unlike his predecessor, he could 'speak on behalf of the Italian citizens' and often did (Pasquino 2015a, 86–7). Though sometimes demotic, his public rhetoric raised the prominence of anti-fascism, constitutional patriotism, and civic virtue. It was credible because his deeds followed his words: in particular, he broke stridently with precedent when he rejected the appointment of a Christian Democrat to a ministerial post 'asserting his lack of competence and integrity for the office' (Pasquino 2015a, 92).

In Chapters 3 and 4 we noted that elites' visible and credible actions can orient society's expectations and choices: Pertini's certainly contributed to strengthening Italy's democracy. The same was done by several similar figures, including among the governing parties: former *azionisti*, often, but also Christian Democrats such as the chair of the parliamentary inquiry on the P2, Tina Anselmi, former partisan and a rare prominent female politician. After an unfit one, Pertini's successors largely followed the precedents he had set. When frictions among the executive, the legislature, and the judiciary arose, as they often did after 1994, the head of state generally had enough credibility and autonomy to 'play the role of referee' (Pasquino 2015a, 93).

The Growing Independence of the Judiciary and the Countermeasures It Attracted

Why were the oil sector bribes discovered? The interests of justice owed the Lockheed case to the oversight function of the US Senate, and its outcome fits well into our general interpretation: but the three magistrates of Genoa ought not to have investigated the earlier, and graver case. The primary reason, quite simply, is that the judges and prosecutors that the republic inherited from the Fascist regime had by then gradually retired or moved up to higher posts or courts, leaving lesser positions and much of the lower courts to younger cohorts (those three magistrates were all born during the war).

These had been schooled and educated by the republic, and matured while the ideas and demands of 1968 were articulated and diffused. Among them, greater numbers than among their elders took the constitution and their own independence—which was both external and internal (i.e., from hierarchical superiors and higher courts), as we said—seriously. Some were also ready to break with convention and investigate the country's elites. This, in summary, is the analysis that the literature on the history of the judiciary offers (Bruti Liberati 1997; Neppi Modona 1997; Guarnieri 2015; see also Colombo 1996, 26–7).

It is compatible with our conceptual framework, for it shows how a formal institution—judicial independence—began to grow flesh around its written bones thanks to the progress made by the transition of Italy's social order, on one hand, and, on the other, to the spread of new ideas, such as the demand for a less archaic, authoritarian, and unequal organization of society. It finds support in the empirical data analysed by Chang et al. (2010, 186, fig. 2), which document that until 1972 'parliamentarians affiliated with opposition parties were much more likely than those affiliated with governing parties to be incriminated by the judiciary [whereas after 1972] deputies in governing parties . . . were more frequently charged', often for crimes with pecuniary motives. The reversal was gradual and one reason for it was that in the 1950s Marxist parliamentarians often took part in workers' or peasants' demonstrations, also to protect them from the harsh public-order policies discussed in Chapter 6. Yet the reversal was primarily the consequence of a decline in the judiciary's subservience to the political power, combined with the naturally lesser incidence of economic crime among opposition parties.

Our conceptual framework however predicts that the less public-spirited segments of Italy's elites would react to the incipient signs of judicial independence, for by virtue of demography the threat to their interests could only grow. In part, the threat was limited ex ante, by the need of parliament's authorization to investigate parliamentarians, as well as by the ordinary jurisdictional rules: the fact that high-level political crime took place mostly in the capital implied that it fell within the jurisdiction of Rome's judicial authorities, which, for this very reason, were particularly docile to external interference (Bruti Liberati 1997; Neppi Modona 1997; Guarnieri 2015; see also Mack Smith 1997, 471). Indeed, the criteria employed by governing parties and factions to allocate power and patronage—criteria unveiled in 1981, never seriously disputed, and quoted by Craveri (2016, 338)—gave to the post of head prosecutor in Rome a value equivalent to 'two ministries', which implies that holders of that critical position could typically be chosen and then influenced. In part, the threat was contained ex post by employing several legal techniques to transfer to Rome the jurisdiction over cases opened elsewhere: techniques which were generally successful because the supreme court, seated in Rome, had the last say on them. The particularly marked decline in judicial efficiency observed during the 1960s, and never thereafter reversed (Bianco and Napolitano 2013, fig. 19.3; Boltho 2013, 116), suggests that this instrument too was used (Colombo 2012, 107), because the funding and organization of the judicial offices fell within the jurisdiction of the political authorities, on which the complexity of legislation equally depended. The decline extended to the civil and commercial courts, of course, yet this was not a disincentive to resorting to this strategy because delayed justice typically harms the weaker litigant more than the stronger one: it certainly benefited deep-pocketed debtors, in particular, because until the early 1990s the legal interest rate was lower than the market rate. When economic elites needed rapid justice, moreover, they could make their agreements subject to arbitration clauses.

The clearest example of those techniques concerns what is often described as the 'biggest scandal of the Italian Republic', namely the P2 (Bull 2015, 298). Shortly after the Milanese judges' findings became public, Rome's judicial authority claimed from them the jurisdiction over both the main case and the ancillary ones based on the evidence contained in the sealed envelopes. The supreme court upheld their claim, whence they rapidly closed and filed all ancillary cases; on the main one they obtained convictions for lesser crimes, and this only in 1996, when society had changed and all protagonists had retired from public life (Colombo 1996, 94–101). The evidence contained in those envelopes mostly concerned high-level corruption and financial crime cases, similar to the oil sector one, and implicated among others the leaderships of IRI, ENI, the DC, and the PSI. One of the two Milanese judges who seized them (Colombo 1996, 94–101) writes that much of that evidence surfaced again during the anti-corruption investigations that began in 1992—the Clean Hands investigations, in which Colombo participated as prosecutor—and served as evidence for numerous prominent convictions.

The Clean Hands investigations shook the country, as we said, and separated its post-war political history into two distinct phases. Had the P2's envelopes remained in the hands of the Milanese authorities, the interruption of the spiral that those investigations provoked could have taken place one decade earlier. Considering how deeply the spiral marked Italy's history during the 1980s, at least part of the damage could have been avoided. Yet it may be asked whether one should lament this or rather marvel at the fact that the P2 could be discovered at all, despite all the obstacles that conspired to prevent it. For instance, the financial police officers who acted on behalf of the Milanese judges received a menacing telephone call from their commander-in-chief, who was a member of the P2, while they were still in the residence of the lodge's leader where they had just discovered and seized its documents

(Colombo 1996, 49).[14] Our reading suggests that the second reaction is more justified than the first. The discovery of the P2 was certainly an unexpected event, because its own strategy included also countermeasures—such as hosting prominent judges among its ranks, and financing the conservative faction of the national judges' association—precisely against the risks posed by the incipient activism of the judiciary. But once the two judges overcame the obstacles that ought to have prevented them from discovering the P2, the interests represented by it made effective use of their informal power to limit the damage. Had they not been able to do this, in other words, Italy would not have risked sinking in the spiral in the first place.

The Bank of Italy

The Bank of Italy contributed to an essential early macroeconomic stabilization in 1947, and then assisted the forces that drove the economic miracle; its stiff monetary tightening of 1963 was politically controversial but brought the economy back onto a sustainable path, which eased stable and still rapid growth until the crises of 1969 and 1973; thereafter it served as a critical force for stability in a very vulnerable policy equilibrium based on debt-financed expansionary policy and the fiscal drag. In Italy's heavily bank-oriented financial system, moreover, bank credit was firms' main source of external finance: the Bank of Italy was also an effective supervisor and guarantor of the economy's central mechanism for allocating capital, which over the 1948–2009 period worked on the whole efficiently (Battilossi et al. 2013). The fact that until the 1990s the banking sector was predominantly state-owned—such that after the early 1960s the country's main lenders became as exposed to nepotism, clientelism, and political interference as IRI, their shareholder—and that in the private sector long-term relationships between firms and banks were often prevalent, did involve risks. But in contrast with the previous nine decades, between 1948 and the Great Recession the country suffered no large-scale banking or financial crises, and when banks failed—relatively rare and often pathological cases, such as Calvi's and Sindona's—retail deposits were never affected (Ciocca 2007, 296 *passim*). The competence and long-earned credibility of its central bank thus were important ingredients of Italy's growth model (see Carli 1996; Barca 1997; Mack Smith 1997; Ciocca 2007; Rossi 2007; Crafts and Magnani 2013; Felice 2015; Quaglia 2015).

---

[14] Ginsborg (2001, 144) reports an officer's description of his supreme commander's words: 'You better know that you've found some lists. I'm in those lists—be careful, because so are all the highest echelons ["of the state", the officer understood]. Watch out, the [financial police] could be overwhelmed by this.'

One might argue that the Bank of Italy should have been more incisive in persuading the governments of the 1970s to shift to a more sustainable and less inflationary fiscal policy, but already in 1974 Carli retorted that in those difficult years refusing to underwrite the desired amount of sovereign debt would have amounted to a 'seditious act'. The question, which is broader than we described it, is unsettled (see Crafts and Magnani 2013, 89, also for Carli's quotation).

The tension between the central bank's mandate to safeguard the credibility of the banking sector and the interests stemming from the degenerating collusion between political and economic elites was no less stark but far less ambivalent, conversely, as the judicial attack of 1979 shows. The bank resisted. By this, it gained in credibility and independence. As Quaglia (2015, 517) writes, in fact, until the creation of the ECB 'in economists' rankings the Bank of Italy used to be awarded fairly high scores [as to] political independence'. The governing parties seem to have accepted that the central bank could not at once be a monetary authority with the domestic and external credibility that Italy's predicament required, and a supervisory authority as pliable to their illegitimate demands as to allow unscrupulous or criminal bankers to be systematically bailed out with public money. For the cause of that judicial attack was the central bank's opposition to the rescue not just of Sindona's but also of Calvi's bank and of a third one, closely associated with the DC, which risked large losses on loans to two entrepreneurs equally tied to the DC (Magnani 2016, 101–4). The withdrawal of that attack, and the eschewal of comparable forms of interference, protected a patrimony of credibility and personnel that proved often critical during the following four decades.

9

The Last Four Decades: The Spiral Unperturbed, Halted, Resumed

The Spiral Unperturbed (1980–1992): a Tipping Point Is Passed – The Rupture of 1992–1994 – The Spiral Resumed (1994–2011) – The Quality of the Rule of Law – Political Accountability – Closing the Circle: Economic Policy, Institutions, and Performance – The Rupture of 2011–2013 and Its Aftermath

The Spiral Unperturbed (1980–1992): a Tipping Point Is Passed

A 'Missed Opportunity'

During the 1980s the republic defeated organized terrorism, social tensions quietened, the governing coalition was stable, if quarrelsome, and a declining, politically isolated PCI was freshly confined to permanent opposition. In 1983 a long international expansionary cycle began, oil prices fell, and macroeconomic stability improved. Large firms reaped the benefits of the labour-saving investments of the previous years, industrial districts reached the peak of their vitality, and from them grew Italy's celebrated medium-sized, medium-technology, export-oriented firms (e.g., Berta 2015).

In this favourable context three domestic factors can be highlighted (see Ciocca 2007; Rossi 2007; Crafts and Magnani 2013). The first was the end of the 'wage-push age' and the onset of less tense industrial relations, sealed in 1980 by the defeat of the PCI-supported strike at Fiat's Turin factory (again, however, the reversal in the balance of power between labour and capital did not lead to the adoption of an institutionalized system of cooperative bargaining). The other two were reforms in the institutions governing macroeconomic management, designed to redress the disequilibria accumulated over the previous decade. One was the choice to participate in the European Monetary System (EMS), which gave a credible anchor to monetary policy and contributed to stabilizing the exchange rate in the second half of the decade. The other was the so-called 'divorce' between the central bank and the treasury, in 1982, which allowed the former to refuse to purchase the latter's bonds that private investors left unsubscribed at issuance auctions, and brought large-scale debt monetization to an end. What in 1974 had seemed a seditious act became explicit policy, aimed at strengthening the government's budget constraint—by raising the cost of future borrowing—and lowering inflation.

Inflation did decline, steadily, but the budget constraint was not strengthened: deficits were high and persistent, as Table 9.1 shows, and public debt nearly doubled as a percentage of GDP (see Balassone et al. 2013). Per capita GDP growth was slower than in the 1970s, but stabler and still slightly higher than in Western Europe and the USA (Vecchi 2017, fig. 7.7). Labour productivity growth decelerated markedly, however, dragged down by TFP (Figure 1.3a), and a gap began to open between Italy's convergence to the productivity frontier and the trajectory of its peers (Figure 1.2).

For these reasons the 1980s are often seen as a 'missed opportunity' to remedy Italy's weaknesses, and especially its macroeconomic disequilibria. We refer particularly to Salvati (2000, 2011), but also, with lesser emphasis, to Ciocca (2007), Rossi (2007), Crafts and Magnani (2013), and Toniolo (2013b).

The hypothesis we drew up in Chapter 4 would conversely predict that greater social, political, and macroeconomic stability would have eased the progression of the spiral that had set in. Virtuous choices were no longer imposed by imperatives that overrode the elites' incentives for opportunistic behaviour, as on the occasion of Pertini's election, and the countervailing forces we just reviewed were too weak and too segmented to constrain the spiral. If 'democratic citizens' could contribute to defending the republic from a visible and urgent danger, in particular, they could hardly impose a complex reform programme upon governing parties largely reluctant about it, because they were progressively engulfed in the spiral and ever less threatened by a weakening and politically isolated Communist opposition: this is true especially of reforms aimed at scarcely visible dangers, such as the institutional ones, or at problems that stemmed from the opportunistic behaviour of ordinary citizens themselves, such as petty corruption, tax evasion, and clientelism. Non-organized citizens can be effective in defending the policies and institutions that already exist, or in demanding reforms that boil down to an essentially binary choice, such as abortion or divorce, but not in forcing the redesign of a country's economic institutions, which is what taking that opportunity would mostly have meant. We imply no determinism, nor wish to absolve the governments of the 1980s of their responsibilities:

171

Table 9.1 Selected Macroeconomic Indicators, 1980–1992

Year	GDP Growth[a]	Per-Capita GDP Growth[a]	Total Investment (% GDP)[a]	Activity Rate[b]	Unemployment Rate[b]	Labour Productivity Growth[a]	TFP Growth[a]	Current Account Deficit (% GDP)[c]	Inflation (CPI)[d]	Debt-to-GDP Ratio[e]	Government Expenditure (% GDP)[b]	Government Revenue (% GDP)[b]
1980	3.4	3.1	26.9	58.7	6.9	1.7	0.02	−2.2	21.1	56.1	41.4	34.4
1981	0.8	0.6	24.8	58.9	7.5	0.4	−1.6	−2.4	17.7	58.5	45.3	34.4
1982	0.4	0.2	24.7	58.8	8.2	−0.6	−2.1	−1.7	16.5	63.1	47.3	37.3
1983	1.2	1.0	23.4	59.1	9.1	0.8	−0.8	0.1	14.6	69.4	49.5	39.4
1984	3.2	3.0	24.9	59.2	9.6	3.7	1.7	−0.7	10.8	74.9	49.6	38.1
1985	2.8	2.7	25.0	59.1	9.6	2.0	0.5	−0.9	9.2	80.9	50.3	37.9
1986	2.9	2.8	24.8	59.2	9.9	1.6	0.3	0.4	5.8	85.1	50.8	38.9
1987	3.2	3.1	26.1	59.8	10.3	1.9	0.5	−0.3	4.7	89.1	50.1	38.6
1988	4.2	4.2	26.9	59.9	10.1	2.9	1.4	−0.8	5.1	90.8	50.8	39.7
1989	3.4	3.4	27.3	60.2	9.7	3.5	1.5	−1.4	6.3	93.3	51.9	40.5
1990	2.0	2.0	27.0	60.2	9.0	0.9	−0.5	−1.4	6.5	95.2	53.3	41.8
1991	1.5	1.5	27.8	60.1	8.6	0.01	−1.0	−2.0	6.2	98.6	54.3	43.0
1992	0.8	0.8	28.2	59.7	8.7	1.7	−0.2	−2.2	5.3	105.5	55.6	45.2

Note: [a] Source: Penn World Table. [b] Source: ISTAT. [c] Source: World Bank. [d] Source: OECD. [e] Source: IMF.

an opportunity did present itself, but it was much harder to take than the literature seems to suggest.

As it is, the spiral ran unfettered until the summer of 1992. The collusion between public powers and private interests deepened, Olsonian distributional coalitions proliferated and rose in influence, the intensity of competition remained low, corruption grew in both gravity and scale, tax evasion spread, organized crime strengthened, political clientelism rose, 'worldview politics' was overshadowed by rent-seeking, political cultures weakened, political accountability declined, and, with it, fell also the efficiency of public services and the quality of the political elite. This is the picture that the historiographical and politico-economic literature almost uniformly draws (Barca 1997; Mack Smith 1997; Salvati 2000, 2011; Ginsborg 2001; Crainz 2003, 2016; Rossi 2007; Ciocca 2007; Di Michele 2008; Boltho 2013; Crafts and Magnani 2013; Toniolo 2013a; Bull 2015; Cotta 2015; Felice 2015; Newell 2015; Varsori 2015; Craveri 2016; Gigliobianco and Toniolo 2017).

A critical component of this equilibrium, both cause and effect of it, was precisely the government's ability to finance its deficits by issuing bonds at rising interest rates, predominantly subscribed by domestic investors (e.g., Ciocca 2007; Rossi 2007; Balassone et al. 2013, fig. 2). For the end of debt monetization saw the onset not of budget discipline but of a tacit exchange between political elites and savers and firms, by which growing public deficits sustained aggregate demand and firms' profits, and were financed progressively less by tax revenue—which rose slowly and was increasingly eroded by evasion—than by high-yield bonds. While this equilibrium dampened firms' incentives to invest in innovation, therefore, as the downturn of TFP and Italy's divergence from the productivity frontier suggest, its reliance on debt-financed deficit spending partly compensated the effects on aggregate growth.

The benefits flowed chiefly to the political and economic elites and the most influential interest groups, but they also percolated to most of society through the pervasive system of particularistic inclusion that had been built ever since the late 1950s, and which was expanded. During this decade inequality dropped, in fact, and average living standards improved (Brandolini and Vecchi 2013; Vecchi 2017).

Although the political elite commanded ever less respect, likewise, it nevertheless enjoyed relatively stable consensus and electoral support (e.g., Bull 2015; Newell 2015). Voters' loyalty was accompanied by high levels of dissatisfaction for the functioning of democracy, the highest recorded among the country's European partners throughout the decade (European Commission 1993, 7 and A14). We see here a reflection of the tension, hypothesized in Chapter 4, between citizens' latent and revealed preferences. The visible rise of high-level corruption and large-scale clientelism probably reached a tipping point during the 1980s, signalling to society that public-spiritedness was not a rational choice, as a result of which opportunistic practices spread more widely across society, also at minute level (reliable estimates are lacking, but the phenomenon is uniformly noted by the literature cited earlier). But although public-spiritedness was less and less supported by (narrow) rationality, many nonetheless resented this 'moral decline' and its damaging effects. Hence the combination of disrespect and consensus for the same elite, seen as both corrupt and irredeemable, or irreplaceable.

The features of this equilibrium can also explain why the neo-liberal revolution was tepid in Italy, even though the country was arguably closer to the Anglo-Saxon 'liberal market economy' model (Hall and Soskice 2001) than other European economies. Relatively free to evade regulations and taxes, widely shielded from competition, often recipient of discretionary government subsidies, and locked into a 'marriage of convenience' with the political establishment, a large part of Italy's economic elites had less reason than their foreign peers to demand deregulation and the reduction of the size of the public sector, inefficient though it was.

This equilibrium collapsed in September 1992. To describe the intervening dozen years a few data and examples will suffice, to draw the outer boundaries of each problem.

Politics

'Cercarono solo voti.' 'They only looked for votes': thus Ciocca (2007, 291) describes the policies pursued by the governing parties up to 1992. Competition was indeed stiff, especially among the DC's main factions and between them and the PSI. Yet, as 'worldview politics' and parties' political cultures began to decline (see Pasquino 2015b), and their entrenchment in the state and state-owned enterprises deepened (Cotta 2015), it was increasingly competition for power and rents. For instance, in 1989–92 Italy was governed by the pact by which the centrist and right-wing factions of the DC allied themselves with the PSI against the large left-wing faction of their own party, whose members nonetheless remained in government (Varsori 2015): to appreciate the extent to which the practice of politics had changed, it is enough to consider that when the Socialists first entered the ruling majority, in 1962–3, their long-term objective was the establishment of socialism. Mirror-like, as parties' grassroots organizations weakened, and increasingly became instruments for patronage and career-making (Cotta 2015), electoral competition was ever more based on marketing, as in a cohesive oligopolistic cartel: dominated by 'fragments of parties without ideals', Carli (1996, 10) writes, politics degenerated to such an extent that 'electoral competition [was] based exclusively on the quantity of financial means [available to them]'.

As parties weakened, distributional coalitions strengthened. They had developed over the previous decades, either naturally, according to the logic that Olson (1965, 1982) illustrates, or under the stimulus of the policies of particularistic inclusion that we have described, and were often instruments of large-scale clientelism.[1] As their bargaining power rose, the DC's and its allies' ability to curb their demands on public resources and coordinate them into a coherent development policy declined (Crafts and Magnani 2013, 91, note 9). Besides the effects on public finances, Italy's main political parties thus began losing the critical characteristic that Olson (1982) attributes to 'encompassing organizations', namely the capacity to promote regulatory and redistribution policies that, while beneficial to their electoral constituencies, are compatible with allocative efficiency. Following North's (1983) criticism of Olson, discussed in Chapter 3, we ascribe this evolution to the logic of Italy's social order: to the strength of the spiral, in our metaphor.

In this setting political polarization rose again (Bull 2015). The 'communist threat' was artificially resurrected, less to hold the governing coalition together than to give it a plausible popular justification and thereby re-weave the ideological veil that had hitherto contributed to hiding the expansion of the spiral. To help disseminate the message the public broadcaster and Berlusconi's private television monopoly—not just tolerated but actively safeguarded by the government (Donovan and Gilbert 2015, 396)—were used (Gundle 2015). '[T]o survive we need a Cold War situation': this statement of a DC minister, uttered in 1959 (see Chapter 6), was much truer in these years. The so-called 'Second Cold War' of the 1980s was much less the cause than the pretext for the recrudescence of anti-communism and political polarization.[2]

The dynamics we just described had effects on the quality of fiscal policy, the public administration, and public services, which can be gauged by the fact that during this decade the growth of public expenditure reflected less the increase in the services provided to society than the rise of their real unit costs: it was predominantly due to 'pure inefficiencies' (Ciocca 2007, 291). Sustained fiscal expansion thus did relatively little to raise the country's productivity and production potential. Indeed, empirical research persuasively suggests that public investments were sometimes made primarily, if not exclusively, to serve as sources of bribes (e.g., Golden and Picci 2006).

The Rule of Law

Party financing was often illegal, in fact, as the anti-corruption investigations that began in 1992 will demonstrate. For instance, the courts ascertained that

---

[1] In Chapter 6 we mentioned the example of the farmers' association, Coldiretti.
[2] Throughout the decade the PCI and the governing parties nonetheless cooperated extensively, in both law-making and local administration.

since the late 1970s virtually every procurement contract made by the agency in charge of road construction and maintenance was tainted by corruption: in agreement with the management of the agency and the public works ministry, 200 firms had joined up in a cartel, through which they decided which tender would be assigned to which firm, at pre-agreed inflated prices, and arranged the paperwork accordingly: one of the culprits confessed that in the agency and the ministry everybody was being paid, 'also the ushers' (Davigo and Mannozzi 2007, 265–7). It also emerged that some firms paid additional bribes to the ministry's or the agency's leadership, to jump the queue that the cartel had set. For corruption had replaced the procurement process to such an extent that it paradoxically recreated a level playing field: a rigid and anti-competitive one, however, which constrained the opportunities of the more productive firms, and led some to engage in what can be defined as second-degree corruption.

Corruption was equally pervasive in the Milan offices of the financial police, the Guardia di finanza (Colombo 1996, 137–45). The practice of taking bribes—to condone tax evasion, typically—was so systematic that in the indictment the prosecutors had to explain why they were not charging the accused also of having set up a joint criminal enterprise, a graver crime than corruption. In those offices, they argued, the organization and command hierarchy of the hypothetical criminal enterprise were so intertwined with the official structure of the financial police as to be indistinguishable from it: consequently, the accused could not be charged of having set up a *separate* criminal organization (which, by law, prevented the graver charge from being raised).[3] In blunter words, they had effectively turned a segment of a public authority into a criminal enterprise.

These were relatively grave cases. Yet few judicial offices were as effective as Milan's in investigating bribery. Between 1983 and 2002, in particular, the prosecution office responsible for the southern tip of Calabria obtained only three convictions for corruption, compared to Milan's 882: relative to the size of the two judicial districts, these numbers translate into ratios, respectively, of 0.76 and 14.07 convictions per 100,000 inhabitants (Davigo and Mannozzi 2007, 74). In that part of Calabria organized crime was particularly powerful, civicness low, clientelism widespread, and public expenditure and transfers intense (Putnam 1993; Gratteri and Nicaso 2016): for each of these reasons corruption could be expected to be more, not nineteen times less, widespread than in Milan. Those cases were grave only relative to those that have been revealed, therefore, but probably not relative to the many that remained undisturbed. Even so, almost 3,000 members of Italy's political and economic

---

[3] Quoted by Davigo and Mannozzi (2007, 281–4).

elites were indicted (Boeri 2010, 3), including six former prime ministers and many senior managers of the main private and state-owned firms (Barbacetto et al. 2012).

As in the case of the oil sector scandal mentioned in Chapter 8, bribes were generally allocated among parties according to pre-defined criteria and often channelled between one single party and one single enterprise, which acted as intermediaries for the two sides of the exchange: the political cartel and the business one (Davigo and Mannozzi 2007; Hine 2015). In Milan and else-where, where they were part of the administration, Communists participated fully in the system.

Corruption was systemic, in sum, and the vicious circles discussed in Chapter 4 pervasive. To highlight the link with the rise of clientelism and the decline of political parties, political cultures, and worldview politics, it suffices to note that the Clean Hands investigations set off from the case of a lesser Milanese public-sector manager, a Socialist, who used the bribes he collected also to pay for the membership fees of hundreds of party members (Rhodes 2015, 310; Davigo 2017, 12). He thus came to effectively own a small but growing segment of the Milanese PSI, on whose strength he planned to enter the municipal executive body and, eventually, national politics. Adverse selection is less a by-product than a physiological feature of a system of political selection in which parties tolerate such practices, as the governing parties and especially the PSI did (see Cotta 2015).

As the literature profusely shows, adverse selection was prevalent among civil servants too: those loyal to the public interest were either sidelined, or eventually absorbed by the spiral (e.g., Davigo and Mannozzi 2007; Davigo 2017). It may be remembered that Calamandrei ([1947] 2004, 235–6) saw the same phenomenon in the Fascist regime.

Italian society was informed. In 1980 Calvino described a country 'based on illegality', as we said in the Preface. One year later, in a celebrated interview, the leader of the PCI denounced that political parties had become 'machines of power and clientelism', organized as federations of factions and 'camarillas', each governed by 'bosses and underbosses', which lacked know-ledge about society and its needs and merely 'managed' disparate interests, including 'shady' ones.[4] The analysis was accurate, as regards both the decline of parties and the rise of corruption and special interest groups. But the resurgence of political polarization and the systemic nature of the incen-tives generated by the spiral allowed these and similar warnings to be written down as partisan and overlooked—including, as we saw, within the Com-munist party itself.

---

[4] Quoted by Di Michele (2008, 299).

After 1984–5 an attempt to increase tax revenue and reduce delinquency was made, but it was half-hearted and accompanied by the repeated concession of amnesties (Ginsborg 2001, 154 *passim*; Chiarini et al. 2013). The incentive to evade taxes thus increased rather than declined, as we suggested in Chapter 3, for the benefits grew, as fiscal pressure rose, and the costs fell, as the state's policies at once revealed its unwillingness or inability to fight tax evasion systematically, and weakened the social norm proscribing it (see Besley et al. 2015).

The same logic underpinned land-use and urban-planning policy, the field on which the battle of 1962–4 had publicly been waged. In 1985 a far-sighted law to protect the country's landscapes was approved, but it was preceded by a wide amnesty for illegal construction and lesser irregularities, covering the whole post-1948 period, in respect of which more than 4 million applications were presented (Berdini 2010, 19).

Collusion and Competition

Collusion between the public authorities and economic elites strengthened. Two clear and related illustrations are offered by the credit sector, still predominantly state-owned, and competition policy. In their study of the allocative efficiency of Italy's banking system, Battilossi et al. (2013, 513) find that during the 1970s 'credit volumes stopped responding to sectoral [growth opportunities[5]] and even showed, after 1982, an adjustment in the wrong direction', namely a shift in the allocation of credit towards sectors with *lower* growth opportunities. Besides physiological errors in lending policies and the 'social' motivations—'the aim of stabilizing employment in problematic sectors'—that informed much of public policy during the 1970s, they ascribe this remarkable shift to collusion: credit policies 'may have been distorted and used to favor politically connected interests'.

As Ciocca (2007, 2014) argues, vigilant and demanding lenders are a significant source of competitive pressure on firms: in the 1980s it weakened significantly, relative to the 1950s and the 1960s. Nor did policy-makers strengthen other determinants of the intensity of competition: pervasive anti-competitive regulation in the product markets was not dismantled, and a modern competition law—modelled on the European Community rules—was adopted only in 1990, partly in response to European pressure. With the support of the economic elites, moreover, the ruling coalition rejected the decentralized enforcement system originally proposed (Toffoletto 1995, 70–9 and 166–79), and granted the power to enforce the new law primarily to a

---

[5] Inferred from price/earnings ratios drawn from stock market data (pp. 494–5).

competition authority instead, whose actual independence was arguably limited (see Pera and Cecchini 2015).[6] The intensity of competition grew noticeably only after the completion of the European single market (Giordano and Zollino 2017), in 1993, suggesting that external forces were again decisive, as in the 1950s.

Inappropriate Institutions and Italy's Incipient Divergence from the Frontier

In Chapter 2 we noted that impersonally enforced rights increase economic efficiency, chiefly by widening the radius of trust, and that competition and the rule of law stimulate firms' growth, innovation, and productivity growth, especially in close-to-frontier economies. In this light, the downturn of TFP and the reversal of Italy's convergence to the frontier are hardly surprising, for during the 1980s the rule of law remained weak and neither the microeconomic nor the macroeconomic determinants of the intensity of competition strengthened—with the notable exceptions, respectively, of the defeat of terrorism and the onset, after 1985, of exchange rate stability (Ciocca 2007; Rossi 2007). Though mostly unchanged, therefore, Italy's institutions became ever less appropriate for the needs of an economy that had approached the productivity frontier (see Figure 1.1).

Productivity collapsed in services, not in manufacturing. But signs of weakness emerged in this sector too, beyond the effects of IRI's continued decline.[7] They are revealed by changes in Italy's competitive position. Federico and Wolf (2013, 345) observe a 'major discontinuity around 1980'. If the post-war decades had seen 'a shift in specialization from traditional textiles and low-technology goods toward medium-technology, most notably engineering products', such that 'Italy seemed poised to converge to the German model', since the 1980s the country 'lost competitiveness in (many) medium-technology products' and relied more 'on exports of low-technology "made in Italy" products (plus some specialized engineering)'. Besides the dynamism of the industrial districts and the medium-sized firms that arose from them, this discontinuity indicates a broader retrenchment of the private sector into lower-technology productions, which went in parallel with a comparatively marked decline in average firm size. In the same vein, Barbiellini Amidei et al. (2013, 384) note that after the mid 1980s the interest of foreign capital 'increased in scale-intensive industries, but decreased in science- and technology-based industries', a trend which 'suggests a diminishing attractiveness of Italian

---

[6] For example, the jurist who led the agency in 1994–7 had previously been a parliamentarian (1983–94), minister (1987–9), and prime minister (1992–3), he resigned from the agency before the end of his mandate, and shortly thereafter he again became minister (1998–2000, 2006–8), prime minister (2000–1), and parliamentarian (2001–6).

[7] A belated attempt to reverse it was cut short by the events of 1992–4 (see Ciocca 2014).

high-technology industries' (a sector in which, despite their decline, IRI's firms were nonetheless responsible for most of R&D expenditure growth: p. 401). Far from converging to the German model, during this decade the country's private sector generally retreated from the frontier.

This, in our reading, was both an effect of the growing inappropriateness of Italy's institutions and a proximate cause of the reversal shown by Figure 1.2. In summary, low competition dampened the incentives for reallocation and innovation; the weakness of the rule of law—through its effects, in particular, on corporate governance standards and the functioning of the domestic financial markets—hampered the efficient allocation of capital; and the availability of corruption, tax evasion, and collusion with public authorities as sources of revenue or profits magnified both effects. All this, in turn, sustained the progress of the spiral.

The South and Organized Crime

The divergence of the South, which had resumed in the early 1970s, accelerated. IRI's large firms established there further weakened, few flexible and efficient small- and mid-sized firms arose around them, and the special development policy became ever more based on current transfers and labour income (Cannari et al. 2010; Iuzzolino et al. 2013), which stoked political clientelism. As Crafts and Magnani (2013, 92) write, '[f]rom being a factor supporting Italian growth, the relative stagnation of the South gradually became a drain on public resources'.

The regional redistribution of resources that this entailed—coupled with the rise, albeit modest, of tax revenue—helped a new populist party, the Northern League, to claim the representation of the more productive North against the 'parasitic' South and the inefficient bureaucracy in Rome (Davis 2015, 62). It won only one seat in the 1987 election, but its manifesto mixing fiscal revolt, ethnicity-based themes, and, eventually, threats of secession, gained support in parts of the Catholic North, mainly from small entrepreneurs, their workers, and the lower middle classes (Passarelli 2015).

With the probable exception of grand corruption, the degeneration we just reviewed took its acutest forms in the South (see Barbagallo and Bruno 1997; Trigilia 2012; Felice 2013; Davis 2015). Both effect and cause of these regions' decline, during the 1980s organized crime strengthened, thanks also to the profits reaped from the drug trade: not just in Sicily, but also in Calabria and Campania, where the camorra and especially the 'ndrangheta became more organized (Paoli 2015). The increase of profits also provoked conflict, however, and a long internecine war for the control of the Sicilian mafia, which eventually came under the control of a particularly aggressive leadership. The organization's ties with parts of the DC were nonetheless preserved, and its engagement in influencing electoral competition and organizing large-scale clientelism persisted (De Feo and De Luca 2013; Alesina et al. 2016). Fuelled by the rise of its investable profits, its involvement in procurement corruption, illegal construction, and formal business activities also rose, and its ties with the economic elites correspondingly deepened (Lupo [1996] 2009).

One significant example was ascertained in 2014, when the supreme court confirmed the seven-year sentence issued to the person, Marcello Dell'Utri, who had served as mediator between Berlusconi and the mafia between 1974 and 1992 (Paoli 2015, note 58). According to the findings of the trial, the main object of his mediation was the payments that Berlusconi regularly made to the organization during that period (Berlusconi was investigated for these payments but was not charged). In the 1970s Berlusconi was a rising Milanese entrepreneur, and paid the organization to protect his nascent activities in Sicily and his own family from kidnappings (Donovan and Gilbert 2015, 395). Notably, however, the trial established that the payments were interrupted neither by the change in the mafia's leadership, nor by the rise in Berlusconi's influence (in 1984–5 he could obtain from the government two very controversial ad hoc measures, two decree-laws[8], protecting his television business: Donovan and Gilbert 2015, 396). Notably, moreover, in the 1980s Dell'Utri became the chief executive officer of Berlusconi's advertising business, the cash-generating core of his media group (Lane 2004), and hence for a long time was Berlusconi's 'right-hand man' (Paoli 2015, 677). In particular, in 1993 Dell'Utri was 'the driving force behind the creation of Forza Italia' (Donovan and Gilbert 2015, 395; see also Ginsborg 2001, 290), the political party that Berlusconi led to victory in March 1994.

In 1982 the mafia killed the police general credited with a decisive contribution in defeating the Red Brigades, Carlo Alberto Dalla Chiesa, who had been appointed prefect of Palermo three months earlier with the mandate to fight organized crime. The shock provoked by his assassination widened the following of the hitherto small anti-mafia movement (Paoli 2015). The reaction led parts of Sicilian society to turn actively against the organization, and sustained the work of the magistrates—among whom were Paolo Borsellino and Giovanni Falcone—who in 1986–7 charged its known leadership and hundreds of its foot soldiers (La Spina 2014; Paoli 2015). This unprecedented 'maxi trial' was based on the analysis that the mafia was a unitary, vertical organization, in which the leadership held command responsibility for its subordinates' actions: an interpretation that had hitherto been largely rejected

---

[8] These are legislative acts having the force of law, which the executive can issue in exceptional circumstances and expire unless ratified by parliament within sixty days.

by the higher courts, which typically acquitted the mafia's higher ranks for absence of evidence on individual crimes (see Falcone 1991). In 1987 the first instance court endorsed this analysis and issued 344 convictions, including life sentences for nineteen mafia leaders (Ginsborg 2001, 209).

The reaction did not come only from circles close to the mafia. Stajano ([1987] 2010) dissects the libellous words that from the pages, again, of the *Corriere* the writer Leonardo Sciascia (1987) addressed to Borsellino and others, accused of 'making a career' out of exaggerated rhetoric about the mafia. A heated debate followed, across the nation, in which voices as heterogeneous as the DC, the PSI, the Sicilian PCI and trade unions, a far-left independent newspaper (*Il manifesto*), and a small grouping of libertarians all took the side of the contrarian Sicilian intellectual. The anti-mafia movement was shaken and suffered rifts. Stajano (2017) reports Falcone as saying, plausibly, that on account of his reputation Sciascia's article had 'set the fight against the mafia back by ten years'.

'They Only Looked for Votes'

To conclude, we return to Ciocca's reproach. Considering the incentives they faced and the opportunities they had, 'they' could scarcely be expected to act otherwise. In the course of the 1970s the spiral had spread its roots deep into society. Thereafter it ran unfettered because the equilibrium was self-perpetuating, such that, in particular, fiscal discipline could not be imposed without depriving the elites of critical instruments—deficit spending and large-scale clientelism—to secure both sustained economic growth and stable political support. And its run was feebly resisted because the forces that could oppose it—parts of the judiciary, the media, civil society, and also of the PCI—lacked either the instruments, the information, or the organization to do so more than episodically, and could rarely coordinate their efforts. Intellectuals and vocal minorities did denounce the degeneration of the country (see Urbinati 2015), and so did some newspapers, but public discourse was heavily influenced by the state- or elite-controlled media, and especially by the public broadcaster and Berlusconi's private television monopoly (Gundle 2015; Mancini 2015). Before 1992 some corruption scandals did emerge, but the political elite could generally block them through the techniques we already discussed. And when public opinion began to show outrage, politicians began to accuse prosecutors of political bias (Bruti Liberati 1997).

In the space of three years, between 1991 and 1994, the equilibrium that we have just described was first shaken, mightily, and then recomposed. The chronology of events guides the next section, while the following ones discuss the causes and effects of the resumption of the spiral.

The Rupture of 1992–1994

una fine così miseranda è l'espressione del fallimento di tutta una nazione.

[such a pitiable end is the expression of the bankruptcy of a whole nation.]

(Norberto Bobbio, 20 January 1993)

The Storm Gathers (1991)

In the course of 1990 discontent found expression in the collection of 600,000 signatures for a set of legislative referenda, which aimed at abandoning the proportional electoral system—judged to be a cause of unresponsive government—in favour of a majoritarian one. The constitutional court allowed only one question to be put to the electorate, however, concerning the selection of parliamentarians: namely, the proposal to reduce the number of preference votes that citizens could express within party lists from four (three, in the smaller electoral districts) to one.[9] Its rationale was that multiple preferences had become an instrument of clientelism (Regalia 2015, 136); in particular, they were the basis for a practice known as '*voto di scambio* (vote of exchange), that is, the routine to use preferences, by voters, as a barter good and, by candidates, as an asset to purchase'.[10]

The proposal was firmly opposed by the governing parties, which sought also to downplay its importance so as to ensure that the threshold for the validity of the vote—half of the electorate—would not be met. The same did their fiercest opponent, notably, the Northern League (Passarelli 2015, 228). The PCI, then undergoing its transformation into a non-communist left-wing party, was hesitant and divided. Only disparate civil society organizations, often Catholic, Confindustria, and a relatively small and diverse group of politicians and intellectuals supported the proposal with determination. Their campaign, alimented by grievances and demands much broader than the referendum question itself concerned, leveraged on the widely perceived cleavage separating an inadequate, clientelistic, and often corrupt political elite from a virtuous civil society. The tacit exchange between the two, based on the policies of particularistic inclusion that we have reviewed, was not discussed.

The referendum was held on 9 June 1991. Voter turnout was 62.5 per cent and 95.6 per cent supported the proposal. The result was a surprise. Ginsborg

---

[9] Under the constitution such referenda can only repeal laws or parts of them.

[10] In party lists numbering dozens of candidates, multiple preferences allowed ballots to be marked by unique numerical combinations (i.e., combinations of the serial numbers of the candidates chosen), making it possible to check voters' compliance with their side of the exchange.

(2001, 174) writes that '[a] different Italy had made its voice heard, one that was much less servile than either government or opposition had imagined'.

In our perspective, the vote was the sign that the expansion of the spiral during the 1980s and its increasingly visible damaging effects had heightened the tension between citizens' opportunistic choices and their latent preferences. In the absence of a credible alternative to the ruling majority, most voters supported it and acted as the incentives flowing from the spiral dictated: but given a chance to express their preferences outside of the dialectic between government and opposition, in a referendum opposed by most of the political elite, those same voters expressed a demand for better government. This was true also of much of the economic elites, as Confindustria's stance shows. Although they benefited from collusion with the governing parties, they suffered from the weight and rigidity of systemic corruption and from the comparative inefficiency of the public sector, in view of the imminent completion of the European single market.

A similar rationale, stemming from the long-term unsustainability of the country's equilibrium, underpinned the government's decision to accept the stringent macroeconomic criteria set forth in the Maastricht Treaty for participating in EMU, each of which Italy was far from meeting. In 1991 the same political elite that presided over that equilibrium chose to bind themselves and their successors to a commitment, the so-called *vincolo esterno*, which was de facto incompatible with it: a commitment, however, that aimed at forcing an improvement in macroeconomic management and economic institutions, and, even more importantly, at anchoring the country to the European integration process (see, e.g., Carli 1996, 399–407; Ciocca 2007, 309 *passim*).

The Equilibrium Is Shaken (1992)

On 30 January 1992 the supreme court upheld the interpretation underpinning the 'maxi trial' against the mafia, confirmed most prison sentences issued against its leaders and foot soldiers, and dealt to the organization a blow both unexpected and unprecedented (Lupo ([1996] 2009).

On 17 February the Milanese Socialist who financed party membership fees with corruption proceeds was arrested while he was collecting a small bribe. His confession set what came to be known as the Clean Hands investigation in motion.

On 12 March the mafia killed the politician who since the 1970s was Andreotti's 'chief agent' in Sicily, and 'had for many years secretly represented mafia interests in Rome': this was both 'reprisal' for not having prevented that judicial blow, and 'a warning to others' (Mack Smith 1997, 478). As Lupo ([1996] 2009, 261–2) writes, with this murder and that of another long-standing political interlocutor, the mafia reacted to the 'inability of the political power to keep firm control over the judiciary [and] ensure the protections that [it] expected'.

The April national election recorded considerable losses by the DC and the successor of the PCI, lesser ones by the PSI, and the rise of the Northern League, which won close to 9 per cent of the vote (Bull 2015). The latter had run on the manifesto described earlier and a public rhetoric of unheard violence and vulgarity, used as a marker of its alterity in respect of the ruling Roman 'partitocracy' (see Cotta 2015; Passarelli 2015).

After the vote the anti-corruption investigations widened, targeted ever more prominent politicians and businessmen, and gradually began to spread beyond Milan. This acceleration reflects the systemic nature of corruption: having penetrated the system, prosecutors could multiply the directions of their investigations, and their progress in turn increased culprits' incentive to seek leniency, or avoid arrest, by confessing before being found or immediately after (see Colombo 1996; Davigo and Mannozzi 2007; Rhodes 2015). In parallel, the popular enthusiasm sparked by the investigations and the support they received from growing parts of the mainstream media constrained the political elite's ability to defend itself.

On 23 May the mafia killed Falcone, with 300 kilograms of explosives. On 19 July it killed Borsellino, in the same way. Having punished its ineffective or disloyal political interlocutors, the organization had turned on its main adversaries. The first murder happened while parliament was in the process of electing the president of the republic: Andreotti was a strong contender, but in a political climate radically changed by the explosion a rare Christian Democrat of untainted reputation was elected. After the second murder, Ginsborg (2001, 263) writes, '[t]he state trembled, and to all Europe it seemed as if Italy was slipping rapidly out of control'. For the same reason a strong reaction followed, however, which fused with popular support for the Clean Hands investigations and gave impetus to both the anti-mafia movement and law enforcement efforts (see La Spina 2014; Paoli 2015). In January 1993 the main leader of the mafia was arrested—near Palermo, where he had lived for decades as a fugitive—and a few months later Andreotti was charged with abetting the organization.

While the most visible, odious, and immediately damaging manifestations of the equilibrium were thrown open before the nation's eyes, its critical pillar—debt-financed fiscal profligacy—cracked. Ciocca (2007, 307–15), then at the central bank, describes the progression of the events, which the newly elected government failed to stem. In the summer vast speculative movements in the currency markets eventually forced the lira—and the British pound—out of the EMS, provoking a depreciation of about 20 per cent over six months; the real interest rates on the sovereign debt—then equivalent to about 105 per cent of GDP—rose to a level that brought the country to the verge of the precipice; at the height of the crisis, in mid September, the government enacted the 'largest and most intense' budget adjustment in the history of the Italian state (Rossi 2007, 79), the net effect of which was equivalent to 5.8 per cent of GDP.

A 'Pitiable End' (1993)

The ruling class nonetheless sought to defend the extant equilibrium. On 5 March 1993 the government adopted a set of decree-laws, which it described as a 'political solution' to the corruption problem (Ginsborg 2001, 275). By then much of the business establishment and more than one third of the members of parliament were under investigation, and almost one third of the cabinet had resigned for the same reason (Ginsborg 2001, 279–80; Di Michele 2008, 356). One decree decriminalized illegal party financing, the most common charge, and lowered the penalties for bribery. The riskiness of the move—88 per cent of the population was then dissatisfied with the functioning of their democracy, a level 20 percentage points higher than the European average (European Commission 1993, A14), and only an estimated 2 per cent trusted political parties (Barbacetto et al. 2012, 127)—suggests a degree of desperation. Public opinion and the press reacted with outrage, in fact, and the president of the republic refused to promulgate the decree.

Already low, the credibility of the government collapsed. The DC, the PSI, and their allies were all dissolving in the meanwhile, under the impetus of the anti-corruption and anti-mafia investigations. Defeated, they changed strategy: bowing to popular pressure, five months after that decree parliamentarians abolished their own immunity from prosecution, which in the previous decades had blocked countless investigations.

In April a fresh referendum on the electoral law was held, which imposed the majoritarian model. The aim was to achieve '[s]olid parliamentary majorities, stable governments, accountability, and alternation in government' (Regalia 2015, 137). Parliament complied, with a law that however mixed the first-past-the-post system, for three quarters of the seats, with the proportional-representation system, for the remainder.

Soon after the referendum a fresh executive was formed, led by the highly respected governor of the central bank. It was the first 'technical', non-partisan executive, based primarily on the support of the president of the republic (see Calise 2015; Pasquino 2015a). It included several technocrats, relied on a broad parliamentary majority, which de facto included also the main left-wing party (the successor of the PCI), and had the mandate to ensure macroeconomic stability and lead the country to early elections, judged urgently necessary.

The left seemed the strongest contender. Except in Milan, gained by the Northern League, its candidates won all main mayoral elections held in June, under a new majoritarian two-round electoral system. The successor of the PCI was heavily tainted by corruption, by European standards, but less than its erstwhile adversaries (Ginsborg 2001, 282). And the League was tainted too, as in January 1993 its leader and its treasurer were charged—and later convicted—for having accepted an illegal financial contribution from a large firm (Ginsborg 2001, 288). Remarkably, the crime had taken place shortly after the party had imposed itself as a significant force, in the April 1992 election.

It is in this context that, a few months after the arrest of its leader, the mafia resorted to an equally unprecedented strategy, reminiscent of that employed by extreme-right terrorism two decades earlier. Bombs exploded on 27 May, in Florence, and on 27 July, in Milan and Rome, which killed ten people, destroyed one museum, and damaged other monumental buildings. But even though further high-profile arrests followed those attacks, the strategy was discontinued.[11]

In the autumn the left prevailed in another wave of mayoral elections, including in Rome. Berlusconi's Forza Italia party was formed then. 'Threatened by the possible victory of the left' at the imminent national election, Hopkin (2015, 327) explains, he 'mobilized his own public image and his corporate resources to reorganize the fragmented center-right into a single electoral coalition, drawing on the emergent Northern League and the [neo-fascist party]'.

A Fresh Political Elite Rises (1994)

His candidacy to the premiership was announced two months before the vote, scheduled for March 1994. Allied with the League and the neo-fascists, he faced a left-wing coalition (chiefly heirs of the PCI) and a smaller centrist one (chiefly heirs of the DC's left wing). Berlusconi ran on a liberal manifesto and resurrected the spectre of communism, claiming that a victory of the left-wing coalition would have put the nation's freedoms at risk. Aided by his campaigning skills and private television monopoly, he went much further than the governing coalitions of the 1980s in artificially reopening that ideological cleavage: his rhetoric often borrowed the tones of the 1948 vote, and deeply marked the campaign. For its part, the left invoked Berlusconi's conflict of interest to deny his fitness for public office. Polarization rarely declined during the following two decades: in the public arena, the centre-left

---

[11] The rationale of this strategy and the reasons why it was abandoned were the subject of repeated, controversial, and thus far inconclusive judicial investigations.

and the centre-right often denied to each other the status of legitimate political adversary.

Berlusconi's coalition won the popular vote but could form a government only thanks to a classical instance of 'molecular' *trasformismo*, namely the switch to its side of a handful of centrist parliamentarians, one of whom was appointed finance minister.

In the summer the government issued another decree-law aiming to obstruct the anti-corruption investigations. Nicknamed the 'save the thieves' decree, it was promulgated but soon repealed under popular outrage (Rhodes 2015, 318–9). But the political risk was offset by its practical effects, for unlike the earlier one this decree was in force for a few days. It caused most suspects of corruption held in pre-trial custody to be immediately freed, and consequently allowed them to communicate and agree mutually convenient defence strategies, or otherwise tamper with the evidence; almost none was rearrested, in fact, and the wave of confessions that had hitherto sustained the Clean Hands investigations markedly declined, and never resumed thereafter (Colombo 1996, 2012; Davigo and Mannozzi 2007, 157–73). Contradicting earlier pledges to support the fight against corruption, this decree signalled a strategy to safeguard the equilibrium that had been shaken in 1992. Notably, the government weathered the scandal.

As the investigations began to implicate Berlusconi's business or political associates, moreover, the governing elite began accusing the magistrates of political bias, in a crescendo of attacks which, once Berlusconi himself was charged, reached peaks unseen in contemporary Western democracies (see Donovan and Gilbert 2015; Guarnieri 2015; Rhodes 2015).

Thus another near-permanent feature of the following two decades set in, next to political polarization: the equally acute polarization between the judiciary and the political class. The two dialectics often mixed and overlapped. The centre-right regularly and very vocally accused its political opponents and the judiciary, or part of it, of colluding against it. The centre-left tended to defend the judiciary, but sometimes joined the centre-right's criticism. The judiciary was a naturally more passive participant in these contests, but polarization and the campaign waged against it opened divisions among magistrates and led several of them to take inappropriate public stances. Some entered politics, on both sides of the spectrum, and two prominent ones even founded small political parties.

The Spiral Resumed (1994–2011)

Berlusconi's victory was not the reason why Italy's equilibrium survived the rupture of 1992–4. Nor was it the fact that once 'corruption inquiries moved to lower levels, affecting small and medium-business owners—ordinary citizens—"people began to say that's enough: you've liberated us from the old political class that sucked our blood, now you can leave us in peace"', as, among others, two protagonists of the investigations—the then head prosecutor of Milan (quoted by Rhodes 2015, 318) and Colombo (e.g., 2012, 85)—maintain. These were rather signs that the equilibrium had resisted.

The reason, in our interpretation, is that the nation was not presented with proposals credible enough to engender the expectation that the spiral would be reversed. Credible enough, as we said in Chapter 4, to lead citizens to behave *as if* public-spiritedness was individually rational and thereby *make* it individually rational to eschew opportunism.

In 1992–4 Italy arguably did have the opportunity to move a decisive step in its transition towards the open-access social order. For one countervailing force—the judiciary, or more precisely segments of it, whose *actual* independence was relatively recent—had powerfully disrupted the status quo; its disruption had brought the long-rising tension between citizens' latent preferences and opportunistic choices to a breaking point, which manifested itself in vast popular support for the investigations; and this prevented the political and economic elites from defending the status quo (indeed, some joined the chorus for change). Of course, many citizens had for long accepted the equilibrium built on particularistic inclusion, weak rule of law, and limited universal opportunities. But when the investigations and the September 1992 currency crisis exposed not just the obscenity but also the vulnerability of that equilibrium, their rational opportunism gave way to the latent preference for a fairer and more efficient organization of society.

To shift to such an equilibrium, however, a *pars construens* had to follow the *pars destruens*. The nation needed to receive proposals equal to such a challenge, which could be left neither to the judiciary nor to the uncoordinated pressure of citizens: the anti-corruption and anti-mafia magistrates could embody the hope for change, in particular, but not carry it to fruition. This was a tall order, as change required credible proposals for a fresh social contract, in effect, aiming to reduce the gap that separated the country's formal institutions from its actual ones, and align them to the needs of a mature democracy and a close-to-frontier economy. Achieving change required a long-term collective effort, moreover, comparable in intensity—but far larger in scope—to that which spread across the agrarian South in 1944–7 (see Chapter 6).

For them to be credible, and therefore capable of changing citizens' expectations, such proposals had to meet at least four conditions. They had to rest on a clear analysis of the extant equilibrium. They had to be comparable in ambition to the reform programme of 1962–4, as the roots of the spiral had spread deep into society. They had to rely on effective organizations, capable of collecting and coordinating society's demands and imposing them upon the political authorities. And they had to be broad-based, capable of transcending the left–right axis: similar, in this, to the limited agreements of which Sen (2009) writes, or indeed to the constitutional compromise of 1946–7, which held firm despite the rising winds of domestic and international polarization. The parallel is legitimate, for in 1992–4 change meant strengthening the rule of law and the supremacy of the public interest over private interests: this was as foundational an enterprise as the constitutional compromise of 1946–7, and ought to have relied on an equally wide and pluralist consensus.

The opportunity was lost because it was either not seen, seemingly, or eschewed. The problem is less that the three contending coalitions of March 1994 were all, in varying degree, tainted by corruption. The problem is that each described it as a pathology, not as a component of a 'harmonious system', in Calvino's words (1980). None had the capacity, the credibility, or the intention to explain that 'system' to the nation and present it with a realistic alternative. None had the strength to impose upon its competitors that foundational agenda—strengthening the rule of law and the supremacy of the public interest—as a common platform.

The strategic aim of Berlusconi's coalition, as the 'save-the-thieves' decree already suggested, was one of essential continuity with the pre-1992 equilibrium. The centrist coalition, small and weak, was heavily tainted by it. This was less true of the left, which still commanded a relatively strong grassroots organization. But not even this coalition appears to have realized that the country needed a reform programme capable of being presented as a genuinely national-constitutional agenda. The left acted as though the March 1994 vote was an ordinary election instead, the first which it could realistically hope to win, and ran on a fairly classical, if prudent, progressive manifesto (see Ginsborg 2001, 282 *passim*).

In one word, if the reformist ideas of 1962–4 lacked the urgency of a profound crisis to impose them, the crisis of 1992–4 lacked the reformist programme that could have turned it into an equilibrium shift. And in both cases, unlike in the rural South of the mid 1940s no large, mass-based party or organization either saw or determinedly sought to take the opportunity for change.

Absent the credible prospect of an equilibrium shift, which alone could have changed their expectations, many voters anticipated the effects of the resumption of the spiral and voted according to the incentives flowing from it. For all Berlusconi's admirable campaigning skills and private television monopoly, anti-communism—five years after the fall of the Berlin Wall, three after the dissolution of the Soviet Union—cannot suffice to explain his coalition's victory. It stemmed from those incentives, which the events of 1992–4 had suspended but not removed, as the behaviour of the Northern League—its involvement in corruption, but also its earlier opposition to the referendum on multiple preferences—already suggested. Berlusconi's votes came mostly from the erstwhile electorate of the DC, the PSI, and their allies, which had all disappeared (Donovan and Gilbert 2015; Hopkin 2015). But even among those voters many, in the heated atmosphere of 1992–4, had clamoured for change. As the prospects of change waned, they chose to support a businessman who had prospered under the old equilibrium precisely because he promised to preserve and stabilize it, while making it more efficient and 'liberal'.

Stability is the critical perspective, diametrically opposed to that we followed thus far. The reason lies in the tension that traversed Italy's amphibious social order, in transition between the limited-access model and the open-access one, which manifested itself in the wide chasm separating the country's formal institutions from its actual ones, namely that intermittently illuminated space in which spun the vicious circles that we have described. For by enforcing the law upon opportunistic practices that had hitherto relied on permissive norms, the judicial investigations had disrupted the balance that allowed the two sets of rules to coexist in a 'harmonious' and predictable system. This created uncertainty and instability, as it was no longer clear which set of institutions prevailed: whether the formal ones, which proscribed corruption and tax evasion, or the actual ones, which often condoned them. Soon after the Clean Hands investigations began a 'drastic drop-off in public construction' occurred, in fact (Chang et al. 2010, 477). This form of instability may seem desirable if it is viewed in a dynamic perspective, that of an equilibrium shift, because rupture opens up opportunities for change; but instability is merely disruptive if it is viewed in the perspective of continuity. Once the prospect of an equilibrium shift dissolved, therefore, much of society opted for a return to stability and predictability.

This explains why Berlusconi's government issued the 'save-the-thieves' decree, a mere two months after taking office, and why the outrage it provoked did not bring it down. This explains why two weeks later it issued another decree-law, which granted a building amnesty as wide as that of 1985 (Berdini 2010), covering all intervening years, and why parliament eventually ratified it. These two decrees are the signal that the forces of continuity had prevailed, and it is under this signal that the so-called Second Republic began. The following sections analyse this period from three converging perspectives—the rule of law, political accountability, and the economic institutions—and seek to answer the questions posed in Chapter 1: why did Italy fail to adjust, and why were its reforms inadequate?

The Quality of the Rule of Law

The Synthetic Indicators

The rule of law is a 'macro' institution decisive for economic and democratic development, as we argued in Chapters 2 and 3. It is also the field in which the most visible effects of the spiral and the vicious circles it alimented manifested themselves. So it is here that the effects of the rupture of 1992–4 must first be investigated.

The evolution of the rule of law and, within this broader notion, that of the state's capacity to contain corruption are illustrated, respectively, by Figures 9.1 and 9.2. Although these indicators synthetize all available ones, including those produced by Transparency International, they are to be read with caution, as we noted in Chapter 1. The clarity of the trends they reveal, nonetheless, the width of the gap that separates Italy from its peers, and the consistency between the two indicators considerably raises their reliability. Both indicators are amply confirmed by the history of the past two decades, moreover. Donovan and Gilbert (2015), Hine (2015), Hopkin (2015), and Rhodes (2015) review the main facts and the essential literature. Here a few indications shall suffice.

Legislation on Corruption

After the two decrees of 1993 and 1994, over the 1996–2011 period Italy's parliament passed more than a dozen laws having the effect of obstructing,

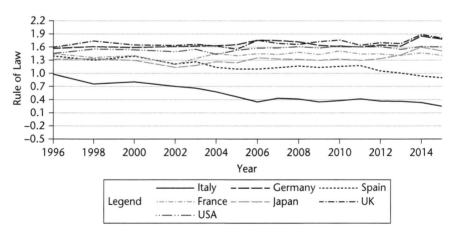

Figure 9.1 Comparative Governance Indicators (Rule of Law), 1996–2015

Rule of law captures perceptions of the extent to which agents have confidence in and abide by the rules of society, and in particular the quality of contract enforcement, property rights, the police, and the courts, as well as the likelihood of crime and violence.
Source: The Worldwide Governance Indicators

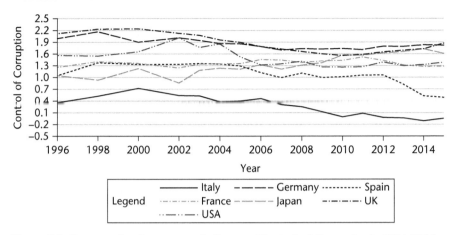

Figure 9.2 Comparative Governance Indicators (Control of Corruption), 1996–2015

Control of corruption captures perceptions of the extent to which public power is exercised for private gain, including both petty and grand forms of corruption, as well as 'capture' of the state by elites and private interests.
Source: The Worldwide Governance Indicators

not strengthening, the repression of corruption and white-collar crime. The majority were passed by centre-right majorities (2001–5 and 2008–11), the rest by centre-left ones (1996–2001 and 2006–8). The latter sternly, and plausibly, criticized the former's laws as motivated by Berlusconi's needs as a defendant in numerous judicial trials, but when it was in power it repealed none of them.[12]

As a result, repressing corruption became considerably harder than it was up to 1994 (Davigo and Mannozzi 2007; Davigo 2017). The problem is well illustrated by a comparison with Finland, which the indicator shown in Figure 9.2 consistently identifies as one of the least corrupt countries in the world (with a score of 2.3 in 2015, in a scale ranging between 2.5 and −2.5, compared to Italy's −0.05). As regards the uncovering of the crime, in 2010 Finland and Italy opened the same number of corruption investigations in per capita terms, 0.4 per 100,000 inhabitants (Vannucci 2012). As regards the punishing of it, data published by the Council of Europe (2016, 80–1) show that in 2015 the number of people serving a final sentence for white-collar crimes—'economic and financial crimes', which includes corruption—was about six times greater in Finland than in Italy, again in per capita terms. Notably, the same data show that in 2015 the share of the total population serving a final prison sentence was *greater* in Italy than in Finland (0.05 and 0.04 per cent, respectively), but the share of prison inmates sentenced for white-collar crimes was *eight times smaller* in Italy than in Finland (0.9 and 7.3 per cent, respectively), implying that Italy's law

---

[12] Nor did the 2011–13 technocratic government (which in 2012 passed an anti-corruption law widely viewed as ineffective: e.g., Davigo 2017).

enforcement system is not generally lenient but is particularly tolerant with such crimes. In sum, if Italy were no more corrupt than Finland its efforts to repress corruption and white-collar crime would have to rise by a factor of six. Not too distant disproportions would emerge from comparisons with other established European democracies. They suggest that in Italy corruption is very seldom detected and even more rarely punished.

Two of the laws that contributed to this result merit a brief description. One, adopted in 2002, effectively decriminalized accounting fraud for all companies but listed ones. Besides other purposes, such as evading taxes and defrauding minority shareholders, falsifying a company's accounts serves also to create the slush funds out of which bribes and illegal political contributions are generally drawn. This law made it easier to hide these crimes, therefore, but also did little to improve Italy's already defective corporate governance standards (see Figure 9.4). After repeated calls by the IMF (e.g., 2014, 13; 2015a, 13) and others, criminal sanctions for accounting fraud were re-established in 2015, by a coalition government. Notably, Confindustria issued no criticism of the 2002 law and gave no support to the 2015 bill: on the contrary, in 1997 its newspaper published a letter of solidarity with Fiat's chief executive officer, found guilty of false accounting, signed by a large part of the economic establishment.[13]

Another law, adopted in 2005, drastically reduced the statute of limitations, namely the time limit that extinguishes one's criminal responsibility unless a final verdict is issued before its expiry. Research quoted by the European Commission (2014, 8) found that as a result of that law in 2006–7 between 10 and 11 per cent of criminal cases were declared time-barred during court proceedings, compared to averages of between 0.1 and 2 per cent in other EU countries. Lowering that time limit strengthened defendants' incentive to engage in delaying tactics, in a country in which the average duration of judicial proceedings was already extremely long, and affected especially corruption cases, which tend to be complex. An estimated two thirds of the 3,200 defendants of the Clean Hands trials benefited from it, in fact (Vannucci 2009, 242).[14] The gravity of the matter was such that, as the European Commission (2014, 3) reports, '[i]n the context of the 2013 European Semester of economic policy coordination, the Council recommended that Italy

---

[13] The verdict became final in 2000 but was later revoked by virtue of the 2002 law. Incidentally, the former senior management of the newspaper—*Il Sole 24 Ore*, published by a listed company controlled (67.5 per cent) by Confindustria—is currently being investigated for false accounting.

[14] Donovan and Gilbert (2015, 404) describe a more recent case, which is worth mentioning because it exemplifies the crudest form of *trasformismo* (on which more later): 'Berlusconi [was] accused of paying €3 million to [a senator] to persuade him to cross the floor in parliament in 2006. [The senator] plea-bargained a 20-month sentence and, in July 2015, Berlusconi was sentenced to three-years' imprisonment for corruption. The statute of limitations was effective from later that year, however.'

strengthen its legal framework for the repression of corruption, including by revising the rules governing limitation periods'. The statute of limitations was extended in June 2017, after a four-year long parliamentary debate, but to levels below the pre-2005 ones.

Parliament did not only promote impunity for corruption, moreover, but also widened the opportunities for it. Barbieri and Giavazzi (2011) show that ad hoc legislation on large public works, often passed ostensibly for reasons of urgency, regularly imposed simplified procurement procedures lacking critical safeguards, and discuss several corruption cases that arose precisely in this sector. Recent ones concern the works to protect Venice from rising tide levels and the 2015 Milan universal exhibition. An earlier one is the object also of research quoted by the European Commission (2014, 13), which compares the per-kilometre construction cost—in millions of euros, at constant prices—of high-speed railway tracks in various countries: Tokyo-Osaka, 9.3; Madrid-Seville, 9.8; Paris-Lyon, 10.2; Rome-Naples, 47.3; Italy (average), 61; Turin-Novara, 74; Novara-Milan, 79.5; Bologna-Florence, 96.4. To better appreciate these disproportions, it may be noted that the—comparatively civic, according to Putnam (1993)—lands on which the Milan-Novara-Turin line runs are flat and not prone to earthquakes, unlike most of the foreign and Italian comparators.

In this field, therefore, for about two decades the work of Italy's parliament has consistently aimed at reducing the gap between the country's formal and actual institutions by bringing the former closer to the latter, not vice versa. Such use of the legislative function attracted the vehement protest of citizens' movements, newspapers, politicians, and intellectuals. But only the judiciary succeeded in partly containing it: a few of those laws were invalidated by the constitutional court, including for breach of the equality principle, upon applications of the lower courts that had to apply them (Guarnieri 2015).

What explains these laws is the re-establishment of the pre-1992 equilibrium. The reason is that in a static perspective a stable inefficient equilibrium is preferable to instability, as we said, and once the prospects for an equilibrium shift vanished this became true also for ordinary citizens. In the presence of an independent and effective judiciary, the gap between formal and actual institutions is a permanent source of tension, instability, and unpredictability: these laws effectively ratified some of the distortions that flew from that tension, and thereby reduced the judiciary's ability to disrupt the extant equilibrium, as it had done in 1992–4.

Compared to the 1980s corruption became more decentralized (e.g., Vannucci 2009, 247–9), due also to the decline of the country's political parties (on which more later). And a second tipping point was probably reached, because elite corruption was effectively avowed: those laws and those attacks on the judiciary amounted to implicit statements that corruption is acceptable, or at least tolerable. The logic discussed in Chapter 4—and especially Tirole's (1996) arguments drawn from the difficulty of (re)building a reputation of integrity—can explain why Italy's political elite chose to give this solution to the tension between law and praxis. Yet this meant shedding what we called 'hypocrisy', namely the necessity of hiding the opportunism of the elites so as to avert its damaging diffusion throughout society. In other words, the veil shielding high-level corruption was repeatedly pierced during the 1980s, shattered in 1992–4, and not rebuilt. This adds weight to the hypothesis that corruption has hence risen, as Figure 9.2 indicates.

Social Tolerance for Corruption, Blackmail, and Trust in the Judiciary

The centre-right and the centre-left could enact and maintain those laws because they provoked neither large protests nor a drop in electoral support. We already explained the underlying logic, but two more proximate reasons can be mentioned. On one hand, after 1994 the *Corriere* and much of the mainstream press gradually shifted from a position of often uncritical support for the anti-corruption magistrates to one of equally often uncritical equidistance between the latter and the politicians accusing them of partisan bias (see Colombo 2012, 207–26). On the other hand, despite the persistence of the myth of a neat distinction between a virtuous civil society and a corrupt elite (Crainz 2003, 2016), social tolerance for corruption grew remarkably.

Among many possible ones, the vicissitudes of two fairly ordinary politicians—both former Christian Democrats, both targets of the Clean Hands investigation—can serve as an example. One in 1993 confessed to having participated in the corruption scheme of the road construction agency mentioned earlier, but was eventually acquitted for a technicality: in 2005 he became the leader of a small centrist party, then in government, and in 2006 was elected to parliament (Barbacetto et al. 2012, 825–6). The other was elected to parliament in 2001, in the ranks of Berlusconi's party, a few days before his six-year sentence for corruption was confirmed by the supreme court: he obtained a reduction of the sentence, its conversion into social work, and the acceptance that his parliamentary service would count as such (Davigo and Mannozzi 2007, 130; Barbacetto et al. 2012, 828). So he served his sentence by serving one parliamentary term, during which many of the laws discussed earlier were passed. In July 2014 he was arrested again, accused of being the mediator of a corruption scheme concerning the works for the 2015 Milan universal exposition, and accepted a three-year prison sentence for this (Ferrarella 2014). Arguably, he responded rationally to the incentives that society had presented him with: corruption is rarely detected, leniently punished, socially tolerated, and widespread, so the benefits of using his know-how in that sector presumably outweighed the costs, not just ex ante but also ex post.

But even more important than his know how was his credibility. For by neither confessing nor implicating others he at once attested his own reliability as a mediator, and safeguarded the blackmail potential of any incriminating information he may have possessed.[15] In 2002 an influential intellectual, former minister and close adviser of Berlusconi, theorized this logic and extended it to a broader sphere: having posited that 'a linear conception of legality' is foreign to politics, he declared that to engage in politics one 'must be vulnerable to blackmail', *ricattabile*, because this assures the other members of the 'system' that one will stand together with them (quoted by Davigo and Mannozzi 2007, 152 note 113). The logic is the same as that which underpinned the power of the P2 (see Colombo 2012, 121–33 and 239–46), and its unspoken premiss is that much of the political system was tainted by illegality.

'Corruption in Italy is a pervasive and systemic phenomenon which affects society as a whole', a Council of Europe report recently concluded (GRECO 2009, 6). Worse, corruption seems now accepted as a physiological component of public life, as we said in the Preface. Under the incentives stemming from the resumption of the spiral, the same population that overwhelmingly supported the Clean Hands investigations and demonstrated in large numbers against the decrees of 1993 and 1994 reacted weakly against the subsequent laws, save for some vocal minorities (see Ginsborg 2001), and responded with growing indifference to the scandals they generated.

This reversal was eased by purposeful action, moreover, by those parts of the political and economic elites that were either directly involved in wrongdoing or had a greater stake in safeguarding the extant equilibrium. They conducted a two-decade long campaign of often ferocious attacks on the judiciary, as we said, aimed at harming its credibility: both directly, by accusing magistrates of bias, and indirectly, by dragging them into political contests. This strategy was largely successful (see Sberna and Vannucci 2013), also because the imprudent or inappropriate conduct of some magistrates confirmed, or at least appeared to corroborate the charges. If in 1992–4 public opinion hailed anti-corruption and anti-mafia prosecutors as the nation's saviours, only 31 per cent of citizens now tend to trust the judicial system, compared to 52 in the EU and 65, 51, and 67 in Britain, France, and Germany, respectively: only Bulgarians, Cypriots, Slovakians, and Slovenians trust their judiciaries less than Italians (European Commission 2015, 30). While social tolerance for corruption increased, therefore, the nation also lost trust in the only authority that had demonstrated the capacity to fight it.

---

[15] Although Italian law does not require an admission of guilt for this idiosyncratic form of plea bargaining (introduced by one of the laws discussed earlier), his acceptance of a three-year sentence for corruption suggests a degree of involvement in the facts.

Tax Evasion

Tax evasion persisted, sustained by the same incentives that operated before the rupture of 1992–4 and fuelled by the amnesties and similar measures that were issued during the 2000s and 2010s (see Galbiati and Zanella 2012; Casaburi and Troiano 2016; Zhang et al. 2016). Tax revenue did rise as a share of GDP, but Chiarini et al. (2013, 282), who analyse the past four decades, note a 'stable gap between the apparent and the effective tax rates, suggesting that taxpayers suffer a stable overburden of fiscal pressure because of tax evasion'.

The estimates of Schneider and Enste (2013) and Buhen and Schneider (2016) indicate that tax evasion is now more than twice as high as in Britain, France, or Germany, as we noted in the Preface. They are corroborated by research commissioned by the European Commission on the 'VAT gap', namely the difference between the amount of value added tax (VAT) theoretically due and actual collections (CASE 2016, 8). This measure therefore estimates the revenue loss due to both delinquencies and insolvencies or miscalculations, but it is properly comparable across member states as VAT rules have been harmonized within the Union. Italy's VAT gap, expressed as a percentage of theoretical revenue (fig. 2.1 and table 2.1), is estimated at 28 per cent in 2014, twice the EU average and between two and three times higher than Britain's (10), France's (14), Germany's (10), and Spain's (9). Nor is a declining trend visible, as the gap was 25 per cent in 2010 and is more or less stable at the current level since then (p. 34).

Unlike in the legislation on corruption, however, in this field a clear difference is discernible between centre-right and centre-left: the latter issued no amnesties, until 2014, and intensified the fight against tax evasion. And as public signals also matter, it is notable that while on 17 February 2004 Prime Minister Berlusconi suggested that evading excessive taxation is legitimate, citing a 33 per cent threshold, in 2007 a finance minister of the centre-left spoke of the 'beauty' of contributing one's share to the provision of public goods. One reason is that the traditional electorate of the centre-left is disproportionately drawn from categories—pensioners, civil servants, workers in regular employment—that have limited scope for evading taxes, which are withheld at the source, and therefore bear the burden of other categories' evasion. But the minister's statement was not part of a battle of ideas in the service, at once, of a credible reform programme—addressing also the quality of the public goods delivered—and of an attempt to impose upon the nation's agenda the broader imperative of strengthening the rule of law, and remained isolated.

Organized Crime

Organized crime became less visible, after the terrorist strategy of 1992–3, but seems increasingly involved in corruption and political clientelism, as both enforcer and participant in illegal pacts (Paoli 2015). Empirical research suggests that it continues to influence political life through violence (Alesina et al. 2016); that it lowers the quality of the political elite (Daniele and Geys 2015); that it distorts the allocation of transfers to local government and the distribution of subsidies (Barone and Narciso 2014); that it depresses firm productivity (Albanese and Marinelli 2013) and foreign investment flows (Daniele and Marani 2011). More generally, Pinotti (2015) estimates that over a thirty-year period the presence of organized crime entails a loss equivalent to 16 per cent of a region's per capita GDP. As we said, its persistence is both symptom and proximate cause of the continuing relative decline of the South.

The repression effort did not slacken but the results obtained reveal the magnitude of the challenge. Paoli (2015, 673–4) writes that since 1991

> over 200 city councils were dismissed, a few two or three times, for being 'polluted' or conditioned by mafia groups. Proving the latter's persistent influence, 25 such councils were dismissed in 2012 alone, including for the first time a regional capital, Reggio Calabria. Numerous investigations in the three affected regions have demonstrated that even regional and national politicians continue to accept, and even seek, mafia electoral support in exchange for various favors. The former president of the region of Sicily [received] a seven-year prison sentence in 2011 for having abetted [the mafia].

The picture is not entirely dark, of course, and for instance Parini (2003) discusses the case of a village in the rural South that repulsed an attempt by organized crime to effectively take control of it. It was a case of broad-based collective action, roughly reminiscent of that we discussed in Chapter 6, if incomparable in scale.

Organized crime is ever less confined to those regions, however, as both empirical research (Calderoni 2011) and judicial findings attest. For example, a recent Milanese investigation, whose conclusions were confirmed in 2014–5 by the supreme court, revealed that the Calabrian 'ndrangheta—now viewed as more dangerous than the Sicilian mafia (Paoli 2015; Gratteri and Nicaso 2016)—is well rooted in Lombardy, and that its military power and 'stable and constant presence' engender similar effects as those traditionally observed in the South, such as the conspiracy of silence (*omertà*) of those vulnerable to its power of intimidation (Procura di Milano 2015, 87–8). Indeed, as part of a separate investigation, a former member of the regional government of Lombardy was recently issued a thirteen-year sentence for having 'bought' thousands of votes controlled by 'ndrangheta groups based in the suburbs of Milan, at a price of €50 each, on the occasion of the 2010 regional elections (Ferrarella 2017).[16] Judicial findings also attest that among the causes that

---

[16] The verdict is not final and, by law, the defendant is still presumed innocent.

allowed this organization to take root in Lombardy is 'the openness of business, political, and professional circles...to enter into mutually beneficial dealings with [it]': in particular, entrepreneurs do not merely 'submit to the 'ndrangheta but do business with it, often taking the initiative in opening contacts with it' (Procura di Milano 2016, 58).

The same is true for social tolerance. At the 2001 election Berlusconi's party fielded Dell'Utri as its candidate in the constituency covering the centre of Milan, which hosts the economic, social, and intellectual elite of a city often described as the 'moral capital' of the nation. It was a first-past-the-post contest and Dell'Utri's main opponent, representing the centre-left, was a professor of constitutional law; at that time the charge of having abetted the mafia had already been validated by an independent judge, and two years earlier Dell'Utri had accepted a two-year sentence for false accounting and tax fraud (Barbacetto et al. 2012, 710–12). He won, with 46 per cent of the vote.[17] This was not the result directly, or even mostly, of tolerance for organized crime. Those votes also stemmed from the polarization between politics and the judiciary, which did not just lower the credibility of the latter, and therefore of the charges brought against Dell'Utri, but also suggested a sort of equivalence between defendants and prosecutors, and, by implication, between illegality and law enforcement. In the eyes of many, in other words, polarization eclipsed the distinction inherent in the republican idea, that between private interests and the public interest.

The Italian Landscape

We end with a closely related matter—building amnesties. Fresh ones were issued in the 2000s, by centre-right majorities, and like those of 1985 and 1994 they undermined the rules they derogated from, engendered the expectation of continued tolerance, fuelled illegal construction, and thus raised pressure for further amnesties. Berdini (2010) illustrates this vicious circle and estimates that since 1948 more than 450,000 new buildings—hosting 6 million people—were constructed entirely illegally, disproportionately in the South. The foundations of this housing stock are depicted in Figure 9.1.

Unlike the amnesty of 1985, moreover, those of the 2000s were not accompanied by equally serious attempts to better protect the peninsula's urban and natural landscapes. In a recent essay on planning policies and practices since the Fascist epoch, an eminent scholar in this field writes of the 'destruction of the Italian landscape', which is 'well-advanced' and proceeds in

---

[17] The author votes in that constituency, and for the remarks that follow relies also on the recollection of conversations with conservative-leaning friends.

the 'general indifference' of society and the state (Benevolo 2012, 78). We turn to the roots of the latter's indifference.

Political Accountability

Political accountability is low in Italy. The curves shown in Figure 9.3, again syntheses of the available indicators, indicate a gap between the country and its European peers that is smaller than that shown by Figures 9.1 and 9.2 but equally persistent. The link between legal and political accountability is indeed structural, as we suggested in Chapter 4, and we shall argue that the latter also declined after 1994. This may seem surprising, as in 1993 a predominantly majoritarian electoral system was adopted, precisely in order to obtain more accountable government, and rotation in power became the norm, after five decades of DC-dominated governments: centre-right coalitions won the 1994, 2001, and 2008 elections, and centre-left ones prevailed, if narrowly, in each of the subsequent ones, those of 1996, 2006, and 2013. Having reached 40 per cent in 1994, moreover, electoral volatility hence remained at levels—between 10 and 20 per cent—about double those of the previous decades (Mershon 2015, fig. 12.1), and the same is true of the parliamentary turnover rate, the fraction of new entrants at each election, which after the exceptional peak of 1994 (69.5 per cent) never fell below 45 per cent (Galasso et al. 2010, fig. 1).

Yet Figure 9.3 is corroborated by its mirror image, the level of confidence in public authorities. If only 31 per cent of citizens now trust the judiciary, the same research (European Commission 2015, 35–36) found even less

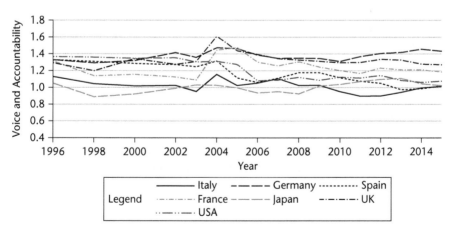

Figure 9.3 Comparative Governance Indicators (Voice and Accountability), 1996–2015

Voice and accountability captures perceptions of the extent to which a country's citizens are able to participate in selecting their government, as well as freedom of expression, freedom of association, and a free media.

Source: The Worldwide Governance Indicators

confidence in either the parliament or the government: 17 and 16 per cent, respectively, about half the levels of one decade earlier (Vassallo 2015, 116) and of current EU averages; within the Union, in particular, only Spaniards trust their executive less than Italians. These findings also reflect the consequences of the Great Recession, naturally, but they are subsequent to the rise of a party, the Five Star Movement (5SM), which in 2013 won one quarter of the vote on the wings, precisely, of popular discontent (Passarelli 2015). Worse, they are consistent with an indirect, but graver indicator of distrust for the public authorities, namely electoral participation, which between 1979 and 2013 declined monotonically from 90 to 75 per cent.

Low political accountability is both a consequence of the resumption of the spiral and the effect of broader phenomena. For the latter we refer chiefly to the analysis of Rosanvallon (2015, ch. I and II), who highlights the rise of the de facto power of executives relative to legislatures, the increasing 'presidentialization' of the former, also in parliamentary democracies, and the difficulty of adjusting the checks-and-balances system to this new setting. Political parties moved closer to the executive, in parallel, and away from society.

In Italy most parties dissolved, as we saw. They were replaced by different political organizations, with smaller structures, membership bases, and grassroots support, which left little space to internal democracy, seldom took the name of 'party', often served chiefly as campaigning machines, and frequently split and merged, giving rise to a more fragmented political system (Cotta 2015; Hopkin 2015; Mershon 2015; Passarelli 2015; Regalia 2015). Most were and still are dominated by a single leader, leading to a degree of 'personalization' of politics significantly more marked than in other mature democracies (Pasquino 2014), and in their hands the political cultures that had hitherto informed the country's public life effectively vanished (Pasquino 2015b). Within them, in one word, the collective action problem became acute. The main heirs of the PCI did partly retain its organization and culture, and in 2008 merged with the successors of the DC's left wing, to form the Partito Democratico (PD). But this party also underwent the same decay (see Revelli 2015), if in lesser measure than its competitors.[18]

Revelli (2013) inscribes these trends into broader ones observed in Western democracies ever since the decline of Fordism. Taking a perspective akin to that of Katz and Mair (2009), both Ignazi (2012) and Revelli (2015) underline how Italian parties gradually retreated from society to entrench themselves into the state, and came to share an interest in increasing their influence within the latter while reducing their own and their elected representatives'

---

[18] The author had a sense of this in 2014–15, while participating in an attempt to foster cooperation between the party and the vital forces of civil society around an important archaeological site in Calabria (see Capussela and Guzzo 2014).

accountability to the electorate. These parties thus lost the capacity to collect society's demands and aspirations, coordinate them into a coherent interpretation of the public interest, and, on its basis, act themselves as a source of pressure for responsive government. A void opened between them and citizens, as we said in the Preface, who overwhelmingly revoked their trust in them.[19]

In parallel, the proximity between political and economic elites grew. In part this is measurable. Commenting on the data analysed by Bandiera et al. (2010) and Galasso et al. (2010), Boeri (2010, 5) writes 'that the Italian political class is increasingly and directly involved in private business and that a large proportion of Italian capitalism is deeply oriented towards politics'. As Cingano and Pinotti (2009) show, moreover, these links also reach the lower ranks. Like much of the literature in this field, they analyse the political connections and performance of a representative sample of firms (they focus on manufacturers having more than fifty employees). But unlike other studies they measure such connections from the presence in firms of employees serving in local government, which also allows them to draw comparisons across Italian provinces. They find that between 1985 and 1997 the share of politically connected firms rose from less than 40 to more than 50 per cent of the sample; that connections with governing parties raised their revenues and profits—but not their productivity—by increasing their sales to the public sector; that this harmed the latter's efficiency in delivering public goods; and that, across provinces, both effects were considerably greater the more widespread corruption was. These findings confirm that the incentives underpinning the long-standing collusion between political and economic elites survived the rupture of 1992–4, and corroborate the hypothesis that its worst degeneration also became more frequent.[20]

More generally, Italy's new parties became more vulnerable to distributional coalitions. If special interest groups had gained in influence during the 1980s, after 1992–4 they 'invaded' the polity and the public administration, as Crafts and Magnani (2013, 104) put it. The reason, they suggest (p. 103), is that such parties no longer absolve the function that Olson (1982) assigns to 'encompassing organizations', namely to maintain interest groups' and their own constituencies' demands within the bounds of allocative efficiency and, more broadly, of a plausible definition of the public interest. As the collective action problem became acuter within them, in other words, Italian parties gradually lost the capacity to help society overcome its own collective action problems.

---

[19] For instance, Demos (2014) recorded a level of trust in parties—3 per cent, down from 8 in 2010—equal to the statistical margin of error of the poll.

[20] Boeri (2010, 4–5) notes also that managers elected to parliament—where their share roughly doubled after 1994 (Galasso et al. 2010, table 2.1)—were twice as likely to be involved in criminal investigations as the average parliamentarian.

The decline of electoral participation and the shrinkage or disappearance of parties' membership bases and grassroots support also raised the relative importance of clientelism, both minute and corporatist. This strengthened the power of factions and the roots of adverse selection within parties, and further increased their dependence on organized interest groups: a dependence that can only have grown after 2014, when the direct public financing of parties—generous and unpopular in equal measure—was replaced by a system based on the partial tax deductibility of supporters' contributions.[21]

In short, as political parties severed their links with society they entrenched themselves deeper into the state and tightened their ties with distributional coalitions and economic elites, losing autonomy vis-à-vis both. In exchange they gained greater control over the public administration (Cassese 2014, 142–5; Piattoni 2015, 165–8), on one hand, and votes, money, and a degree of benevolence from the mainstream media, on the other (for the latter is still mostly controlled by finance and industry, with the notable exception of the *Corriere*, acquired by a publisher in 2016). Policy-making thus became less transparent, in only apparent contradiction with the parallel mediatization of political life, the phenomenon which the political scientist Giovanni Sartori called *videocracy* (namely, 'the hegemonic role of television in dictating the content and style of politics': Urbinati 2015, 604).

In most of these respects the deterioration of political parties was already under way in the 1980s. A clear sign of its acceleration is that Italy's new parties proved worse than their predecessors in either selecting candidates for elected office or commanding their loyalty. Galasso et al. (2010) analyse public data—including education, income, career, involvement in criminal investigations—concerning all parliamentarians elected during the 1948–2008 period, and measure their quality through plausible objective criteria. They conclude (p. 82, fig. 2.3, and table 3.3) that

> the switch from the First to the Second Republic led to a dramatic worsening of the quality of the cohorts of politicians who have entered Parliament after 1994 [and went] hand in hand with a dramatic decrease of the average level of education of newly elected MPs, which . . . has been a staple of the Second Republic.

Parliamentarians also proved remarkably more inclined towards molecular *trasformismo*, which is typically associated, both historically and functionally, with clientelism (Valbruzzi 2015). Its plainest form, party switching, is exactly measurable. Between 1948 and 1994 the percentage of parliamentarians that

---

[21] Contributions are limited to €30,000 per year. In addition, taxpayers can direct the treasury to transfer 0.2 per cent of their taxes to a party: in 2016 only 2.4 per cent of them exercised this option, however, raising an aggregate of €11.7 million, which is one order of magnitude below the average yearly public transfers under the previous system.

in the course of one legislature moved from one parliamentary group to another never exceeded 10 per cent, and was generally much lower (Valbruzzi 2015, fig. 3.1). In the 2008–13 legislature and the current one it was 19 and 35 per cent, respectively (OpenPolis 2017). In the conclusions of his study of political selection, Besley (2005, 58) writes that 'no society can run effective public institutions while ignoring the quality of who is recruited to public office and what they stand for'. In Italy the former fell 'dramatically' and the latter is increasingly unclear.

That fall is the effect not just of low accountability, Besley's reasoning suggests, but also of low competition, both within parties and among them. For despite the polarization that set in afresh after 1994, competition among Italy's cartel-like parties was arguably limited, precisely because they shared an interest in preserving their entrenchment in the state and lowering their own and the public authorities' accountability to the electorate (Ignazi 2012; Revelli 2013, 2015). The legislation on corruption offers a clear example, as despite their Manichaean rhetoric during electoral campaigns the policies of the centre-right and the centre-left differed little.

Finally, the votes of 2006, 2008, and 2013 were held under an electoral law that (unconstitutionally) gave voters no say in selecting parliamentarians, leaving it entirely to party leaders and intra-party negotiations.[22] Again, that law was adopted by the centre-right, vehemently denounced by the centre-left, but left unchanged by it after it won the 2006 election. So it was also by design that political accountability remained low and intra-party competition lost all transparency: faced by pervasive distrust, rather than seeking to regain citizens' confidence by making itself more vulnerable to their pressure, the political elite opted for further insulating itself from it. The same rationale underpins part of the two vast and partly similar constitutional reforms—one adopted by the centre-right, one by the centre-left—that were defeated by popular referenda in 2006 and 2016 (see Pasquino and Valbruzzi 2017).

This defensive strategy, unsurprising in a ruling class 'unable to exercise hegemony' (Newell 2015, 13), is consistent with the parallel deliberate erosion of the rule of law. Just as legal and political accountability mutually reinforce each other in the 'good' equilibrium, as we called it in Chapter 4, so too both must be constrained if political and economic rents are to be protected from creative destruction. Indeed, the laws openly promoting impunity for corruption could hardly have been passed in the presence of an effective system of political accountability.

Of course, other factors also played a role. Berlusconi's private television monopoly polarized political coverage and raised the partisanship of most

---

[22] The primaries by which the PD selected candidates for the 2013 election were little more than a gesture (see, more broadly, Cotta 2015, 50).

mainstream media, severely denting their credibility as guardians of the public interest. Equally, the progress of Italians' cultural sophistication presumably lagged the growing complexity of their society, making them less demanding and engaged citizens and less perceptive judges of events and policies than other European electorates: only about one third of them read at least one book per year or one newspaper per day (De Mauro 2014, 79–90), in particular, and recent OECD research (cited by Vecchi 2017, 207) found that as much as 59 per cent of adults have no more than bare functional literacy and numeracy, a share twice as high the next worst country in the sample. Based on these data, De Mauro (2014, 103–6) argues that less than one third of the population possess the literacy skills—such as the ability to understand a newspaper article—that are required to take active part in social life. *Governare è far credere*, 'to govern is to make believe'. The maxim drawn from Machiavelli's *Prince* was certainly at play, as education nourishes critical reflection, and it certainly helps explaining Italian elites' secular neglect for universal education. But these factors eased, not caused, the phenomena we described.

Before moving to their effects on economic performance some less palpable consequences may be mentioned. In a book titled *On Rules* (Colombo [2008] 2015), the former magistrate who discovered the P2 and played a major role in the Clean Hands investigations describes Italy as a 'vertical' society, hierarchical and unequal, still far from the model designed by its constitution. From the link between democracy and the rule of law he draws a similar parallel between two traits of the country's contemporary culture, the weakness of the ethic of rules and the ethic of responsibility, both widely recognized, and the fact that inequality is often interiorized by citizens: it is also for this reason that in the Preface we suggested an analogy with Sen's discussion of the 'adaptive preferences' of the deprived (1999, 62–3; 2009, 282–4). Writing from the vantage point of republican political theory, and of its notion of freedom as non-domination, Viroli's essay on *Berlusconi's Italy* ([2010] 2012) describes a country subject to the 'enormous' power of one man, which generated a court around him: domination breeds servility, he posits, and offers persuasive illustrations. Though reached from quite different routes, especially as regards the relationship between culture and institutions, these authors' conclusions are consonant with ours. That enormous power, in particular, has its roots in the spiral. But it seemed useful to mention them also because they might resonate in readers familiar with the country, and help them link our analysis with what they saw: next, perhaps, to ordinary examples of public-spiritedness.[23]

---

[23] Moro (2013) in fact remarks that since the turn of the century the practices of active citizenship have become more widespread. He suggests a correlation with the decline of parties' membership bases; estimates that such practices involve between 7 and 12 per cent of the

Closing the Circle: Economic Policy, Institutions, and Performance

On this background an answer to the questions posed in Chapter 1 can be advanced. As we noted there, the crisis of September 1992, the Maastricht Treaty, and the adoption of the euro radically changed the framework for economic policy. In parallel, the external environment was being changed equally profoundly by the ICT revolution, the acceleration of globalization, and the rise of China and other emerging economies. Italy reached this juncture with inappropriate economic institutions, as the synchrony between their evolution and its convergence to the productivity frontier had been broken already in the 1960s, and with a growth model which had already caused it to begin diverging from its peers (Figure 1.2). More than the latter, therefore, the country needed adjustment to turn those shocks into growth opportunities.

The literature discussed in Chapter 1 explains why they became fetters instead, and why structural weaknesses that had hitherto been compatible with comparatively high growth—the small size of firms, their specialization in low-technology, labour-intensive sectors, 'oppressive' regulation, low human capital (e.g., Crafts and Magnani 2013, 92–101)—became increasingly binding constraints. The urgency of reform was clear. The many reforms enacted since the early 1990s were targeted at such weaknesses, and besides anchoring the country to the European integration process the adoption of the euro was itself a 'commitment technology', intended to lock in the reform programme (p. 100). The question by which we closed Chapter 1 is why the results were inadequate.

Our hypothesis is that adjustment was hindered by the resumption of the spiral, whose effects went beyond—or, at least, can be described with greater precision than by referring to—the direct consequences of the weakness of the rule of law, which undermined the effectiveness of the reforms of formal institutions, and the more general observation that the prevalence of distributional coalitions tends both to lead to institutional sclerosis and to 'slow down a society's capacity to adopt new technologies and to reallocate resources in response to changing conditions' (Olson 1982, 74). To establish this interpretation a model would have to be built—based on Chapter 4—and empirically tested. In its absence we illustrate the hypothesis discursively, drawing on a brief analysis of three areas: the main developments in the public sector; the promotion of competition; and the allocation of resources.

---

population, a share comparable to the European average (p. 155); and notes that their protagonists—such as non-profit associations and civil society organizations—enjoy high levels of trust, often far higher than any public authority (table 4.3).

Table 9.2 lays out the broader context. One critical variable for joining the EMU, inflation, gradually declined—thanks largely to a form of tripartite incomes policy agreed in 1993, which linked wage rises to programmed inflation—and then stabilized at the lowest levels of the post-war period. Investment was sustained, the employment rate slowly rose, but unemployment remained high. Net exports benefited from a 30 per cent nominal devaluation over the 1992–5 period. And while the growth of TFP, labour productivity, and per capita GDP fell, profits rose to remarkably high levels and were often used to reduce firms' debts—leverage declined from 60 to 35 per cent between 1993 and 2000—and 'consolidate control' over firms in the hands of majority shareholders (Ciocca 2007, 334).

Having won the 1996 election, the centre-left set the achievement of EMU membership in 1999 as its main priority. Though opposed by Berlusconi's party, the Northern League, and part of the economic elites (Fiat's president argued against it), this policy rested on wide popular support (Ginsborg 2001, 306–7). To meet the other two criteria of the Maastricht Treaty, concerning public deficit and debt, the government relied relatively less on containing primary expenditure than on raising the tax burden—which peaked in 1997, when the primary surplus also peaked at 6.6 per cent of GDP—and especially on the convergence of the interest rates on Italy's debt to the level of its peers (e.g., Rossi 2007). Having joined the euro and de facto locked in this critical saving, the tax burden slowly declined and primary expenditure resumed its rise, which continued up to the 2008 crisis at rates close to the Eurozone average (Lorenzani and Reitano 2015, fig. 2.1).

In parallel, the debt-to-GDP ratio declined steadily: from 121 to 104 per cent, its nadir, between 1994 and 2004. A significant contribution came from a vast privatization programme, which between 1985 and 2009 raised proceeds equivalent to 12 per cent of the 2004 GDP (Ciocca 2014, 277). The state lowered its share in ENI and the electricity utility to about 30 per cent, in particular, and, above all, having sold its banks and most of its firms, it liquidated IRI, which had been the pillar of Italy's mixed-economy model.

Reforms enacted between 1995 and 2011 stabilized long-term pension liabilities below 15 per cent of GDP (Ferrera and Jessoula 2015, fig. 38.1). But greater cuts in primary expenditure were judged 'socially and politically unsustainable' (Rossi 2007, 108). More importantly, in the 1990s and especially in the 2000s, the effort to increase the efficiency of public expenditure and adjust its composition was weak. So the inefficiency of the public administration remained a serious competitive disadvantage (Bianco and Napolitano 2013; Piattoni 2015), and the budget continued to reflect 'ineffective public spending policies, failing to support more sustainable growth based on physical infrastructure, human capital, and innovation' (Lorenzani and Reitano 2015, 8). In particular, both original sins of Italy's welfare system persisted

Table 9.2 Selected Macroeconomic Indicators, 1993–2007

Year	GDP Growth[a]	Per-Capita GDP Growth[a]	Total Investment (% GDP)[a]	Activity Rate[b]	Unemployment Rate[b]	Labour Productivity Growth[a]	TFP Growth[a]	Current Account Deficit (% GDP)[c]	Inflation (CPI)[d]	Debt-to-GDP Ratio[e]	Government Expenditure (% GDP)[b]	Government Revenue (% GDP)[b]
1993	−0.8	−0.9	26.0	59.5	9.7	2.1	−0.3	0.7	4.6	115.7	56.6	46.6
1994	2.1	2.1	26.7	59.2	10.6	4.4	2.2	1.2	4.0	121.2	53.8	44.7
1995	2.9	2.9	28.4	59.2	11.2	3.1	1.6	2.1	5.2	120.9	52.7	45.3
1996	1.3	1.3	27.0	59.6	11.8	0.4	−0.6	3.0	4.0	120.2	52.6	45.7
1997	1.9	1.9	26.0	59.8	11.2	2.1	0.6	2.6	2.0	117.4	50.3	47.7
1998	1.69	1.7	24.2	60.6	11.3	0.1	−0.6	1.6	2.0	114.3	49.0	46.2
1999	1.5	1.5	24.4	61.2	10.9	0.8	−0.3	1.1	1.7	113.1	48.1	46.4
2000	3.7	3.5	24.7	61.8	10.0	2.8	1.6	0.1	2.5	108.6	46.2	45.4
2001	1.8	1.4	23.9	62.3	9.0	0.4	−0.5	0.5	2.8	108.3	48.1	45.0
2002	0.2	−0.3	25.0	62.8	8.5	−1.1	−2.0	−0.3	2.5	105.3	47.4	44.5
2003	0.1	−0.4	25.1	62.9	8.4	−0.9	−1.8	−0.6	2.7	104.1	48.6	45.1
2004	1.6	1.0	26.2	62.6	8.0	1.0	−0.2	−0.4	2.2	103.7	48.0	44.5
2005	0.9	0.4	27.0	62.4	7.7	0.6	−0.7	−0.9	2.0	105.7	48.5	44.2
2006	2.0	1.5	0.3	62.6	6.8	−0.04	−0.6	−1.5	2.1	106.3	49.2	45.8
2007	1.5	1.1	0.3	62.4	6.1	0.1	−0.7	−1.4	1.8	103.4	48.4	46.9

Note. [a] Source: Penn World Table. [b] Source: ISTAT. [c] Source: World Bank. [d] Source: OECD. [e] Source: IMF.

(Ferrera et al. 2012, fig. 1.1 and 1.2): its functional distortion towards the risks of old age, and its distributive distortion, which is the direct consequence of the policy of particularistic inclusion pursued, with varying aims, ever since the 1950s. The distributive distortion peaked between the 1980s and the 1990s, reaching a comparatively 'exceptional' degree of segmentation and differentiation among professional categories, and thereafter began an 'extremely slow' adjustment (pp. 9–11). Only the pension reform of 2011—adopted by a technocratic government to avert an incipient debt crisis—significantly dented it; but the comparatively disproportionate prevalence of pensions over expenses for family benefits and services, unemployment protection, and poverty relief remained (Ferrera and Jessoula 2015, 507 *passim*).

We may begin to correlate these choices to the equilibrium that had re-established itself after the rupture of 1992–4, and in particular to the increased influence of distributional coalitions and the tighter proximity of political and economic elites, joined by the common objective of limiting political and economic creative destruction. Distributional coalitions and economic elites—part of which opposed the commitment device represented by EMU—certainly did not encourage stiffer cuts to primary expenditure, from which they drew rents. In the presence of widespread corruption, the model proposed by Aghion et al. (2016) suggests that the ensuing rise of tax pressure depressed growth. Tax evasion presumably adjusted upwards, as the 'gap between the apparent and the effective tax rates' remained stable (Chiarini et al. 2013, 282), and the related disincentive against firm growth (Bobbio 2016) likewise intensified.

The effects were broader, however. On one hand, the effort to adjust the composition of public expenditure was hindered not just by distributional coalitions but also by the priority of preserving the system of particularistic inclusion, which remained critical for political consensus: a priority which was cast aside only during severe crises, as in 2011, and which was at least partly shared by the economic elites, despite its effects on growth, by reason of their mutually beneficial collusion with the political elite. On the other hand, collusion, the influence of distributional coalitions, and the low accountability of the political elite hampered the effort to improve the efficiency of the public administration, which was also a source of rents for each of them. This effort was de facto incompatible with the contemporary tolerant policy on corruption, moreover, and was also hindered by the parallel polarization between the judiciary and the political elite, for in that climate attempts to raise judicial efficiency by adjusting the delicate balance between magistrates' independence and accountability sparked prohibitive controversies. Political and economic elites anyway had little interest in improving the effectiveness of the power that could enforce legal accountability upon them, as we noted already in Chapter 8. So, although judicial efficiency improved somewhat during the 2000s, as measured by the length of civil proceedings (Bianco and Napolitano 2013, fig. 19.3), it remained extremely low in comparative terms (World Bank 2016, 35).

The consequences for TFP and aggregate growth are likely to have been significant. Empirical research recently published by the IMF and the Bank of Italy suggests that the inefficiency of the public administration, in general, and of the judiciary, in particular, hinder the growth of firms' size and productivity (Giacomelli and Menon 2013; Esposito et al. 2014; Giordano et al. 2015). And continuity in spending policies and execution deprived the economy of both a short-term stimulus, as fiscal multipliers vary, and of sustained support for productivity growth, through greater and better investment in human capital and innovation.

We turn to competition. Its intensity grew in these two decades, but arguably not enough to spur innovation and reallocation to the degree that the economy needed (Gigliobianco and Toniolo 2017). Its growth appears to have been predominantly due to external sources of competitive pressure, moreover, just like during the economic miracle. Giordano and Zollino (2017) estimate firms' mark-ups—the difference between prices and marginal costs, which is a rent that tends to fall as competition rises—and observe a decline after the completion of the European single market, in 1993, and a further drop after the adoption of the euro. Remarkably, they also find (pp. 19–21) that the reduction in workers' rents—namely, their share of mark-ups—was 'almost double' the reduction of firms' rents, and that in the regulated services sector, where important privatizations took place, the decline in mark-ups was 'significantly' smaller than in manufacturing, and was disproportionately borne by workers: these firms, they conclude, 'seemed to have maintained substantial market power and the result of privatizations has thereby been a reallocation of rents from wages to profits instead of a drastic increase in competition in the goods market'.

Crafts and Magnani (2013, 97) note that the privatization programme 'was mainly aimed at reducing public debt', and that 'opportunities to introduce competition in utilities...were missed, and regulation was inadequate'. In part, this can be explained by the fact that the state found itself in a conflict of interests, as it was at once the seller of the future profit streams generated by those companies, and their future regulator. The weakness of the rule of law and the inefficiency of the public administration—both endogenous to the equilibrium, in our reading—then hampered the effectiveness of this (admittedly complex) regulatory effort. At a deeper level, however, regulatory policy was also undermined by the collusion between political and economic elites—which grew after 1992–4, we argued. As Cavazzuti (2017) shows, 'internal protectionism' dates back from the 1950s, when the European Common Market gradually precluded external protectionism: taking forms that changed with the economic and institutional context, this practice persistently aimed at shielding at least the upper echelons of Italian industry from at least the internal sources of competitive pressure. This form of protectionism, the main offspring of collusion, was also observable in these two decades, Cavazzuti argues, and one of its effects was precisely the tendency of Italian entrepreneurs to 'seek refuge' in sectors still 'shielded from internal and external competition', such as regulated utilities (p. 526). 'Seeking refuge' is an apt metaphor for these entrepreneurs' strategy, whose prospects were constrained by the reasons mentioned earlier and those we shall discuss presently.

A mirroring picture emerges from a comprehensive OECD analysis (2017, 20) of the skills endowment of the Italian economy:

> Italy is currently trapped in a low-skill equilibrium—a situation in which the low supply of skills is accompanied by low demand from firms. While many, relatively large, companies compete in the global markets successfully, many others have low-skilled managers and workers with relatively low levels of productivity. The low levels of skills of managers and workers are coupled with low investment in productivity-enhancing work practices and in technologies requiring workers to use high-skills.

Grillo (2017) considers a different perspective, equally consistent with our approach. Greater competition was meant to stimulate the reallocation of resources from sectors and firms having lesser prospects of productivity growth to ones with greater potential. This required flexible factor markets. Italy's labour market did become more flexible, after reforms enacted in 1997 and 2003 (e.g., Vesan 2015), but the social protection system and in particular the unemployment insurance system were not made more universalistic (for the reasons, endogenous to the equilibrium, discussed earlier). So the resistance to flexibility remained strong. And as employment protection remained largely based on wage supplementation schemes, often ad hoc, which safeguard workplaces through a state-funded temporary reduction of the firms' labour costs, their effect was to protect from exit and reallocation especially the less productive firms. Contemporary empirical research, which Grillo (2017) does not cite, supports this argument (Calligaris et al. 2016, 38–9). This tension between a progressively more flexible labour legislation and Italy's persistently segmented social protection system thus was another channel through which particularistic inclusion weighed on the country's growth.

We turn, to conclude, to the allocation of resources. TFP grows with technological and organizational innovation, as well as through the reallocation of resources to more innovative or productive firms or sectors. This second channel can be stimulated by competition, but may be hindered by frictions in the markets for production factors, leading to their misallocation. Remarkably, even though the intensity of competition grew over the past two decades, if insufficiently, Calligaris et al. (2016, 32) do not find that misallocation declined, as theory would predict, but that it increased 'significantly': 'if in 2013 misallocation had remained at its 1995 level, Italian productivity would have been 10% higher in manufacturing and a hefty 67% higher in services'. Misallocation grew far more within each geographical area, industry sector, and size class, than between different areas, sectors, and classes, suggesting that systemic, horizontal causes were at play. Notably, misallocation was particularly pronounced in the 'core of the Italian productive system' (p. 43), namely among large firms and in the North-West, where most of them are based.

One of such systemic causes is likely to be the persisting underdevelopment of Italy's capital markets (e.g. Pinelli et al. 2016; Cavazzuti 2017, 523–5), which is largely due, in our reading, to the fact that repeated reforms of their *formal* institutions were undermined by the weakness of the rule of law. Another is that collusion and other socially undesirable routes to profits provided an alternative strategy to this growing number of less productive firms, and thus progressively increased the constituency that opposed *actual* reform. A third cause, closely related, is that suggested by Baumol (1990) and Acemoglu (1995), namely the reallocation of talent away from socially desirable activities by reason of the rise of the rewards of rent-seeking relative to those of productive entrepreneurship. The latter two reasons are likely to have affected especially large firms, among which misallocation grew more, as collusion with the political power was a more readily available strategy.

Finally, these mutually reinforcing dynamics also affected Italy's more productive and innovative firms, by strengthening their incentive to adapt to the logic of the equilibrium, raising their collective action problem, and thus further reducing the constituency for *actual* reform. Figure 9.4 can help illustrate the argument. It indicates that in Italy corporate governance practices—for which we chose two indicators of outcomes—are gravely inferior to those prevailing among its peers. In such a context, entrepreneurs who do not engage in opportunistic practices tend to suffer both a competitive disadvantage relative to those who do, as well as the system-wide effects of the ensuing low trust in the reliability of firms' financial statements and of their commitment to protect minority shareholders, which raises the cost of capital, and constrains its availability, for all firms. In other words, Figure 9.4 suggests that in the trade-off discussed in Chapter 4, between sound corporate governance practices and predatory ones, Italian capitalism settled on an equilibrium consistent with the other components of the spiral.

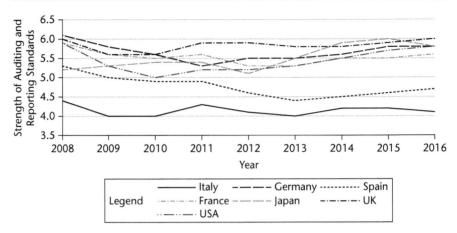

Figure 9.4a Selected Corporate Governance Indicators (Strength of Auditing and Reporting Standards), 2008–2016

Strength of Auditing and Reporting Standards: In your country, how would you assess financial auditing and reporting standards regarding company financial performance? [1 = extremely weak; 7 = extremely strong]
Source: Global Competitiveness Report

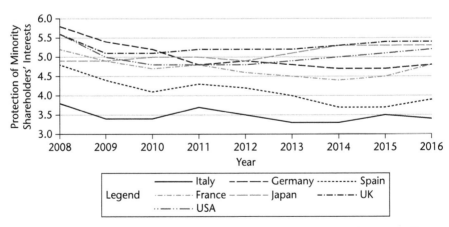

Figure 9.4b Selected Corporate Governance Indicators (Protection of Minority Shareholders' Interests), 2008–2016

Protection of Minority Shareholders' Interests: In your country, to what extent are the interests of minority shareholders protected by the legal system? [1 = not protected at all; 7 = fully protected]
Source: Global Competitiveness Report

The Rupture of 2011–2013 and Its Aftermath

Plausibly, just before the 2001 election *The Economist* wrote that Berlusconi's victory 'would be unthinkable in any self-respecting democracy', on account of his conflict of interests and numerous criminal trials.[24] He won decisively, then and in 2008.

In late 2011, as a debt crisis approached, he resigned, under pressure both internal and external (Donovan and Gilbert 2015, 404). The technocratic government that averted the crisis, at the cost also of a stiff budget adjustment, relied on his support too. In 2013 he lost to the centre-left, if by a handful of votes, and that summer his sentence for tax fraud was confirmed by the supreme court.

In several respects the 2013 election marked a rupture comparable to that of two decades earlier. Electoral volatility marginally exceeded 40 per cent, the 1994 peak, reaching 'one of the highest [values] observed in an established democracy' (Mershon 2015, 152). Parliamentary turnover, 65 per cent, was just below the 1994 peak. The 25 per cent won by the 5SM was a 'spectacular' result for a new entrant (Hopkin 2015, 335), which transformed the country's political system into a tri-polar one, for the moment at least, and brought into the halls of parliament a lively cohort of ordinary citizens and a loud call for clean politics. At the end of the year a fresh and unusually young leadership took over the PD, finally, through an open contest in which 2.8 million supporters voted: it promised change, elevated Matteo Renzi to the premiership, and won an unprecedented 41 per cent at the polls for the European Parliament, in May 2014.

Shall this rupture lead to a better outcome? Nothing seems less certain. After a decade dominated by the 'worst Prime Minister' since the war (Boltho 2013, 123), government effectiveness improved—in an exceptionally difficult macroeconomic context, as Table 9.3 shows, especially in 2011–14. Yet the signs of a credible determination to break the logic of the spiral, without which citizens' expectations cannot begin to change, were few and feeble. In particular, the laws that raised the statute of limitations and reversed the decriminalization of false accounting were the result of long parliamentary debates wholly centred on short-term political tactics, with no trace of the battle of ideas that could have been waged on them.

The signs of continuity were neither overwhelming nor particularly grave compared to the recent past, but their strength as drivers of society's incentives and expectations is inertial: absent a greater opposing force they prevail. We mention some examples, chosen for their clarity.

---

[24] Quoted by Ginsborg (2001, 317–8).

Table 9.3 Selected Macroeconomic Indicators, 2008–2015

Year	GDP Growth[a]	Per-Capita GDP Growth[a]	Total Investment (% GDP)[a]	Activity Rate[b]	Unemployment Rate[b]	Labour Productivity Growth[a]	TFP Growth[a]	Current Account Deficit (% GDP)[c]	Inflation (CPI)[d]	Debt-to-GDP Ratio[e]	Government Expenditure (% GDP)[b]	Government Revenue (% GDP)[b]
2008	−1.0	−1.3	27.9	62.9	6.7	−0.2	−1.9	−2.8	3.3	106.1	49.4	46.7
2009	−5.5	−5.7	25.8	62.35	7.7	−1.8	−4.5	−1.8	0.8	116.4	52.5	47.1
2010	1.7	1.5	25.1	62.0	8.4	2.5	1.2	−3.4	1.5	119.3	51.2	46.6
2011	0.6	0.4	26.1	62.0	8.4	0.8	−0.1	−3.0	2.8	120.8	49.1	45.7
2012	−2.8	−2.9	24.2	63.5	10.6	−0.01	−1.9	−0.4	3.0	127.0	50.8	47.8
2013	−1.7	−1.8	22.3	63.3	12.1	0.4	−1.0	1.0	1.2	129.0[e]	51.0	48.1
2014	−0.4	−0.5	21.0	63.9	12.7	−0.3	−0.8	1.8	0.2	131.8[e]	51.2	48.2
2015	0.8[c]	0.9[c]	17.3[c]	64.0	11.9	—	—	1.4	0.03	132.0[e]	50.5	47.9

Note: [a] Source: Penn World Table. [b] Source: ISTAT. [c] Source: World Bank. [d] Source: OECD. [e] Source: IMF.

Further attempts to improve the composition of the budget and contain primary expenditure growth, named 'spending reviews', led to little more than a freeze of the wage bill. The diagnosis and proposals for more ambitious measures are available, Lorenzani and Reitano (2015, 29) remark, but 'Italy appears to be still lacking the willingness to push forward [their] operationalisation'. In parallel, capital expenditure declined steeply (fig. 2.5).

In the persisting absence of a fresh policy for its development (Felice 2013; Iuzzolino et al. 2013), expenditure cuts weighed disproportionately on the South (Trigilia and Viesti 2016). These regions are a vast reservoir of underused resources and the main locus of Italy's potential for rapid, convergence-led growth (see Trigilia 2012). Their relative decline continues, conversely. Worse, Vecchi (2017, 283 and fig. 7.6) documents the incipient 'polarization' of the country, as the South and the Centre-North are both diverging and becoming more homogenous within themselves.

Equally worryingly, between 2008 and 2015 the tertiary education system—critical also for breeding an engaged and demanding citizenry—has lost about one fifth of its students, teachers, courses, and funding: a disinvestment greater than in any other troubled Eurozone economy bar Greece, effected by the country in which the share of graduates among young adults was already the lowest in the Union (Viesti 2016).[25] Economic elites raised no significant criticism against this policy, notably, which both confirms the 'low-skills trap' noted by the OECD (2017) and suggests that defensive growth strategies remain prevalent among firms.

In 2014 the government issued a decree bringing 'a general decriminalization of all tax-related offences' (Visco 2015). It was adopted on 24 December, ahead of two days on which newspapers traditionally are not published, but the outcry nevertheless forced its withdrawal (some of its measures were later revised and enacted, however). In December 2015 the government trebled—from €1,000 to €3,000—the threshold within which cash payments are permissible. Limiting the use of cash can be an effective policy against tax and regulatory evasion (Rogoff 2016), conversely: in the same months France, where the informal economy is two thirds smaller as a share of GDP, lowered the threshold from €3,000 to €1,000.

Finally, on 16 March 2017 a bipartisan majority in the senate refused to expel from its ranks, as the law requires, a senator convicted for embezzlement of public funds. The day before Campania's administration approved a bill allegedly amounting to an amnesty covering up to 67,000 illegal buildings. These are the product of a flow which never stopped and is accelerating, in relative terms, as in this sector the informal economy seems to have

---

[25] In 2015–17 a reform to improve school performance was approved, however; the OECD's PISA results released in late 2016 are no less disappointing than previous ones.

suffered comparatively less from the Great Recession: in 2015 for every 100 authorized buildings constructed, twenty illegal ones were also built; the ratio was below fifteen in 2004, is now close to fifty in the South, and above sixty in Campania (ISTAT 2017, 132 and 136). In August the government challenged that de facto amnesty before the constitutional court. But the mere announcement can be presumed to have stimulated further construction, in the expectation of tolerance both formal and informal, raising pressure for it. Indeed, in May the senate gave preliminary approval to a bill making the demolition of illegal buildings—already extremely rare (Berdini 2010)—more difficult. The destructive chase between amnesties and illegal construction continues, therefore.[26]

These choices speak of a political elite that is still acting within the logic of the spiral, as Moro did when he chose to cover up the 1964 coup. By reason also of its lower average quality, however, the current elite seems even more deeply trapped into that logic, as the apparent attempt to stimulate growth in the informal economy reveals, and might have lost sight of the country's future, as its policies on budget composition, tertiary education, the South, and the 'Italian landscape' suggest.

An indirect confirmation that continuity prevailed can be drawn from electoral participation, which fell in virtually all polls—European, regional, municipal—held since 2013, often considerably. Most ominously, in the 2014 regional elections in comparatively civic Emilia-Romagna turnout decreased to 38 per cent, 30 percentage points below the previous election and 6 below comparatively uncivic Calabria. Only the constitutional referendum of 2016 contradicted this trend. Thanks also to a long, heated, heavily politicized, but fairly informative campaign, turnout reached an encouraging 65 per cent, 13 percentage points higher than in the constitutional referendum of 2006.

We conclude with some remarks on the protagonists, who at the time of writing are preparing for the general election scheduled for early 2018. Campania is administered by the PD, and since 2013 Italy is governed by coalitions joining the PD, in dominant position, some centrist formations, and variable segments of the centre-right: in late 2013 Berlusconi's party moved into opposition, next to a small grouping of nationalists and neo-fascists and, to their right, the increasingly xenophobic Northern League (see Passarelli 2015). The shift of the PD towards the political centre opened a space to its left, which is currently occupied by a handful of small separate formations. The largest opposition force is the 5SM. Although this is a populist party openly critical of representative democracy, it arguably has several potential futures

---

[26] Mirroring the state's 'indifference' for it, the protection of Italy's landscapes is one of the sectors in which active citizenship—see note 23—is engaged (Moro 2013, 151–2).

still within its chords. Unlike that of Italy's right and centre-right, in particular, its populism has civic traits that might evolve into more constructive political proposals than the mere simplistic castigation of elite corruption. But the party appears vulnerable to the incentives flowing from the spiral: it remains a leader-dominated organization, lacking either a political culture or a workable selection system, and it is relatively closed to grassroots participation, which is ring-fenced into a limited-access website.

Conclusions

Clysterium donare; postea seignare; ensuitte purgare.
[Pastiche parodying medical jargon]
(Molière, *Le Malade imaginaire*, 1673)

The medics repeat that prescription thirteen times, to no avail. They could because the patient's illness was imaginary. Italy's is not. Those interested in the matter have read more than thirteen times that the country must cut taxes, improve education, and similar reasonable prescriptions. The one conclusion that can be stated with confidence, despite the limitations of our analysis, is that greater attention should be devoted to the country's apparent inability to reform itself.

The other conclusions are four. The first is that without the credible prospect of an equilibrium shift even well-designed reforms of Italy's political or economic institutions are likely to yield limited benefits, because they will be undermined by the incentives flowing from the vicious circles that we have described. The second is that the country's political and economic elites are unlikely to be either willing or able to promote an equilibrium shift, because creative destruction would endanger their rents, because they are subject to insufficient pressure from society, and because the ideas, intermediate organizations, and broad-based support that such a programme would require are still lacking.

Incremental reforms could relax these constraints. There is ample margin for gradually strengthening the rule of law and the promotion of competition, for example, which would improve efficiency, incentives, and expectations. Rosanvallon (2015) suggests plausible ways to raise political accountability and stimulate civic engagement. And from Pettit (2012) one can draw a broader republican reform programme, which could significantly improve the quality of Italy's democracy. Yet precisely because these measures run counter to the logic of the extant equilibrium, they are unlikely to be adopted or implemented with determination. They face the same collective action problem that they seek to overcome.

Likewise, the equilibrium does remain exposed to endogenously generated shocks, such as that of 1992–4, as well as to external sources of pressure, such as the European *vincolo esterno*. But these can open opportunities for an equilibrium shift, not accomplish it. And promising though they were, the opportunities of the 1990s were missed precisely by reason of those constraints.

The third conclusion, consequently, is that absent an external shock the country is likely to remain on the current equilibrium for as long as its material and moral consequences will be tolerable. Inequality, poverty, and vulnerability are rising, Vecchi (2017) documents. The tipping point is unlikely to be imminent, however, because Italy's democracy seems nevertheless vital enough to react before it is reached. But in our reading it will do so through measures that are less likely to uproot the causes of decline than assuage its symptoms. So a critical juncture might be approaching.

The fourth conclusion, implicit in the first two, is that a strategy to reverse Italy's resistible decline should focus on the variable that is freer from the grip of extant equilibrium, namely ideas. We sketch the battle of ideas from which such a strategy could begin. For the rest, we refer to our remarks on the reasons why the critical junctures of 1962–4 and 1992–4 were missed. To go beyond is to risk trespassing into fiction.[1]

What would be needed is a reliable diagnosis of Italy's equilibrium and its inefficiencies, and proposals for incremental reforms—of either formal institutions or of their enforcement characteristics—chosen for both their efficiency gains and their capacity, if implemented, to attest to the credibility of the programme and induce a change of expectations. In other words, reforms at once realistic and sharply inconsistent with the logic of the spiral (reducing corruption or illegal construction are obvious, if ambitious, examples).

On this basis two parallel discussions could begin. One, aimed at the general population, would seek to persuade it—leveraging on the tension between latent and revealed preferences—that deliberate political action based on the proposed reforms can achieve an equilibrium shift. The other is the discussion suggested by Rodrik (2014), aimed at those parts of the political and economic elites whose opportunities are constrained by the extant equilibrium, for whom greater creative destruction, or at least the removal of some inefficiencies, would yield a net gain. Recall, in this respect, that the extant equilibrium does not rest upon agreements or common strategies but on the convergence of different interests: were parts of society to revise their assessment of their

---

[1] But we would nonetheless suggest that republican political theory, on which Pettit's (2012) proposals rest, could provide useful ideas for that battle, and that the debate would benefit from being opened to the public opinions of other European nations.

own interests, therefore, resistance to reform would weaken. Note, moreover, that the two discussions could be mutually reinforcing: the more ordinary citizens embrace the reform programme the more it is likely to spread among elites too, and vice versa.

The result could be a revised, clearer, and more realistic set of proposals, and an at least potential reformist coalition comprising also part of the elites. This would create an incentive for political entrepreneurs to lead, organize, and extend such a coalition. Other political parties could respond to its emergence by adopting at least part of the reform programme. Some reforms would thus rely on broad-based support, and their implementation could achieve tangible results. If so, society's expectations would begin to change and the opportunity for an equilibrium shift could open.

This is a long-term strategy, of course, and each of its passages faces a collective action problem. But the sequence goes from the lowest—that faced by the initial debate—to the highest obstacle, and its dynamic is potentially self-reinforcing. For if their direction is inverted vicious circles turn into virtuous ones.

References

Abramovitz, Moses. 1986. 'Catching Up, Forging Ahead, and Falling Behind'. *Journal of Economic History* 46 (2): 385–406.

Acanfora, Paolo. 2015. 'The Catholic Right'. In *The Oxford Handbook of Italian Politics*, edited by Erik Jones and Gianfranco Pasquino, pp. 425–39. New York: Oxford University Press.

Acemoglu, Daron. 1995. 'Reward Structures and the Allocation of Talent'. *European Economic Review* 39 (1): 17–33.

Acemoglu, Daron. 2003. 'Why Not a Political Coase Theorem? Social Conflict, Commitment and Politics'. *Journal of Comparative Economics* 31 (4): 620–52.

Acemoglu, Daron. 2005. 'Constitutions, Politics, and Economics: A Review Essay on Persson and Tabellini's *The Economic Effects of Constitutions*'. *Journal of Economic Literature* 43 (4): 1025–48.

Acemoglu, Daron, and Matthew Jackson. 2015. 'History, Expectations, and Leadership in the Evolution of Social Norms'. *Review of Economic Studies* 82 (2): 423–56.

Acemoglu, Daron, and Matthew Jackson. 2016. 'Social Norms and the Enforcement of Laws'. *Journal of the European Economic Association*, forthcoming. URL: http://economics.mit.edu/files/11376.

Acemoglu, Daron, and James Robinson. 2006. 'Economic Backwardness in Political Perspective'. *American Political Science Review* 100 (1): 115–31.

Acemoglu, Daron, and James Robinson. 2012. *Why Nations Fail: The Origins of Power, Prosperity and Poverty*. New York: Crown.

Acemoglu, Daron, and James Robinson. 2013. 'Economics versus Politics: Pitfalls of Policy Advice'. *Journal of Economic Perspectives* 27 (2): 173–92.

Acemoglu, Daron, Simon Johnson, and James Robinson. 2001. 'The Colonial Origins of Comparative Development: An Empirical Investigation'. *American Economic Review* 91 (5): 1369–401.

Acemoglu, Daron, Simon Johnson, and James Robinson. 2005. 'Institutions as a Fundamental Cause of Long-Run Growth'. In *Handbook of Economic Growth*, edited by Philippe Aghion and Steven Durlauf, pp. 385–472. Amsterdam: Elsevier.

Acemoglu, Daron, Philippe Aghion, and Fabrizio Zilibotti. 2006. 'Distance to Frontier, Selection, and Economic Growth'. *Journal of the European Economic Association* 4 (1): 37–74.

Acemoglu, Daron, David Ticchi, and Andrea Vindigni. 2011. 'Emergence and Persistence of Inefficient States'. *Journal of the European Economic Association* 9 (2): 177–208.

Acemoglu, Daron, Suresh Naidu, Pascual Restrepo, and James Robinson. 2014. 'Democracy Does Cause Growth'. NBER Working Paper No. 20004. URL: www.nber.org/papers/w20004.

Acemoglu, Daron, Georgy Egorov, and Konstantin Sonin. 2015. 'Political Economy in a Changing World'. *Journal of Political Economy* 123 (5): 1038–86.

Aghion, Philippe, and Ufuk Akcigit. 2017. 'Innovation and Growth: The Schumpeterian Perspective'. In *Economics without Borders: Economic Research for European Policy Challenges*, edited by Laszlo Matyas et al., pp. 29–72. Cambridge: Cambridge University Press.

Aghion, Philippe, and Rachel Griffith. 2005. *Competition and Growth: Reconciling Theory and Evidence*. Cambridge, MA: MIT Press.

Aghion, Philippe, and Peter Howitt. 2006. 'Joseph Schumpeter Lecture: Appropriate Growth Theory: A Unifying Framework', *Journal of the European Economic Association* 4 (2–3): 269–314.

Aghion, Philippe, and Peter Howitt. 2009. *The Economics of Growth*. Cambridge, MA: MIT Press.

Aghion, Philippe, Alberto Alesina, and Francesco Trebbi. 2008. 'Democracy, Technology and Growth'. In *Institutions and Economic Performance*, edited by Elhanan Helpman, pp. 511–43. Cambridge, MA: Harvard University Press.

Aghion, Philippe, Ufuk Akcigit, and Peter Howitt. 2014. 'What Do We Learn from Schumpeterian Growth Theory?'. In *Handbook of Economic Growth*, edited by Philippe Aghion and Steven Durlauf, Vol. 2B, pp. 515–63. Amsterdam: Elsevier.

Aghion, Philippe, Ufuk Akcigit, Julia Cagé, and William Kerr. 2016. 'Taxation, Corruption, and Growth'. *European Economic Review* 86: 24–51.

Aghion, Philippe, Yann Algan, Pierre Cahuc, and Andrei Shleifer. 2010. 'Regulation and Distrust'. *Quarterly Journal of Economics* 125 (3): 1015–49.

Agosti, Aldo. 2015. 'Alcide De Gasperi and Palmiro Togliatti'. In *The Oxford Handbook of Italian Politics*, edited by Erik Jones and Gianfranco Pasquino, pp. 341–57. New York: Oxford University Press.

Akerlof, George. 2015. 'Anger and Enforcement'. Warwick University working paper, 1 February. URL: www2.warwick.ac.uk/fac/soc/economics/staff/rakerlof/anger_and_enforcement_2-1-15.pdf.

Akerlof, George, and Robert Shiller. 2015. *Phishing for Phools: The Economics of Manipulation and Deception*. Princeton, NJ: Princeton University Press.

Akerlof, George, and Dennis Snower. 2016. 'Bread and Bullets'. *Journal of Economic Behavior and Organization* 126: 58–71.

Albanese, Giuseppe, and Giuseppe Marinelli. 2013. 'Organized Crime and Productivity: Evidence from Firm-Level Data'. *Rivista Italiana degli Economisti* 18 (3): 367–94.

Alesina, Alberto, and Eliana La Ferrara. 2002. 'Who Trusts Others?'. *Journal of Public Economics* 85 (2): 207–34.

Alesina, Alberto, Salvatore Piccolo, and Paolo Pinotti. 2016. 'Organized Crime, Violence, and Politics'. NBER Working Paper No. 22093. URL: www.nber.org/papers/w22093.

Allum, Felicia, and Renate Siebert. 2003. 'Conclusion: Organized Crime and Democracy: "Uncivil" or "Civil" Society?'. In *Organized Crime and the Challenge to Democracy*, edited by Felicia Allum and Renate Siebert, pp. 195–203. Abingdon: Routledge.

Almond, Gabriel, and Sydney Verba. 1963. *The Civic Culture: Political Attitudes and Democracy in Five Nations*. Princeton, NJ: Princeton University Press.

Amatori, Franco, Matteo Bugamelli, and Andrea Colli. 2013. 'Technology, Firm Size, and Entrepreneurship'. In *The Oxford Handbook of the Italian Economy since Unification*, edited by Gianni Toniolo, pp. 455–84. New York: Oxford University Press.

Armao, Fabio. 2003. 'Why Is Organized Crime So Successful?'. In *Organized Crime and the Challenge to Democracy*, edited by Felicia Allum and Renate Siebert, pp. 25–35. Abingdon: Routledge.

Arrighetti, Alessandro, and Gilberto Seravalli. 1997. 'Istituzioni e dualismo dimensionale dell'industria italiana'. In *Storia del capitalismo italiano*, edited by Fabrizio Barca, pp. 265–333. Rome: Donzelli.

Arrow, Kenneth. 1972. 'Gifts and Exchanges'. *Philosophy and Public Affairs* 1 (4): 343–62.

Balassone, Fabrizio, Maura Francese, and Angelo Pace. 2013. 'Public Debt and Economic Growth: Italy's First 150 Years'. In *The Oxford Handbook of the Italian Economy since Unification*, edited by Gianni Toniolo, pp. 516–32. New York: Oxford University Press.

Baldini, Gianfranco. 2015. 'Christian Democracy: *The* Italian Party'. In *The Oxford Handbook of Italian Politics*, edited by Erik Jones and Gianfranco Pasquino, pp. 173–83. New York: Oxford University Press.

Banca d'Italia. 2016. 'Relazione annuale, anno 2015—CXXII esercizio', Rome, 31 May. URL: www.bancaditalia.it/pubblicazioni/relazione-annuale/2015/index.html.

Bandiera, Oriana. 2003. 'Land Reform, the Market for Protection, and the Origins of the Sicilian Mafia: Theory and Evidence'. *Journal of Law, Economics, and Organization* 19 (1): 218–44.

Bandiera, Oriana, Luigi Guiso, Andrea Prat, and Raffaella Sadun. 2010. 'Italian Managers: Fidelity or Performance?'. In *The Ruling Class: Management and Politics in Modern Italy*, edited by Tito Boeri, Antonio Merlo, and Andrea Prat, pp. 107–99. New York: Oxford University Press.

Banfield, Edward. 1958. *The Moral Basis of a Backward Society*. Glencoe: Free Press.

Banti, Alberto Mario. 1996. *Storia della borghesia italiana. L'età liberale (1861–1922)*. Rome: Donzelli.

Barbacetto, Gianni, Peter Gomez, and Marco Travaglio. 2012. *Mani pulite*, 2nd ed. Milan: Editori Riuniti.

Barbagallo, Francesco, and Giovanni Bruno. 1997. 'Espansione e deriva del Mezzogiorno'. In *Storia dell'Italia Repubblicana*, edited by Francesco Barbagallo, vol. 3, *L'Italia nella crisi mondiale. L'ultimo ventennio*, tome 2, *Istituzioni, politiche, culture*, pp. 401–70. Turin: Einaudi.

Barbiellini Amidei, Federico, John Cantwell, and Anna Spadavecchia. 2013. 'Innovation and Foreign Technology'. In *The Oxford Handbook of the Italian Economy since Unification*, edited by Gianni Toniolo, pp. 378–416. New York: Oxford University Press.

Barbieri, Giorgio, and Francesco Giavazzi. 2014. *Corruzione a norma di legge. La lobby delle grandi opera che affonda l'Italia*. Milan: Rizzoli.

Barca, Fabrizio. 1997. 'Compromesso senza riforme nel capitalismo italiano'. In *Storia del capitalismo italiano*, edited by Fabrizio Barca, pp. 3–115. Rome: Donzelli.

References

Barca, Fabrizio. 2006. *Italia frenata: Paradossi e lezioni della politica per lo sviluppo*. Rome: Donzelli.

Barca, Fabrizio, and Sandro Trento. 1997. 'La parabola delle partecipazioni statali: una missione tradita', In *Storia del capitalismo italiano*, edited by Fabrizio Barca, pp. 185–236. Rome: Donzelli.

Barone, Guglielmo, and Sauro Mocetti. 2014. 'Inequality and Trust: New Evidence from Panel Data'. Banca d'Italia Working Paper No. 973. URL: www.bancaditalia.it/pubblicazioni/temi-discussione/2014/2014-0973/index.html?com.dotmarketing.htmlpage.language=1.

Barone, Guglielmo, and Gaia Narciso. 2014. 'Organized Crime and Business Subsidies: Where Does the Money Go?'. *Journal of Urban Economics* 86: 98–110.

Basu, Kaushik. 2015. 'The Republic of Beliefs: A New Approach to "Law and Economics"'. World Bank Policy Research Working Paper 7259. URL: http://documents. worldbank.org/curated/en/2015/05/24454378/republic-beliefs-new-approach-'law-economics'.

Battilossi, Stefano, Alfredo Gigliobianco, and Giuseppe Marinelli. 2013. 'Resource Allocation by the Banking System'. In *The Oxford Handbook of the Italian Economy since Unification*, edited by Gianni Toniolo, pp. 485–515. New York: Oxford University Press.

Baumol, William. 1990. 'Entrepreneurship: Productive, Unproductive and Destructive'. *Journal of Political Economy* 98 (5): 893–921.

Bellucci, Paolo. 2015. 'Communists'. In *The Oxford Handbook of Italian Politics*, edited by Erik Jones and Gianfranco Pasquino, pp. 184–96. New York: Oxford University Press.

Bénabou, Roland, and Jean Tirole. 2011. 'Laws and Norms'. NBER Working Paper No. 17579. URL: www.nber.org/papers/w17579.

Benevolo, Leonardo. 2012. *Il tracollo dell'urbanistica italiana*. Rome-Bari: Laterza.

Berdini, Paolo. 2010. *Breve storia dell'abuso edilizio in Italia: dal ventennio fascista al prossimo futuro*. Rome: Donzelli.

Bernardi, Emanuele. 2015. 'Aldo Moro and Enrico Berlinguer'. In *The Oxford Handbook of Italian Politics*, edited by Erik Jones and Gianfranco Pasquino, pp. 368–77. New York: Oxford University Press.

Berta, Giuseppe. 2015. 'Industry and the Firm'. In *The Oxford Handbook of Italian Politics*, edited by Erik Jones and Gianfranco Pasquino, pp. 478–90. New York: Oxford University Press.

Bertola, Giuseppe, and Paolo Sestito. 2013. 'Human Capital'. In *The Oxford Handbook of the Italian Economy since Unification*, edited by Gianni Toniolo, pp. 249–70. New York: Oxford University Press.

Besley, Timothy. 2005. 'Political Selection'. *Journal of Economic Perspectives* 19 (3): 43–60.

Besley, Timothy, and Robin Burgess. 2001. 'Political Agency, Government Responsiveness and the Role of the Media'. *European Economic Review* 45 (4): 629–40.

Besley, Timothy, and Robin Burgess. 2002. 'The Political Economy of Government Responsiveness: Theory and Evidence from India'. *Quarterly Journal of Economics* 117 (4): 1415–51.

Besley, Timothy, Anders Jensen, and Torsten Persson. 2015. 'Norms, Enforcement, and Tax Evasion'. CEPR Discussion Paper No. 10372. URL: http://cepr.org/active/publications/discussion_papers/dp.php?dpno=10372.

Bevilacqua, Piero. 2005. *Breve storia dell'Italia meridionale*. 2nd ed. Rome: Donzelli.

Bianco, Magda, and Giulio Napolitano. 2013. 'Why the Italian Administrative System Is a Source of Competitive Disadvantage'. In *The Oxford Handbook of the Italian Economy since Unification*, edited by Gianni Toniolo, pp. 533–68. New York: Oxford University Press.

Bidner, Chris, and Patrick Francois. 2013. 'The Emergence of Political Accountability'. *Quarterly Journal of Economics* 128 (3): 1397–448.

Bisin, Alberto, and Thierry Verdier. 2011. 'The Economics of Cultural Transmission and Socialization'. In *Handbook of Social Economics*, edited by Jess Benhabib, Alberto Bisin, and Matthew Jackson, Vol. 1A, pp. 339–416. Amsterdam: Elsevier.

Bloch, Marc. [1946] 1990. *L'étrange défaite*. Paris: Gallimard, repr. 1990.

Blyth, Mark. 2013. *Austerity: The History of a Dangerous Idea*. New York: Oxford University Press.

Bobbio, Emmanuele. 2016. 'Tax Evasion, Firm Dynamics and Growth'. Banca d'Italia Occasional Paper No. 357. URL: www.bancaditalia.it/pubblicazioni/qef/2016-0357/QEF_357_16.pdf.

Boeri, Tito. 2010. 'Introduction'. In *The Ruling Class: Management and Politics in Modern Italy*, edited by Tito Boeri, Antonio Merlo, and Andrea Prat, pp. 1–6. New York: Oxford University Press.

Boeri, Tito, Riccardo Faini, Andrea Ichino, Giuseppe Pisauro, and Carlo Scarpa (eds). 2005. *Oltre il declino*. Bologna: Il Mulino.

Boltho, Andrea. 2013. 'Italy, Germany, Japan: From Economic Miracles to Virtual Stagnation'. In *The Oxford Handbook of the Italian Economy since Unification*, edited by Gianni Toniolo, pp. 108–33. New York: Oxford University Press.

Bordignon, Fabio, Luigi Ceccarini, and Ilvo Diamanti. 2018. *Le divergenze parallele. L'Italia: dal voto devoto al voto liquido*. Roma-Bari: Laterza.

Boucheron, Patrick. 2013. *Conjurer la peur. Sienne, 1338. Essay sur la force politique des images*. Paris: Seuil.

Brandolini, Andrea, and Giovanni Vecchi. 2013. 'Standards of Living'. In *The Oxford Handbook of the Italian Economy since Unification*, edited by Gianni Toniolo, pp. 227–48. New York: Oxford University Press.

Braudel, Fernand. [1989] 1994. *Le Modèle italien*. Paris: Flammarion, repr. 1994.

Bressanelli, Edoardo, and David Natali. 2019. 'Introduction'. *Contemporary Italian Politics* 11 (3): pp. 208–19.

Broadberry, Stephen, Claire Giordano, and Francesco Zollino. 2013. 'Productivity'. In *The Oxford Handbook of the Italian Economy since Unification*, edited by Gianni Toniolo, pp. 187–226. New York: Oxford University Press.

Brunnermeier, Markus, Harold James, and Jean-Pierre Landau. 2016. *The Euro and the Battle of Ideas*. Princeton, NJ: Princeton University Press.

Brusco, Sebastiano, and Sergio Paba. 1997. 'Per una storia dei distretti industriali italiani dal secondo dopoguerra agli anni novanta'. In *Storia del capitalismo italiano*, edited by Fabrizio Barca, pp. 335–88. Rome: Donzelli.

Bruti Liberati, Edmondo. 1997. 'La magistratura dall'attuazione della Costituzione agli anni novanta'. In *Storia dell'Italia Repubblicana*, edited by Francesco Barbagallo, vol. 3, *L'Italia nella crisi mondiale. L'ultimo ventennio*, tome 2, *Istituzioni, politiche, culture*, pp. 141–237. Turin: Einaudi.

Buhen, Andreas, and Friedrich Schneider. 2016. 'Size and Development of Tax Evasion in 38 OECD Economies: What Do We (Not) Know?'. *Journal of Economics and Political Economy* 3 (1): 1–11.

Bull, Martin. 2015. 'The Pentapartito'. In *The Oxford Handbook of Italian Politics*, edited by Erik Jones and Gianfranco Pasquino, pp. 296–308. New York: Oxford University Press.

Calamandrei, Piero. [1947] 2004. 'Patologia della corruzione parlamentare'. *Il Ponte* 3 (10), October 1947, in *Costituzione e leggi di Antigone*, pp. 233–51. Milan: Sansoni.

Calderoni, Francesco. 2011. 'Where is the Mafia in Italy? Measuring the Presence of the Mafia across Italian Provinces'. *Global Crime* 12 (1): 41–69.

Calise, Mauro. 2015. 'Government and Prime Minister'. In *The Oxford Handbook of Italian Politics*, edited by Erik Jones and Gianfranco Pasquino, pp. 95–106. New York: Oxford University Press.

Calligaris, Sara, Massimo Del Gatto, Fadi Hassan, Gianmarco Ottaviano, and Fabiano Schivardi. 2016. 'Italy's Productivity Conundrum: A Study on Resource Misallocation in Italy'. European Commission Discussion Paper No. 030. URL: https://ec.europa.eu/info/publications/economy-finance/italys-productivity-conundrum-study-resource-misallocation-italy_en.

Calvino, Italo. 1980. 'Apologo sull'onestà nel paese dei corrotti'. *La Repubblica*, 15 March.

Cannari, Luigi, Marco Magnani, and Guido Pellegrini. 2010. *Critica della ragione meridionale. Il Sud e le politiche pubbliche*. Rome-Bari: Laterza.

Capussela, Andrea Lorenzo, and Piero Guzzo. 2014. 'The Sybaris Project: Ancient Cities, New Politics, and Public Engagement in Southern Italy'. *LSE Impact Blog*, 11 October. URL: http://blogs.lse.ac.uk/impactofsocialsciences/2014/10/11/sybaris-project-ancient-cities-new-politics/.

Cardoza, Anthony. 2015. 'The Risorgimento'. In *The Oxford Handbook of Italian Politics*, edited by Erik Jones and Gianfranco Pasquino, pp. 16–25. New York: Oxford University Press.

Carey, John, and Matthew Shugart. 1995. 'Incentives to Cultivate a Personal Vote'. *Electoral studies* 14 (4): 417–39.

Carli, Guido. 1996. *Cinquant'anni di vita italiana*. 2nd ed. Rome-Bari: Laterza.

Casaburi, Lorenzo, and Ugo Troiano. 2016. 'Ghost-House Busters: The Electoral Response to a Large Anti Tax Evasion Program'. *Quarterly Journal of Economics* 131 (1): 273–314.

CASE (Center for Social and Economic Research). 2016. 'Study and Reports on the VAT Gap in the EU-28 Member States'. Warsaw, 23 August. URL: https://ec.europa.eu/taxation_customs/sites/taxation/files/2016-09_vat-gap-report_final.pdf.

Cassese, Sabino. 2014. *Governare gli italiani. Storia dello Stato*. Bologna: Il Mulino.

Castronovo, Valerio. 2015. 'Gianni Agnelli and Enrico Mattei'. In *The Oxford Handbook of Italian Politics*, edited by Erik Jones and Gianfranco Pasquino, pp. 358–67. New York: Oxford University Press.

Cavazzuti, Filippo. 2016. 'Gli effimeri anni ottanta: la mancanza di regole e il vuoto degli istituti di controllo'. November, forthcoming.

Cavazzuti, Filippo. 2017. 'Un racconto di economia politica sul protezionismo interno'. In *Concorrenza, mercato e crescita: il lungo periodo*, edited by Alfredo Gigliobianco and Gianni Toniolo, pp. 491–532. Venice: Marsilio.

Cento Bull, Anna. 2015. 'Terrorist Movements'. In *The Oxford Handbook of Italian Politics*, edited by Erik Jones and Gianfranco Pasquino, pp. 656–67. New York: Oxford University Press.

Cento Bull, Anna, and Philip Cooke. 2013. *Ending Terrorism in Italy*. Abingdon: Routledge.

Chabod, Federico. [1950] 1961. *L'Italia contemporanea (1918–1948)*. Turin: Einaudi.

Chang, Eric, Miriam Golden, and Seth Hill. 2010. 'Legislative Malfeasance and Political Accountability'. *World Politics*, 62 (2): 177–220.

Chang, Ha-Joon. 2002. 'Breaking the Mould: An Institutionalist Political Economy Alternative to the Neo-Liberal Theory of the Market and the State'. *Cambridge Journal of Economics* 26 (5): 539–59.

Chang, Ha-Joon. 2008. *Bad Samaritans: The Myth of Free Trade and the Secret History of Capitalism*. New York: Bloomsbury.

Chang, Ha-Joon. 2011a. 'Institutions and Economic Development: Theory, Policy and History'. *Journal of Institutional Economics* 7 (4): 473–98.

Chang, Ha-Joon. 2011b. 'Reply to the Comments on "Institutions and Economic Development: Theory, Policy and History" '. *Journal of Institutional Economics* 7 (4): 595–613.

Chiarini, Bruno, Elisabetta Marzano, and Friedrich Schneider. 2013. 'Tax Rates and Tax Evasion: An Empirical Analysis of the Long-Run Aspects in Italy'. *European Journal of Law and Economics* 35 (2): 273–93.

Ciaccarone, Giuseppe, and Enrico Saltari. 2015. 'Cyclical Downturn or Structural Disease? The Decline of the Italian Economy in the Last Twenty Years'. *Journal of Modern Italian Studies* 20 (2): 228–44.

Ciano, Galeazzo. 1990. *Diario 1937–1943*. Edited by Renzo De Felice. Milan: Rizzoli.

Cingano, Federico, and Paolo Pinotti. 2009. 'Politicians at Work. The Private Returns and Social Costs of Political Connection'. Banca d'Italia Working Paper No. 709. URL: www.bancaditalia.it/pubblicazioni/temi-discussione/2009/2009-0709/index.html?com.dotmarketing.htmlpage.language=1.

Ciocca, Pierluigi. 2003. 'L'economia italiana: un problema di crescita'. *Bollettino Economico* 41 (November): 81–94.

Ciocca, Pierluigi. 2007. *Ricchi per sempre? Una storia economica d'Italia (1796–2005)*. Turin: Bollati Boringhieri.

Ciocca, Pierluigi. 2012. 'Centocinquant'anni: per una "teoria della storia economica" d'Italia'. *Rivista di storia economica* 28 (1): 9–25.

Ciocca, Pierluigi. 2014. *L'IRI nella economia italiana*. Rome-Bari: Laterza.

Clausen, Bianca, Aart Kraay, and Zsolt Nyiri. 2011. 'Corruption and Confidence in Public Institutions: Evidence from a Global Survey'. *World Bank Economic Review* 25 (2): 212–49.

Collier, Paul. 2016. 'The Cultural Foundations of Economic Failure: A Conceptual Toolkit'. *Journal of Economic Behavior and Organization* 126 (B): 5–34.

Collotti, Enzo. 2003. *Il Fascismo e gli ebrei. Le leggi razziali del 1939*. Rome-Bari: Laterza.

Colombo, Gherardo. 1996. *Il vizio della memoria*. Milan: Feltrinelli.

Colombo, Gherardo. [2008] 2015. *On Rules*. Translated by Elisabetta Zoni. Amsterdam: Amsterdam University Press.

Colombo, Gherardo. 2012. *Farla franca. La legge è uguale per tutti?* Milan: Longanesi.

Commissione parlamentare d'inchiesta sulla loggia massonica P2. 1984. 'Relazione di maggioranza'. Doc. XXIII n. 2, 12 July, rapporteur Tina Anselmi. URL: www.senato. it/service/PDF/PDFServer/BGT/909679.pdf.

Committeri, Marco. 1999. 'Errori e omissioni nella bilancia dei pagamenti, esportazioni di capitali e aperture finanziaria dell'Italia'. Banca d'Italia Working Paper No. 352. URL: www.bancaditalia.it/pubblicazioni/temi-discussione/1999/1999-0352/index. html.

Conti, Davide. 2017. *Gli uomini di Mussolini. Prefetti, questori e criminali di guerra dal fascismo alla Repubblica italiana*. Turin: Einaudi.

Conti, Nicolò. 2015. 'Socialists, Republicans, and Radicals'. In *The Oxford Handbook of Italian Politics*, edited by Erik Jones and Gianfranco Pasquino, pp. 197–210. New York: Oxford University Press.

Cotta, Maurizio. 2015. 'Partitocracy: Parties and their Critics in Italian Political Life'. In *The Oxford Handbook of Italian Politics*, edited by Erik Jones and Gianfranco Pasquino, pp. 41–52. New York: Oxford University Press.

Council of Europe. 2016. *Annual Penal Statistics. SPACE I: Prison Populations*. Strasbourg: Council of Europe. URL: http://wp.unil.ch/space/2017/04/space-i-2015-report/.

Coyle, Diane. 2014. *GDP: A Brief but Affectionate History*. Princeton, NJ: Princeton University Press.

Crafts, Nicholas, and Marco Magnani. 2013. 'The Golden Age and the Second Globalization in Italy'. In *The Oxford Handbook of the Italian Economy since Unification*, edited by Gianni Toniolo, pp. 69–107. New York: Oxford University Press.

Crainz, Guido. 2003. *Il paese mancato. Dal miracolo economico agli anni ottanta*. Rome: Donzelli.

Crainz, Guido. 2016. *Storia della Repubblica. L'Italia dalla Liberazione ad oggi*. Rome: Donzelli.

Craveri, Piero. 2016. *L'arte del non governo. L'inesorabile decline della Repubblica italiana*. Venice: Marsilio.

Çule, Monika, and Murray Fulton. 2009. 'Business Culture and Tax Evasion: Why Corruption and the Unofficial Economy Can Persist'. *Journal of Economic Behavior and Organization* 72 (3): 811–22.

Daniele, Gianmarco, and Benny Geys. 2015. 'Organised Crime, Institutions and Political Quality: Empirical Evidence from Italian Municipalities'. *Economic Journal*, 125 (586): 233–55.

Daniele, Vittorio, and Ugo Marani. 2011. 'Organized Crime, the Quality of Local Institutions and FDI in Italy: A Panel Data Analysis'. *European Journal of Political Economy* 27 (1): 132–42.

Daveri, Francesco, and Maria Parisi. 2010. 'Experience, Innovation and Productivity: Empirical Evidence from Italy's Slowdown'. CESifo Working Paper No. 3123. URL: www.cesifo-group.de/portal/page/portal/DocBase_Content/WP/WP-CESifo_Working_ Papers/wp-cesifo-2010/wp-cesifo-2010-07/cesifo1_wp3123.pdf.

Davigo, Piercamillo. 2017. *Il sistema della corruzione*. Rome-Bari: Laterza.

Davigo, Piercamillo, and Grazia Mannozzi. 2007. *La corruzione in Italia. Percezione sociale e controllo penale*. Rome-Bari: Laterza.

Davis, John. 2015. 'A Tale of Two Italys? The "Southern Question" Past and Present'. In *The Oxford Handbook of Italian Politics*, edited by Erik Jones and Gianfranco Pasquino, pp. 53–68. New York: Oxford University Press.

de Blasio, Guido, and Giorgio Nuzzo. 2012. 'Capitale Sociale e Disuguaglianza in Italia'. Banca d'Italia Occasional Paper No. 116. URL: www.bancaditalia.it/pubblicazioni/qef/2012-0116/index.html.

de Blasio, Guido, Diego Scalise, and Paolo Sestito. 2014. 'Universalism vs. Particularism: A Round Trip from Sociology to Economics'. Banca d'Italia Occasional Paper No. 212. URL: www.bancaditalia.it/pubblicazioni/qef/2014-0212/index.html?com.dotmarketing.htmlpage.language=1.

de Cecco, Marcello. 2000. *L'economia di Lucignolo: opportunità e vincoli dello sviluppo italiano*. Rome: Donzelli.

de Cecco, Marcello. 2013. 'The Italian Economy Seen from Abroad'. In *The Oxford Handbook of the Italian Economy since Unification*, edited by Gianni Toniolo, pp. 134–54. New York: Oxford University Press.

De Feo, Giuseppe, and Giacomo De Luca. 2013. 'Mafia in the ballot box'. URL: https://pure.strath.ac.uk/portal/files/28322264/20131109defeodelucaWP.pdf.

de Grauwe, Paul. 2017. *The Limits of the Market: The Pendulum between Government and Market*. Oxford: Oxford University Press.

De Luna, Giovanni. 2006. *Storia del Partito d'Azione*. Turin: UTET.

De Mauro, Tullio. 1970. *Storia linguistica dell'Italia unita*. 2nd ed. Roma-Bari: Laterza, repr. 2011.

De Mauro, Tullio. 2014. *Storia linguistica dell'Italia repubblicana: dal 1946 ai giorni nostri*. Rome-Bari: Laterza.

Del Pero, Mario. 2015. 'Italy and the Atlantic Alliance'. In *The Oxford Handbook of Italian Politics*, edited by Erik Jones and Gianfranco Pasquino, pp. 685–96. New York: Oxford University Press.

Della Porta, Donatella. 2015. 'Social Movements'. In *The Oxford Handbook of Italian Politics*, edited by Erik Jones and Gianfranco Pasquino, pp. 645–55. New York: Oxford University Press.

Della Sala, Vincent. 2015. '*Gli Esami Non Finiscono Mai*: Italy and the European Union'. In *The Oxford Handbook of Italian Politics*, edited by Erik Jones and Gianfranco Pasquino, pp. 697–707. New York: Oxford University Press.

Demos. 2014. 'Gli italiani e lo Stato: Rapporto 2014'. 29 December. URL: www.demos.it/a01077.php.

di Belgiojoso, Cristina. [1848] 1977. *Il 1848 a Milano e a Venezia*. Edited and translated by Sandro Bortone, 1977. Republished, 2011. Milan: Feltrinelli.

Di Michele, Andrea. 2008. *Storia dell'Italia repubblicana (1948–2008)*. Milan: Garzanti.

Di Nino, Virginia, Barry Eichengreen, and Massimo Sbracia. 2013. 'Real Exchange Rates, Trade, and Growth'. In *The Oxford Handbook of the Italian Economy since Unification*, edited by Gianni Toniolo, pp. 351–77. New York: Oxford University Press.

Diamond, Jared. 1997. *Guns, Germs and Steel: The Fate of Human Societies*. New York: Norton.

Djankov, Simeon, Rafael La Porta, Florencio Lopez-de-Silanes, and Andrei Shleifer. 2002. 'The Regulation of Entry'. *Quarterly Journal of Economics* 117 (1): 1–37.

Djankov, Simeon, Rafael La Porta, Florencio Lopez-de-Silanes, and Andrei Shleifer. 2003. 'Courts'. *Quarterly Journal of Economics* 118 (2): 453–517.

Donovan, Mark, and Mark Gilbert. 2015. 'Silvio Berlusconi and Romano Prodi'. In *The Oxford Handbook of Italian Politics*, edited by Erik Jones and Gianfranco Pasquino, pp. 394–406. New York: Oxford University Press.

Drake, Richard. 2003. *Apostles and Agitators: Italy's Marxist Revolutionary Tradition*. Cambridge, MA: Harvard University Press.

Eco, Umberto. 2011. 'L'italiano di domani'. URL: http://presidenti.quirinale.it/ napolitano/qrnw/statico/eventi/2011-02-lett/doc/Eco.pdf.

Emmott, Bill. 2012. *Good Italy, Bad Italy: Why Italy Must Conquer its Demons to Face the Future*. New Haven, CT: Yale University Press.

Esposito, Gianluca, Sergi Lanau, and Sebastiaan Pompe. 2014. 'Judicial System Reform in Italy: A Key to Growth'. IMF Working Paper No. 14/32. URL: www.imf.org/external/ pubs/ft/wp/2014/wp1432.pdf.

European Commission. 1993. 'Eurobarometre 39. Juin 1993'. URL: http://ec.europa.eu/ public_opinion/archives/eb/eb39/eb39_fr.pdf.

European Commission. 2014. *Report from the Commission to the Council and the European Parliament—EU Anti-corruption Report*. Annex 12, Italy. Doc. COM (2014) 38 final, 3 February.

European Commission. 2015. 'Standard Eurobarometer 83. Spring 2015. Table of Results'. URL: http://ec.europa.eu/public_opinion/archives/eb/eb83/eb83_anx_ en.pdf.

Favretto, Ilaria. 2015. 'The "Opening to the Left"'. In *The Oxford Handbook of Italian Politics*, edited by Erik Jones and Gianfranco Pasquino, pp. 268–82. New York: Oxford University Press.

Federico, Giovanni, and Nikolaus Wolf. 2013. 'A Long-Run Perspective on Comparative Advantage'. In *The Oxford Handbook of the Italian Economy since Unification*, edited by Gianni Toniolo, pp. 327–50. New York: Oxford University Press.

Feld, Lars, and Stefan Voigt. 2003. 'Economic Growth and Judicial Independence: Cross Country Evidence Using a New Set of Indicators'. *European Journal of Political Economy* 19 (3): 497–527.

Felice, Emanuele. 2013. *Perché il Sud è rimasto indietro*. Bologna: Il Mulino.

Felice, Emanuele. 2015. *Ascesa e declino. Storia economica d'Italia*. Bologna: Il Mulino.

Ferrarella, Luigi. 2014. 'Patteggiano tutti anche Greganti'. *Corriere della sera*, 31 October.

Ferrarella, Luigi. 2017. ''Ndrangheta, 13 anni all'ex assessore lombardo'. *Corriere della sera*, 9 February.

Ferraresi, Franco. 1996. *Threats to Democracy: The Radical Right in Italy after the War*. Princeton, NJ: Princeton University Press.

Ferrera, Maurizio, and Matteo Jessoula. 2015. 'The Welfare State: Pensions and Health Care'. In *The Oxford Handbook of Italian Politics*, edited by Erik Jones and Gianfranco Pasquino, pp. 504–17. New York: Oxford University Press.

Ferrera, Maurizio, Valeria Fargion, and Matteo Jessoula. 2012. *Alle radici del welfare all'italiana. Origini e futuro di un modello sociale squilibrato*. Venice: Marsilio.

Filippin, Antonio, Carlo Fiorio, and Eliana Viviano. 2013. 'The Effect of Tax Enforcement on Tax Morale'. Banca d'Italia Working Paper No. 937. URL: www.bancaditalia. it/pubblicazioni/temi-discussione/2013/2013-0937/index.html?com.dotmarketing. htmlpage.language=1.

Frankel, Jeffrey, and David Romer. 1999. 'Does Trade Cause Growth?'. *American Economic Review* 89 (3): 379–99.

Franzinelli, Mimmo. 2014. *Il piano Solo. I servizi segreti, il centro-sinistra e il «golpe» del 1964*. 2nd ed. Milan: Mondadori.

Franzinelli, Mimmo, and Alessandro Giacone (eds). 2013. *Il centrosinistra alla prova. Il primo governo Moro nei documenti e nelle parole dei protagonisti (novembre 1963 – agosto 1964)*. Milan: Feltrinelli.

Fukuyama, Francis. 2000. 'Social Capital and Civil Society'. IMF Working Paper No. 00/74. URL: www.imf.org/external/pubs/cat/longres.aspx?sk=3547.

Gadda, Carlo Emilio. [1967] 1990. *Eros e Priapo*. Milan: Garzanti, repr. 1990.

Galante Garrone, Alessandro. 1996. *L'Italia corrotta. 1895–1996*. Rome: Editori Riuniti.

Galasso, Vincenzo, Massimiliano Landi, Andrea Mattozzi, and Antonio Merlo. 2010. 'The Labour Market of Italian Politicians'. In *The Ruling Class: Management and Politics in Modern Italy*, edited by Tito Boeri, Antonio Merlo, and Andrea Prat, pp. 7–104. New York: Oxford University Press.

Galbiati, Roberto, and Giulio Zanella. 2012. 'The Tax Evasion Social Multiplier: Evidence from Italy'. *Journal of Public Economics* 96 (5–6): 485–94.

Gambetta, Diego. 1993. *The Sicilian Mafia: The Business of Private Protection*. Cambridge, MA: Harvard University Press.

Gambetta, Diego. 2009. *Codes of the Underworld: How Criminals Communicate*. Princeton, NJ: Princeton University Press.

Garin, Eugenio. [1965] 1993. *Scienza e vita civile nel Rinascimento italiano*. Rome-Bari: Laterza, repr. 1993.

Gerschenkron, Alexander. 1962. *Economic Backwardness in Historical Perspective, a Book of Essays*. Cambridge, MA: Harvard University Press.

Gerschenkron, Alexander. 1970. *Europe in the Russian Mirror: Four Lectures in Economic History*. Cambridge: Cambridge University Press.

Giacomelli, Silvia, and Carlo Menon. 2013. 'Firm Size and Judicial Efficiency: Evidence from the Neighbour's Court'. Banca d'Italia Working Paper No. 898. URL: www. bancaditalia.it/pubblicazioni/temi-discussione/2013/2013-0898/index.html?com. dotmarketing.htmlpage.language=1.

Giavazzi, Francesco, Ivan Petkov, and Fabio Schiantarelli. 2014. 'Culture: Persistence and Evolution'. NBER Working Paper No. 20174. URL: www.nber.org/papers/ w20174.

Gigliobianco, Alfredo, and Gianni Toniolo. 2017. 'Concorrenza e crescita in Italia'. In *Concorrenza, mercato e crescita: il lungo periodo*, edited by Alfredo Gigliobianco and Gianni Toniolo, pp. 3–39. Venice: Marsilio.

Gilens, Martin, and Benjamin Page. 2014. 'Testing Theories of American Politics: Elites, Interest Groups, and Average Citizens'. *Perspectives on Politics* 12 (3): 564–81.

Ginsborg, Paul. 1990. *A History of Contemporary Italy: Society and Politics 1943–1988*. London: Penguin.

Ginsborg, Paul. 2001. *Italy and its Discontents: Family, Civil Society, State 1980–2001*. London: Penguin.

Giordano, Claire, and Francesco Zollino. 2017. 'Macroeconomic estimates of Italy's mark-ups in the long run, 1861–2012'. Banca d'Italia Economic History Working Paper No. 39. URL: www.bancaditalia.it/pubblicazioni/quaderni-storia/2017-0039/index.html?com.dotmarketing.htmlpage.language=1.

Giordano, Raffaella, Sergi Lanau, Pietro Tommasino, and Petia Topalova. 2015. 'Does Public Sector Inefficiency Constrain Firm Productivity: Evidence from Italian Provinces'. IMF Working Paper No. 15/168. URL: www.imf.org/external/pubs/cat/longres.aspx?sk=43106.0.

Giunta, Anna, and Salvatore Rossi. 2017. *Che cosa sa fare l'Italia: la nostra economia dopo la grande crisi*. Rome-Bari: Laterza.

Glaeser, Edward, Bruce Sacerdote, and Jose Scheinkman. 1996. 'Crime and Social Interactions'. *Quarterly Journal of Economics* 111 (2): 507–48.

Glaeser, Edward, Rafael La Porta, Florencio Lopez-de-Silanes, and Andrei Shleifer. 2004. 'Do Institutions Cause Growth?'. *Journal of Economic Growth* 9 (3): 271–303.

Golden, Miriam. 2003. 'Electoral Connections: The Effects of the Personal Vote on Political Patronage, Bureaucracy and Legislation in Postwar Italy'. *British Journal of Political Science* 33 (2): 189–212.

Golden, Miriam, and Paasha Mahdavi. 2015. 'The Institutional Components of Political Corruption'. In *Routledge Handbook of Comparative Political Institutions*, edited by Jennifer Gandhi and Rubén Ruiz-Rufino, pp. 404–20. Abingdon: Routledge.

Golden, Miriam, and Lucio Picci. 2006. 'Corruption and the Management of Public Works in Italy'. In *The Handbook of Economic Corruption*, edited by Susan Rose-Ackerman, pp. 457–83. Cheltenham: Edward Elgar.

Gollwitzer Franke, Sophia, and Marc Quintyn. 2012. 'Institutional Transformations, Polity and Economic Outcomes: Testing the North-Wallis-Weingast Doorsteps Framework'. IMF Working Paper No. WP/12/87. URL: www.imf.org/external/pubs/cat/longres.aspx?sk=25799.0.

Gomellini, Matteo, and Cormac Ó Gráda. 2013. 'Migrations'. In *The Oxford Handbook of the Italian Economy since Unification*, edited by Gianni Toniolo, pp. 271–302. New York: Oxford University Press.

Gordon, Robert. 2015. 'Secular Stagnation: A Supply-Side View'. *American Economic Review, Papers and Proceedings* 105 (5): 54–9.

Gorga, Andrea (ed.). 2018. 'Le misure della cd. Pace Fiscale nel dl 119/2018'. Osservatorio conti pubblici italiani, 12 November. URL: https://osservatoriocpi.unicatt.it/cpi-archivio-studi-e-analisi-le-misure-della-cd-pace-fiscale-nel-dl-119-2018-1118.

Gorga, Andrea (ed.). 2019. 'Reddito di cittadinanza: generoso con i single e parsimonioso con le famiglie numerose'. Osservatorio conti pubblici italiani, 11 February. URL: https://osservatoriocpi.unicatt.it/cpi-archivio-studi-e-analisi-reddito-di-cittadinanza-generoso-con-i-single-e-parsimonioso.

Gotor, Miguel. 2011. *Il memoriale della Repubblica. Gli scritti di Aldo Moro nella prigionia e l'anatomia del potere italiano*. Torino: Einaudi.

Gramsci, Antonio. [1929–35] 2011. *Prison Notebooks*. Edited by Joseph Buttigieg, translated by Joseph Buttigieg and Antonio Callari, 1992, 1996, 2007. New York: Columbia University Press, repr. 2011.

Gratteri, Nicola, and Antonio Nicaso. 2016. *Padrini e padroni*. Milan: Mondadori.

GRECO (Group of States against Corruption). 2009. 'Evaluation Report on Italy'. 2 July. Strasbourg: Council of Europe. URL: www.coe.int/t/dghl/monitoring/greco/evaluations/round2/GrecoEval1-2(2008)2_Italy_EN.pdf.

Greif, Avner. 1994. 'Cultural Beliefs and the Organization of Society: A Historical and Theoretical Reflection on Collectivist and Individualist Societies'. *Journal of Political Economy* 102 (5): 912–50.

Greif, Avner. 2006. *Institutions and the Path to the Modern Economy: Lessons from Medieval Trade*. New York: Cambridge University Press.

Greif, Avner, and David Laitin. 2004. 'A Theory of Endogenous Institutional Change'. *American Political Science Review* 98 (4): 633–52.

Grillo, Michele. 2017. 'Tutela della concorrenza e diffusione sociale del rischio'. In *Concorrenza, mercato e crescita: il lungo periodo*, edited by Alfredo Gigliobianco and Gianni Toniolo, pp. 533–61. Venice: Marsilio.

Guarnieri, Carlo. 2015. 'The Courts'. In *The Oxford Handbook of Italian Politics*, edited by Erik Jones and Gianfranco Pasquino, pp. 120–31. New York: Oxford University Press.

Guiso, Luigi, and Paolo Pinotti. 2013. 'Democratization and Civic Capital'. In *The Oxford Handbook of the Italian Economy since Unification*, edited by Gianni Toniolo, pp. 303–23. New York: Oxford University Press.

Guiso, Luigi, Paola Sapienza, and Luigi Zingales. 2015. 'Long Term Persistence'. Working paper, 15 September. *Journal of the European Economic Association*, forthcoming. URL: http://faculty.chicagobooth.edu/luigi.zingales/papers/research/Long-term-Persistence.pdf.

Gundle, Stephen. 2015. 'Cinema and Television'. In *The Oxford Handbook of Italian Politics*, edited by Erik Jones and Gianfranco Pasquino, pp. 569–82. New York: Oxford University Press.

Hall, Peter, and David Soskice. 2001. 'An Introduction to Varieties of Capitalism'. In *Varieties of Capitalism: The Institutional Foundations of Comparative Advantage*, edited by Peter Hall and David Soskice, pp. 1–70. Oxford: Oxford University Press.

Hardin, Russell. 1971. 'Collective Action as an Agreeable n-Prisoners' Dilemma'. *Science* 76: 472–81.

Hassan, Fadi, and Gianmarco Ottaviano. 2013. 'Productivity in Italy: The Great Unlearning'. *VOX*, 30 November. URL: www.voxeu.org/article/productivity-italy-great-unlearning.

Helliwell, John, Shun Wang, and Jinwen Xu. 2014. 'How Durable Are Social Norms? Immigrant Trust and Generosity in 132 Countries'. NBER Working Paper No. 19855. URL: www.nber.org/papers/w19855.

Hellman, Stephen. 2015. 'The Compromesso Storico'. In *The Oxford Handbook of Italian Politics*, edited by Erik Jones and Gianfranco Pasquino, pp. 283–95. New York: Oxford University Press.

Hine, David. 2015. 'Public Ethics and Political Corruption in Italy'. In *The Oxford Handbook of Italian Politics*, edited by Erik Jones and Gianfranco Pasquino, pp. 608–20. New York: Oxford University Press.

Hirschman, Albert. 1970. *Exit, Voice, and Loyalty: Responses to Decline in Firms, Organizations, and the State*. Cambridge, MA: Harvard University Press.

Hirschman, Albert. 1982. *Shifting Involvements: Private Interest and Public Action*. Princeton, NJ: Princeton University Press.

Hobsbawm, Eric. 1994. *Age of Extremes: The Short Twentieth Century 1914–1991*. London: Penguin.

Hoff, Karla, and Joseph Stiglitz. 2008. 'Exiting a Lawless State'. *Economic Journal* 118 (531): 1474–97.

Hoff, Karla, and Joseph Stiglitz. 2016. 'Striving for Balance in Economics: Towards a Theory of the Social Determination of Behavior'. *Journal of Economic Behavior and Organization* 126 (B): 25–57.

Hopkin, Jonathan. 2015. 'Bipolarity (and After)'. In *The Oxford Handbook of Italian Politics*, edited by Erik Jones and Gianfranco Pasquino, pp. 325–38. New York: Oxford University Press.

Ignazi, Piero. 2012. *Forza senza legittimità. Il vicolo cieco dei partiti*. Rome-Bari: Laterza.

Ignazi, Piero. 2015. 'Fascists and Post-Fascists'. In *The Oxford Handbook of Italian Politics*, edited by Erik Jones and Gianfranco Pasquino, pp. 211–23. New York: Oxford University Press.

IMF (International Monetary Fund). 2014. 'Italy – 2014 Article IV consultation'. Country Report No. 14/283, September. URL: www.imf.org/external/pubs/cat/longres.aspx?sk=41925.0.

IMF (International Monetary Fund). 2015a. 'Italy – 2015 Article IV consultation'. Country No. Report 15/166, July. URL: www.imf.org/external/pubs/cat/longres.aspx?sk=43046.0.

IMF (International Monetary Fund). 2015b. 'Italy – Selected issues'. Country Report No. 15/167, July. URL: www.imf.org/external/pubs/cat/longres.aspx?sk=43047.0.

IMF (International Monetary Fund). 2016. 'Corruption: Costs and Mitigating Strategies'. Staff Discussion Note No. SDN/16/05. URL: www.imf.org/external/pubs/cat/longres.aspx?sk=43888.

IMF (International Monetary Fund). 2017. 'Italy – 2017 Article IV consultation'. Country No. Report 17/237, July. URL: www.imf.org/en/Publications/CR/Issues/2017/07/27/Italy-2017-Article-IV-Consultation-Press-Release-Staff-Report-and-Statement-by-the-Executive-45139.

IMF (International Monetary Fund). 2018. 'Italy – 2018 Article IV Consultation'. Country Report n. 19/40, 18 December. URL: https://www.imf.org/en/Publications/CR/Issues/2019/02/06/Italy-2018-Article-IV-Consultation-Press-Release-Staff-Report-and-Statement-by-the-Executive-46579.

IMF (International Monetary Fund). 2019. 'Italy – 2018 Article IV Consultation – Supplementary Information'. 17 January. URL: https://www.imf.org/en/Publications/CR/Issues/2019/02/06/Italy-2018-Article-IV-Consultation-Press-Release-Staff-Report-and-Statement-by-the-Executive-46579.

ISTAT (Istituto nazionale di statistica). 2017. 'Rapporto Bes 2016: il benessere equo e sostenibile in Italia'. Rome. URL: www.istat.it/it/archivio/194029.

Italia nostra. 2018. 'Grave approvare condono Ischia nel Decreto Genova'. Communiqué 15 November. URL: https://www.italianostra.org/approvato-il-decreto-genova-la-nota-di-italia-nostra/.

Iuzzolino, Giovanni, Guido Pellegrini, and Gianfranco Viesti. 2013. 'Regional Convergence'. In *The Oxford Handbook of the Italian Economy since Unification*, edited by Gianni Toniolo, pp. 571–98. New York: Oxford University Press.

James, Harold, and Kevin O'Rourke. 2013. 'Italy and the First Age of Globalization, 1861–1940'. In *The Oxford Handbook of the Italian Economy since Unification*, edited by Gianni Toniolo, pp. 37–68. New York: Oxford University Press.

Jones, Erik, and Gianfranco Pasquino (eds). 2015. *The Oxford Handbook of Italian Politics*. New York: Oxford University Press.

Katz, Richard, and Peter Mair. 2009. 'The Cartel Party Thesis Revisited'. *Perspectives on Politics* 7 (4): 753–66.

Kaufmann, Daniel, Aart Kraay, and Massimo Mastruzzi. 2010. 'The Worldwide Governance Indicators: Methodology and Analytical Issues'. World Bank Policy Research Working Paper No. 5430. URL: http://elibrary.worldbank.org/doi/abs/10.1596/1813-9450-5430.

Keefer, Philip, and Razvan Vlaicu. 2007. 'Democracy, Credibility and Clientelism'. *Journal of Law, Economics, and Organization* 24 (2): 371–406.

La Malfa, Ugo. 1962. *Verso una politica di piano*. Napoli: ESI.

La Porta, Rafael, Florencio Lopez-de-Silanes, Andrei Shleifer, and Robert Vishny. 1998. 'Law and Finance'. *Journal of Political Economy* 106 (6): 1113–55.

La Spina, Antonio. 2014. 'The Fight Against the Italian Mafia'. In *Oxford Handbook of Organized Crime*, edited by Letizia Paoli, pp. 593–611. New York: Oxford University Press.

Landes, David. 1998. *The Wealth and Poverty of Nations: Why Some Are So Rich and Some So Poor*. New York: Norton.

Lane, David. 2004. *Berlusconi's Shadow: Crime, Justice and the Pursuit of Power*. London: Penguin.

Le Goff, Jacques. 1979. 'The Usurer and Purgatory'. In *The Dawn of Modern Banking*, edited by Fredi Chiappelli, pp. 25–53. New Haven, CT: Yale University Press.

Legambiente. 2018. 'Approvato dl Genova con i condoni edilizi'. Communiqué 15 November. URL: https://www.legambiente.it/approvato-dl-genova-con-i-condoni-edilizi/.

Levi, Carlo. [1950] 1951. *The Watch*. Translated by John Farrar. New York: Farrar, Straus and Young.

Linz, Juan, and Alfred Stepan. 1996. 'Toward Consolidated Democracies'. *Journal of Democracy* 7 (2): 14–33.

Lodato, Saverio, and Roberto Scarpinato. 2008. *Il ritorno del Principe. Criminalità, corruzione, mafia: il potere in Italia*. Milan: Chiarelettere.

Lorenzani, Dimitri, and Vito Reitano. 2015. 'Italy's Spending Maze Runner: An analysis of the structure and evolution of public expenditure in Italy'. European Commission Discussion Paper No. 023. URL: https://ec.europa.eu/info/sites/info/files/file_import/dp023_en_2.pdf.

Lupo, Salvatore. [1996] 2009. *History of the Mafia*. Translated by Anthony Shugaar. New York: Columbia University Press.

Mack Smith, Denis. 1997. *Modern Italy: A Political History*. 3rd ed. New Haven, CT: Yale University Press.

Magnani, Marco. 1997. 'Alla ricerca di regole nelle relazioni industriali: breve storia di due fallimenti'. In *Storia del capitalismo italiano*, edited by Fabrizio Barca, pp. 501–44. Rome: Donzelli.

Magnani, Marco. 2016. *Sindona. Biografia degli anni Settanta*. Turin: Einaudi.

Magnani, Marco [Magnani(II)]. 2013. *Sette anni di vacche sobrie. Come sarà l'Italia del 2020? Sfide e opportunità di crescita per sopravvivere alla crisi*. Novara: UTET.

Manasse, Paolo. 2013. 'The Roots of the Italian Stagnation'. CEPR Policy Insight No. 66. URL: http://cepr.org/content/roots-italian-stagnation.

Mancini, Paolo. 2015. 'The Press'. In *The Oxford Handbook of Italian Politics*, edited by Erik Jones and Gianfranco Pasquino, pp. 583–93. New York: Oxford University Press.

Manzoni, Alessandro. [1840] 1972. *The Betrothed*. Translated by Bruce Penman, 1972. London: Penguin.

Marchetti, Piergaetano. 1997. 'Diritto societario e disciplina della concorrenza'. In *Storia del capitalismo italiano*, edited by Fabrizio Barca, pp. 467–99. Rome: Donzelli.

Marchetti, Piergaetano. 2011. 'La regolamentazione delle società quotate'. In *Dall'Unità ai giorni nostri: 150 anni di borsa in Italia*, edited by CONSOB, pp. 43–73. Rome: CONSOB.

Mattheier, Klaus. 2000. 'Die Durchsetzung der deutschen Hochsprache im 19. und beginnenden 20. Jahrundert: sprachgeographisch, sprachsoziologisch.' In *Handbücher zur Sprach- und Kommunikations-wissenschaft*, edited by Armin Burkardt, Hugo Steger, and Herbert Ernst Wiegand, vol. 2, *Sprachgeschichte*, pp. 1951–66. Berlin: de Gruyter.

Matthews, Dylan. 2016. 'Remember that Study Saying America is an Oligarchy? 3 Rebuttals say it's Wrong.' *Vox*, 9 May. URL: www.vox.com/2016/5/9/11502464/gilens-page-oligarchy-study.

Melloni, Alberto. 2015. 'The Italian Catholic Hierarchy'. In *The Oxford Handbook of Italian Politics*, edited by Erik Jones and Gianfranco Pasquino, pp. 409–24. New York: Oxford University Press.

Mershon, Carol. 2015. 'Party Systems in Post-World War II Italy'. In *The Oxford Handbook of Italian Politics*, edited by Erik Jones and Gianfranco Pasquino, pp. 144–58. New York: Oxford University Press.

Milanović, Branko. 2016. *Global Inequality: A New Approach for the Age of Globalization*. Cambridge, MA: Harvard University Press.

Mill, John Stuart. [1848] 2008. *Principles of Political Economy*. Oxford: Oxford University Press.

Moro, Giovanni. 2013. *Cittadinanza attiva e qualità della democrazia*. Rome: Carocci.

Mudde, Cas, and Cristóbal Rovira Kaltwasser. 2013. 'Populism'. In *The Oxford Handbook of Political Ideologies*, edited by Michael Freeden and Marc Stears, pp. 493–512. Oxford: Oxford University Press.

Mukand, Sharun, and Dani Rodrik. 2015. 'The Political Economy of Liberal Democracy'. NBER Working Paper No. 21540. URL: www.nber.org/papers/w21540.

Mukand, Sharun, and Dani Rodrik. 2016. 'Ideas versus Interests. A Unified Political Economy Framework'. 10 April. URL: http://drodrik.scholar.harvard.edu/publications/ideas-versus-interests.

Müller, Jan-Werner. 2016. *What is Populism?* Philadelphia, PA: University of Pennsylvania Press.

Nardozzi, Giangiacomo. 2004. *Miracolo e declino; L'Italia tra concorrenza e protezione.* Rome-Bari: Laterza.

Neppi Modona, Guido. 1997. 'La magistratura dalla Liberazione agli anni cinquanta. Il difficile cammino verso l'indipendenza'. In *Storia dell'Italia Repubblicana*, edited by Francesco Barbagallo, vol. 3, *L'Italia nella crisi mondiale. L'ultimo ventennio*, tome 2, *Istituzioni, politiche, culture*, pp. 83–137. Turin: Einaudi.

Newell, James. 2015. 'La Classe Dirigente'. In *The Oxford Handbook of Italian Politics*, edited by Erik Jones and Gianfranco Pasquino, pp. 3–15. New York: Oxford University Press.

North, Douglass. 1983. 'A Theory of Economic Change'. *Science* 219: 163–4.

North, Douglass. 1990. *Institutions, Institutional Change, and Economic Performance.* Cambridge: Cambridge University Press.

North, Douglass. 1991. 'Institutions'. *Journal of Economic Perspectives* 5 (1): 97–112.

North, Douglass. 1994. 'Economic Performance through Time'. *American Economic Review* 84 (3): 359–68.

North, Douglass. 2005. *Understanding the Process of Economic Change.* Princeton, NJ: Princeton University Press.

North, Douglass, and Robert Thomas. 1973. *The Rise of the Western World.* Cambridge: Cambridge University Press.

North, Douglass, John Wallis, and Barry Weingast. 2009. *Violence and Social Orders: A Conceptual Framework for Interpreting Recorded Human History.* Cambridge: Cambridge University Press.

North, Douglass, John Wallis, Steven Webb, and Barry Weingast (eds). 2012. *In The Shadow of Violence: Politics, Economics, and the Problems of Development.* Cambridge: Cambridge University Press.

Novelli, Claudio. 2000. *Il Partito d'Azione e gli Italiani. Moralità, politica e cittadinanza nella storia repubblicana.* Milan: Nuova Italia.

OECD (Organisation for Economic Co-operation and Development). 2017. *OECD Skills Strategy Diagnostic Report: Italy 2017.* Paris: OECD.

Oliva, Federico. 1997. 'L'uso del suolo: scarsità indotta e rendita'. In *Storia del capitalismo italiano*, edited by Fabrizio Barca, pp. 545–77. Rome: Donzelli.

Olson, Mancur. 1965. *The Logic of Collective Action: Public Goods and the Theory of Groups.* Cambridge, MA: Harvard University Press.

Olson, Mancur. 1982. *The Rise and Decline of Nations: Economic Growth, Stagflation, and Social Rigidities.* New Haven, CT: Yale University Press.

Onida, Fabrizio, Giuseppe Berta, and Mario Perugini. 2013. 'Old and New Italian Manufacturing Multinational Firms'. In *The Oxford Handbook of the Italian Economy since Unification*, edited by Gianni Toniolo, pp. 417–51. New York: Oxford University Press.

OpenPolis. 2017. 'Parlamentari'. Web page, accessed on 18 August. URL: https://parlamento17.openpolis.it/i-gruppi-in-parlamento/camera.

Orsina, Giovanni. 2015. 'Liberalism and Liberals'. In *The Oxford Handbook of Italian Politics*, edited by Erik Jones and Gianfranco Pasquino, pp. 240–52. New York: Oxford University Press.

Ortoleva, Peppino. 1997a. 'I media. Comunicazione e potere'. In *Storia dell'Italia Repubblicana*, edited by Francesco Barbagallo, vol. 3, *L'Italia nella crisi mondiale. L'ultimo ventennio*, tome 2, *Istituzioni, politiche, culture*, pp. 865–84. Turin: Einaudi.

Ortoleva, Peppino. 1997b. 'Il capitalismo italiano e i mezzi di comunicazione di massa'. In *Storia del capitalismo italiano*, edited by Fabrizio Barca, pp. 237–64. Rome: Donzelli.

Ostellino, Piero. 2011. 'L'immagine e la dignità del paese'. *Corriere della Sera*, 19 January.

Ostrom, Elinor. 1990. *Governing the Commons: The Evolution of Institutions for Collective Action*. New York: Cambridge University Press.

Ostrom, Elinor. 2000. 'Collective Action and the Evolution of Social Norms'. *Journal of Economic Perspectives* 14 (3): 137–58.

Ostrom, Elinor. 2010. 'Analyzing Collective Action'. *Agricultural Economics* 41 (1): 155–66.

Paccagnella, Marco, and Paolo Sestito. 2014. 'School Cheating and Social Capital'. Banca d'Italia Working Paper No. 952. URL: www.bancaditalia.it/pubblicazioni/temi-discussione/2014/2014-0952/index.html?com.dotmarketing.htmlpage.language=1.

Paoli, Letizia. 1995. 'The Banco Ambrosiano Case: An Investigation into the Underestimation of the Relations between Organized and Economic Crime'. *Crime, Law and Social Change* 23 (4): 345–65.

Paoli, Letizia. 2015. 'Mafia, Camorra, and 'Ndrangheta'. In *The Oxford Handbook of Italian Politics*, edited by Erik Jones and Gianfranco Pasquino, pp. 668–82. New York: Oxford University Press.

Parini, Ercole Giap. 2003. 'Civil Resistance: Society Fights Back . . . '. In *Organized Crime and the Challenge to Democracy*, edited by Felicia Allum and Renate Siebert, pp. 130–42. Abingdon: Routledge.

Pasolini, Pier Paolo. 1975. 'Bisognerebbe processare i gerarchi Dc'. *Il Mondo*, 28 August 1975.

Pasquino, Gianfranco. 2014. 'Italy: The Triumph of Personalist Parties'. *Politics and Policy* 42 (4): 548–66.

Pasquino, Gianfranco. 2015a. 'The Presidents of the Republic'. In *The Oxford Handbook of Italian Politics*, edited by Erik Jones and Gianfranco Pasquino, pp. 82–94. New York: Oxford University Press.

Pasquino, Gianfranco (ed.). 2015b. 'La scomparsa delle culture politiche in Italia'. Monographic issue, *Paradoxa* 9 (4).

Pasquino, Gianfranco, and Marco Valbruzzi. 2017. 'Italy Says No: The 2016 Constitutional Referendum and its Consequences'. *Journal of Modern Italian Studies* 22 (2): 145–62.

Pasquino, Gianfranco. 2018. 'Not a normal election: roots and consequences'. *Journal of Modern Italian Studies* 23 (4): pp. 347–61.

Pasquino, Gianfranco. 2019. 'The state of the Italian Republic'. *Contemporary Italian Politics* 11 (2): pp. 195–204.

Passarelli, Gianluca. 2015. 'Populism and the Lega Nord'. In *The Oxford Handbook of Italian Politics*, edited by Erik Jones and Gianfranco Pasquino, pp. 224–39. New York: Oxford University Press.

Passarelli, Gianluca, and Dario Tuorto. 2018. *La Lega di Salvini. Estrema destra di governo*. Bologna: Il Mulino.

Pavone, Claudio. [1994] 2013. *A Civil War: A History of the Italian Resistance*. Translated by Peter Levy, 2013. London: Verso.

Pavone, Claudio. 1995. *Alle origini della Repubblica. Scritti su fascismo, antifascismo e continuità dello Stato*. Turin: Bollati Boringhieri.

Peli, Santo. 2004. *La Resistenza in Italia. Storia e critica*. Turin: Einaudi.

Pellegrino, Bruno, and Luigi Zingales. 2014. 'Diagnosing the Italian Disease'. Chicago Booth Working Paper, September. URL: http://faculty.chicagobooth.edu/luigi.zingales/papers/research/Diagnosing.pdf.

Pera, Alberto, and Marco Cecchini. 2015. *La rivoluzione incompiuta. 25 anni di Antitrust in Italia*. Rome: Fazi.

Persson, Anna, Bo Rothstein, and Jan Teorell. 2013. 'Why Anticorruption Reforms Fail: Systemic Corruption as a Collective Action Problem'. *Governance* 26 (3): 449–71.

Persson, Torsten, and Guido Tabellini. 2000. *Political Economics: Explaining Public Policy*. Cambridge, MA: MIT Press.

Persson, Torsten, and Guido Tabellini. 2003. *The Economic Effects of Constitutions*. Cambridge, MA: MIT Press.

Pettit, Philip. 2012. *On the People's Terms: A Republican Theory and Model of Democracy*. Cambridge: Cambridge University Press.

Piattoni, Simona. 2015. 'Bureaucracy'. In *The Oxford Handbook of Italian Politics*, edited by Erik Jones and Gianfranco Pasquino, pp. 159–70. New York: Oxford University Press.

Piketty, Thomas. [2013] 2014. *Capital in the Twenty-First Century*. Translated by Arthur Goldhammer, 2014. Cambridge, MA: Harvard University Press.

Pinelli, Dino, István Székely, and Janos Varga. 2016. 'Exploring Italy's Growth Challenge: A Model-Based Exercise'. European Commission Discussion Paper No. 041. URL: https://ec.europa.eu/info/sites/info/files/file_import/dp041_en_2.pdf.

Pinotti, Paolo. 2012. 'Trust, Regulation and Market Failures'. *Review of Economics and Statistics*, 94 (3): 650–78.

Pinotti, Paolo. 2015. 'The Economic Consequences of Organized Crime: Evidence from Southern Italy'. *Economic Journal* 125 (586): 203–32.

Pombeni, Paolo. 2015. 'Christian Democracy in Power, 1946–63'. In *The Oxford Handbook of Italian Politics*, edited by Erik Jones and Gianfranco Pasquino, pp. 255–67. New York: Oxford University Press.

Procura di Milano. 2015. 'Bilancio di responsabilità sociale 2014/2015'. Milan. URL: URL: www.procura.milano.giustizia.it/files/BRS-Procura-2015.pdf.

Procura di Milano. 2016. 'Bilancio di responsabilità sociale 2016'. Milan. URL: www.procura.milano.giustizia.it/files/BRS-Procura-2016.pdf.

Putnam, Robert. 1993. *Making Democracy Work: Civic Traditions in Modern Italy*. Princeton, NJ: Princeton University Press.

Putnam, Robert. 1995. 'Bowling Alone: America's Declining Social Capital'. *Journal of Democracy* 6 (1): 65–78.

Putnam, Robert. 2000. *Bowling Alone: The Collapse and Revival of American Community*. New York: Simon and Schuster.

Quaglia, Lucia. 2015. 'The Bank of Italy'. In *The Oxford Handbook of Italian Politics*, edited by Erik Jones and Gianfranco Pasquino, pp. 518–27. New York: Oxford University Press.

References

Regalia, Marta. 2015. 'Electoral Systems'. In *The Oxford Handbook of Italian Politics*, edited by Erik Jones and Gianfranco Pasquino, pp. 132–43. New York: Oxford University Press.

Regini, Marino. 2015. 'Trade Unions'. In *The Oxford Handbook of Italian Politics*, edited by Erik Jones and Gianfranco Pasquino, pp. 528–40. New York: Oxford University Press.

Revelli, Marco. 2013. *Finale di partito*. Turin: Einaudi.

Revelli, Marco. 2015. *Dentro e contro. Quando il populismo è di governo*. Rome-Bari: Laterza.

Revelli, Nuto. 2003. *Le due guerre. Guerra fascista e Guerra partigiana*. Turin: Einaudi.

Rhodes, Martin. 2015. 'Tangentopoli: More than 20 Years On'. In *The Oxford Handbook of Italian Politics*, edited by Erik Jones and Gianfranco Pasquino, pp. 309–24. New York: Oxford University Press.

Rodrik, Dani. 2008. 'Second-Best Institutions'. *American Economic Review, Papers and Proceedings* 98 (2): 100–4.

Rodrik, Dani. 2011. *The Globalization Paradox: Democracy and the Future of the World Economy*. New York: Norton.

Rodrik, Dani. 2014. 'When Ideas Trump Interests: Preferences, Worldviews, and Policy Innovations'. *Journal of Economic Perspectives* 28 (1): 189–208.

Rodrik, Dani. 2015. *Economic Rules: The Rights and Wrongs of the Dismal Science*. New York: Norton.

Rodrik, Dani, Arvind Subramanian, and Francesco Trebbi. 2004. 'Institutions Rule: the Primacy of Institutions over Geography and Integration in Economic Development'. *Journal of Economic Growth* 9 (2): 131–65.

Rogoff, Kenneth. 2016. *The Curse of Cash*. Princeton, NJ: Princeton University Press.

Rosanvallon, Pierre. 2006. *La Contre-démocratie. La politique à l'âge de la défiance*. Paris: Seuil.

Rosanvallon, Pierre. 2015. *Le bon gouvernement*. Paris: Seuil.

Rose-Ackerman, Susan. 2006. 'Introduction and Overview'. In *The Handbook of Economic Corruption*, edited by Susan Rose-Ackerman, pp. xiv–xxxviii. Cheltenham: Edward Elgar.

Rossi, Salvatore. 2007. *La politica economica italiana 1968–2007*. 4th ed. Rome-Bari: Laterza.

Rossi Doria, Anna. 1983. *Il ministro e i contadini. Decreti Gullo e lotte nel Mezzogiorno*. Rome: Bulzoni.

Rothstein, Bo. 2005. *Social Traps and the Problem of Trust*. New York: Cambridge University Press.

Rothstein, Bo, and Dietlind Stolle. 2008. 'The State and Social Capital: An Institutional Theory of Generalized Trust'. *Comparative Politics* 40 (4): 441–59.

Rothstein, Bo, and Eric Uslaner. 2005. 'All for All: Equality and Social Trust'. *World Politics* 58 (1): 41–72.

Salvadori, Massimo. 2013. *Storia d'Italia. Crisi di regime e crisi di sistema 1861–2013*. 4th ed. Bologna: Il Mulino.

Salvati, Michele. 1984. *Economia e politica dal dopoguerra ad oggi*. Milan: Garzanti.

Salvati, Michele. 2000. *Occasioni mancate: Economia e politica in Italia dagli anni 60 ad oggi*. Rome-Bari: Laterza.

Salvati, Michele. 2011. *Tre pezzi facili sull'Italia. Democrazia, crisi economica, Berlusconi*. Bologna: Il Mulino.

Satyanath, Shanker, Nico Voigtländer, and Hans-Joakim Voth. 2013. 'Bowling for Fascism: Social Capital and the Rise of the Nazi Party'. NBER Working Paper No. 19201. URL: www.nber.org/papers/w19201.pdf.

Sberna, Salvatore, and Alberto Vannucci. 2013. '"It's the Politics, Stupid!": The Politicization of Anti-Corruption in Italy'. *Crime, Law and Social Change* 60 (5): 565–93.

Schefter, Martin. 1977. 'Party and Patronage: Germany, England, and Italy'. *Politics and Society* 7 (4): 403–51.

Schelling, Thomas. 1980. *The Strategy of Conflict*. 2nd ed. Cambridge, MA: Harvard University Press.

Schneider, Friedrich, and Dominik Enste. 2013. *The Shadow Economy: An International Survey*. 2nd ed. Cambridge: Cambridge University Press.

Sciascia, Leonardo. 1987. 'I professionisti dell'antimafia'. *Corriere della Sera*, 10 January.

Sen, Amartya. 1967. 'Isolation, Assurance, and the Social Rate of Discount'. *Quarterly Journal of Economics* 81 (1): 112–24.

Sen, Amartya. 1999. *Development as Freedom*. Oxford: Oxford University Press.

Sen, Amartya. 2004. 'How Does Culture Matter?'. In *Culture and Public Action*, edited by Vijayendra Rao and Michael Walton, pp. 37–58. Stanford, CA: Stanford University Press.

Sen, Amartya. 2009. *The Idea of Justice*. London: Penguin.

Seravalli, Gilberto. 1999. *Teatro regio, teatro comunale. Società, istituzioni e politica a Modena e a Parma*. Rome: Donzelli.

Siciliano, Giovanni. 2011. '150 anni di borsa in Italia: uno sguardo d'insieme'. In *Dall'Unità ai giorni nostri: 150 anni di borsa in Italia*, edited by CONSOB, pp. 13–39. Rome: CONSOB.

Solow, Robert. 1956. 'A Contribution to the Theory of Economic Growth'. *Quarterly Journal of Economics* 70 (1): 65–94.

Stajano, Corrado. 1991. *Un eroe borghese*. Turin: Einaudi.

Stajano, Corrado. [1987] 2010. 'I lumi di Sciascia'. In *L'Italia ferita*, pp. 99–105. Pordenone: Cinemazero.

Stajano, Corrado. 1997. 'Portella della Ginestra, anatomia di una strage politica'. *Corriere della Sera*, 3 June.

Stajano, Corrado. 2017. 'Stragi di mafia, un filo rosso'. *Corriere della Sera*, 4 June.

Stiglitz, Joseph. 2012. *The Price of Inequality*. London: Penguin.

Stockemer, Daniel, Bernadette La Montagne, and Lyle Scruggs. 2013. 'Bribes and Ballots: The Impact of Corruption on Voter Turnout in Democracies'. *International Political Science Review* 34 (1): 74–90.

Stolfi, Francesco, and Mark Hallerberg. 2016. 'Clientelistic Budget Cycles: Evidence from Health Policy in the Italian Regions'. *Journal of European Public Policy* 23 (6): 833–50.

Sundström, Aksel, and Daniel Stockemer. 2015. 'Regional Variation in Voter Turnout in Europe: The Impact of Corruption Perceptions'. *Electoral Studies* 40 (4): 158–69.

Svolik, Milan. 2015. 'Equilibrium analysis of political institutions'. In *Routledge Handbook of Comparative Political Institutions*, edited by Jennifer Gandhi and Rubén Ruiz-Rufino, pp. 70–83. Abingdon: Routledge.

Tabellini, Guido. 2010. 'Culture and Institutions: Economic Development in the Regions of Europe'. *Journal of the European Economic Association* 8 (4): 677–716.

Tarrow, Sidney. 1967. *Peasant Communism in Southern Italy*. New Haven, CT: Yale University Press.

Tarrow, Sidney. 1989. *Democracy and Disorder. Protest and Politics in Italy, 1965–1975*. Oxford: Oxford University Press.

Tarrow, Sidney. 1996. 'Making Social Science Work across Space and Time: A Critical Reflection on Robert Putnam's *Making Democracy Work*'. *American Political Science Review* 90 (2): 389–97.

Teodori, Massimo. 2015. 'The Laity'. In *The Oxford Handbook of Italian Politics*, edited by Erik Jones and Gianfranco Pasquino, pp. 453–62. New York: Oxford University Press.

Tirole, Jean. 1996. 'A Theory of Collective Reputations (with Applications to the Persistence of Corruption and to Firm Quality)'. *Review of Economic Studies* 63 (1): 1–22.

Toffoletto, Alberto. 1995. *Il risarcimento del danno nel sistema delle sanzioni per la violazione della normativa antitrust*. Milan: Guerini.

Tomasi di Lampedusa, Giuseppe. [1958] 2007. *The Leopard*. Translated by Archibald Colquhoun, 1960. New York: Random House, repr. 2007.

Toniolo, Gianni. 2012. 'Il declino economico dell'Italia'. In *Il modello di sviluppo dell'economia italiana quarant'anni dopo*, edited by Marcello Messori and Damiano Bruno Silipo, pp. 1–18. Milano: EGEA.

Toniolo, Gianni (ed.). 2013a. *The Oxford Handbook of the Italian Economy since Unification*. New York: Oxford University Press.

Toniolo, Gianni. 2013b. 'An Overview of Italy's Economic Growth'. In *The Oxford Handbook of the Italian Economy since Unification*, edited by Gianni Toniolo, pp. 3–36. New York: Oxford University Press.

Toniolo, Gianni, and Vincenzo Visco (eds). 2004. *Il declino economico dell'Italia. Cause e rimedi*. Milan: Bruno Mondadori.

Trigilia, Carlo. 2012. *Non c'è Nord senza Sud. Perché la crescita dell'Italia si decide nel Mezzogiorno*. Bologna: Il Mulino.

Trigilia, Carlo, and Gianfranco Viesti. 2016. 'La crisi del Mezzogiorno e gli effetti perversi delle politiche'. *Il Mulino* (1): 52–61.

Urbinati, Nadia. 2015. 'The Intellectuals'. In *The Oxford Handbook of Italian Politics*, edited by Erik Jones and Gianfranco Pasquino, pp. 594–607. New York: Oxford University Press.

Valbruzzi, Marco. 2015. 'Trasformismo'. In *The Oxford Handbook of Italian Politics*, edited by Erik Jones and Gianfranco Pasquino, pp. 26–40. New York: Oxford University Press.

Valbruzzi, Marco, and Rinaldo Vignati (eds). 2018. *Il vicolo cieco. Le elezioni del 4 marzo 2018*. Bologna: Il Mulino.

van Aaken, Anne, Lars Feld, and Stefan Voigt. 2010. 'Do Independent Prosecutors Deter Political Corruption? An Empirical Evaluation Across Seventy-Eight Countries'. *American Law and Economics Review* 12 (1): 204–44.

Vannucci, Alberto. 2009. 'The Controversial Legacy of "*Mani Pulite*": A Critical Analysis of Italian Corruption and Anti-Corruption Politics'. *Bulletin of Italian Politics* 1 (2): 233–64.

Vannucci, Alberto. 2012. 'Così la corruzione prospera'. *lavoce.info*, 19 June. URL: www.lavoce.info/archives/27773/cosi-la-corruzione-prospera/.

Varese, Federico. 2014. 'Protection and Extortion'. In *Oxford Handbook of Organized Crime*, edited by Letizia Paoli, pp. 343–58. New York: Oxford University Press.

Varsori, Antonio. 2015. 'Bettino Craxi and Giulio Andreotti'. In *The Oxford Handbook of Italian Politics*, edited by Erik Jones and Gianfranco Pasquino, pp. 378–93. New York: Oxford University Press.

Vassallo, Salvatore. 2015. 'Parliament'. In *The Oxford Handbook of Italian Politics*, edited by Erik Jones and Gianfranco Pasquino, pp. 107–19. New York: Oxford University Press.

Vecchi, Giovanni. 2017. *Measuring Wellbeing: A History of Italian Living Standards*. Oxford: Oxford University Press.

Vesan, Patrick. 2015. 'Labor Market Policy and Politics'. In *The Oxford Handbook of Italian Politics*, edited by Erik Jones and Gianfranco Pasquino, pp. 491–503. New York: Oxford University Press.

Viesti, Gianfranco. 2016. 'Il declino del sistema universitario italiano'. In *Università in declino. Un'indagine sugli atenei da Nord a Sud*, edited by Gianfranco Viesti, pp. 3–56. Rome: Donzelli.

Viroli, Maurizio. [2010] 2012. *The Liberty of Servants: Berlusconi's Italy*. Translated by Antony Shugaar. Princeton, NJ: Princeton University Press.

Visco, Vincenzo. 2015. 'Se l'evasione non è un reato'. *lavoce.info*, 7 January. URL: www.lavoce.info/archives/32223/se-levasione-non-reato/.

Winters, Jeffrey, and Benjamin Page. 2009. 'Oligarchy in the United States?'. *Perspectives on Politics* 7 (4): 731–51.

World Bank. 2016. *Doing Business 2016: Measuring Regulatory Quality and Efficiency*. Washington, DC: World Bank.

Zhang, Nan, Giulia Andrighetto, Stefania Ottone, Ferruccio Ponzano, and Sven Steinmo. 2016. ' "Willing to Pay?" Tax Compliance in Britain and Italy: An Experimental Analysis'. *PLoS ONE* 11 (2). doi:10.1371/journal.pone.0150277.

Name Index

General Index